Human Resource Planning

Human Resource Planning
A Business Planning Approach

Donald W. Jarrell
Drexel University

Prentice Hall, Englewood Cliffs, New Jersey 07632

Library of Congress Cataloging-in-Publication Data

Jarrell, Donald W.
    Human resource planning: a business planning approach / Donald W.
Jarrell.
            p. cm.
    Includes bibliographical references and index.
    ISBN 0-13-446485-0
    1. Manpower planning. I. Title.
HF5549.5.M3J38   1992
    658.3'01—dc20

92-1498
CIP

Acquisitions editor: Alison Reeves
Copy editor: Mary Louise Byrd
Editorial assistant: Diane Peirano
Cover design: Bruce Kenselaar
Pre-press buyer: Trudy Pisciotti
Manufacturing buyer: Bob Anderson

© 1993 by Prentice-Hall, Inc.
A Simon & Schuster Company
Englewood Cliffs, New Jersey 07632

Printed in the United States of America
10   9   8   7   6   5   4   3   2

ISBN 0-13-446485-0

Prentice-Hall International (UK) Limited, *London*
Prentice-Hall of Australia Pty. Limited, *Sydney*
Prentice-Hall Canada Inc., *Toronto*
Prentice-Hall Hispanoamericana, S.A., *Mexico*
Prentice-Hall of India Private Limited, *New Delhi*
Prentice-Hall of Japan, Inc., *Tokyo*
Simon & Schuster Asia Pte. Ltd., *Singapore*
Editora Prentice-Hall do Brasil, Ltda., *Rio de Janeiro*

Contents

Preface and Acknowledgments   **ix**

Introduction   **xi**

PART 1—BUSINESS PLANNING OVERVIEW   **1**

Chapter 1, An Introduction to Business Planning   **3**

Business Planning Practice, 3
Business Planning Concepts, 10
Universality of Planning Practice and Theory, 16
Summary, 16
Learning Exercises, 17
Endnotes, 18

Chapter 2, Strategic Business Planning   **21**

Strategic Planning Concepts, 21
Strategic Planning Process, 27
The Human Resource Role in Strategic Planning, 51
Summary, 61
Learning Exercises, 62
Appendix: Glossary of Behavioral Change Techniques
   Useful for Planning, 63
Endnotes, 65

Chapter 3, Tactical and Operational Business Planning   **73**

Tactical Planning, 74
   Tactical Planning Concepts, 74
   Tactical Planning Process, 89
   The Human Resource Role in Tactical Planning, 91

Operational Planning, 93
   Operational Planning Concepts, 94
   Operational Planning Process, 96
   The Human Resource Role in Operational Planning, 97
Summary, 98
Learning Exercises, 99
Endnotes, 101

**PART 2—HUMAN RESOURCE PLANNING: STRATEGIC
AND TACTICAL STAGES**   **107**

Chapter 4, Strategic Planning for Human Resources   **109**

Necessary Conditions for Strategic Planning for Human Resources, 110
The Elements of Strategic Planning for Human Resources, 113
Strategic Human Resource Planning Process, 146
Summary, 153
Learning Exercises, 155
Endnotes, 157

Chapter 5, Tactical Planning for Human Resources   **174**

Tactical Human Resource Planning Concepts, 174
Tactical Human Resource Planning Process, 180
Summary, 181
Learning Exercises, 182
Endnotes, 183

**PART 3—OPERATIONAL PLANNING FOR HUMAN
RESOURCES**   **185**

**Chapter 6, Meeting the Information Needs of Human
Resource Planning**   **187**

An Information System for Human Resources, 187
An Information System for Human Resource Planning, 190
Managing an HRIS for Human Resource Planning, 194
Suggested Improvements for HRISs, 196
Summary, 199
Learning Exercises, 200
Endnotes, 201

Chapter 7, Defining the Future   **204**

Futures Analysis, 204
Further Definition of Specific Variables, 208
Summary, 216
Learning Exercises, 217
Endnotes, 218

Chapter 8, Evaluating Human Resources   **221**

The Role of Evaluation in Planning, 221
A Supportive Setting for Evaluation, 223
A Philosophy of Evaluation, 224
An Approach to Evaluation, 225
What to Measure, 227
Standards for the Evaluation, 228
Methods of Evaluation, 229
The Evaluator(s), 244
Using the Evaluation, 245
Summary, 246
Learning Exercises, 247
Appendix: Glossary of Employee Attributes, 249
Endnotes, 250

Chapter 9, Determining Flows of Human Resources   **256**

Views of Human Resources Flows, 257
Identifying Human Resource Flows and Their Effects, 266
Summary, 274
Learning Exercises, 276
Endnotes, 277

**Chapter 10, Planning for the Management of Human
Resource Flows**   **281**

Key Individuals and Groups, 282
Support Structure for Flows, 289
Strategy-Driven Flows of Human Resources, 292
Summary, 295
Learning Exercises, 296
Appendix 1: Guide for an Analysis of the Effects of Human
    Resource Flows, 298
Appendix 2: Glossary of Procedures and Programs Used
    in the Management of Human Resource Flows, 299
Endnotes, 301

Closure   **305**

PART 4—CASES   **307**

1. Lehman Brothers, 308
2. Bolling Laboratories, Inc., 311
3. Shuckman Interiors, Inc., 318
4. Bank of America, 326
5. Westview Company, Inc., 333
6. Apex Manufacturing Company, Inc., 337

7. Northeast Data Resources, Inc., 343
8. Deft Research and Development, Inc., 351
9. Chase Manhattan Bank, 362
10. Sun Microsystems, Inc., 376

Index   **397**

Preface
and Acknowledgments

This book was written in response to a need. For a number of years I have felt that human resource planning lacked a clear definition. It has been many things to many people—all different. Without a clear definition, research and sharing of ideas derived from practice are dissipated and lack focus. This book is an attempt to structure and shape a body of material that will meet the needs of students and practitioners of the field. In writing the book, I have used information from a broad range of subject areas. In some instances I have had to be inventive: The needed material had not been developed and I had to fill the gaps with my own ideas. I trust the reader will find this book a useful beginning toward an increased understanding of the field and its potential.

I want to acknowledge the help of some indispensable people—I could not have written the book without their help. My wife, Joanne, has been a continual partner in this task. She has been sometime co-author, consummate editor, and constructive critic. She was unswerving in her belief that we could do it.

My colleague at Drexel, Paul Kessler, has been taskmaster, reviewer of the entire manuscript, and always optimistic, even when he had to read some very rough first drafts.

My colleagues, students, and former students at Drexel have given me moral support and encouragement. The library staff have been patient, professional, and competent.

A number of people have graciously given permission to reprint their materials. Their contributions are acknowledged within the book. To all these persons, my heartfelt thanks!

Introduction

Human Resource Planning: A Business Planning Approach

Capital? You've got to have it....But it's people that will make the difference. That's why at General Motors, management and labor together are implementing what amounts to a "people" revolution. It's a revolution in which each side recognizes that people, not fixed assets or technology, are the deciding factor in the bottom line....

Alan Smith,
Executive Vice President,
General Motors Corporation,
December 6, 1988[1]

In today's organizations, human resource issues are replacing capital resource issues as the guiding force of organizations.[2] Employees are becoming the most important resources of the organization. This rise to prominence of human resources is caused by the combined effect of two events: a backlog of unsolved problems in human resource management and a dramatic increase in knowledge of human resources.

The backlog of problems has been caused by too little attention to the management of human resources in the past. Finance, general management, marketing, production, and research and development all received much more attention than human resource management.[3] Awareness of the inadequacies of human resource management has come as we compared our success in this area with that of organizations in other countries where human resources were considered critical to success. Organizations in the United States have considerable catching up to do. They have "people problems" galore.

Fortunately, the raw material needed to solve many of these problems is available. Knowledge of human resources has been increasing rapidly in recent years. This increase in knowledge is the result of a number of factors, including government regulation that requires organizations to demonstrate the validity of their human resource systems, the increasing use of the computer to support human resource information systems, a rapidly expanding and readily available human resource literature, rising expectations of chief executive officers for the human resource function, and the movement into human resources of highly trained practitioners who both use and generate knowledge. For these and other reasons, knowledge is virtually exploding upon the human resource scene. As knowledge expands, new applications in the human resource field occur almost daily.

Planning for human resources, to be effective, must be done at all levels of the organization and must involve most persons in the organization. It must be coextensive with the business planning process. Business planning has as its purpose preparation by an organization for the future. Including human resource planning in business planning ensures that preparations for the future are extended to the human resources of the organization.

Human resource considerations are part of every business decision. Human resource planning allows the organization to adapt its decisions in a timely and efficient manner to changes in the economy and in society at large. Considering human resources throughout the business planning process can significantly lower costs and can increase the value of investments in human resources.[4]

Beyond the monetary aspects of human resource planning are ethical considerations. Human resources are people, fellow human beings. The time to consider the quality of the work life of these people is at the business planning stage, when the hands of decision makers are not tied by commitments of resources to other areas of planning. Provision of a work life of outstanding quality is as important a social contribution for an organization as is the production of quality products and services.

The coincidence of a backlog of need for knowledge and a worthwhile supply of knowledge ensures that the next quarter century or more will be a time of opportunity for organizations that manage their human resources effectively. Organizations can seize this opportunity if their approach to human resource management is well thought out and sound.

Introducing human resource planning into the business planning process will be a new adventure for many organizations. There will be a need for managers who understand both human resources and accepted business planning theory and practice.[5] A knowledge of human resources and of business planning can be a passport into the fast-paced world of professional management.

Endnotes

[1]Alan Smith, remarks at the University Club of Chicago, Chicago, December 6, 1988. Copies of these remarks were mailed by John W. McNulty, Vice President, Public Relations, to university faculty across the United States. See also the discussion of the

role of people in the new GM strategy in Roy S. Roberts, "Remarks on Getting Back to the Basics of Competition: People," *Executive Speeches*, 2, no. 11 (June 1988), 17–21.

[2]Barbara E. Heiken, James W. Randell, Jr., and Robert N. Lear, "Using Information Technology for Strategic Human Resource Planning," *Information Strategy: The Executive's Journal*, 2, no. 4 (Summer 1986), 8–14.

[3]A survey of 500 large U.S. corporations found that human resources was a secondary consideration in planning as compared to the other functions cited here. James S. Ang and Jess H. Chua, "Long Range Planning in Large United States Corporations—A Survey," *Long Range Planning*, 12, no. 2 (April, 1979), 99–102.

[4]For a dramatic example of failure to consider human resources at the business planning stage, see W. E. Bright, "How One Company Manages Its Human Resources," *Harvard Business Review*, 54, no. 1 (January-February, 1976), 81–93.

[5]A survey by Heidrick and Struggles, Inc., a Chicago-based executive search firm, showed that the average salary of human resource executives who did human resource planning was 50 percent higher than those who did not plan. *Business Week*, February 26, 1979, pp. 116–121. In a survey by Korn/Ferry International and Columbia University Graduate School of Business, when top executives of corporations were asked to list the ideal skills needed by their chief executive officer, they listed as most important "strategy formulation" and as next in importance "human resource management." See *Wall Street Journal*, March 9, 1990, p. R33.

Part 1

Business Planning Overview

Human resource planning can be completely successful only if it is fully integrated with business planning. Such integration cannot occur unless human resource planners influence and are influenced by the business planning effort in an organization.

To take an active part in business planning, human resource specialists need to know the basic concepts of business planning. Other managers need to understand human resource applications to business planning. Part I of the text will prepare you in both respects. Chapter 1 provides an overview of the basic ideas of business planning. Chapter 2 discusses human resource applications in strategic planning, the first of three stages of business planning. Chapter 3 considers human resource applications in the other two stages of business planning—tactical planning and operational planning.

Chapter 1

An Introduction
to Business Planning

Imagine that you are to assist with the planning for a large manufacturing firm. The firm has plants across the United States and in foreign countries and has relationships with a vast number of outside people and organizations. What are the planning tasks that need to be done? Where do you start in the planning process? These are the questions this chapter tries to answer. The chapter discusses two main topics, business planning practice and business planning concepts.

BUSINESS PLANNING PRACTICE

Some countries rely heavily on centralized planning and control of their economies to produce goods and services. In countries with centrally directed economies, the government establishes an economic plan for the economy as a whole and resources are allocated to producing organizations in accordance with the plan. Planning by individual economic organizations must be consistent with the overall economic plan.

Other countries, the United States among them, have unplanned economies; that is, they have no central direction of their economies. These countries rely on private enterprise and the free market to produce the goods and services needed to satisfy consumers. In countries with free enterprise economies, most planning is done by organizations acting independently of each other, not by state or federal governments. Planning by these organizations in free enterprise economies is known as business planning. In these economies, business planning serves as a directive force in much the same way that centralized planning does in socialist countries.

Planning in the United States

Business planning first began to receive widespread attention in the academic community and in professionally managed firms after World War II.[1] Often, planning has been a response to major economic events. Events such as the energy crisis of the 1970s, growing competition from developing foreign countries, and the realization of the European Community caused increasing numbers of managers to see the world economy as interdependent and turbulent. They began to consider planning as an answer.[2]

Business organizations with professional management almost always do business planning.[3] And planning is becoming more widespread among smaller industrial, consumer, and service firms, which often lack professional management.[4] As the practice of business planning spreads, it is gradually becoming both more formal and more comprehensive. For example, consider the following:

- Most firms that plan have written plans.[5]
- Many large organizations have a central planning unit that does not plan but that contributes to the smooth functioning of the planning process by providing expert advice on planning and by absorbing some of the often massive underlying work of planning.[6]
- Larger firms often use computer-based models for planning.[7]
- Environmental surveillance has become a common element in planning processes.[8]
- The scope of surveillance frequently includes both broad economic conditions and detailed scenarios for segments of the environment.[9]
- Most organizations have plans that cover various functional areas of the organization.[10]

Planning has not affected all functional areas of management uniformly. The most emphasis has been given to finance. A survey of 500 large U.S. corporations found that financial planning models were used in most firms using or developing corporate planning models[11] Financial statements typically are a part of each division's long-range plan[12] Accountants have far more responsibility for business planning strategy than any other professional group.[13]

General management and marketing, followed by production and research and development, also have been given emphasis in planning. External relations, human resource management, and procurement have occupied secondary roles.[14]

From an overall perspective, considering both small and large firms, planning in the United States is in its infancy. But a few firms have extensive experience in planning. What views of planning are shared by these veteran planners? A study of business planning in ten large, well-managed firms with extensive experience in planning produced the following conclusions:

- Planning is critical for good management.
- There are wide variations in planning procedures used in different organizations.

- There is no single best system for planning.
- Planning systems tend to evolve through a trial-and-error process.
- It is critical to have top management deeply involved in planning.
- Planning is expensive, but the benefits outweigh the costs.[15]

Stages of Planning

Planning in its most highly developed form is done in three stages: strategic, tactical, and operational. These stages of planning have a hierarchical relationship to each other, with strategic planning being the most comprehensive. It establishes the limits within which tactical planning takes place. Tactical planning, the next most comprehensive, sets the limits within which operational planning occurs. Operational planning provides closure for the planning process.

Strategic planning, as its name implies, concerns planning that enables the organization to take advantage of opportunities for gain in the world in which the organization operates. Strategic planners take an outsider's view of the organization and the outside world, a stance that allows them to examine objectively the opportunities and hazards of the environment relevant to the organization. They also examine the capabilities and limitations of the organization for dealing with the environment. They then choose appropriate objectives and strategies for the organization.

In contrast to strategic planning, *tactical planning* involves an insider's view of the organization as a whole. Tactical planners determine how to deploy resources to organization units and job positions so as to implement the strategies and achieve the objectives of strategic planning. Deployment of resources in an organization is accomplished through organization design, organization culture, budgetary processes, and policies.

In contrast to strategic planning, and like tactical planning, *operational planning* involves an insider's view of the organization. And, in contrast to both strategic planning and tactical planning, operational planning involves a specific organization unit, not the organization as a whole. Organization direction is set through strategic planning, resources are deployed through tactical planning, and resources are applied to everyday operations through operational planning. Operational planners determine how to use with maximum efficiency the resources assigned in earlier stages of planning.

In practice, the stages of planning have a phased relationship to each other; it is easier to think of strategic planning first, tactical planning second, and operational planning third. However, the stages of planning must interact. Feedback obtained from implementation of plans in each stage will influence future planning in its own stage as well as in other stages. No stage of planning should take precedence in the planning process. Optimum planning occurs when the best overall set of business plans, including plans in all three stages of planning, is achieved.

Use of the stages of planning frequently is hampered because the relationship of the stages with the managerial hierarchy and the time periods of planning is not understood.

Stages of Planning and the Managerial Hierarchy

It is tempting to draw parallels between the planning hierarchy and the managerial levels in an organization—to say that strategic planning is done by top-level managers, that tactical planning is done by intermediate-level managers, and that operational planning is done by lower-level managers. It is true that the jobs of top-level managers tend to prepare them for strategic planning, the jobs of intermediate-level managers for tactical planning, and those of lower-level managers for operational planning. But these persons tend to have positional biases and may be too close to their work to plan objectively for the organization. Including other persons from the organization in the planning effort helps to offset these positional biases and to obtain a more representative organization viewpoint among planners.

Lower-level employees may need training to enable them to participate constructively in strategic planning. For example, they can be provided with results of surveys conducted by outside consultants about the environment and about organization strengths and weaknesses.

It is, therefore, a mistake to draw a parallel between the planning hierarchy and the managerial hierarchy. An effective team of persons should be assembled to perform planning in each of its stages. Persons should be assigned to these teams because they can contribute to the team's effectiveness, not simply because they hold a given position in the organization.

Stages of Planning and Time Periods of Planning

It also is tempting to assume that strategic planning is long-range planning, that tactical planning is medium-range planning, and that operational planning is short-run planning. Such an assumption is never appropriate. Stage plans and time plans are different and serve different purposes.[16]

The distinct purposes of stage plans and time plans must be recognized if they are to complement each other properly and if each is to serve its purpose well. It is especially important to remember that time is *not* an explicit consideration in stage planning. Stage plans are to set a direction for the organization. They are atemporal. They need *not* be done on a periodic basis. New strategic, tactical, and operational plans should be developed only when current plans seem to be ineffective or when changes in the organization or the environment indicate that the current stage plans are out of date.[17]

In contrast to stage plans, time plans have as their purpose the management of time. They are prepared for carefully selected periods of time appropriate to the technology of the organization and are repeated periodically. Time plans perform two important functions that stage plans cannot provide:

- Time plans provide the specifics of what is to be done and when to achieve the objectives of the stage plans. Time plans stipulate goals associated with specific time periods and implement detailed control mechanisms and annual budgets.
- Time plans force planners to consider all appropriate time periods in planning. This function is extremely important in the United States, where planners tend to exaggerate the importance of strategic planning and to take for granted time planning, especially long-range planning.[18]

Exhibit 1-1 makes clear the distinction between stage planning and time planning. Time plans are subordinate to stage plans. They are developed subsequent to stage plans and within the constraints of the choices made during stage planning. However, the importance of time plans should not be minimized. Stage plans without corresponding time plans are one-dimensional. Time plans are necessary to complete the planning process. They specify the details of "what" and "when" that fulfill the stage plans. Further, they form the basis by which achievement of the stage plans can be measured.

Type of Planning	Purpose and Expected Outcomes of Planning
Strategic	To provide direction, via broad objectives, and to indicate how—the strategies by which—these objectives are to be achieved.
Long run	To indicate *what* the firm is to have achieved —its long-run goals—within a specific time period long enough to allow fundamental change in the organization.
Tactical	To promote the proper deployment of resources through organization design, organization culture, budgetary processes, and policies.
Medium range	To indicate *what* the firm is to have achieved—its medium-run goals—within a specified time period long enough to allow organization growth.
Operational	To promote the efficient use of allocated resources by performing operational planning functions.
Short run	To indicate *what* the firm is to have achieved—its short-run goals—within a specified time period long enough to allow change in production schedules.

Exhibit 1-1. Comparison of Stage Planning and Time Period Planning

Levels of Planning

Strategic, tactical, and operational planning must be done at the enterprise level and at all primary levels of departmentation. A primary level of departmentation is the first level from the top at which the division of the organization into units occurs. For complex organizations, planning will typically be done at the following levels:[19]

- Enterprise level—the organization as a whole.
- Functional level—the first level of departmentation by function. Functional units at the first level typically report to the chief executive officer. Examples of functions often reporting at this level are finance, human resources, marketing, and production.
- Group level—the first level of departmentation by kind of business. Groups typically report to the chief executive officer. A group includes two or more closely related businesses.[20]
- Business unit level—the second level of departmentation by kind of business. Business units typically report to the chief executive officer of a group. A business unit manufactures, services, or sells a single product or service or several closely related products or services.

Not all organizations will have all these levels within their structure. Exhibit 1-2 illustrates possible combinations. All organizations are likely to have both an enterprise and a functional level. Only multibusiness organizations will have group and business unit levels.

Levels of Planning and the Managerial Hierarchy

As with the stages of planning, it is tempting to draw parallels between the levels of planning and the managerial levels in an organization—for example, to say that planning at the enterprise level is done by the organization's chief executive officer, that planning at the functional level is done by the function chief executive officers, that planning at the group level is done by the group chief executive officers, and that planning at the business unit level is done by the business unit chief executive officers. Although the executives for each of these levels of planning will certainly be involved, planning cannot be done by these persons alone.[21] Planning for each level should have representation from other planning levels. Overlap of the membership of planning groups for the different levels will help to ensure coordination of planning at the different levels and the achievement of an integrated set of business plans.

Full responsibility for planning should not be assumed by higher level executives alone. These executives represent only some of the various viewpoints and interests that determine the quality and acceptability

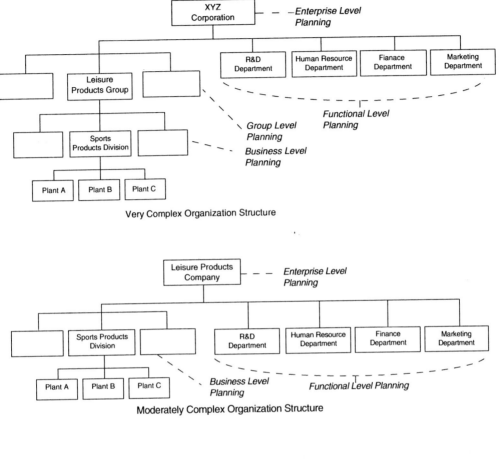

Very Complex Organization Structure

Moderately Complex Organization Structure

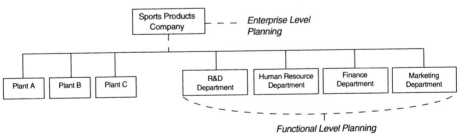

Simple Organization Structure

Exhibit 1-2. Illustrative Planning Levels for Organizations with Very Complex, Moderately Complex, and Simple Structures

of planning outcomes. All persons in the organization should be considered potential participants on planning committees at the various levels. If training and development are available for potential participants, many persons can be included who would otherwise lack the skills and knowledge needed to contribute fully to the planning effort.

Planning by Units of the Organization

Organizations are divided into many parts, such as wholly owned companies, product groups, divisions, regions, locations, plants, departments, sections, and work teams. In addition to taking part in the organizational business planning, each of these units must do further planning.

Planning by subordinate units for their own actions may be comprehensive or narrow, depending on whether they act in a proactive or a reactive manner, that is, whether the units anticipate events and initiate appropriate action before events occur or respond to events after they occur. Proactive organization units must do extensive strategic, tactical, and operational planning to guide their initiatives.

The plans of different organization units must be integrated into a meaningful whole that is consistent with business planning at the enterprise, functional, group, and business unit levels. This integration may be achieved in one or more ways:

1. Provide for overlapping memberships of organizationwide planning groups and organization unit planning groups.
2. Establish standing plans—statements of objectives, principles, policies, standard methods, standard operating procedures, and/or rules—consistent with organizationwide plans to guide planning by organization units.
3. Establish positions in the managerial hierarchy with authority to approve or require modification of organization unit plans.

BUSINESS PLANNING CONCEPTS

Evolution of Planning Concepts

As organizations plan, they learn from each other, from management consultants, and from researchers. Ideas that prove successful in one organization are adopted by other organizations.

Ideas used in organizations are studied by researchers to determine why they are or are not successful. Those ideas that work become accepted concepts of planning and are taught in universities to soon-to-be practitioners who apply the ideas. And the cycle continues. This process produces a continual building of new concepts. Some of the more basic of these are presented here.

Business Planning Terms

In order to be able to discuss planning concepts, some terms must be understood by the reader. Listed here are some of the basic elements of business planning:

- Organization
- Organization identity
- Strategies
- Operations
- Organization philosophy
- Environment
- Tactics
- Objectives

The definitions of these terms follow.

An ORGANIZATION is a collection of human, material, and capital resources sociotechnically arranged to allow their use to accomplish a productive end. Organizations include private, profit-seeking corporations, partnerships, and sole proprietorships; private, nonprofit organizations; and government agencies.

ORGANIZATION PHILOSOPHY is a commitment of the organization[22] to a set of principles that allocates responsibilities of the organization toward the various stakeholders of the organization. An organization philosophy serves as an ethical guide for conducting the affairs of the organization.

ORGANIZATION IDENTITY is that set of characteristics that makes a particular organization unique, that distinguishes it from other organizations.

The organization exists in and is part of a larger world from which the organization obtains resources. ENVIRONMENT is this larger world.

STRATEGIES are sets of activities carried out by an organization. These sets of activities are selected as appropriate ways for the organization to deal with the environment.

TACTICS, like strategies, are sets of activities carried out by an organization. These activities, however, are concerned with the internal affairs of the organization. They are selected as appropriate ways to administer the organization in order to support its strategies.

OPERATIONS, like tactics, are sets of internal activities carried out by an organization. They are selected as appropriate ways for units of the organization to carry out their day-to-day activities to implement the organization tactics and to support the environmental strategies.

OBJECTIVES are long-term enduring ends that drive an organization's efforts as it deals with the environment, manages its internal affairs, and conducts its daily operations. Objectives, like strategies, tactics, and operations, describe intended activities of the organization.

Objectives are necessary to provide a focus for human behavior in carrying out activities. To provide an even sharper focus for behavior, objectives often are restated as goals. Goals differ from objectives in that they are time-bound, are readily measurable, and are targets deliberately chosen for pursuit by the organiza-

Concept	Military Planning Usage
Strategy	Set of activities chosen to secure maximum military advantage by capitalizing on strengths and weaknesses of enemy forces relative to one's own forces.
Tactic	Set of activities aimed at deploying troops on the field of battle to implement chosen strategies.
Operation	Set of specific activities, such as selecting, scheduling, and transporting, aimed at carrying out troop deployment tactics.
Concept	Business Planning Usage
Strategy	Set of activities chosen to secure maximum gain by capitalizing on opportunities and problems in the environment, relevant to organization capabilities.
Tactic	Set of activities aimed at deploying organization resources to implement chosen strategies.
Operation	Set of specific activities aimed at carrying out resource deployment tactics.

Exhibit 1-3. Comparison of the Stages of Planning, as Defined in the Military and in Business

tion.[23] An example will make clear the distinction between an objective and a goal. "Increased sales" is an objective; "growth in total dollars of sales for the year 1990 of 13 percent" is a goal.

Strategies, tactics, and operations are terms borrowed from military planning, which served as a model for business planning. Exhibit 1-3 shows this relationship. A review of this exhibit will further the reader's understanding of these terms.

Theoretical Foundations of Business Planning

Terms mean little until they are put to work in a theory. Theory allows the systematic organization of knowledge such that it can be applied to a wide variety of circumstances to analyze, predict, and otherwise explain the nature of phenomena. Two theories of organizations help to structure business planning: the open systems theory and the self-producing systems theory.

Open Systems Theory

The open systems theory has been, and continues to be, very influential in the industrialized countries of the world. In this theory an *organization* is in continual interaction with its *environment*, importing energy and resources (inputs), transforming energy and resources into products and services (outputs), and exporting these products and services to the environment. It engages in exchanges with other systems—suppliers, customers, creditors, labor markets, unions, government agencies—to obtain necessary inputs and to dispose of outputs. To exist, the organization must engage in this exchange process.

Whether the organization continues to exist, and how well it exists, depend on how effectively the organization deals with its environment. Hence, the term *open systems*, for these systems depend for their continued existence on remaining open to the environment.[24]

Because the well-being of an organization depends on its dealings with the environment, it must manage these interactions carefully. An organization does this by erecting boundaries between itself and the environment to allow control of the kinds of interactions that may occur. Only those interactions are allowed in which the exchanges that occur are in the interest of the organization.

Because environment is central to the open systems theory,[25] planning begins with *environmental analysis*—a study of the opportunities and the problems in the environment for the organization. Once environmental analysis has been done, *organization identity* is established. Organization identity is determined by what the organization does or is able to do. Just as people in our society tend to be defined by their occupations or professions, so, too, do organizations tend to be defined by what they do. And just as the capacities of people are measured by the various skills they possess and by the extent to which those skills are compatible with the demands of their professions, capacities of organizations are measured by the effectiveness of the various subsystems of the organization and by the extent to which the capacities of the subsystems are congruent with the demands of the environment. This concept of organization as a set of subsystems.in relationship to environment is shown in Exhibit 1-4.

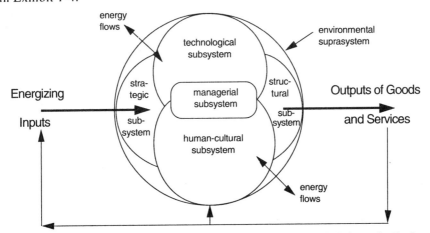

Exhibit 1-4.   Organization as a Set of Independent Subsystems in Relation to Its Environment
Source: Fremont E. Kast and James E. Rosenzweig, *Contingency Views of Organization and Management* (New York: Science Research Associates, 1973), p. 14.

Once environmental analysis has been completed and organization identity established, appropriate *objectives* and corresponding *strategies, tactics,* and *operations* of the organization may be determined. Objectives, and goals based on these objectives, typically are defined in terms of inputs, outputs, or, more commonly, a combination of the two. For example, open systems objectives often are stated in terms of the profitability of organization activities and corresponding goals are stated in terms of rate of return on assets or sales.

To summarize, in the open systems theory of organization, the environment is the source of all threat and opportunity. Organization identity, objectives, strategies, tactics, and operations—all are defined in relationship to the environment. The environment is a "mirror" used by planners to determine the present various states of the organization. Desired changes in these states are projected for the future as objectives and are attained through the choice of appropriate strategies, tactics, and operations.

Self-Producing Systems Theory

The self-producing systems theory was first published in the United States in the 1970s.[26] According to this theory, the aim of a system is the maintenance of system identity through *autopoiesis* (self-production). This view has had less application to social organizations than has the open systems theory. However, it adds several worthwhile ideas to the open systems view.

A major contribution of the self-producing systems view is to point out that the way a system actually operates and the way it appears to operate to an outside observer often are different.[27] By insisting on seeing systems as they actually are, proponents of the self-producing systems theory have provided a perhaps more accurate—certainly a more complex and therefore a more difficult to use—view of organizations.

In the self-producing systems view, organizations are neither open nor closed to the environment but are an inseparable part of the environment. All systems are part of every other system. A system becomes identifiable as a system only when it is capable of autonomous action in relation to the universe of other systems. Autonomous action requires that the system have organization—that is, that the system have relatively stable relations among its components. When changes occur in the universe at large, systems attempt to maintain organization and therefore self-identity, in spite of this change. They maintain organization and identity by engaging in continuous circular patterns of interaction whereby change in one element of the system is coupled with changes elsewhere in the system. These circular patterns of interaction are always self-referential in that a system can only enter into interactions consistent with the pattern of relations that define its organization, that is, with its identity.

Maintenance of system identity through self-production is central to understanding the self-producing systems theory. It may be helpful to illustrate this idea. All autopoietic systems continuously reproduce themselves. The person you recognize as "Joe" is not in point of fact the same person from minute to minute. The components of the living system "Joe," through processes of metabolism, growth, and molecular replication, will shortly cease to exist, having been replaced by other components. You will continue to recognize the living system as Joe, however, because the relations among Joe's components remain consistent with the system you identify as Joe. Joe is continually being reproduced following a blueprint that establishes Joe's identity. In fact, this immutability of component relations is necessary for Joe's continued existence as a living system.[28]

Just as the system "Joe" does not depend for its identity on keeping a given set of components, the organization you know as "Your Place of Work" does not depend for its identity on keeping the same people,[29] machines, or even buildings. Its identity depends, instead, on the relations among people and those other components remaining consistent with the organization you know as Your Place of Work. Its entire appearance and purpose may change while "it" survives. Like living systems, maintenance of identity is not a matter of choice for organizations; it is necessary to their continued existence.

The self-producing systems view of organization is complex. Unfortunately little can be done to reduce its complexity, for the theory does not allow the simplifying assumption of viewing the organization as it appears to an outside observer. Fortunately, if we look only at those aspects of the theory needed for business planning—that is, the relationships among the elements of business planning—the theory becomes less complex. As indicated earlier, *organization* (system) and *environment* are inseparable in the self-producing systems view. To discover *organization identity*, one must trace the circular pattern of interactions through which the system maintains its identity in the presence of change.

Self-producing systems are not concerned with producing a product or service as such.[30] The sole aim of a self-producing system is the maintenance of self-identity, and all actions allowed by the system support this single purpose.[31] Though there are no explicit objectives or strategies, *apparent objectives* and *strategies* may be inferred by observing the behaviors of self-producing systems.

A Comparison of the Theories

In spite of their being very dissimilar ways to describe the organization, both the open systems theory and the self-producing systems theory are tenable. The difference between the two is in the viewpoints taken of the organization, but both viewpoints can be useful to business planners.

In the open systems view, an organization is an *allopoietic* (other-producing) system. In the self-producing systems view, an organization is an *autopoietic* (self-producing) system. In actual fact, organizations usually are created allopoietic, to produce a product or service. Once created, they become also autopoietic, continually creating themselves. Organizations, therefore, can be fully understood only by using both the open systems and the self-producing systems theories.

UNIVERSALITY OF PLANNING PRACTICE AND THEORY

This chapter has concentrated on business planning practice in the United States. However, business planning practice and theory are similar among organizations in the developed, free enterprise countries of the world. This is both evidenced by, and aided by, several facts. Management consulting firms are international in their operations. Foreign students in increasing numbers are studying planning in MBA programs in the United States. There is a well-developed planning literature, and this literature is decidedly international in scope.[32] Professional approaches to business planning are much the same, whether the planner lives in the United States or in another of the developed, free enterprise countries.

SUMMARY

In the past, rapid growth and vast opportunity in domestic markets have allowed many firms in the United States to avoid planning. But recent events have forced firms in ever increasing numbers to turn to planning to improve their ability to compete. Organizations appear to be learning to plan more effectively. Planning is being done by larger numbers of firms. Planning is becoming more formal and complex.

All employees of the organization should be considered for participation in the various stages and levels of planning. Inclusion should be based on their ability to contribute to the planning effort.

The stages of planning are time-independent and should not be confused with long-range, medium-range, and short-range planning. Stage planning and time-period planning are complementary and distinct.

Organization units plan for the actions of their own units. They may do extensive planning in all its stages or do only limited planning. Their separate plans must be consistent with overall plans for the organization.

The elements of business planning are organization, organization philosophy, organization identity, environment, strategies, tactics, operations, and objectives. The relationships among these elements are established through a coordinated set of strategic, tactical, and operational plans at all planning levels. Depending on the complexity of the structure of an organization, planning may be done at the enterprise, function, group, or business unit level.

Two theories helpful in seeing the relationships among the elements of business planning and in determining what these relationships should be are the open systems theory of organizations and the self-producing systems theory of organizations. The open systems theory sees organizations as creations of people, designed to do certain things and to achieve certain objectives. The self-producing systems theory sees organizations as living, evolving systems, concerned with maintaining identity. Although these theories are different ways of looking at organizations, they complement each other well.

LEARNING EXERCISES

Small-Group Case Discussion

All members of the class or study group should read Case 1, "Lehman Brothers." When everyone has completed reading the case, groups of three should be formed through random assignment of members of the class or study group.

Each participant in your discussion group should lead the discussion of one of the questions/activities. The discussion leader for each question should appoint a member of the group to serve as note taker for the group, making notes about outcomes of the discussion. These notes should be brief and should be made as the discussion proceeds; note taking should not interfere with the discussion.

The discussion leader should monitor the time allowed for discussion and should summarize the position of the group, as needed, during the discussion. This summary helps to provide direction and to promote consensus and allows the note taker to check the accuracy of his or her notes. Before closing the discussion, the discussion leader should again summarize the discussion.

The note taker will be asked to report the consensus or viewpoints of the discussion group to the class or study group.

1. Lehman Brothers was discontinued as a separate business in 1984 when Shearson took over Lehman Brothers Kuhn Loeb, Inc. What appears to have been the immediate reason for the action taken by Shearson Lehman Hutton Holdings, Inc., in 1990, described in Case 1?
2. Why do you suppose Shearson Lehman Hutton Holdings, Inc., was unable to build an identity that would promote cohesion of its employees? What are the necessary ingredients or preconditions for building an organization identity?
3. What, if anything, in your opinion, does the Lehman name represent? Do you think this effort to resurrect the Lehman name will be successful?

Activity

Secure a recent issue of several business newspapers or business journals, such as the *Wall Street Journal, Business Week, Fortune,* or *Forbes.* (Most libraries hold these.) Scan several articles in each. Does it appear that planning is a topic of current interest? How much attention is given to strategic planning as compared to tactical and operational planning? Copy references that you believe are concerned with each of the stages of planning and compare these with the text discussion of strategic, tactical, and operational planning. Were you correct in your application of the terms in classifying your material?

Discussion Question

1. Are both the open systems theory and the self-producing systems theory equally valid for explaining the behavior of an organization? Explain your answer. Take an organization with which you are familiar and describe the organization in terms of each theory. Which theory lends itself more readily to a "factual" description and which to a "feeling" description. How much overlap in content is there between the two descriptions? Does this suggest that each theory may be suited for different kinds of planning issues? Explain your answer.

Endnotes

[1] A specific date when business planning began is difficult to establish. Leontiades observed in 1980 that separate, specialized units to do planning had only recently emerged. See Milton Leontiades, *Strategies for Diversification and Change* (Boston: Little, Brown, 1980), p. 115. Andrews observes that strategic planning, a cornerstone of the business planning process, was first introduced into General Electric Company in 1970. The concept had been discussed in universities some years before. Kenneth R. Andrews, *The Concept of Corporate Strategy* (Homewood, IL: Irwin, 1987), pp. 8–9.

[2] See, for example, "Planning for Future Perfect," *Sales and Marketing Report*, February 6, 1978, pp. 27–31.

[3] James S. Ang and Jess H. Chua, "Long Range Planning in Large United States Corporations—A Survey," *Long Range Planning*, 12, no. 2 (April 1979), pp. 99–102.

[4] "Planning for Future Perfect."

[5] Parmanand Kumar, "Long-Range Planning Practices by U.S. Companies," *Managerial Planning*, 26, no. 4 (January/February 1978), 31–33, 38.

[6] James K. Brown and Rochelle O'Connor, *Planning and the Corporate Planning Director*, Report No. 627 (New York:The Conference Board, 1974), pp. 54–56.

[7] Howard A. Karten, "Study Says DP-Assisted Planning Makes the Grade," *Computerworld*, December 18, 1978, p. 15.

[8] Ronald J. Kudia, "The Components of Strategic Planning," *Long Range Planning*, 11, no. 6 (December 1978), 48–52

[9] Philip S. Thomas, "Environmental Scanning—The State of The Art," *Long Range Planning*, 13, no. 1 (February 1980), 20–28.

[10] Kudia, "The Components of Strategic Planning."

[11] Ang and Chua, "Long Range Planning in Large United States Corporations."

[12] Kudia, "The Components of Strategic Planning."

[13] Gordon Pearson, "Business Strategy Should Not Be Bureaucratic," *Accountancy*, 97, no. 1112 (April 1986), 109–12.

[14] Yezdi M. Godiwalla, Wayne A. Meinhart, and William D. Warde, "Environmental Scanning—Does It Help The Chief Executive?," *Long Range Planning*, 13, no. 5 (October 1980), 87–99.

[15] Harold W. Henry, "Then and Now: A Look at Strategic Planning Systems," *Journal of Business Strategy*, 1, no. 3 (Winter 1981), 64–69.

[16] For a discussion of the way chief executive officers distinguish between strategic planning and long-range planning, see Ruth Gilbert Shaeffer, *Developing Strategic Leadership* (New York: The Conference Board, 1984), pp. 2–5.

[17]The issues management process usually serves as a barometer of the currency of stage plans; if issues management is no longer able to keep strategic plans up to date, it is time to do additional strategic and/or tactical planning. See Chapter 2 for a discussion of issues management.

[18]See Richard T. Pascale, "Our Curious Addiction to Corporate Grand Strategy," *Fortune*, January 25, 1982, pp. 115–16; Dennis C. King and Walter G. Beevor, "Long-Range Thinking," *Personnel Journal*, 57, no. 10 (October 1978), 542 –45.

[19]In some organizations the organization structure may be divided at the top level into units based on geographic region or technological type. In these organizations business planning must be done for these levels.

[20]The group is similar to a division. In some organizations related businesses may be combined in wholly owned subsidiary corporations.

[21]The most important activity distinguishing executives from other managers in an organization may be the planning activity. See Patrick Calby, "Analysis of Management and Professional Jobs for Systematic Career Planning and Development," Ph.D. dissertation, Loyola University of Chicago, 1984.

[22]It is useful to speak of organizations as though they "do" things. Obviously, it is people who use organizations to do things.

[23]Many readers will have learned to define "goals" as this chapter has defined "objectives" and vice versa. There does not appear to be agreement about which is a broad aim of an organization and which is a specific aim. See the discussion in Rochelle O'Connor, *Corporate Guides to Long-Range Planning*, Report No. 687 (New York: The Conference Board, 1976), p. 67.

[24]Organizations are open systems but are not necessarily negentropic systems. To be a *negentropic* system—that is, to avoid evolution toward a condition of increasing disorder—an organization must not only be open to the environment but also must be both a net importer of energy in some form from the environment and be capable of using this energy to achieve increased order and complexity. For further discussion of this point, see Lloyd R. Amey, *Corporate Planning: A Systems View* (New York: Praeger, 1986), appendix pp. 10–11.

[25]Romanelli and Tushman have identified three prominent models of organizational evolution. E. Romanelli and M. L. Tushman, "Inertia, Environments and Strategic Choice: A Quasi-Experimental Design for Comparative-Longitudinal Research," *Management Science*, 32, no. 5 (May 1986), 608–21. In all of these models, environment plays a critical role. See Barbara W. Keats and Michael A. Hitt, "A Causal Model of Linkages Among Environmental Dimensions, Macro Organizational Characteristics, and Performance," *Academy of Management Journal*, 31, no. 3 (September 1988), 572.

[26]Francisco J. Varela, *Principles of Biological Autonomy* (New York: North Holland, 1979).

[27]See, for example, ibid., pp. 167–69.

[28]Humberto R. Maturana and Francisco J. Varela, *Autopoiesis and Cognition: The Realization of the Living* (Boston: Reidel, 1980), p. 9.

[29]For a parallel discussion of the ability of tradition to outlive the leaders of an organization, see J. Douglas Brown, *The Human Nature of Organizations* (New York: AMACOM, 1973), pp. 68–69.

[30]That is, they are not "goal-directed." Humberto L. Maturana, "Conclusions," in Maturana and Varela, *Autopoiesis and Cognition,* p. 51. An exception may occur: If goal direction becomes an element of organization identity, then organizations may be said to be goal-directed.

[31]The concern of an organization to maintain its identity was observed by Selznick. "As an

organization acquires a self, a distinctive entity, it becomes an institution. This [process of becoming an institution] involves the taking on of values, ways of acting and believing, that are deemed important for their own sake. From then on self-maintenance becomes more than bare organizational survival; it becomes a struggle to preserve the uniqueness of the group in the face of new problems and altered circumstances." Philip Selznick, *Leadership in Administration: A Sociological Interpretation* (New York: Harper & Row, 1957), p. 21. See also pp. 16–22.

[32]Professional journals available in the United States that regularly publish articles about business planning in other countries include *Academy of Management Journal, Chief Executive, Forbes, Harvard Business Review, Human Resource Planning; International Journal of Manpower* (UK), *International Management* (UK), *International Studies of Management & Organization, Journal of Business Strategy, Journal of International Business Studies, Long Range Planning* (UK), *Management Japan* (Japan), *Management Today* (UK), and *Strategic Management Journal* (UK).

Chapter 2

Strategic Business Planning

The importance of strategic planning to the business planning process may be illustrated by the well-known jest about the pilot who told his passengers in midflight that he had some bad news and some good news. The bad news was that he didn't know where they were going. The good news was that he was getting them there in a hurry. Strategic planning ensures that the organization knows where it is going. Without strategic planning, tactical planning and operational planning can only ensure that the organization gets to an unknown, perhaps undesirable, destination.

Strategic planning in complex organizations may be done at the enterprise, functional, group, and business unit levels of organization. The majority of examples in this chapter are drawn from the enterprise level. Where such examples are not appropriate for other levels of planning, examples will be provided for those other levels as well.

The human resource professional who wishes to participate in strategic planning should be informed about strategic planning concepts, the strategic planning process, and the role of human resources in the process.

STRATEGIC PLANNING CONCEPTS

Four concepts provide structure for, and therefore simplify, strategic planning.[1] These are:

- Strategic business units
- Distinctive competence
- Strategic group mapping
- Experience curves

Strategic business units provide a way for complex and diversified organizations to divide the responsibility for strategic planning and implementation among different people in the organization. *Distinctive competence* provides a way of understanding the organization's strengths and weaknesses in dealing with its environment. *Strategic group mapping* provides a way of understanding the strategies used by other firms producing the same products or services. *Experience curves* provide a way of understanding the effects of being first in the market with a new product. Each of these ideas will be discussed in turn.

Strategic Business Units

Parts of an organization that face similar competitive challenges and opportunities in the marketplace, and therefore may use similar strategies, may be combined into a single unit called a *strategic business unit*.[2] Persons employed in each strategic business unit specialize in selected areas of competitive proficiency. This makes the task of achieving competitive advantage manageable. Exhibit 2-1 illustrates the strategic business unit.

Part A of Exhibit 2-1 shows a partial organization chart for Products, Inc.,[3] a firm that produces five types of products: agricultural products, industrial supplies, office equipment, sporting goods, and leisure products. Originally, each of these products was grouped into a separate product division, and all five product divisions reported to a vice president of operations. The chief executive officer and the vice president of operations oversaw the strategic planning for all these diverse products as well as for the company as a whole.

Because the strategic considerations of some of the product divisions were similar, the divisions were grouped into strategic business units and a vice president was appointed to head each group. This reorganization is shown in Part B of Exhibit 2-1. The firm must now support an additional vice presidency—a worthwhile investment because it allows for better strategic planning.

With the revised organization structure in effect, the two strategic business units (Exhibit 2-1, Part B) will concentrate on achieving competitive advantage in their respective lines of business. Enterprise-level strategic planning will concentrate on strategic planning for the organization as a whole. It will concentrate on questions such as:

- What is out there in the environment?
- What are the proper strategies for dealing with the environment?
- How can responsibility for management of these strategies be allocated among the strategic business units?
- Is our present business unit configuration appropriate for meeting the challenges of the environment?

Once these questions have been answered, the corporation sets about the task of developing an appropriate business unit configuration through acquisition,

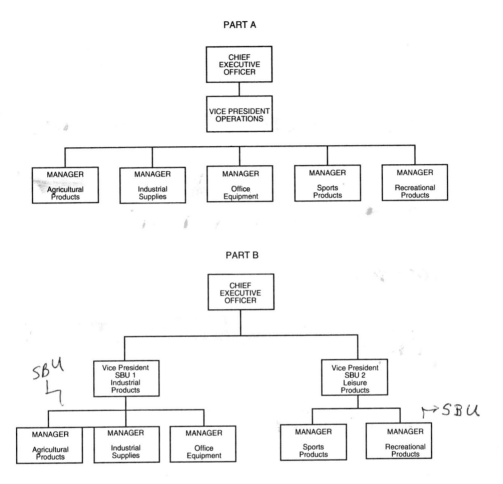

Exhibit 2-1. Organization Chart of Products, Inc., before and after Division into Strategic Business Units

divestiture, growth, or downsizing.[4] The new configuration initiates another cycle of realigned responsibilities for lines of business and new organizationwide strategic planning. And the cycle continues.

Successful companies change their organization structure frequently.[5] The strategic business unit is a dynamic tool of strategic management that allows reorganization as necessary to cope with a turbulent environment.

Distinctive Competence

The idea of *distinctive competence* was first used by Philip Selznick in 1957.[6] He used the term to describe an organization's relative strengths—that set of things that an organization did especially well *in comparison to its competitors*. Raymond Miles and Charles Snow popularized the idea of distinctive competence by relating strategic orientations of organizations to distinctive competences of the organizations. They developed a classification that included four strategic orientations:

- Defender—This type of organization has a narrow product market domain. Top managers are highly expert in their organization's limited area of operation but do not tend to search outside their domain for new opportunities. As a result of this narrow focus, this type of organization seldom needs to make major adjustments in its technology, structure, or methods of operation. Instead, it devotes primary attention to improving the efficiency of its existing operations.

- Prospector—This type of organization almost continually searches for market opportunities, and it regularly experiments with potential responses to emerging environmental trends. Thus, it often is a creator of change and uncertainty, to which its competitors must respond. However, because of its strong concern for product and market innovation, this type of organization usually is not highly efficient.

- Analyzer—This type of organization attempts to maintain a stable, limited line of products or services, while at the same time moving quickly to follow a carefully selected set of the more promising new developments in the industry. It seldom is "first in" with new products or services. However, by carefully monitoring the actions of major competitors in areas compatible with its stable product market base, the organization frequently can be "second in" with a more cost-efficient product or service.

- Reactor—This type of organization does not appear to have a consistent product-market orientation. It is usually not as aggressive in maintaining established products and markets as some of its competitors, nor is it willing to take as many risks as other competitors. Rather, the organization responds in those areas where it is forced to do so by environmental pressures.[7]

In a study published in 1980, Snow and Lawrence Hrebiniak extended the work of Miles and Snow by demonstrating that organizations in similar environments often could enjoy equal success while pursuing different strategies if the organizations had distinctive competences appropriate to their strategies.[8] The study included a survey of 88 companies in four industries. Two of the industries, automotive and air transportation, had environments characterized by low uncertainty, and two, plastics and semiconductors, had environments characterized by high uncertainty. Top managers in the firms reported that all four strategic types were represented in each of the industries. The distinctive competences used by the strategic types were:

- Defenders—Strength in general management, financial management, production, and applied engineering.
- Prospectors—Strength in general management, financial management, marketing/selling, and basic engineering.
- Analyzers—Strength in general management, production, and financial management. Other strengths varied considerably among industries.
- Reactors—As expected, no logical or consistent pattern of distinctive competence.[9]

Defenders, prospectors, and analyzers generally showed varying degrees of success. Reactors generally were unsuccessful, except in the air transportation industry, where competition was limited by government regulation. Reactors performed second only to analyzers in this industry.[10]

This study demonstrates that firms gain a competitive advantage by seeing that the environments they choose to operate in, the strategic orientation they choose to adopt, and the distinctive competences they choose to develop all are suited to one another.[11]

Strategic Group Mapping

In *strategic group mapping* an organization plots the position of each competitor on a graph. The graph shows the strategies used by each organization and the success of those strategies. An example of a strategic group map for the retail jewelry industry is shown in Exhibit 2-2. The manner in which strategic group mapping is accomplished will be illustrated by reference to this example.

Typically, four steps are involved. First, two key strategic variables are selected as the basis for defining the industry's strategic groups.[12] For the retail jewelry industry these variables are the extensiveness of merchandise offered for sale and the quality of the merchandise offered for sale, as indicated by the price of the merchandise. These two variables are used as axes for a two-dimensional map. Second, each firm is plotted on the map. For example, a firm selling a small variety of high-quality jewelry would be plotted in the upper left quadrant of the map. All firms in the jewelry industry are plotted in the same manner.

Third, groupings of firms are identified. When all firms are plotted it will appear that firms tend to cluster at a small number of points on the map. Firms located at the same position on the map form strategic groups. Because the firms in a group have similar extent of merchandise offered for sale and quality of merchandise, they are likely to adopt similar strategies. Finally, characteristics of strategic groups, such as market share, profitability, and location, are shown by the use of appropriate location symbols. In the map of Exhibit 2-2, relative share of the market is indicated by the size of the circle used as a location symbol.[13]

Strategic group mapping is especially useful to a firm doing strategic planning in a highly complex industry.[14] An industry is a group of firms that produce the same or similar products or services. A complex industry has many firms of many types. Because firms in the same strategic group generally resemble each other closely, strategic group mapping reduces the complexity of the industry by allowing the consideration of a few strategic groups rather than many firms. This similarity can aid in the identification of strategic opportunities in the industry. Following are several examples:

- Because firms in the same strategic group tend to behave similarly, it may be possible to predict how an entire group of firms will respond to future events, such as an increase in the purchase of jewelry as an investment. This knowledge may allow the identification of opportunities associated with this change.

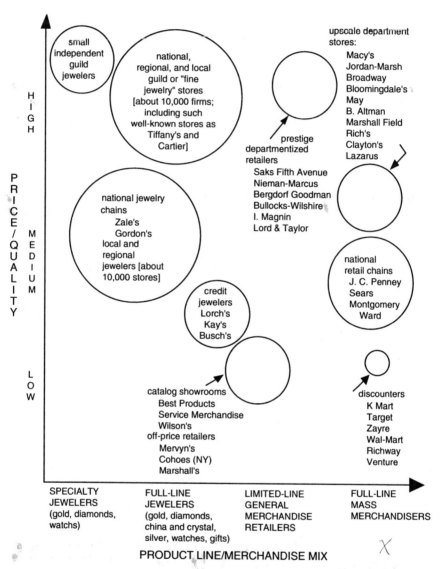

Exhibit 2-2.   Illustrative Strategic Group Map of Competitors in the Retail Jewelry Industry

Source: Arthur A. Thompson, Jr., and A. J. Strickland III, *Strategy Formulation and Implementation: Tasks of The General Manager,* 3rd ed. (Plano, TX: Business Publications, 1986), p. 101.

- Because entry barriers tend to vary among strategic groups, strategic group mapping helps to identify strategic groups where entry may be more readily accomplished.
- Because firms in different strategic groups often differ in their vulnerability to competition, strategic group mapping helps to reveal opportunities for expansion of the market of substitute products.[15]

By knowing its competition, a firm may plan its strategies in order to have an advantage over its competitors.

Experience Curves

An *experience curve* expresses the idea that as an organization gains experience in the use of a process, it becomes more proficient in carrying out the process. This idea was popularized by Boston Consulting Group in the late 1960s. On the basis of the Group's experiences with client firms, Bruce D. Henderson, president, estimated that unit costs tended to decline by a fixed percentage, usually in the order of 20 to 30 percent,[16] each time the number of units produced doubled.[17] This decline was attributed to the combined effects of learning,[18] specialization, increased scale of operation, increased capital investment, and incremental gains associated with debugging and otherwise making bit-by-bit improvements in state-of-the-art technology.[19]

Because unit costs may decline markedly with experience, strategies to increase the probability of being first in the market with a new product deserve consideration by a firm. By entering a market first, a cost advantage can be gained over potential competitors and this cost advantage can be used to deter the entry of others into the market. This strategy is especially useful in a market where price is an important consideration to purchasers of the product. A firm may keep out potential competitors either by lowering product price as the firm's unit costs decline or by threatening a price war if competitors enter the market.

In situations where a firm finds itself in a position of being a later entrant into the market, it must decide about its willingness and ability to accept possible initial losses to gain market share.

One disadvantage of pursuing a strategy intended to protect an initial market position is that experience can become a negative value and a detriment in the long run if it leads to undue commitment to existing plants and processes.[20]

There is increasing recognition, especially among Japanese producers, that the experience curve need not be fixed.[21] The rate at which people learn a new process may be changed sharply by the promotion of conditions in organizations that favor learning, such as creation of moderate pressure to produce, provision of motivation to learn, and lowering of turnover rates.[22]

The experience curve can be used to explain when new technologies should be introduced or to understand the competitive advantage of entire industries and national economies.

STRATEGIC PLANNING PROCESS

Planning is an iterative process. As the process unfolds, it changes form. The order of the steps for planning presented here is only a rough guide. It may prove necessary to perform two or more steps together. And some steps may need to be done only as a basis for performing other steps when the initial steps may be finished. For example, the objectives of planning must be known before participants can be selected; but participants no doubt will wish to refine the initially stated objectives. The order given is a beginning point for the process.

The following steps should be carried out in strategic planning:

- Establish objectives for the planning process.
- Identify participants and define their responsibilities.
- Choose an organization philosophy.
- Study the environment.
- Establish organization identity.
- Establish organization objectives.
- Establish organization strategies.
- Implement the chosen strategies.
- Evaluate the planning effort.
- Manage the issues arising under the strategic plan.

Establishing Objectives for the Planning Process

Deciding in advance on the purpose or purposes of planning is the most important of the steps of strategic planning. Planning often fails because those planning do not define the objectives. Setting objectives gives direction to the process and provides criteria for evaluating the planning effort.

There are two types of planning objectives: process objectives and product objectives. *Process objectives* are changes we wish to produce in the knowledge, understanding, attitudes, or values of people by involving those people in the planning process. It is not necessary for a final written plan to be drafted and implemented for process objectives to be achieved. For example, increased ability to make day-to-day decisions on the job as a result of taking part in decision making during planning is a process objective.

In contrast, *product objectives* require the completion of a plan. They are changes that occur because an explicit, written plan was communicated to stakeholders and was implemented. Better understanding by stakeholders of organization activities is a product objective.

Planning may be conducted for process objectives alone, for product objectives alone, or for both kinds of objectives. Most organizations will have both process and product objectives. Listed here are some possible objectives of the planning process. They range from objectives that are almost entirely process to those that are almost entirely product; in between are those that are both process and product in nature.

Process 1. To promote acceptance of intended future courses of action
Process 2. To provide a vehicle through which the organization can "learn"from its experience and adapt accordingly

3. To draw agreement from the management levels as to what they will be trying to accomplish[23]
4. To improve the quality of decision making in the organization
5. To achieve greater efficiency of resource allocation and utilization
6. To achieve coordination, integration, or cohesion of subunits of the organization
7. To develop a frame of reference for making current decisions[24]
8. To correct past errors in decision making
9. To improve the performance of the organization in some respect
10. To deal with uncertainty and change in the environment
11. To deal with external pressures or threats in the environment
12. To control and/or to manage growth of the organization and its businesses
13. To determine and implement appropriate future courses of action

An unrealistically long list of objectives will not provide focus for the planning effort. The list of objectives can be kept manageable in size by subjecting each proposed objective to three questions.

Is this objective basic enough to merit inclusion on the list? An objective is basic if achieving the objective will, in turn, lead to the achievement of other objectives. For example, in some organizations, objective 2, (to provide a vehicle…)will itself lead to the achievement of objective 4 (to improve the quality…). Only basic objectives should be chosen.

Would actions taken to achieve this objective conflict with the achievement of other, more desirable objectives? For example, objective 6 (to correct past errors…), by focusing attention on mistakes, may inhibit the experimentation needed to achieve objective 2.

Is this objective worth the necessary expenditure of organization time and money to achieve? If the final list of objectives includes only those that are basic, that produce little discord with other objectives, and are ones planners will support, the list will be short and will provide a sharp focus for planning.

Identifying Participants and Their Responsibilities

People in an organization participate in planning by influencing the planning process in some way. Few or many members of an organization may participate. At the one extreme, the chief executive officer and his or her staff may do all planning. At the other extreme, every member of the organization may take some part in planning. Most frequently the number of participants falls in between these extremes. People influence the planning process in various ways. They may approve the work of others who do the actual work of planning, they may serve on a committee that does the actual planning, they may give suggestions to the committee, they may respond to surveys of various kinds, they may serve on task forces to do specific planning tasks, and they may carry out the plan finally developed.

In deciding who should participate in planning, every member of the organization should be considered a potential participant. In most organizations, those members assigned to a strategic planning committee will do the actual work of planning. But every member of the organization may be able to contribute in some way to the work of the committee.

Selecting Members of the Strategic Planning Committee

Persons should be chosen for membership on the strategic planning committee who have knowledge, skills, and personal characteristics that allow them to contribute to the planning effort.

Two kinds of knowledge are especially useful on the committee: knowledge about a specialized function of the organization and knowledge about the organization as a whole.[25] Knowledge about the organization as a whole includes both knowledge about the management of business organizations in general and knowledge about the particular managerial requirements of the specific organization.

Interpersonal skills of value are tact, persuasiveness, ability to listen to others, and ability to command respect. These characteristics help a member to get consideration of his or her ideas by other persons on the committee.

An attitude toward one's work that complements well all of these interpersonal skills is activity stance. The appropriate activity stance for a professional serving on a planning committee is proactive. A proactive stance is a readiness to anticipate events and to initiate appropriate action before events occur rather than merely respond to events after they occur. To be proactive requires that one be able to "read" a situation and to see what needs doing; to be reactive only requires that one react to a problem after the problem is apparent.

Careful selection of the persons to serve on the committee is necessary, as size of the committee is critical for committee effectiveness. Large groups tend to become unwieldy; and individuals lack a feeling of responsibility and sense of involvement in large groups. In large and complex organizations, it will be especially difficult to represent all parts of the organization and also keep committee size to manageable proportions. The use of appropriate conferencing techniques allows larger committees, numbering perhaps 1,000 or more. In traditional practice, committee size ranges from less than 10 to as many as 100.[26]

It will be useful to find persons for planning who can perform multiple functions in the planning group or persons who can be trained to perform multiple functions so that the requisite planning expertise can be obtained while keeping the size of the group to a minimum. For example, persons may be found who have knowledge or skills useful for planning, occupy positions of influence, and can represent the views of several interest groups. Or representatives of interest groups may be trained to enhance their planning skills and knowledge. Or persons with critical planning skills or knowledge may be trained to enhance their ability to influence others.

Choosing an Organization Philosophy

An organization philosophy is a commitment of the organization to a set of principles that allocates the responsibilities of the organization toward its various stakeholders. Stakeholders of an organization may include employees, investors, major lenders, traditional customers, unions, the local community, environmentalists, consumer advocates, government agencies, and the public at large.[27]

Need for an Organization Philosophy

An organization philosophy serves as an ethical and practical guide for conducting the affairs of the organization. The set of principles contained in an organization philosophy provides a formula for reconciling the needs of the various stakeholders and the needs of the organization as a whole.[28]

An organization philosophy is necessary for strategic planning. It serves as a vehicle for expressing the values of the organization in its strategic plans. The philosophy provides an answer to the questions, How much sacrifice of stakeholder well-being will be tolerated to enhance the well-being of the organization as a whole, and how much sacrifice of organization well-being will be tolerated to enhance the well-being of the stakeholders? How much responsibility does the organization owe to its stakeholders, and how much responsibility do stakeholders owe to the organization?

Substance of a Philosophy

The values expressed by a philosophy are abstract. The words of an organization philosophy can only partly state the feelings of organization members who develop the philosophy. What matters in an organization philosophy is the collective agreement of organization planners about the basic responsibilities of an organization.

First, an organization philosophy should deal with the fundamental purposes of the organization. Organization members must find and articulate those reasons for the existence of the organization beyond narrow self-interest. Second, the organization philosophy should state the trade-offs to be made where the needs of various stakeholders and of the organization are in conflict—that is, where obtaining one set of needs requires a sacrifice in other sets of needs.

Tenure of a Philosophy

An organization philosophy will remain unchanged so long as the basic purposes of the organization remain unchanged. But organizations do exist in a changing world, and an organization philosophy must be able to change with the world around it. No organization philosophy can commit an organization irrevocably to a given set of trade-offs among stakeholder and organization needs. For this reason, an organization philosophy needs to be reviewed periodically. Whether or not the philosophy is changed, the occasion of a review provides an opportunity to rededicate the organization to its principles.

Choosing a Philosophy

In choosing a philosophy, two basic points should be considered. First, the values of top management cannot be successfully imposed on an organization. Top management must, at a minimum, consider the values of other stakeholders in the organization when choosing a philosophy.[29] Second, human values are likely to "fit" the organization as it is seen by the various stakeholders. People see organizations as anthropomorphous—as resembling a human.[30] Human values may be used with little change as the values of an organization. In the past, organization philosophies often have been statements of the beliefs of founders of organizations.[31] For example, IBM's philosophy is that set of values put down on paper by its founder, Thomas J. Watson, Sr. These values became the foundation for the entire organization.[32]

For established organizations that have no organization philosophy or that wish to revise their organization philosophy, a committee of admired and respected individuals may be used to define the values and beliefs of the organization. If these members are held in esteem by all important stakeholder groups, the values and beliefs they articulate will be the values and beliefs of many stakeholders of the organization.[33]

An organization philosophy must be that of the entire organization in the sense that the entire organization must either accept or acquiesce in the philosophy. Unless the values contained in a statement of philosophy are satisfying to organization stakeholders and practiced by most persons in the organization, they become empty slogans.

Studying the Environment

A study of the environment is done to discover information of relevance for the organization. The steps in an environmental study are setting objectives for the study, determining the scope of the study, conducting the study, and summarizing the results of the study.

Setting Objectives for the Study

The objectives of a study effort should be defined carefully before the study begins. Both process and product objectives should be included. This will help to focus attention on areas of real concern to planners.

One very important process objective (a desired change in people who participate in the study process) is to bring about an accurate view of the environment by top management.[34] This can be accomplished in part by requiring top management to participate directly in an environmental study. Product objectives (specific kinds of information we wish to produce for use in planning) will vary considerably with the planning needs of the organization. For example, information may be needed in an organization about expected changes in the lifestyles of consumers. This information will help to determine changes in demand for the organization's different products and therefore the appropriateness of different objectives and strategies for the organization.

Determining the Scope of the Study

Before conducting a study of the environment, a decision should be made as to how extensive the study is to be. Two questions need to be answered: How often will the environment be studied? How much of the environment will be studied? Liam Fahey and William King have identified three study models used by organizations to answer these questions: the irregular, the regular, and the continuous.[35]

The *irregular model* is designed to react to a crisis. It requires that a study be conducted each time an unanticipated major event occurs. The study is limited to a determination of what the event means for the organization and what immediate or short-term defensive measures need to be taken. The *regular model* is not a response to a specific event but entails a regular review of selected events in the environment, such as changes in consumer preferences. Its purpose typically is to monitor those events likely to affect particular decisions or challenges confronting the organization so that adjustments in organization actions can be made as necessary.

The *continuous model* is neither a response to a specific event nor a review of selected events. This model entails the continuous monitoring of all those sectors of the environment of importance to the organization to allow a determination of the appropriate future course of the organization. Unlike the first two models, which are retrospective, this model is prospective, in that the information will be used to make decisions about courses of action. Also unlike the first two models, this model requires a commitment to planning commensurate with the commitment to continuous study envisioned by this model.

An organization may use the irregular model and the regular model either alone or together. The continuous model is sufficient when used alone.

Conducting the Study

A comprehensive study of the environment should consist of two parts: a study of characteristics of organization relationships in the environment and a study of characteristics of sectors of the environment.[36] Each part of the study requires a different approach.[37] The discussion that follows is based on a continuous model, although the procedures described may be followed for the regular and the irregular models as well.

Study of Relationships

A study of relationships involves that part of the environment—people and groups of people, other organizations or government agencies—with which the organization interacts.[38] To identify relationships of the organization with other entities, planners may

1. Audit a random sample of organization records to determine with what outside persons, groups, and other organizations the focal organization has direct contacts. Likely sources of information are job descriptions of boundary maintenance positions, correspondence files, records of telephone calls placed, unit telephone directories, supplier lists, purchaser lists, and employee memberships in external organizations paid by the employer.

    To determine with what additional outside persons, groups, and other organizations the focal organization has indirect contacts, interviews may be conducted with persons in boundary maintenance positions, such as general managers and staff specialists, who have continued relationships with outside persons, groups, and organizations.
2. Determine the type(s) of relationship(s) between each external entity and the organization, taking into consideration the direction of the relationship, that is, organization $\rightarrow$ external entity, organization $\leftarrow$ external entity, or organization $\leftrightarrow$ external entity.[39] Possible kinds of relationships are alliance, attacking, control, contractual, defending, dependence, familial, neighbor, purchasing, rapport, selling, support, symbiotic, and combinations.[40]
3. Determine the objects of exchange of each relationship.[41]
4. Assess the importance to the organization and the stability of each relationship. In some cases the help of activity area specialists will be necessary.

Study of Sectors

In order to reduce the study of the environment to manageable proportions, we divide it into sectors—economic, cultural, social, technological, demographic, political, legal, infrastructure, and ecological. To identify characteristics of the sectors, planners may

1. Develop a listing of the major activities performed in all primary functions of the organization and its various businesses.[42] For example, a primary function of most manufacturing businesses would be marketing. Activities that might be performed in connection with marketing are marketing research, product design, selection of distributors or outlets, physical distribution, personal selling, advertising and promotion, and pricing.[43]
2. Determine the sectors of the environment likely to be of importance to the organization, given the activities identified. For a large and complex organization, most sectors of the environment may be relevant. For smaller or less complex organizations, only one or two sectors may be relevant.
3. Develop a reasonably complete list of environmental characteristics for all relevant sectors of the environment. The following illustrates such a listing for the demographic sector:[44]

Population density	Demographic growth rate
Population mobility	Population growth rate
Birth rate	Population distribution by age
Death rate	Population distribution by sex
Immigration rate	Population distribution by family
Emigration rate	construction

   To ensure completeness, this list should be prepared by referring to a number of published lists.[45]
4. Determine which characteristics from step 3 are important for carrying out the activities from step 1. For example, the characteristic "population distribution by age" may be considered important for the "personal selling" activity of the marketing function. The resulting list should be updated periodically to ensure that all important characteristics are included.
5. Determine the current state, direction and rate of change, and expected future trends of each important characteristic. Some characteristics may require further study. For example, if "population distribution by age" is shifting toward older age groups, it may be useful to know whether this shift is caused by past intergenerational differences in birth rates or by an increase in average life span. Sources of information about environmental sectors are abundant.[46]

At times the process of identifying sector characteristics may need the help of activity area specialists.

Interpreting the Results

The results of the study have more practical value if the findings are interpreted in terms that have meaning for planning. Each characteristic identified can be classified according to whether it embodies[47]

- A *threat* to the objective of effective operation of the organization

- A *constraint* on the operations of the organization and therefore a potential threat to the objective of effective operation
- A *problem* for the organization—a situation that requires a solution to prevent it from becoming a constraint or a threat
- A *negative symptom* that serves as the basis for a forecast of an approaching problem, constraint, or threat
- A *neutral condition* that has the potential to become either a positive or a negative influence on the objective of effective operation of the organization
- A *positive symptom* that serves as the basis for a forecast of an approaching opportunity, a lifting of constraints, or an assist to the objective of effective operation of the organization
- An *opportunity* for the organization—a situation that allows action to turn opportunity into a lifting of constraints or an assist to the objective of effective operation of the organization
- A *removal of constraints* on the organization and therefore a potential assist to the objective of effective operation of the organization
- An *assist* to the objective of effective operation of the organization

Summarizing the Results

Environments are complex. Even that portion of the environment of concern to an organization, the organization domain, is complex. If planners are to consider the environment as they plan, they must be able to envision the environment. A summary report of the organization domain can assist planners to envision it as an integrated, manageable whole.[48]

Perhaps the most effective report is simply a tabular listing of major opportunities, threats, and constraints to the organization. These should be classified according to how important they are and according to whether the opportunity, threat, or constraint arises out of a relationship or out of a sector of the environment. This listing should represent a consensus report of the planning committee and should be intended for the committee's own use. A sample report is shown in Exhibit 2-3. For a complex organization, such a report is likely to include 25 or more items.[49]

Establishing Organization Identity

Organization identity has been defined as that set of characteristics that make an organization unique. There are three complementary means of discovering organization identity. Planners may look at the ability of the organization to deal with the environment, conduct formal studies of the organization itself, or learn the organization through experience. One of these means will not suffice alone in discovering organization identity. Planners must choose a combination of these to arrive at a final determination.

Summary Report of Strategic Planning Committee
Environmental Scanning Study
E. C. Corporation*

Characteristics of Relationships

Items of Major Importance

- Threat to viability of many present units from deterioration of services provided by major cities.
- _____
- _____

Items of Importance

- Increased threat of foreign and domestic competition as size of market segment increases.
- _____
- _____

Characteristics of Sectors

Items of Major Importance

- Opportunities for expansion into new service areas as a result of pending national legislation in the health care field.
- _____
- _____

Items of Importance

- Expected opportunities created by decline in proportion of families that own their own home.
- _____
- _____

*To the author's knowledge, not an actual company.

Exhibit 2-3.   Sample Summary Report of Environmental Scanning for E. C. Corporation

Using an Environmental Mirror

The *open systems theory* of organizations defines organization identity in terms of the ability of an organization to cope with its environment.[50] This approach is similar to our discovering what we look like by viewing ourselves in a mirror. Planners learn what the organization is like by viewing it in the mirror of the environment. Looking in the mirror of the environment, planners ask

How are we seen by persons outside the organization?
How are we doing out there?
What is our market share?
What has been the trend in our sales?
Do people see us as a good place to work?

Ability to cope with the environment, in the open systems view, largely depends on an organization having subsystems that are appropriate for their environment and for each other. In this view, organizations are composed of interrelated and complex subsystems. Thus organizations contain individuals (who are systems on their own account), who belong to groups or departments, which, in turn, belong to larger organization divisions, and so on.[51] Organization subsystems frequently studied in this connection are strategy, technology, human resources, structure, and decision making.

This view of an organization as a set of interrelated subsystems interacting with its environment is shown in Exhibit 2-4. Firm A illustrates the idea of congruence of organization subsystems with the environment and with each other. Firm A is operating in a stable and certain environment.[52] The characteristics of the subsystems of firm A are well suited for this environment.[53] Firm A has few lines of business, it follows a cost leadership product pricing strategy, it uses a technology with structured jobs, it uses few specialist and professional employees, it has a structure with a few closely related units, and its managers make individual decisions. The identity of firm A, as seen in the environmental mirror, is of a firm with subsystems that allow it to cope well with its environment.

Firm B illustrates an organization with subsystems that are not entirely appropriate for its environment and with each other.[54] The firm is operating in a turbulent and unpredictable environment. It is well suited for this environment in that it has many lines of business, it follows a product innovation and differentiation strategy, it has a structure with many dissimilar units,[55] and it makes collaborative decisions. But firm B is attempting to operate in a turbulent environment with a technology of structured jobs and with few specialists and professional employees. Its technology and its personnel will be unsuited both for its environment and for its other subsystem characteristics. For example, collaboration in decision making will be unsuccessful because employees with the necessary specialties are not available to help with the complex and difficult decisions involved in introducing the many new products. The identity of firm B, as seen in the envi-

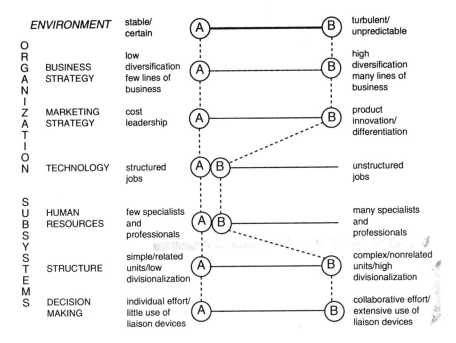

Exhibit 2-4. Congruence and Incongruence Among Organization Subsystems

ronmental mirror, is of a firm with subsystems that do not allow it to cope well with its environment.

Research suggests that ability to cope with the environment is an important measure of organization identity because the environment is critical to organization success.[56] However, open systems approaches to planning have not encouraged an extensive knowledge of the organization. It may be, in fact, that planners in U.S. organizations know the environment better than they know their own organizations.

Studies of the Organization Itself

The *self-producing systems theory* suggests that organizations are much more than an image in a mirror called the environment. Whereas organizations are initially only somewhat mechanical entities created to produce a product or service, as they continue to exist, they assume a complex existence of their own, similar in many respects to living organisms. As such, they assume an identity too complex to be understood by analyses that consider only the way they deal with the environment. Studies of the organization itself and deliberate attempts to get to know the organization through experience can add to planners' knowledge of the organization and thus its identity.

The focus of most of our discussion here will be on people, as people can tell us about organization identity. However, organization identity is created by all components of the organization, not just by people. Organization identity is a product of the relationships among people, buildings, capital resources, holdings of land, equipment, and intangible assets of the organization.

There are many possible approaches to the study of organizations. Two that are especially useful for disclosing the identity of a self-producing system are culture analysis and semantic analysis.

Studying Organization Identity Through Culture

The people involved provide the best evidence of organization identity, for people act out organization identity.[57] This acting out of organization identity is called organization culture.[58]

Organization culture may be studied by examining

- The words and behaviors common to members of an organization that distinguish them from people outside the organization
- The words that form the organization history
- The assumptions underlying the words and behaviors

The purpose of most words and behaviors in organization life is not to express culture but to accomplish work. Therefore, careful attention is necessary to observe those words and behaviors that do express culture. Observed over a period of time, words and behaviors can help flesh out an understanding of culture obtained through the examination of organization history and cultural assumptions.

Particularly revealing sources of information about organizations are the formal and informal histories—those created by the people of the organization—about the organization: reports, accounts, narratives, communications, myths, legends, and stories. Formal histories are those preserved by conscious decision. Informal histories are those preserved by oral tradition—that is, by being passed from one person to another by word of mouth. Both formal and informal histories contain inaccuracies and consciously embellished historical facts. For example, organization heroes are remembered as larger than life. That history is reinterpreted suggests that the reinterpretation serves to enhance organization identity. Informal histories may be particularly revealing of organization identity because remembering the history normally is not an assigned part of the work of people in the organization. Because people spontaneously choose to preserve the information by repeating it, such information likely expresses values important to them.

Much of the culture of an organization with a well-established identity may cease to be articulated by words or behaviors because the part of organization identity underlying the culture is so accepted that it is taken for granted. For example, in organizations with lifetime employment policies, members of the organization make a "tenure" assumption that once someone has been accepted he or she is likely to remain in the organization unless he or she fails in a major way. This assumption will not normally be called into question.[59] An examination of the basic assumptions on which a culture is based will reveal these latent features of culture and can be used to supplement a study of the words and behaviors and of the history of an organization.

Edgar Schein suggests that the basic assumptions underlying culture may be uncovered by questioning the basic beliefs of people. For the topics of belief listed below, he suggests questions similar to those indicated:[60]

Relationship of organization to environment	Do people view the relationship of organization to environment as one of dominance, submission, servitude, harmonizing, cooperation, or what?
Nature of reality and truth	What are the linguistic and behavioral rules that define what is real and what is not? What is a "fact"? How is truth determined? Is truth invented, discovered, or revealed?
Nature of time and space	Are time and space linear or cyclic? Are they measured by clock and yardstick or by accomplishment and utilization? Are they owned or merely occupied? What constitutes public and private space and time?
Nature of human beings	What does it mean to be "human"? What attributes are considered intrinsic or ultimate to human beings? Are humans perfectible?
Nature of human activity	Given answers to the above questions, what are human beings to do? Are they to be active or passive? Self-developmental or fatalistic? What is work and what is play?
Nature of human relationships	How are human beings to relate to each other? Are they to conserve or distribute power and love? Are their relationships to be competitive or cooperative? Individualistic, group collaborative, or communal? Governed by lineal authority, law, or charisma?

These questions may be used as a checklist to guide an examination of the words and behaviors used in organizations. They also may be used in the design of interview guides and questionnaires to survey persons familiar with the organization culture.

By examining the words, behaviors, and histories that emanate from the people of an organization, and by examining the basic assumptions behind the culture, inferences may be drawn about the organization identity that drives the culture. If the heroes of the culture are enterprising problem solvers, so, too, is the organization an ingenious problem solver. If the themes of stories about the organization are about socially responsible behavior, the organization is seen as socially responsible. Recurrent themes from independent sources are particularly persuasive—for example, themes that are common to stories told by persons who have little direct social contact. These are likely to have arisen out of a shared organization identity.

Studying Organization Identity Through Semantics

A more direct way of studying organization identity is to determine the meaning of the organization to organization participants. Charles Osgood, George Suci, and Percy Tannenbaum developed a method for doing this, called semantic differentiation.[61] Semantics is the study of meaning in language. Usually we state what an idea means to us by using other ideas, as in the definition just given for semantics. *Semantic differentiation* is a method for establishing dimensions for the entire range of meaning and for locating a particular idea within that range.

Semantic differentiation has proven to be a powerful and relatively simple way of describing ideas that are so rich in meaning that we find it difficult to express this meaning in a concise way. For example, assume that you are asked to describe XYZ Corporation, your place of work. You are likely to find this a time-consuming task. You also are likely to describe different aspects of XYZ Corporation than another employee.

In their research, Osgood, Suci, and Tannenbaum asked respondents to check off on each of a set of interval scales, a point they felt was most descriptive of an idea such as "organization." This set of scales was called a semantic differential. End points of each scale were described or "anchored" by bipolar adjectives suggesting opposite or polar amounts of a characteristic. The accompanying example shows scales anchored by the bipolar adjectives good/bad, weak/strong, and inactive/active used to describe "organization."

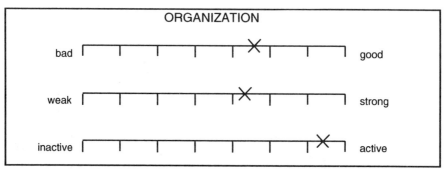

Osgood, Suci, and Tannenbaum, by repeating their research and using a large number of carefully selected respondents, scales, and ideas, were able to find a small number of representative scales[62] (12 is the number most frequently used) that could be used with almost all groups of people to describe almost every idea in everyday use.[63]

In actual use, a semantic differential used to measure the meaning of ideas useful for planning, such as the organization, its objectives, and its strategies, would need to be supplemented. The set of scales identified by Osgood, Suci, and Tannenbaum does not define in appropriate depth the entire range of meaning. This supplementation usually is done in a two-stage process. First, a procedure developed by Harry Triandis, called the triad procedure, is used to generate pairs of potentially relevant bipolar adjectives.[64] Next, a factor analysis is conducted to reduce the scales based on these adjectives to a number practical for use in a questionnaire.[65]

Three examples of the ways the semantic differential may be used in strategic planning are

- To compare the meaning of the organization, its objectives, and its strategies to planners with the meaning of the same ideas to other organization members. This will help to ensure that the ways planners think are representative of the thinking of organization members-at-large.
- To compare the meaning of implicit objectives and strategies with official strategies.
- To compare the meaning of the organization with the meaning of its objectives and strategies. This can help to determine whether the objectives and strategies are suited to the organization.

Getting to Know The Organization Through Participant Observation

The identity of an organization can never be captured fully by observational studies. Planners must become participant observers to truly understand their organization. Participant observation requires creative use of a wide range of observational techniques: prolonged face-to-face contact with the members of groups; penetration of "fronts" erected to present idealistic, false, or taken-for-granted images of a setting or the people in it; direct participation in group activities; and an emphasis on intensive work with group members rather than on the use of survey techniques.[66]

The self-producing systems theory suggests that participant observation be guided by the following additional recommendations:

- The organization and its environment must be studied together and by the same persons. An essential idea of the self-producing systems theory is that the organization is an inseparable part of its environment[67] and that organization identity cannot be understood apart from the environment.[68]
- The contacts of the participant observers must be wide enough to include the network of relations both within the organization and between the organization and its environment. It is the relations that aid in understanding the organization identity. Such contacts may require surmounting many different social and physical barriers.
- Learning about the organization through experience must come over a period of time so that the recursive cycles by which the organization adapts to change can be observed. Ideally, this experience would begin in the early stages of organization, while the organization is discovering its initial identity.

- All relationships must be observed with emphasis on the effect of change on the relationships. Participant observers should note which relationships among and between organization components—the artifacts, the objects, and the people of the organization and of the environment—are adjusted when change occurs. They should then try to determine what these adjustments or failures to adjust reveal about organization identity.
- The focus of the study is the organization, not its components. Organization identity controls all choices in the organization about relationships. What must be observed, then, is the nature of the relationships within the organization and its environment, not the characteristics of the components themselves.

Getting to Know the Organization by Changing It

In addition to observing the effects of naturally occurring change, planners may take advantage of their participant status and introduce planned change. This type of change is likely to produce the most profound learning. Managers as participant observers learn, along with the organization, its identity and its implicit objectives and strategies. Kurt Lewin has observed that if you wish to understand a system, you should try to change it.[69]

Establishing Organization Objectives and Strategies

Once the environment and the organization are known, objectives and strategies appropriate for the organization and its environment may be established. Objectives are desired future states of the organization. Strategies are ways the organization is to act to achieve those desired states.

Planners, in selecting objectives for the organization, should ensure that the objectives reflect the philosophy of the organization and can serve as a rallying point for the efforts of organization members. Objectives should be stated as broad, continuing aims or purposes of the organization.

Objectives for the enterprise level may be set in such areas as financial payoffs to stockholders in the form of dividends and capital gains, financial payoffs to employees in the form of compensation and benefits, employee quality of work life, quality of goods and services produced, social responsibility, long-term stability of the organization, and ability of the organization to withstand adversity. Objectives for the function, group, or business unit levels may be set in such areas as socially responsible operations and use of resources, competitive ability, profitability, revenue growth, cash flows, financial strength, industry leadership, product and resource market reputation, operating efficiency, overall size and degree of diversification, technological capability, and degree of vulnerability to recession.[70]

Once objectives have been chosen, strategies are selected that state how the organization will cope with the environment to achieve the objectives. Following are some examples of strategies intended for enterprise-level planning. Most are appropriate also for group- and business-level planning:

- Concentration on the current business(es)

- Marketing and product development ranging from cosmetic to substantial modifications of an existing product
- Innovation that creates new products and makes existing products obsolete
- Horizontal integration (entering related lines of business)
- Vertical integration (entering lines of business of present input suppliers and/or present output distributors)
- Joint venture/joint ownership; concentric diversification (diversification centered around a core strength)
- Conglomerate diversification (diversification in unrelated lines of business)
- Retrenchment, turnaround, divestiture, and/or liquidation
- Combination strategies[71]

Functions, like groups and businesses, use resources and produce an output. Strategies for functions must state how the function intends to maintain acceptance of its outputs and to secure necessary resources. This will differ greatly, depending on the function involved.

In choosing strategies, it must be kept in mind that the strategies must match both the organization and the environment. Matching the characteristics of organization and strategy alone will do little to affect organization performance. Neither will a matching of the characteristics of organization and environment. Organization, environment, and strategies all must be closely aligned or performance will suffer.[72]

Implementing Objectives and Strategies

The implementation of objectives and strategies in organizations is not easily accomplished. Even in organizations with highly developed planning systems, objectives and strategies often are not carried out.[73] How, then, can planners ensure that the objectives and strategies developed by the planning group will be implemented? The self-producing systems theory offers a guide.

An organization, though created by humans, soon realizes a life of its own. The organization continues to exist by ensuring that all change is consistent with its own identity. Organization objectives and strategies are central to organization identity. An organization, therefore, will accept objectives and strategies only if they are consistent with its identity. To ensure that the objectives and strategies that emerge from the planning process are consistent with organization identity, planners must involve the entire organization in the planning process.

The Crescive Approach to Strategy Implementation

Involving the entire organization in the planning process may be done by adopting a crescive approach to planning. A *crescive* (from the Latin crescere, "to grow") *approach* is one in which objectives and strategies are "grown" within the organization.[74] A parallel may be drawn between the growth of objectives and strategies in organizations and the growth of plants in a garden. What grows or doesn't grow in the garden is the product of many factors, including the amount of rainfall, soil conditions, and ambient temperature. The good gardener knows the garden, what is more likely to grow there and what is not, what will encourage the growth process and what will not. The good gardener encourages growth of a particular kind but recognizes that each plant requires special treatment. In the crescive approach to the implementation of objectives and strategies, the primary task of organization planners is to create in the organization a fertile, well-tended soil within which their strategies may be "grown."

The intensive focus of effort and information during planning produces ideas for objectives and strategies that would not otherwise occur. In the crescive approach, planners accept that the objectives and strategies they choose cannot be installed, but must develop, in their organizations. The groundwork for the acceptance of these objectives and strategies is laid long before the objectives and strategies are to be implemented.

If the organization is to accept the ideas of planners, the organization as a whole must share as much as possible the information and experiences of planners. And planners must use the ideas of others in the organization as they plan. The objectives and strategies chosen by planners are seeds to be planted in the organization. These objectives and strategies will be accepted and implemented only if the organization is a fertile soil for growing these particular seeds. The task of planners in implementing objectives and strategies is to foster those internal conditions that promote their growth:

- Planners must share widely their own knowledge of the organization and its environment and must encourage others to do the same. Every person associated with the organization and its environment must be encouraged to serve as a sensor, gathering information and remaining open to new and discrepant information. Ideas must be judged not by the author of the idea but by the merit of the idea. Organization leaders must collect and use this information and disseminate the information to others.

- Planners must create a climate within which a wide variety of reality-based objectives and strategies can emerge in a wide variety of places. They can do this by building flexible structures, creating opportunities for direct contact between persons in the organization and persons in the organization environment, fostering experiences that promote growth of organization members, hiring creative people and rotating them through positions that allow contact with others in the organization, providing seed funding for good ideas, ensuring minimal encumbrance by bureaucratic approval cycles, remaining tolerant of failure where planning and effort are adequate, and giving favorable publicity to innovations.

- Planners must promote organization learning by choosing experiences for the organization, such as joint ventures, for their long-term developmental effect, not solely for an immediate gain from the experience. Organizations determine "who" they are vis à vis their experiences. As participant observers, planners learn, along with the organization, its identity and its implicit objectives and strategies.

- The paths that organization leaders choose for their organizations should be selected with an eye toward developing implicit objectives and strategies for the organization. For maximum developmental effect, these experiences should

  - Have a high probability of success. Success tends to cause realistic aspiration levels in people and thus promotes reality-based planning.

- Include experiences in new environments where new experiences and new challenges are likely.

Evaluating the Planning Effort

Planning is not something to be completed within a given time. It is a continuous process of deliberation and testing. As organizations plan, they learn. The learning process may be quite extensive in complex organizations with extensive domains,[75] requiring years to perfect, during which extensive modification of management systems must occur.[76] Evaluation must be used as feedback to modify the planning process for future use.

Both the planning process and planning outcomes should be evaluated. In evaluating the planning process, reactions of both planners and other employees should be measured. At the end of each planning cycle, members of each planning committee should critique the planning process used and should make plans for revision of the process in future cycles. A questionnaire may be distributed to planning participants in advance to stimulate their thinking about needed changes. Exhibit 2-5 is an example of such a form. At the end of each planning cycle a similar form may be sent to all employees in the organization. Because employees must implement any planned changes, their reaction to the way planning is done is important. Exhibit 2-6 is an example of a form that may be used with employees.

Occasionally the planning process should be evaluated by outside organization behavior and planning consultants. Persons in the organization may be too close to the process to see its strengths and weaknesses objectively.

The manner in which the planning outcomes are evaluated will depend on the objectives established at the beginning of the planning process. If, for example, an expected outcome of planning is learning, tests of learning may be administered to participants. These tests can determine both how much planners are learning and whether they are gaining important knowledge. If an expected outcome of planning is to improve the profitability of the organization, an estimate should be made of the dollar amounts of both the benefits and costs of planning.

Where possible, before-and-after measures should be used for evaluations of both the planning process and the planning outcomes. For example, learning tests may be administered to planners before a planning cycle begins and at the end of the cycle. And the profitability of a business may be compared for two comparable years, one before and one after planning. Control groups should be used if possible. For example, in a large organization, planning may be started in one business or function first. Thus, effects of planning will be more apparent when that one business or function can be compared with other businesses or functions that do not plan.

Evaluation can be expensive, but it often increases the rate of improvement of the planning process and usually is a good investment.

XYZ Organization
Evaluation Form for Planners
Planning Effort, Current Year

Please place a check in the appropriate box for each of the items listed below. Use the space at the bottom to explain your answer if appropriate to do so.

	very little	little	some	much	very much
1. How much did you learn about planning as a science during this planning effort?					
2. How much did you learn about the XYZ organization during this planning effort?					
3. How much did you learn about the XYZ environment during this planning effort?					
4. To what extent did your attitudes and beliefs about others change as a result of this planning effort?					
5. To what extent did your values change as a result of this planning effort?					
6. To what extent will the performance of the organization change during the next 5 years as a result of this planning effort?					

Exhibit 2-5. Sample Questions to Allow Planners to State Their Reactions to a Planning Effort

XYZ Organization
Evaluation Form for All Employees
Planning Effort, Current Year

Please place a check in the appropriate box for each of the items listed below. Use the space at the bottom to explain your answer if appropriate to do so.

	very little	little	some	much	very much
1. How much of the information you received during planning was of interest to you?					
2. How much did you learn about the XYZ organization as a result of information communicated to you during planning?					
3. How much did you learn about the XYZ competition during this planning effort?					
4. In future planning cycles, how much information would you like about planning?					
5. In your opinion, is there a desire among employees for greater participation in planning than was allowed this time?					

Exhibit 2-6. Sample Questions to Allow Employees to State Their Reactions to a Planning Effort

Issues Management

Observation of the issues that arise under strategic plans is another measure of the effectiveness of the strategic planning process. Issues arise only when plans for dealing with the organization domain are incomplete. An issue is any event occurring in the environment that is not provided for in the strategic plans of the organization. Observation of issues is done as part of an issues management process. Issues management is a procedure for dealing with issues that arise in the external environment.

Issues will arise with the best of plans.[77] An issue may arise because planners' views of the environment are inaccurate. An inaccurate view of the environment may be the result of an omission during an environmental study[78] or of environmental changes that occurred after the environmental study was conducted. An issue may arise because planners' views of the organization are inaccurate. They may have spent much time learning about the environment but little time learning about the organization. An issue may arise because the information gathered during an environmental study was not properly linked to strategic plans for the organization.

Issues management serves two purposes in the strategic planning process: to monitor and correct the process that produces the organization's strategic plans and to deal with specific issues in a manner that furthers the organization's strategic plans.[79] Three steps are involved in issues management:

- Issue discovery
- Issue analysis
- Accommodation

Issue discovery is the observation and identification of events that are of concern to the organization, given its current range of operations, but were not anticipated in the strategic plans. For example, the 1988 federal law banning general use of the polygraph by employers was an issue for many employers. But for other employers with an effective strategic planning process that included human resource planning, this was not an issue. These employers had established strategic objectives for their human resources and were aware, as a result of environmental analysis, of the rising tide of sentiment in the United States opposing invasion of the privacy of employees. As a result, most of these employers already had discontinued use of the polygraph in favor of the less invasive honesty tests.

When an issue has been discovered, *analysis* is necessary to determine the implications of the issue for the planning process and to determine what actions, if any, are necessary to deal with the issue. To illustrate, in 1987, when the bill banning use of the polygraph in employment first became an issue to some employers, those employers were required to answer two questions regarding this proposed legislation:

- In what respects, if at all, should we modify our approach to strategic planning to ensure that sweeping social changes, such as those that resulted in public insistence that the use of the polygraph be banned, are considered in our planning process? The focus here is not on the specific issue as such, but on the implications of this issue for the completeness and the balance of the strategic plans.
- What public position and what actions should be taken by the organization to deal with this specific issue in a manner consistent with our strategic plans? Should we publicly oppose the legislation? Should we discontinue use of the polygraph in employment? Should we draft a policy statement outlining the right of our employees to privacy?

The final step in issues management, *accommodation*, is very important because it brings to completion the issues management process. At the Atlantic Richfield Company this step is considered to be the fundamental responsibility of the issues management team.[80]

Accommodation to the issue may occur in three ways. First, an organization may alter its strategic planning process to account for the issue by modifying the planning process so that issues of this type do not occur in the future. If, for example, it is determined during the issue analysis phase of issues management that changing values of the U.S. population are not receiving enough attention in the organization's environmental study, more information sources focusing attention on the social sector can be included in the material reviewed by the environmental study group. Second, an organization may alter its current operations to account for the issue. The organization might draft a policy statement on employee rights to privacy. Third, an organization may participate in public forums, shaping and resolving an issue by advocacy of the organization's interests.[81] This may be done through lobbying, writing to officials, advertising, and personal contacts.

THE HUMAN RESOURCE ROLE IN STRATEGIC PLANNING

The human resource department should play an important role in all levels of strategic planning. The primary contributions of the human resource department to strategic planning are

- The service of the human resource executive on the strategic planning committee
- The services of human resource specialists in helping to
  - Design the process to bring about behavioral change
  - Select those who plan
  - Train those who plan
  - Manage planned change

The Human Resource Executive on the Strategic Planning Committee

Should the Human Resource Executive Be on the Committee?

An activity or function should be represented on the committee only if the contribution made by the representative warrants the expense of inclusion on the committee. The contribution of a representative depends in part on how important the activity or function is to the organization and on the knowledge and skills that the representative brings to the committee.

The importance of an activity or function is determined by the technology of the organization. A technology is an ordered arrangement of methods for modifying data, people, and/or things to produce a product or service. Different technologies require the use of different proportions of three resources: human resources, capital resources, and land.[82] In general, technologies that modify data and people must accumulate and use relatively large amounts of human resource capabilities (dedication, knowledge, and skills of employees), whereas technologies that modify things use relatively large amounts of capital resources and/or land. For example, certified public accounting firms and hospitals, which modify data and people, respectively, normally are human resource intensive, whereas steel fabricators and farms, which modify things, normally are capital goods intensive and land intensive, respectively.

Though no direct data are available, it seems clear that the economies of industrialized countries are making increasing use of technologies that modify data and people and decreasing use of technologies that modify things. This trend toward human resource–intensive technologies is causing organization success to be increasingly dependent on the wise use of human resources. If human resources are important to the successful use of the chosen technology of an organization, it makes sense to pay careful attention to the impact of human resources on strategic plans. This requires that a human resource executive be on the strategic planning committee so that human resources can be considered at an early stage when plans are still flexible and the best use of human resources is possible.

A few firms, such as SmithKline Beecham Corporation, IBM Corporation, and American Express, have outstanding HR professionals taking part in strategic planning. The integral involvement of those executives in the future of their organizations occurred because they were both accomplished human resource professionals and accomplished business managers. They achieved influence in their organizations by foreseeing the human resource impact on the various paths their businesses might follow.[83]

Unfortunately today in most organizations the HR executive is not a member of the strategic planning committee.[84] Human resource executives frequently have shortcomings that prevent their performing effectively. George Gordon identified three basic shortcomings that prevent the HR executive from being an effective part of the strategic planning committee:

- The failure to recognize the financial implications of HR issues. For example, when the HR person does engage in planning, the focus is on abstract concepts or cost alone, with no consideration of the impact on business performance.
- Shortfalls in the business knowledge and skill base of the HR executive, and an ignorance of other parts of the company.
- Underutilization of the tools available to the HR function.[85]

If the human resource executive is to take his or her rightful place on the strategic planning committee, these shortcomings must be remedied. The human resource executive needs to have or to develop the skills required for meaningful contributions to the strategic planning committee. Future human resource executives still in universities and colleges have an advantage that practicing human resource executives do not have. These future executives are being exposed to a broader based education that includes courses in both general management and human resource administration. They will be in a position to contribute in ways that will expand still further the role and influence of the human resource function on the direction of the business.

The Role of the Human Resource Executive on the Committee

The role of the HR executive on the committee can vary from a wide-ranging leadership role to a more limited, supportive role.[86] Those human resource executives who possess good business knowledge can exercise a wide-ranging leadership role, initiating and championing effectively sound ideas about future directions the business may take with due regard for the human resource implications of those ideas. HR executives with only a knowledge of their field can perform in a more limited supportive role. These executives may evaluate the ideas of other members of the committee in light of their full breadth of knowledge in the human resource field.

Human Resource Specialist Support for Strategic Planning

Specialists in the human resource department have a variety of skills that may be useful to the strategic planning committee. Some of these skills are

Group process/behavioral change skills
Staffing skills
Training and development skills
Program implementation skills

Program evaluation skills
Employment communication skills
Organization design skills
Organization development skills

Of these, the four most useful for strategic planning are group process/behavioral change skills, staffing skills, training and development skills, and program implementation skills. Human resource specialists, acting as consultants to the committee, can help design the planning process for behavioral change, can help select those who plan, can help train those who plan, and can help manage the planned change.

Designing the Planning Process for Behavioral Change

Strategic planning offers the organization an especially valuable opportunity to achieve behavioral change. Participants in the planning process take part in an activity quite different from their daily activities. They are allowed a view of the organization and environment that cannot be seen from the confines of their jobs. These activities and observations can be an opportunity for phenomenal personal growth.

Planning participants grow in terms of their skills, knowledge, understanding, attitudes, and/or values. The amount and kinds of personal growth that employees experience during the planning process will depend on the extent of participation allowed in planning and the behavior change techniques used in planning.

Extent of Participation

The extent of participation allowed in initial cycles of planning should be consistent with the way the organization is run. If the organization is tightly controlled by the chief executive officer, strategic planning also should be under his or her tight control. If the organization is participatively managed, strategic planning also should be conducted in a participative manner. Strategic planning is a major effort and will itself produce changes for an organization. If normal authority relationships are disrupted in the planning process, the capacity of the organization to absorb change may be exceeded. As the organization becomes accustomed to planning, more participation should be allowed.

The extent of participation may be gauged along two dimensions—which persons are allowed to participate and what these persons are allowed to do. As shown in Exhibit 2-7, five combinations of persons comprising the planning group are possible. Which of these combinations is chosen depends in part on the extent to which the CEO wishes to share control over the planning process. Persons in the chief executive office, that is, the chief executive officer and the CEO's staff, may do the planning. A second possibility is planning by the CEO and planning experts.

Persons Involved in the Planning Process	Control over Plan and Process Can Be		
	Retained by Person(s) Ultimately Accountable for Planning Results (Assumed to Be the Chief Executive Officer)	Shared with Persons Who Help to Plan; Planning Parameters Are Set by Persons Accountable for Results	Relinquished to Persons Who Help to Prepare the Plan
Chief executive officer and support staff (CEO)	X		
CEO and planning experts (PEXs)	X	X	
CEO, PEXs, and influentials (INFs)	X	X	X
CEO, PEXs, INFs, and interest group representatives (REPs)		X	X
All persons in the organization			X

Exhibit 2-7. Possible Combinations of Strategic Planning Committee Composition and Control

The planning experts are selected from among persons within the organization for the knowledge and/or the skills they can contribute to the planning effort. A third possibility is planning by the CEO, selected planning experts, and persons of influence within the organization. These influential persons are selected for their influence with persons who must conduct the planning or carry out the plan. A fourth possibility is planning by the CEO, selected planning experts, selected influentials, and selected persons who can represent the views of interest groups within the organization. A final possibility, practical only in smaller organizations, is a planning group composed of everyone in the organization.

What the persons who participate in planning are allowed to do also depends in part on the extent to which the chief executive officer is willing to share control over the planning process. The chief executive (and staff) can do the planning and present the completed plan to others in the organization, with or without an attempt to persuade them to accept the plan. Or the CEO may share control by inviting questions about the plan from others in the organization; by presenting a tentative plan, subject to change by others; or by presenting his or her goals for the planning process and getting ideas from others prior to planning. Or the chief executive can allow others to do the planning, with or without his or her review and participation. If the chief executive allows others to do the planning, limits may be set for their work through the use of planning manuals and planning guidelines, by setting organization objectives prior to planning, and/or by stating the assumptions within which planning is to occur. Finally, the chief executive may simply join the committee in planning without setting prior constraints on the outcome.[87]

Behavior Change Techniques

Behavior change techniques may be used to allow planners to experience personal growth as a by-product of their planning experience. These techniques should be chosen so that desired kinds of growth and development occur. Four especially important kinds of growth that may occur among planners are learning, understanding, attitude change, and value change.

Learning is a receiving of information that causes a permanent change in the way people organize their thinking. Learning allows people to acquire additional

Kinds of Change	Examples of Changes
Learning	Planners learn to view the organization as a dynamic system. Planners learn to think of employees as people and as human resources.
Understanding	New knowledge of organizations as dynamic systems allows managers to see ways they may change the organization in their daily work. Learning to view employees as human resources causes managers to see ways of investing in human resources.
Attitude change	Production managers and marketing managers begin to react (think, feel, behave) in a more positive way toward each other. Planners become relatively less positive in their reactions to the concept "efficiency" and relatively more positive in their reactions to the concept "effectiveness."
Value change	Planners begin assigning relatively more value to corporate profits and to quality of work life and relatively less value to quantity of product produced.

Exhibit 2-8. Examples of Behavioral Change That May Occur Among Planners During Strategic Planning

Behavior Change	Behavior Change Technique to Be Used	

Learning/ Understanding	Directed learning
	  Briefing reports
	  Traditional meetings
	  Expert lectures
	  Films
	  Programmed instruction
	
	Semidirected learning
	  Instrumented training
	  Role playing
	  Research reports
	  Nominal group meetings
	  Conferences
	  Case studies
		Discovery learning
		  Self-study
		  Sensitivity training
		  Team building
		  Simulations
		  Primary field research
		  Job rotation

Attitude change	Sensitivity training Team building Simulations Primary field research Job rotation Instrumented training	Role playing Research reports Nominal group meetings Conferences Case studies
Value change	Self-study Primary field research	Job rotation

Exhibit 2-9. Behavior Change Techniques Appropriate for Various Kinds of Behavior Change

skills and knowledge. Understanding is a synergistic effect that may occur with learning. Understanding is the assimilation of information, relating this information to other information one already knows, and drawing conclusions based on the relationship. Attitude change is a change in the degree to which people think, feel, or behave positively or negatively toward something. Value change is a change in the degree of worth or excellence assigned to various social goals or ends. Exhibit 2-8 provides examples of each of these kinds of personal growth.

Once the kinds of growth experiences appropriate for the planning group have been selected, training techniques are chosen to produce the desired growth experiences. Training techniques are shown in Exhibit 2-9. In the exhibit, techniques are grouped according to the kind of behavior change they tend to promote. Techniques to promote learning and understanding are further grouped by type of learning promoted: discovery learning, semidirected learning, and directed learning. The techniques in the three groups differ according to the amount of choice given the learner.

Discovery learning techniques allow the learner to choose information to be learned from among a range of available information. Directed learning techniques give the learner little choice in the information to be learned. Discovery learning techniques tend to produce more learning than directed learning techniques but they tend to be more expensive and, of course, they allow less control over what is learned.[88] Discovery learning techniques promote understanding to a greater degree than do directed learning techniques.

Experiential techniques, those that require participants to take an active part, tend to promote attitude change.[89] Techniques that require appropriate experiences over an extended period of time tend to produce value change. Techniques to produce attitude change and value change require a more complex training design and are more expensive than are techniques to promote learning.

The techniques shown in Exhibit 2-9 are described in the appendix to this chapter.

Human Resource Specialist Assistance

Organization behavior specialists and training specialists can help planners to assess the advantages and disadvantages of participation and to establish an overall design for the planning process that will allow the desired amount of participation—the numbers of people who are to participate and how much those persons are to be allowed to do. These specialists can suggest and help to implement participative methods to give the desired effects.

Within the overall design, behavior specialists and training specialists can assist in the choice of behavior change techniques that will allow planning tasks to be accomplished while promoting growth of planners. Behavior change techniques differ greatly in what they do.[90] It is therefore important to seek professional help in choosing techniques.

Selecting Those Who Plan

There is considerable anecdotal evidence that some persons are more adept at planning than others. Michael Porter, a widely respected consultant in the area of business planning, says

> Strategic planning is not something a manager automatically picks up, no matter how successful he's been. Certain people are more adaptable to that orientation. Certain people have qualities of mind or approaches to thinking about the world that are more consistent with the kind of thinking that has to be done in planning.[91]

Kenichi Ohmae, a director of the management consulting firm McKinsey and Company, who has served as consultant for many large Japanese companies, says the key to the strategic wisdom displayed by Japanese organizations in recent years often can be attributed to a strategist of great natural talent.

How do they do it? The answer is easy. They may not have a strategic planning staff, but they do have a strategist of great natural talent, usually the founder or chief executive. Often—especially in Japan, where there is no business school—these outstanding strategists have had little or no formal business education.... But they have an intuitive grasp of the basic elements of strategy. They have an idiosyncratic mode of thinking in which company, customers, and competition merge in a dynamic interaction out of which a comprehensive set of objectives and plans for action eventually crystallizes.[92]

These two eminent consultants, one with experience in large U.S. businesses and the other in large Japanese businesses, are referring to quite different planning processes. Porter, on the one hand, is speaking of the highly analytical, environment-oriented, planning style used in the United States; Ohmae, on the other hand, is speaking of the highly experiential, intuitive, organization-oriented planning style used in Japan.[93] For Porter, planning is, or should be, a highly advanced science. For Ohmae, planning is, or should be, a highly creative art. Yet both are in agreement that managers differ in their innate planning abilities.

Is it necessary to decide whether to approach planning analytically or intuitively? Superior planners probably use both approaches. Ohmae cautions that it would be a mistake to believe that analysis is useless to the strategist. To the contrary! "Strategists do not reject analysis. Indeed they can hardly do without it. But they use it only to stimulate the creative process."[94]

Superior planning does not come from executives who lack planning skills and vision. How do organizations get managers who can plan? Staffing specialists in the human resource department can help in two ways. First, they may use planning ability as one criterion for hiring managers. Behavior-based interviews[95] and structured ratings of the previous training and experience of job applicants[96] can be used to select applicants who have successfully performed planning tasks similar to those needed in the hiring organization. Thus, through selection at time of hiring, the organization creates a pool of persons with planning ability. When planners are needed, staffing specialists may select from that pool those persons with the best skills for the current planning task.[97]

Second, the staffing specialist can help locate among present employees those persons who have specific planning skills. Through interviews, training and experience ratings, and/or performance appraisal records, these people can be identified.

Training Those Who Plan

Although both Porter and Ohmae believe that individuals differ in their innate ability to plan, both recognize that ability to plan can be improved with training. Porter says, in regard to learning the analytical approach to planning:

Certain kinds of training, like...studying planning and being exposed to it in an academic context, are helpful...I tell my clients, if you don't have people who...know or have learned what this thinking is...like, then you better not expect people to pick it up. ...There has to be some way in which people learn this different way of thinking and this different analytical style. ...I've suggested that, for the first year, a company hold a management meeting. Ask each of the division managers to give a short presentation of their strategy. You know you've got one or two people who really understand the concept. Listening to someone else in a business they are familiar with can provide an excellent example to be followed.[98]

Ohmae says in regard to improving one's innate abilities to plan using an intuitive, creative approach:

To become an effective strategist requires constant practice in strategic thinking. It is a daily discipline, not a resource that can be left dormant in normal times and tapped at will in an emergency. ...The drafting of a strategy is simply the logical extension of one's usual thinking processes. It is a matter of a long-term philosophy, not of short-term expedient. In a very real sense, it represents the expression of an attitude to life. But like every creative activity, the art of strategic thinking is practiced most successfully when certain operating principles are kept in mind....[99]

These principles Ohmae describes as first, remaining flexible in one's behavior by being constantly aware of the full range of alternatives available and the costs and benefits of each alternative; second, resisting the urge to search for the perfect strategy, while missing an opportunity for timely introduction of the strategy; and, third, avoiding excessive attention to the details of a strategy, concentrating instead on choice of the basic course of action.[100]

Planners can improve their ability to plan. Training and development specialists in the human resource department can establish appropriate training programs. These citations from Porter and Ohmae suggest that, to improve planners' analytical skills, seminars, workshops, assigned readings, and meetings would be helpful; to improve planners' intuitive abilities, job rotation, mentoring, and on-the-job training would be helpful. Each method should be evaluated carefully to be sure that the training is accomplishing its purpose.

Managing Planned Change

A final area in which the human resource department can contribute to the planning process is in managing the change that is expected to occur as a result of planning. Some organization behavior specialists, called change agents, have skills that enable them to reduce resistance to change. Their observation skills allow them to infer the causes of behavior and the likely effects of change. They can recommend ways to introduce change that will minimize the negative effects of change. They can help planners to understand what the change means to persons affected by the change; they can help to develop the interpersonal skills that planners will need to effect the change; and they can help make organization changes needed to accommodate the change.

But change agents are not miracle workers. Minimizing the negative impacts of change may not be enough. Planned change may be resisted. Resistance to change occurs when people reject change for reasons unrelated to the merits of the change. If resistance to change is likely, change agents can be most helpful if they are called in at an early stage of planning, before the planning process is actually underway. At this point they can recommend ways to plan that will help to build the trust between planners and nonplanners that allows rational evaluation of the work of planners and acceptance of the plan on its own merit.

SUMMARY

Strategic business planning is done at enterprise, group, business unit, and function levels. The examples used throughout most of the chapter are of enterprise-level strategic planning. However, the discussion can be applied to planning at other levels as well.

Members of a strategic planning committee typically represent a function or activity. A function or activity tends to be represented on the committee if the technology of the organization causes the function or activity to be important to organization performance. The human resource function usually is more important in organizations with technologies that modify data and people and less important in organizations with technologies that modify things.

The human resource executive serving on a strategic planning committee may perform a leadership or supportive role. A leadership role requires that the executive be able to apply both human resource knowledge and generalist business knowledge in a proactive manner.

The steps of strategic planning are: establish objectives for the planning process, identify planning participants, choose an organization philosophy, study the environment, determine organization identity, establish organization objectives and strategies, implement objectives and strategies, evaluate the planning effort, and manage the issues arising under the plan. The emphasis of planning will differ, depending on whether the organization adopts an open systems or a self-producing systems approach to planning. The open systems approach emphasizes the environment, the self-producing systems approach emphasizes the organization. The open systems and self-producing systems approaches are compatible and both may be used simultaneously.

The human resource department can provide support for the strategic planning process through help in designing the planning process for behavioral change, selecting and developing the persons who are to do the strategic planning, and managing the planned change.

LEARNING EXERCISES

Case Analysis

If you have the opportunity for small-group discussion, you may use the procedure suggested for Case 1 in Chapter 1.

For Case 2, "Bolling Laboratories," answer the questions or take the following actions:

1. Based on the information provided in the case, what strategic concepts appear immediately applicable to Bolling Laboratories? Explain your answer.

2. Select a level of the organization on which to focus initial strategic planning effort and state why you chose that particular level.

3. For planning at the level chosen, indicate who (what persons in the organization) should do what, and in what order. For each action step recommended, be as specific in your recommendations as possible. If, for example, you recommend that, as one action step, further study of the environment be done, what persons or departments would be responsible for the study, what areas of the environment would be studied, and which areas would be studied first?

Discussion Questions

1. When organizations initiate the strategic planning process, they sometimes bring in outside consultants to establish a structure for planning. These structures often are elaborate and complex. What advantages and disadvantages do you see with this approach to planning?

2. Is strategic planning in modern industrialized economies becoming easier or more difficult? Explain your answer carefully.

3. Marshall W. Meyer and Lynne G. Zucker, *Permanently Failing Organizations* (Newbury Park, CA: Sage Publications, 1989), argue that many organizations in the advanced economy of the United States are "permanently failing" in the sense that they no longer are able to compete. These organizations are kept from closing by persons and other organizations with a vested interest in their continuance. Does this suggest that organization identity may have a "down" side to the extent that it causes an organization to outlive its usefulness? Explain your answer carefully. (Consult the Meyer and Zucker book if possible.)

APPENDIX
GLOSSARY OF BEHAVIOR CHANGE TECHNIQUES
USEFUL FOR PLANNING

Briefing Report. A report prepared by a subject matter expert or management analyst to inform a decision maker, task force, or committee about a topic being considered. Report content is determined by the preparer's understanding of what the recipient needs to know to make the decision or to accomplish the task.

Case Study. Training in which a group of trainees, usually from diverse backgrounds, read and discuss a case. Learning occurs primarily through the sharing of ideas by trainees. The role of the trainer, though not demanding, is vital to the success of the training. It typically consists of four tasks: selecting study participants (trainees), choosing an appropriate case or cases, providing a structure for group discussion, and providing closure for the experience.

Conference. An assemblage of people, with designated leader(s), for the purpose of information exchange. The leader assumes primary responsibility for the process and content of information exchange. As compared to a meeting, a conference implies more persons in attendance, held for a longer period of time, and covering fewer topics in more depth.

Expert Lecture. Lecture by a subject matter expert with appropriate credentials to one or more trainees for the purpose of sharing the lecturer's expertise with trainees. Normally aided by appropriate audiovisual techniques. .

Film. Film depicting an event or series of events in an appropriate setting and depicting appropriate role model behavior. Shown to one or more trainees for dramatic and socialization effects. Normally preceded by preparatory remarks and followed by discussion and closure.

Instrumented Training. Group process training conducted by a process consultant with structure provided by a self-scoring or computer-scored questionnaire. Questionnaire serves the purpose of directing attention and interest of trainees in preselected areas and of collecting data for group use in discussion. Discussion is conducted by the process consultant. Structure for the discussion is provided by the questionnaire. As a result, process consultant requires less use of group process skills. Training lacks the flexibility of sensitivity training and team building but, where questionnaire is well suited to group needs, can have dramatic behavior change effects, especially with appropriate provision for transfer of learning to the job.

Job Rotation. Movement of trainees among jobs with the primary purpose of allowing them to become acquainted with the technology, structure, culture, and other employees of an organization. Performance on the jobs used in training is secondary to the training objectives.

Nominal Group Meetings. Traditional group meeting modified so that the group is a group in name only. Does not require that the group meet face to face. This modification is intended to avoid the loss of individual objectivity and of individual responsibility for group outcomes that usually occurs in traditional group meetings. The synergistic effects of joint action by individuals are retained by giving individuals feedback about group opinions. Best known of the nominal group techniques is the Delphi technique.

Primary Field Research. Training in which nonprofessionals are asked to participate in collecting data and information about a problem. The training purpose is to encourage an objective look and the development of an accurate understanding by the trainees of the causes of a problem. This training purpose usually will be secondary to the research purpose of gathering accurate information.

Programmed Instruction. Training aided by printed materials or a computer in lieu of a trainer. This printed material or computer is enabled to serve as a quasi-instructor by a predesigned program developed to anticipate the responses of given trainees and to use those responses to guide trainees through a planned sequence of learning experiences. The program can adapt the learning experiences to individual trainee needs so that a minimum amount of time is required for training each trainee.

Research Reports. Channeling of reports by an objective, disinterested, and competent researcher directly to trainees without censorship of research findings or interpretation of meaning of research results.

Role Playing. Group process training in which trainees are asked to accept the social role and current situation of a fictitious or actual person at a very specific point in that person's life. Trainee is then asked to behave as he or she normally would in this role and situation, starting at the given point in the role person's life. The purpose of role playing is to collect specific data about behavior of individual trainees in selected situations for analysis in a group setting. Role playing usually is accompanied by lectures or social modeling examples intended to provide trainees with new ways to behave and thus to cope better with problems encountered in the role plays. Role plays often are videotaped for additional feedback and for reinforcement of appropriate behaviors. Lacks flexibility because of the necessity of developing roles to fit the training need but, where appropriate, is one of the most powerful training techniques available.

Sensitivity Training. Group process training conducted by a process consultant using a variety of techniques to encourage trainees to become sensitive to the feelings of others and to become capable of responding appropriately to those feelings. Requires an unusually competent process consultant, usually with extensive training experience, able to understand and to intervene appropriately in group processes. Training typically has no structure other than that provided by trainees. This lack of structure allows trainer to observe individual behaviors and to intervene as appropriate to create opportunities for the growth and development of individual interpersonal skills. Sensitivity training was once quite popular and was the forerunner of many current personal growth methods. These other forms of personal growth training have largely replaced sensitivity training.

Simulations. Any of various kinds of training experiences intended to approximate real-life experiences not readily available to trainees in everyday life. Examples of experiences for which simulations are useful are management of a company (in a so-called management game), which is an experience not available to most persons, and aviation accidents (in pilot cockpit simulations), which are rare and therefore not within the experience background of most trainees.

Team Building. Group process training, conducted by a process consultant, in which the focus is on helping individual members of a group understand how and why other members of the group behave as they do. Such training usually involves the implicit assumption that with understanding comes acceptance, and this does seem to be the usual outcome of such training. Such training allows a group of individuals to work together more efficiently to the extent that the training enables team members to predict better how other members of the team will behave in given situations. To the extent that acceptance of individual behavior occurs, interpersonal hostility and conflict may be lessened.

Traditional Meeting. Assemblage of two or more persons with an agenda and a designated leader. Leader is responsible for seeing that all items on the agenda are reported on or discussed and that closure is provided for all agenda items within the time allowed for the meeting. As compared to a conference, a meeting usually implies fewer persons in attendance for a shorter period of time and covering topics in less depth.

Endnotes

[1]David F. Scott, Jr., and Berry Waldron suggest that the three dominant planning concepts are the strategic business unit, the experience curve, and the market share grid. See "Strategic Planning and Corporate Growth," *Business Forum*, 10, no. 9 (Winter 1985), 10–15.

[2]Peter Patel and Michael Younger, "A Frame of Reference for Strategy Development," *Long Range Planning*, 11, no. 2 (April 1978), 6–12.

[3]To the author's knowledge, not an actual firm.

[4]Patel and Younger, pp. 6–12.

[5]Peters and Waterman found that America's best-run companies reorganized continuously. Thomas J. Peters and Robert H. Waterman, Jr., *In Search of Excellence: Lessons from America's Best-Run Companies* (New York: Harper & Row, 1982), p. 311.

[6]See p. 317 of Charles C. Snow and Lawrence G. Hrebiniak, "Strategy, Distinctive Competence, and Organizational Performance," *Administrative Science Quarterly*, 25, no. 2 (June 1980), 317–336; Philip Selznick, *Leadership in Administration* (New York: Harper & Row, 1957), pp. 42–56.

[7]These strategic types were first described in Raymond E. Miles and Charles C. Snow, *Organizational Strategy, Structure, and Process* (New York: McGraw-Hill Book Co., 1978), pp. 28–30. They were presented in slightly revised form in Snow and Hrebiniak, "Strategy, Distinctive Competence, and Organizational Performance."

[8]See Snow and Hrebiniak, p. 333.

[9]Ibid., pp. 326–331.

[10] Ibid., pp. 331–332.

[11]It seems unlikely that firms can readily shift from being one of these strategic types to being another of the types. The self-producing-theory of organizations suggests that firms probably develop early in their history a self-identity that is highly resistant to change. This identity seems likely to shape the kinds of strategic orientations and, to a lesser extent, the distinctive competencies possible for a firm. Therefore, planners must identify, more so than shape, the strategic type and the distinctive competencies of the organization. The organization then must choose environments that correspond to its strategic orientation and its distinctive competences.

[12]The statistical procedure cluster analysis may be used to do strategic mapping. If cluster analysis is used, more than two strategic variables may be used to create strategic groups.

[13]Arthur A. Thompson, Jr., and A. J. Strickland III, *Strategy Formulation and Implementation: Tasks of the General Manager,* 3rd ed. (Plano, TX: Business Publications, 1986), p. 101.

[14]Michael E. Porter, *Competitive Strategy: Techniques for Analyzing Industries and Competitors* (New York: Free Press, 1980), pp. 129–132.

[15]Ibid., p. 102.

[16]These are unit value added costs only, that is, they are total costs less the cost of all purchased components, divided by total units of output. Another curve, the learning

curve, behaves in similar fashion and is used to show the behavior of unit labor costs with increasing use of a process. See David A. Aaker, *Developing Business Strategies* (New York: John Wiley, 1984), pp. 204–208.

[17]This rate tends to vary inversely with the complexity of the learning process so that, unless steps are taken to increase the capability of persons to learn complex tasks, a unit cost decline rate of close to zero percent is a practical possibility. See Gordon B. Carlson, Harold A. Bolz, and Hewitt H. Young, editorial consultants, *Production Handbook*, 3rd ed. (New York: Ronald Press, 1972), pp. 1–54–1–55.

[18]The experience curve can be an especially powerful idea when learning rates and forgetting rates are incorporated into the curve. See Shlomo Globerson and Nissan Levin, "Incorporating Forgetting into Learning Curves," *International Journal of Operations and Production Management*, 7, no. 4 (1987), 80–94.

[19]Arthur A. Thompson, Jr., and A.J. Strickland III, *Strategy Formulation and Implementation: Tasks of The General Manager*, 3rd ed. (Plano, TX: Business Publications, 1986), pp. 111.

[20]Frederick W. Gluck, "Taking the Mystique Out of Planning," *Across the Board*, 22, no. 7–8 (July–August 1985), 56–61.

[21]Kenichi Ohmae, *The Mind of the Strategist* (New York: McGraw-Hill Book Co., 1982), p. 117.

[22]Variables such as the complexity of tasks performed, the level of pressure under which people work, the willingness to share ideas, the characteristics of persons who serve as gatekeepers to control access to sources of information and to publication outlets, turnover rates, and cycle times of repetition of events are likely to affect experience curves. If experience curves are important strategic considerations for their firms, human resource departments should monitor and observe these variables for possible effects on learning and forgetting.

[23]Rochelle O'Connor, *Corporate Guides to Long-Range Planning*, Conference Board Report No. 687 (New York: The Conference Board, 1976), p. 11.

[24]Ibid.

[25]The extent to which the human resource executive can recognize the financial implications of human resource activities (George G. Gordon, "Getting in Step," *Personnel Administrator*, 32, no. 4 (April 1987), 44–48, 134) and the human resource executive's grasp of the language and practice of strategic business planning (Raymond E. Miles and Charles C. Snow, "Designing Strategic Human Resource Systems," *Organizational Dynamics*, 13, no. 1 (Summer 1984), 36–52) are additional kinds of knowledge important to the HR executive serving on the strategic planning committee.

[26]See p. 33 of Henry C. Egerton and James K. Brown, "Some Perspectives on Business Planning," *The Conference Board Record*, 8, no. 8 (August 1971), 32–36.

[27]See p. 266 of Lee Dyer: "Bringing Human Resources into the Strategy Formulation Process," and "Linking Human Resource and Business Strategies," *Human Resource Planning*, 7, no. 2 (1984), 79–84. Mansfield identifies the following groups of persons as having an interest in a typical manufacturing company: owners or shareholders, managers, nonmanagerial employees, trade unions, suppliers, distributors, consumers, creditors, employers' associations, the public at large, and the government. See Roger Mansfield, *Company Strategy and Organizational Design* (New York: St. Martin's Press, 1986), pp. 22–23.

[28]Compare p. 395 of Philip H. Mirvis, "Formulating and Implementing Human Resource Strategy: A Model of How To Do It," *Human Resource Management*, 24, no. 4 (Winter 1985), 385–412.

[29]Dyer, "Bringing Human Resources into the Strategy Formulation Process," p. 266.

[30]The emotional ties between people and organizations suggest that organizations are in some sense seen as human. For an excellent discussion of the emotional ties of people to artifacts, see ch. 5, "On the Experience of Loss," in Harry Levinson, *The Great Jackass Fallacy* (Boston: Division of Research, Graduate School of Business Administration, Harvard University, 1973), pp. 66–86. Caporael suggests that people use anthropomorphism as a default vehicle for understanding things that they find otherwise inexplicable. L. R. Caporael, "Anthropomorphism and Mechanomorphism: Two Faces of the Human Machine," *Computers in Human Behavior*, 2, no. 3 (1986), pp. 215–234.

[31]Peters and Waterman state that all the excellent companies they studied were value-driven and that the values were laid down, in virtually all of the companies, by an influential leader. See *In Search of Excellence*, p. 287.

[32]F. G. "Buck" Rodgers, *The IBM Way* (New York: Harper & Row, 1986), p. 9.

[33]Compare the experience of First Chicago Corporation. See "Turnaround at First Chicago," pp. 19–37, in Stanley M. Davis, *Managing Corporate Culture* (Cambridge, MA: Ballinger, 1984).

[34]Javidan has shown that top management's interpretation of the environment may be a key factor in deciding *how much* planning should be done by the organization. Mansour Javidan, "The Impact of Environmental Uncertainty on Long-Range Planning Practices of the U.S. Savings and Loan Industry,".*Strategic Management Journal*, 5, no. 4 (October/December, 1984), 381–392. This finding also is partly supported by the research of Miller and Friesen, who demonstrated that more successful Canadian and U.S. firms increased analysis and innovation when environmental dynamism increased. Danny Miller and Peter H. Friesen, "Strategy-Making and Environment: The Third Link," *Strategic Management Journal*, 4, no. 3 (July/September, 1983), 221–235.

[35]See pp. 62–63 of Liam Fahey and William R. King, "Environmental Scanning for Corporate Planning," *Business Horizons*, 20, no. 4 (August 1977), 61–71.

[36]Most writers suggest that when studying the environment, the *environment* be separated into two segments. The names of the segments vary. Both Schmid (p. 308) and Fombrun and Astley (pp. 48–49) refer to the segments as the task environment and the general environment. See Hillel Schmid, "Managing the Environment: Strategies for Executives in Human Service Organizations," *Human Systems Management*, 6, no. 4 (1986), 307–315; Charles Fombrun and W. Graham Astley, "Beyond Corporate Strategy," *Journal of Business Strategy*, 3, no. 4 (Spring 1983), 47–54. De Vasconcellos Filho (p. 23) identifies two external environments, an operational environment and a macro environment. See Paulo de Vasconcellos Filho, "Environmental Analysis for Strategic Planning," *Managerial Planning*, 33, no. 4 (January-February 1985), 23–30, 36.

[37]The following works were especially helpful in developing the study models used for this section: de Vasconcellos Filho, "Environmental Analysis"; Schmid, "Managing the Environment"; Fombrun and Astley, "Beyond Corporate Strategy"; Constance S. Bates, "Mapping the Environment: An Operational Environmental Analysis Model," *Long Range Planning*, 18, no. 5 (October 1985), 97–107; Subhash C. Jain, "Environmental Scanning in U.S. Corporations," *Long Range Planning*, 17, no. 2 (April 1984), 117–128; Francis Joseph Aguilar, *Scanning the Business Environment* (New York: Macmillan, 1967); D.E. Hussey, "Corporate Planning and The Environment," in D. E. Hussey, ed., *The Corporate Planners' Yearbook, 1978–9* (Oxford: Pergamon Press, 1978), pp. 3–16; Lena Lupica, "Environmental Scanning at AT & T," in Jay S.

Mendell, ed., *Nonextrapolative Methods in Business Forecasting* (Westport, CT: Quorum Books, 1985), pp. 115–123.

[38]De Vasconcellos Filho, "Environmental Analysis," p. 23.

[39]Ibid., p. 26.

[40]Compare Schmid, "Managing the Environment," pp. 308–309.

[41]De Vasconcellos Filho, "Environmental Analysis," p. 26.

[42]If the organization also prepares a listing of the activities performed in the major functions of various businesses it is considering adding, the organization may determine, using the process described, whether adding the business would require it to operate in an environment markedly different from its present environment.

[43]See p. 35 of Edward C. Bursk and William Morton, "What Is Marketing?" pp. 35–46 of Steuart Henderson Britt, *Marketing Manager's Handbook* (Chicago: Dartnell Corp., 1973).

[44]De Vasconcellos Filho, "Environmental Analysis," p. 25.

[45]See ibid.; Bates, "Mapping the Environment"; Jain, "Environmental Scanning"; Fombrun and Astley, "Beyond Corporate Strategy"; Schmid, Managing the Environment"; Aguilar, *Scanning the Business Environment*; Hussey, "Corporate Planning and the Environment"; and Lupica, "Environmental Scanning." See also D. E. Hussey, *Corporate Planning Theory and Practice* (Oxford: Pergamon Press, 1982), pp. 43–54; Charles Fombrun, "Environmental Trends Create New Pressures on Human Resources," *Journal of Business Strategy*, 3, no. 1 (Summer 1982); John Diffenbach, "Corporate Environmental Analysis in Large U.S. Corporations," *Long Range Planning*, 16, no. 3 (June 1983), 107–116; John F. Preble, "Corporate Use of Environmental Scanning," *University of Michigan Business Review*, 30, no. 5 (September 1978), 12–17; R. T. Lenz and Jack L. Engledow, "Environmental Analysis Units and Strategic Decision-Making: A Field Study of 'Leading-Edge' Corporations," *Strategic Management Journal*, 7, no. 1 (January/February 1986), 69–89; and Gene R. Laczniak and Robert F. Lusch, "Environment and Strategy in 1995: A Survey of High-Level Executives," *The Journal of Consumer Marketing*, 3, no. 2 (Spring 1986), 27–45.

[46]For sources of information, see Jain, "Environmental Scanning," p. 124.

[47]This scale is adapted from de Vasconcellos Filho, "Environmental Analysis," pp. 28–29.

[48]Some writers recommend "mapping" the environment. See, for example, Bates, "Mapping the Environment"; and de Vasconcellos Filho, "Environmental Analysis."

[49]A similar report for Sears included 25 items in 1985. See p. 127 of William C. Ashley, "Strategic Issues Forecasting and Monitoring at Sears," in Jay S. Mendell, ed., *Nonextrapolative Methods in Business Forecasting* (Westport, CT: Quorum Books, 1985), pp. 125–132.

[50]Thompson and Strickland, in a note on p. 46 of their text say, "Note how thoroughly the approach to defining the business is grounded in *external* considerations as opposed to internal considerations. (Emphasis theirs.) Arthur A. Thompson, Jr., and A. J. Strickland III, *Strategy Formulation and Administration*, 3rd ed. (Plano, TX: Business Publications, 1986). See also Gareth Morgan, *Images of Organization* (Beverly Hills, CA: Sage Publications, 1986), p. 45.

[51]Morgan, *Images of Organization*, p. 45.

[52]This environmental characteristic often is referred to as dynamism. Other features of the environment are munificence and complexity. These other features appear to be less important to organization effectiveness and have received somewhat less attention than has dynamism. See pp. 572–574 of Barbara W. Keats and Michael A. Hitt, "A Causal Model of Linkages Among Environmental Dimensions, Macro Organizational

Characteristics, and Performance," *Academy of Management Journal*, 31, no. 3 (September 1988), 570–598

[53]Ibid.; Danny Miller, "Relating Porter's Business Strategies to Environment and Structure: Analysis and Performance Implications," *Academy of Management Journal*, 31, no. 2 (June 1988), 280–308; Danny Miller, "Strategy Making and Structure: Analysis and Implications for Performance," *Academy of Management Journal*, 30, no. 1 (March 1987), 7–32. .

[54]Ibid.

[55]Keats and Hitt, "Causal Model of Linkages," found that, contrary to traditional organization theory, organizations in unstable environments tended to have lower levels of diversification and divisionalization than organizations in stable environments. They suggest that executives, by reducing diversification and divisionalization to enable better control of the organization, are unwittingly sacrificing market performance for operating performance. They suggest basing executive compensation on market performance rather than on operating performance to encourage executives to give more attention to market performance. See pp. 584–585, and 591.

[56]The dominant model of organization evolution is an external control model that suggests that the external environment is the controlling influence in organization evolution, not managerial actions or organization inertia. This model is supported by research. See ibid., pp. 571–574, and 587–588, see also E. Romanelli and M. L. Tushman, "Inertia, Environments, and Strategic Choice: A Quasi-Experimental Design for Comparative-Longitudinal Research," *Management Science*, 32, no. 5 (May 1986), 608–621.

[57]Morgan, *Images of Organization*, pp. 241–243.

[58]Karl E. Weick, *The Social Psychology of Organizing* (Reading, MA: Addison-Wesley, 1979), pp. 1–5, 13, 164–166.

[59]Edgar H. Schein, *Organizational Culture and Leadership* (San Francisco: Jossey-Bass, 1985), p. 13.

[60]Ibid., p. 86. See also Florence Rockwood Kluckohn and Fred L. Strodtbeck, *Variations in Value Orientations* (Evanston, IL: Row, Peterson, 1961), pp. 10–20, and 80–90.

[61]Charles E. Osgood, George J. Suci, and Percy H. Tannenbaum, *The Measurement of Meaning* (Urbana: University of Illinois Press, 1961).

[62]These scales represent factors that were described by Osgood, Suci, and Tannenbaum as evaluation, potency, and activity. Ibid., p. 74.

[63]Ibid., pp. 325–326.

[64]Harry C. Triandis and Keith M. Kilty, *Cultural Influences on the Perception of Implicative Relationship Among Concepts and the Analysis of Values*, Group Effectiveness Research Laboratory Technical Report No. 56 (Urbana: Group Effectiveness Research Laboratory, 1968).

[65]For an excellent illustration of the use of this two-stage process to extend the semantic differential technique, see Andrew A. Haried, "The Semantic Dimensions of Financial Statements," *Journal of Accounting Research*, 10, no. 2 (Autumn 1972), 376–391. See also Andrew A. Haried, "Measurement of Meaning in Financial Reports," *Journal of Accounting Research*, 11, no. 1 (Spring 1973), 117–145.

[66]For a discussion of the origins and the requirements of participant observation, see Alan L. Wilkins and William G. Ouchi, "Efficient Cultures: Exploring the Relationship between Culture and Organization Performance,"*Administrative Science Quarterly*, 28, no. 3 (September 1983), 468–481.

[67]In Theory Z terms, the "whole organization" consists of not only the corporation but also

of its suppliers, customers, and community. William G. Ouchi, *Theory Z: How American Business Can Meet the Japanese Challenge* (Reading, MA: Addison-Wesley, 1981), p. 98.

[68]Weick points out two often overlooked advantages of dealing with environments in real time and as one with the organization rather than attempting to capture the "enacted environment" in our studies. First, we are dealing with a material world, not with "current personal definitions of the situation." Second, we deal with the world as it is, not as the anachronistic, dated, belated stimulus that comprises the enacted environment. Weick, *The Social Psychology of Organizing*, p. 166.

[69]K. Lewin, "Group Decision and Social Change," in G. E. Swanson, T. N. Newcomb, and E. L. Hartley, eds., *Readings in Social Psychology*, rev. ed. (New York: Holt, Rinehart & Winston, 1952), pp. 330–344.

[70] These objectives are an adaptation of a list by Thompson. See Thompson and A. J. Strickland, *Strategy Formulation and Implementation*, p. 51.

[71]John A. Pearce II, "Selecting Among Alternative Grand Strategies," *California Management Review*, 24, no. 3 (Spring 1982), 23–31.

[72]Miller, "Relating Porter's Business Strategies," pp. 303–304.

[73]Van Cauwenbergh and van Robaeys contend that several widely accepted ideas about strategic planning need to be questioned, including the assumption that corporate planning can fully serve the strategic needs of an organization. Rather, strategy is not a matter for corporate planners alone, but strategies result from individual decisions at different levels and strategy typically is spread throughout the organization. See A. van Cauwenbergh and N. van Robaeys, "The Functioning of Management at the Corporate Level," *Journal of General Management*, 5, no. 3 (Spring 1980), 19–29.

[74]See David R. Brodwin and L. J. Bourgeois III, "Five Steps to Strategic Action," in Glenn Carroll and David Vogel, *Strategy and Organization: A West Coast Perspective* (Boston: Pitman, 1984), pp. 167–181. There is considerable indirect support in the literature for a crescive approach to the development of objectives and strategies. Henry Mintzberg suggests a process for strategy formulation remarkably similar to the crescive approach. He calls this process the "crafting of policy" by the organization. Mintzberg believes that sound strategy typically emerges or forms rather than being created. Moreover, effective strategies can show up in the strangest places and develop through the most unexpected means. To manage within this context of emerging strategies is to create a climate within which a wide variety of strategies can emerge in a wide variety of places. See Henry Mintzberg, "Crafting Strategy,"*Harvard Business Review*, 65, no. 4 (July–August 1987), 66–74. Similar also is Quinn's logical incremental approach to strategic change and development. See James Brian Quinn, *Strategies for Change: Logical Incrementalism* (Homewood, IL: Irwin, 1980). See also van Cauwenbergh and van Robaeys, "The Functioning of Management at the Corporate Level."

[75]B. L. T. Hedberg, P. C. Nystrom, and W. H. Starbuck, "Camping on Seesaws—Prescriptions for a Self-Designing Organization,".*Administrative Science Quarterly*, 21, no. 1 (1976), 41–65.

[76]Lloyd R. Amey, *Corporate Planning: A Systems View* (New York: Prager, 1986), p. 7; R. L. Ackoff, *Redesigning the Future* (New York: Wiley-Interscience, 1974), chap. 2.

[77] Stubbart has aptly phrased the problem: "We have too many places to look and too few theories of how significant environmental change can be linked to the firm's plans." Charles Stubbart, "Are Environmental Scanning Units Effective?" *Long Range Planning*, 15, no. 3 (June 1982), 139–145.

[78]An issue caused by an omission at the time an environmental scan was conducted is

termed a discontinuity in the projected view of the environment. See Charles B. Arrington, Jr., and Richard N. Sawaya, "Managing Public Affairs: Issues Management in an Uncertain Environment," *California Management Review*, 26, no. 4 (Summer, 1984), 148–160.

[79] C. B. Arrington, Jr., and R. N. Sawaya, "Issues Management in an Uncertain Environment," *Long Range Planning*, 17, no. 6 (December 1984), 17–24.

[80] Arrington and Sawaya, "Managing Public Affairs," p. 157.

[81] Arrington and Sawaya, "Issues Management in an Uncertain Environment," p. 17.

[82] The term *space* may now be more appropriate for this resource than the older term *land*. The essential idea defining this resource was the right to use geographic space both to allow the assembly and location of human and capital resources and to allow the capture and use of dispersed mineral and energy resources (especially solar energy for farming). The term space seems better suited for an age when humans are no longer either landbound or earthbound.

[83] See George G. Gordon, "Getting in Step," *Personnel Administrator*, 32, no. 4 (April 1987), 44–48, 134, for a discussion of human resource practice at IBM and American Express.

[84] Burack, reporting in 1985, on a survey of HR and strategic business planners in 53 diverse organizations in the United States and Canada, found that human resource planning was accorded an active role in the strategic business planning process in only a small proportion of organizations. See Elmer H. Burack, "Linking Corporate Business and Human Resource Planning: Strategic Issues and Concerns," *Human Resource Planning*, 8, no. 3 (1985), 133–145. Nkomo, reporting in 1986, on a survey of 264 directors of personnel/human resources, found that only 14.8 percent prepare plans that are fully integrated with strategic business plans, but this percentage increased among larger firms. See Stella M. Nkomo, "The Theory and Practice of HR Planning: The Gap Still Remains," *Personnel Administrator*, 31, no. 8 (August, 1986), pp. 71–84.

[85] Gordon, "Getting in Step," p. 46.

[86] For an excellent example of the various possible roles of human resource executives in business planning, see, "The Human Resource Executive and Corporate Planning...A Personnel Symposium," *Personnel*, 54, no. 5 (September–October, 1977), 12–22.

[87] See Robert Tannenbaum and Warren H. Schmidt, "How to Choose a Leadership Pattern," *Harvard Business Review*, 51, no. 3 (May–June 1973), 162–175, 178–180.

[88] For a discussion of the importance of the meaningfulness of material for learning and remembering, see William McGehee and Paul W. Thayer, *Training in Business and Industry* (New York: John Wiley, 1961), pp. 162–163.

[89] One of the most firmly established phenomena in contemporary attitude research is that behavior has a causal impact on attitudes and values rather than the reverse. See Adam Kuper and Jessica Kuper, eds., *The Social Science Encyclopedia* (London: Routledge and Kegan Paul, 1985), p. 51.

[90] See pp. 5-40–5-51 of Max H. Forster, "Training and Development Programs, Methods, and Facilities," in Dale Yoder and Herbert G. Heneman, Jr., *ASPA Handbook of Personnel and Industrial Relations*, vol. V, Training and Development (Washington, DC: Bureau of National Affairs, 1977), pp. 5-35–5-56.

[91] Malcolm W. Pennington and Steve M. Cohen, "Michael E. Porter Speaks of Strategy," *Planning Review*, 10, no. 1 (January 1982), 8–12, 36–39.

[92] Ohmae, *The Mind of the Strategist*, p. 2.

[93] Ohmae feels, however, that in Japan the natural strategist is being replaced in favor of "rational, by-the-numbers strategic and financial planners," ibid., p. 3.

[94]Ibid., p. 4.

[95]In behavior-based interviews, candidates are chosen on the basis of behaviors displayed during the interview. Behaviors used to select among candidates are those known as a result of job analysis to be displayed by exceptional employees, but not by other employees. For a description of the behavior-based interview, see Tom Janz, "Initial Comparisons of Patterned Behavior Description Interviews versus Unstructured Interviews," *Journal of Applied Psychology*, 67, no. 5 (October, 1982), 577–580; Christopher Orpen, "Patterned Behavior Description Interviews versus Unstructured Interviews: A Comparative Validity Study," *Journal of Applied Psychology*, 70, no. 4 (November, 1985), 774–776.

[96]Structured ratings of training and experience have been shown to be valid. Several easily applied methods for rating training and experience of applicants are available. See Michael A. McDaniel, Frank L. Schmidt, and John E. Hunter, "A Meta-Analysis of the Validity of Methods for Rating Training and Experience in Personnel Selection," *Personnel Psychology*, 41, no. 2 (Summer 1988), 283–314.

[97]Where many people in the organization are expected to help with planning, ability to plan might be used as one criterion for hiring into other, perhaps all, positions in the organization.

[98]Pennington and Cohen, "Michael E. Porter Speaks," p. 36.

[99]Ohmae, "The Mind of the Strategist," pp. 78–79.

[100]Ibid., pp. 79–82.

Chapter 3

Tactical and Operational
Business Planning

To set the stage for this chapter on tactical and operational planning, let's review the idea of strategic planning. Strategic planning establishes a direction suited to the unique nature of the organization and its environment. This direction is made explicit by the choice of appropriate objectives and strategies.

Once a desired direction has been established by strategic planning, this direction must be realized through tactical and operational planning. Tactical planners prepare for the deployment of resources within organization units and job positions. Operational planners prepare for the optimum use of the resources assigned. The combined result of all three stages of planning is effective use of environmental opportunities.[1]

Tactical planning and operational planning are in many ways less glamorous than is strategic planning. They lack its excitement. They are not at the interface of the organization and the outside world and they don't make big decisions directing the organization in its relationship with the outside world. In contrast, tactical planning and operational planning have a stay-at-home image because their focus is internal. Nevertheless, strategic planning will have diminished value unless it is followed up by these companion planning stages.

This chapter addresses tactical planning and then operational planning. For each stage of planning, concepts, process, and the role of the human resource function are discussed.

TACTICAL PLANNING

Tactical Planning Concepts

Tactical planning serves as a bridge between, and draws its essence from, strategic planning and operational planning. Tactical planning, therefore, is a simple topic, with a limited conceptual base.[2]

The concept to be discussed here is the distributive structure. A product of tactical planning, the *distributive structure* is a complex internal regulatory mechanism that helps to ensure that organization resources are deployed appropriately for the environment in which the organization operates.[3] An organization develops structures for a variety of reasons, many not at all related to tactical planning. But when an organization begins to do tactical planning, certain structures must be chosen and made to serve as tactical structures. The design of these structures must be dictated by the needs of the tactical plan. Other reasons for the design of structures may have to be abandoned or compromised.

Three tactical structures largely determine the deployment of human, material, and capital resources at enterprise, group, and business unit levels. These are organization structure, organization culture, and budget systems. At the functional level, these three structures are replaced by policy statements as the deployment mechanism.

Organization structure formally assigns authority and responsibility to job holders. By their influence on the design of organization structure, tactical planners ensure that the kinds of authority and responsibility assigned to persons in the organization are appropriate for the carrying out of strategic plans. *Organization culture* informally identifies organization heroes and creates norms of proper behavior. By influencing the formation of organization culture, tactical planners ensure informal support for strategic objectives and strategies. *Financial budgets* determine how the financial resources of the organization will be spent. By their influence on budgetary processes, tactical planners ensure that strategic plans are properly financed. *Policy statements* serve as a guide for the way decisions are made. When policy statements are made a part of tactical planning, planners ensure that decisions made in the organization are supportive of strategic plans.

This chapter discusses tactical planning at enterprise, group, and business unit levels of the organization and the roles of organization structure, organization culture, and budget systems in this planning. The examples used will be of enterprise level tactical planning. The discussion can be applied to planning at group and business unit levels as well. Policy as a distributive structure is discussed in Chapter 5.

Organization Structure

Organization structure can be viewed as a way of dividing up the work of the organization and putting it back together again in a manner that promotes the attainment of strategic objectives. It can be more narrowly viewed as a plan defining all job positions in the organization and locating those job positions within the organization by hierarchic level and by organization unit.

Structure design is one of the primary ways that organizations adapt to changes in their strategies. Aligning structure with strategy involves "continual tinkering" with organization design.[4] The primary ways that organization structure can be used to channel resources to achieve strategic objectives are the following:

- Assign *more job positions* in the organization to work crucial to the attainment of strategic objectives.[5]
- Create *specialized job positions* that allow emphasis on work crucial to the attainment of strategic objectives.[6]
- Assign to *high-level job positions* work crucial to the attainment of strategic objectives.

An example of an organization structure designed to emphasize work crucial to the attainment of strategic objectives is shown in Exhibit 3-1. Part A of the exhibit shows a partial organization chart for Products, Inc.,[7] prior to initiation of a formal strategic plan. Following the implementation of strategic planning and an introduction to experience curve thinking in 1985, strategic planners in the firm decided to increase the number of times the firm is first in the market with a new product. Emphasis on the research function was felt to be necessary to achieve this objective. Part B of the exhibit shows the organization structure as revised to promote research. The new structure, as compared to the previous structure, promotes research in the following ways:

- More job positions in the organization have been assigned to the research function. Before the reorganization, there were 1 director of research and 13 researchers. After the reorganization, there were 1 vice president of research, 5 directors of research, and 24 researchers.
- Job positions have been created that allow specialization in research work. After the reorganization, each of the 5 directors of research, along with their assigned researchers, specialized in research on one product line. For this kind of research, increased specialization probably will improve research output.
- High-level job positions have been assigned research work. After the reorganization, a vice president for research reported directly to the chief executive officer.

Design of Organization Structure

Modern-day interest in the connection between strategy and organization structure began with Alfred Chandler's classic study of organization structure, published in 1962.[8] On the basis of an historical study of 70 firms, Chandler concluded that organization structure normally was dictated by strategy. He recognized, however, that organization structure often lagged considerably behind strat-

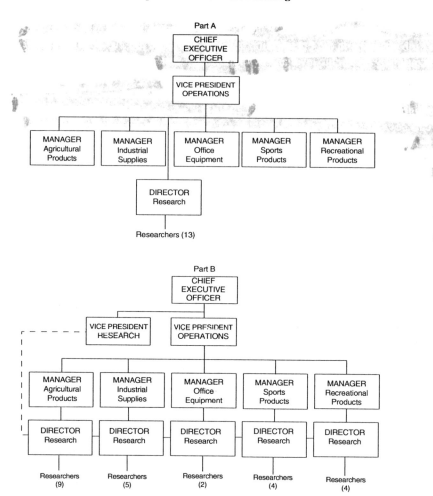

Exhibit 3-1. Organization Structure of Products, Inc., Before and After Tactical Planning.

egy.[9] He also recognized that, on occasion, strategy followed structure.[10] Chandler's views appear to be consistent with most current thinking.[11]

Because strategy and organization structure have a mutually dependent relationship, their mutual effects must be considered. During *strategic* planning, the effect of structure on strategy should be considered. At the stage where organization identity is established, planners must not allow current organization structure to unduly color their thinking about organization identity.[12] Planners must visualize what the organization could be with *other* organization forms.

During *tactical* planning, the effect of strategy on structure should be considered. When making tactical plans for organization structure, planners must determine which of two possible conditions exist:

- The strategies to be supported by the structural change have been implemented.
- The strategies to be supported by the structural change have not yet been implemented.

Each of these situations calls for a different approach to the design of organization structure—a retrospective approach, when strategies have already been implemented, or a prospective approach, when strategies have yet to be implemented. In either event, four tasks must be completed:

1. Assess the consistency of the current organization structure with requirements of the new strategies.
2. Divide the organization into primary segments.
3. Define a detailed organization structure.
4. Test the proposed structure, revising it as necessary.[13]

Retrospective Approach

Under the retrospective approach, new strategies have been introduced with the old structure still in place. The old structure likely will not fit the new strategies. Tactical planners will need to assess the old structure to determine what problems are being caused by implementation of the new strategies and, if necessary, develop a new structure to correct these problems.

The example of Exhibit 3-1, Part B, may be used to illustrate the application of the retrospective approach. As shown in the exhibit, Products, Inc., is engaged in the sales, service, and distribution of a wide range of products. It is organized according to type of product produced and kind of function performed. Each of the divisions does business in at least one foreign country. Recently, organization planners adopted a strategy of further expansion into global markets with an initial concentration on European markets. This strategy is intended to help ensure the long-run stability of the organization.[14]

Step one of the retrospective approach was carried out after one year of emphasis on global expansion, during which time several divisions experienced modest success by further expansion into European markets. Interviews with selected corporate-level and division-level managers revealed the following structurally related problems:

- Divisions that had experienced success within a country often were of little help to other divisions in gaining access to markets within the country.
- Division personnel who were successful in U.S. operations often were unsuccessful in operations outside the United States.
- An inordinate amount of the time of key persons in each division was required for expansion into foreign markets, causing loss of competitive position in markets in the United States.
- Division managers found that they and their staffs were required to become involved in day-to-day operations to obtain the emphasis necessary for expansion into foreign

markets. This caused a breakdown of the autonomy needed for the long-run development of persons at lower levels of the organization.

Step two of the redesign process required dividing the organization into primary segments. The manner in which this is done is critical, because changing the organization design to allow the contingencies arising out of an organization's strategic orientation to be isolated within a region or regions of the organization structure must also allow other contingencies of organization to be resolved within other regions of structure.[15]

There are two basic ways to divide an organization—according to the nature of the markets served and according to the kinds of work done.[16] Each of these bases can be further subdivided into three bases of division, commonly called bases of departmentation. According to the nature of the markets served, these are: kind of product or service provided, kind of customer served, and geographic region served. According to the kind of work done, these are: kind of product or service produced, kind of function performed, and kind of technology used.[17]

Each form of departmentation has strengths and weaknesses. The final choice should further the carrying out of strategies in the following ways:

- Allow specialization in activities important to the carrying out of strategies
- Aid coordination of such activities
- Focus attention on strategic objectives
- Allow strategic decisions to be made in a timely and effective manner
- Be a sound investment of organization resources

The process of selecting a final basis of departmentation was fairly subjective in the case of Products, Inc. And, as in most complex organizations, the final structure utilized not one but several primary bases of departmentation.[18] This occurs because demands are placed on organization structure as a result of contingencies other than strategic contingencies and these demands also must be served.[19] The aim of tactical planners in structural redesign is to find an appropriate region of the organization structure within which to isolate and deal with those contingencies involving strategic orientation of the organization. The choice of planners in Products, Inc., was to isolate contingencies of its global expansion strategy within functional and geographically based segments of the organization, as shown in Exhibit 3-2.

The new structure differs from the old in two ways. First, the new structure places all European operations under a vice president responsible for European operations. These operations are grouped under the Industrial Products Division (all agricultural products, industrial supplies, and office equipment) or the Consumer Products Division (all sports products and recreational products). Grouping of European operations under one vice president who reports to the CEO will ensure that this part of the organization receives the attention it deserves and should further the coordination of activities within the division.

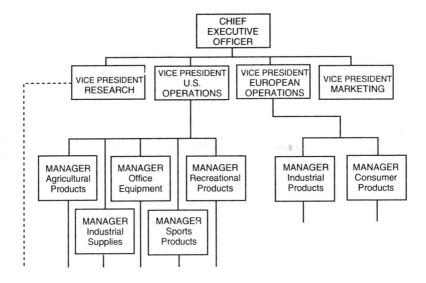

Exhibit 3-2. New Organization Structure of Products, Inc., to Accommodate Its New Strategic Orientation

Second, the new structure establishes an office of vice president for marketing at the corporate level. This has the effect of elevating the attention given to marketing in recognition of the fact that the marketing function will play a key part in the success of the new strategy. Also, it will allow the development of strength in marketing throughout the organization. It was felt that a strength in marketing was necessary to spearhead the push into European markets and, eventually, into other global markets as well.

Once the preferred bases of primary-level departmentation were selected, the next step in the design process was the definition of the associated detailed organization structure. Individuals from a tactical planning committee were assigned responsibility for liaison with task forces of persons selected from affected areas of Products, Inc. These task forces designed the organization structure for each of the newly identified major segments of the organization. Much the same procedure that had been used at the primary level to define problems encountered with the current structure and to select a basis for primary segmentation was repeated in this step.

The last step in the design process was a rigorous test of the proposed structure, contrasting the performance of the proposed structure against that of the current structure.[20] Simulated projects and activities were developed for this purpose. Included were ones essential to implementing the new strategies and similar to actual projects and activities conducted in the recent past. The following measures of performance were used to compare performance under the new structure with that under the old: estimated time required for completion of the projects and activities, estimated time and accountabilities of key persons, and projected quality of the work performed. The results allowed a determination of whether the proposed new structure was likely to reduce the severity of the problems experienced by a misfit of strategy and current organization structure and, if so, whether the gain justified the additional expenditure required.

Prospective Approach

Under the prospective approach, new strategies have been developed but *not* implemented. The old structure likely will not fit the new strategies. Tactical planners must anticipate demands that the strategies will place on the structure and design a new structure that is capable of meeting those demands. This new organization design must be tested prior to its installation as well as in later use. The example that follows illustrates how the tactical planners of Products, Inc., would have proceeded had they redesigned the organization structure prior to the implementation of their global expansion strategy.

In step one, tactical planners reflected on the demands the new global expansion strategy would be expected to make on the organization. To ensure consideration of all aspects of organization during this reflective process, they used a model—that is, a representation of the organization showing the relationships among organization components. The particular model used was a portion of the Van de Ven–Ferry set of organization design modules,[21] as shown in Exhibit 3-3.

```
          MODULE 1                              MODULE 2
 ┌──────────────────────────┐     ┌──────────────────────────────┐
 │  MACROORGANIZATION DESIGN│     │  DESIGN OF ORGANIZATION UNITS│
 │ Structural configuration │     │ Unit specialization          │
 │   Vertical, horizontal,  │     │ Personnel composition        │
 │     and spacial          │     │ Unit standardization         │
 │     differentiation      │     │ Unit decision making         │
 │   Forms of departmentation│    │ Unit performance norms       │
 │   Administrative intensity│    │   and standards              │
 │ Distribution of power    │     │                              │
 │   and authority          │     │                              │
 │   among decision makers  │     │                              │
 └──────────────────────────┘     └──────────────────────────────┘

          MODULE 3                              MODULE 4
 ┌──────────────────────────┐     ┌──────────────────────────────┐
 │ DESIGN OF JOBS OR POSITIONS│   │DESIGN OF INTERUNIT RELATIONSHIPS│
 │ Job specialization       │     │ Intensity of relationships   │
 │ Job expertise            │     │ Formalization of relationships│
 │ Job standardization      │     │ Complexity of relationships  │
 │ Job discretion           │     │ Centralization of relationships│
 │ Job incentives           │     │                              │
 └──────────────────────────┘     └──────────────────────────────┘
```

Exhibit 3-3. Organization Design Modules
Source: Andrew H. Van de Ven and Diane L. Ferry, *Measuring and Assessing Organizations*, (New York: John Wiley, 1980), pp. 10–13.

Planners started with the Macroorganization Design module and followed through the modules in sequence. For each element of a module, two questions were asked: What characteristics of this element are required by the new strategy, and, as a result, what is required of a new optimal structure? Also, how well does our current structure meet these requirements? (Had the change in structure been extensive, they would have used more details of each element than are provided in the exhibit. Andrew Van de Ven and Diane Ferry provide such detail in their book, including an elaborate questionnaire.[22] For major changes in structure, the planners would have engaged the services of an outside organization development consultant to help them with this reflective process.[23])

Once the reflective process was complete, planners selected a basis for primary departmentation and a detailed organization structure that most closely fit the characteristics of the optimal structure identified. These steps are similar to the steps in the retrospective approach and will not be repeated here. As the final step in the design process, the proposed structure was tested prior to its implementation. Again, as in the retrospective approach, simulated projects and activities were used. However, the performance of the proposed structure was compared not only with the performance of the current structure but also with optimum-performance benchmark levels. This additional study was warranted because the organization was changing simultaneously both its strategies and its structure.

A benchmark is a standard of performance based on data from outside organizations.[24] Benchmark levels are established through formal study of competitors (if they are willing) or noncompetitors. The procedure for obtaining benchmark measures is as follows:

- Determine what activities are critical for the new strategies to be implemented.
- Develop key measures of performance for each of these activities.
- Determine, by scanning publications and by conferring with experts in the activity areas, what firms with activities similar to yours are best at the activities.
- Ask those firms to allow you to observe their operations and to compare your data with similar data about activities in their firms.[25]

Such testing is costly, but it helps to ensure that the structure finally adopted is the best possible one for the strategies the organization intends to use.

Comparison of the Approaches

Both the retrospective approach and the prospective approach test the suitability of the current organization structure for the new strategies. Those parts of the current structure that are still appropriate can be retained. Each approach has its weaknesses and its strengths.

The retrospective approach does not allow a thoroughgoing fit of organization structure to strategy. It only corrects the structural problems that appear when new strategies are implemented. Using this approach, the organization accepts a possible decline in performance during the period before structural changes are made. But, by waiting until the full ramifications of the change in strategy for current structure are apparent, the retrospective approach permits a greatly simplified change process. Only those changes intended to correct the known problems of the old structure are implemented. Acceptance of the change in structure is likely because the new structure has the limited purpose of correcting known problems.

The prospective approach is a somewhat more complex and costly approach. It allows, however, a thoroughgoing and objective search for the optimum structure. The structure finally developed is likely to be better than that produced using the retrospective approach. Both strategy and structure change are introduced at the same time. In highly competitive markets this may result in a loss of market position because the organization will need to delay the introduction of new strategies until the new structure is in place.

Which of these approaches is preferable depends in part on how much of a misfit is anticipated between the new strategy and the existing structure. If the misfit is expected to be pronounced, delay in changing the structure could cause extensive financial and competitive losses to the organization and also could cause the organization to reject the needed strategic changes. In this instance the prospective approach is preferable. If the misfit is not expected to be pronounced, it probably is advisable to introduce the new strategies and correct problems with the existing structure when and if they occur.

Organization Culture

Organizations are groups of people and other resources set aside from the rest of the environment to serve some particular and distinct purpose. In healthy organizations, members recognize and institutionalize the distinctive nature of the organization by developing a culture.[26] Organization culture is that group of values and beliefs that set the members of the organization apart from outsiders. Culture formation is the visible sign of transition that an organization exhibits as it develops its own distinctive identity.

Organization culture is expressed by symbols, ceremonies, observances, and myths.[27] This expression can be formal, as in an organization mission statement, or informal, as in an exchange of letters in the "Letters to the Editor" column of an employee publication.

Proper design of culture furthers informal support for the strategic plans. Some organizations have begun to use culture to promote the attainment of strategic objectives by altering the culture in response to changing requirements of the organization. In a healthy organization, the business strategy is developed within the context of a mutually supporting culture.[28]

Origins of Culture

Organization identity determines organization culture. This concept is illustrated in the 1981–83 attempt to change the culture of the First National Bank of Chicago. Stanley Davis reports that the key to successful change was recognition of the importance of organization identity to culture:

> As we interviewed managers during this transition, one compelling theme emerged. First and foremost was the need to establish an institutional identity that had somehow gotten lost or obscured to both customers and employees. It was this commitment to institutional identity that would become the organizing principle of First Chicago's new culture.[29]

But what are the forces that cause people to enact a common organization identity and thus produce a common culture? The culture formation process is complex. Here are some key points:

1. People have difficulty explaining organizations. Therefore, they envision organizations as anthropomorphic,[30] as thinking, feeling, and acting in a human manner.[31]
2. Because people anthropomorphize organizations, they act out an organization identity by behaving as they believe the organization thinks and feels.
3. Given the anthropomorphic qualities of organization identity, organization identity and personal identity have close parallels. As an individual enacts organization identity, he or she tries to reproduce in the organization his or her own idealized self-image or, failing that, tries to reproduce one of his or her other favored "possible selves." Possible selves are embodiments of the hopes and fears of the individual, representing what the individual might become, would like to become, and is afraid of becoming.[32]
4. But the individual acts out organization identity in a social setting. Others also are trying to reproduce the organization in their own images. An individual tends to reinforce selectively enactments by others consistent with the individual's own self-image. Alliances are formed among persons with similar preferred possible selves. A supportive network is built around an agreed-on view of what the collective enactments of organization identity should be.[33] This phenomenon is the basis for culture formation.
5. If many or most persons in the organization agree on what the organization should be, the enactments of organization identity will share many common features. An organization culture is established.

Both organization identity and organization culture have their genesis in the kinds of people who work in the organization.

Cultural Evolution

Benjamin Schneider contends that the kinds of people who work in an organization are functions of an attraction-selection-attrition (ASA) cycle. Persons who fit into the organization tend to be attracted to, selected for employment, and

retained in the organization, whereas those who do not fit are not attracted, selected, or retained. He believes it is in this ASA cycle that we find the growth and
development of organization climate and culture.[34]

In terms of the culture formation process described above, persons will be
attracted, selected, and retained by the organization if their self-images, and hence
their desires for organization identity, are compatible with the self-images of persons already in an organization. Persons will not be attracted, selected, and
retained by the organization if their self-images, and hence their desires for organization identity, are not compatible with the self-images of persons already in an
organization. Over a period of time every organization develops a strong culture.
Culture becomes stronger the longer the cycle is at work.

It is obvious that some long-lived organizations have weak cultures and
some relatively short-lived organizations have strong cultures. And it appears that
organizations with high turnover, which should allow full rein for the operation of
the ASA cycle, often have weaker cultures than do organizations with low
turnover. How can this be explained? Perhaps there are obstacles that sometimes
prevent the formation of culture.

In a 1986 study Jon Pierce found that employees who felt they "made a difference" in their organizations internalized and acted out the organization's values
and traditions. Employees who felt they did not "make a difference" ignored or
even resisted the organization's values and traditions.[35] If the individual lacks the
authority or freedom to influence the organization to any significant degree and
cannot find other persons with similar or compatible self-images with whom to
unite as a power bloc, he or she will be unable to reproduce one of his or her "possible selves" and therefore will be unable to identify with the organization. Thus,
such persons will not act out the organization identity.

Contrary to Schneider's theory, persons who find it impossible to express
themselves (their self-images) through their organization do not necessarily leave
the organization. More often they stay and simply give up trying to build organization identity. They only "work for the organization"; they no longer believe in it.
Davis has expressed this phenomenon of noninvolvement in the form of a cultural
principle: If guiding beliefs do not drive the strategies and actions of an organization, then daily beliefs will. Guiding beliefs involve areas of major importance to
an individual; daily beliefs involve the minutiae of daily life, such as the belief that
the water cooler is the best place to go for the straight story at work.[36]

If an individual who is trying to express himself or herself through the organization is surrounded by persons who are no longer trying to express themselves,
the insulating effect of these persons presents a further obstacle to cultural influence. The individual can find no reinforcement for the expression of guiding
beliefs, only for daily beliefs. Persons may continue indefinitely in an organization
able to express only daily beliefs through the organization.

In sum, organization culture may evolve and become stronger under favorable conditions. Where obstacles to evolution exist, organizations may never
develop a strong culture.

Managing Culture

Because evolution of culture is neither fixed nor inevitable, organizations should take steps to manage the culture-formation process. The deliberate attempt to manage organization culture as a tactical tool is a relatively new phenomenon. Its use appears to be widespread.[37] Tactical planners must look at the culture of the organization and decide their aim concerning the culture—whether to maintain the culture as it is, to strengthen the culture, or to modify the culture. Several methods are available for managing culture so that it contributes to the tactical planning process.

First, planners themselves may act as "culture bearers." To serve as culture bearers, planners must determine the identity desired for the organization. This step is performed as part of the strategic planning process. Planners then must behave in ways appropriate to this organization identity as they perform their jobs in the organization.

Second, people may be hired who have desires for an organization identity similar to that needed to achieve the strategic objectives. Candidates should be screened not simply for what they can and will do for the organization but also for what they believe and value. The kinds of people hired determine, within narrow limits, the culture of the organization. If the people hired are similar in their desires for organization identity with most persons already in the organization, this practice will allow for the maintenance and strengthening of an existing culture. If the people hired have desires for organization identity different from most persons already in the organization, this practice will allow for the modification of an existing culture. In either event, persons who most closely approximate in their behavior the desired culture should be used as models for selecting new employees.

People making hiring decisions tend to hire people like themselves.[38] Hiring processes that allow these model employees a voice in determining who gets hired, such as internal referral, can help to ensure that the possible selves of employees will overlap, increasing the opportunities for reinforcement of cultural enactments.

Third, employees must be allowed to express their self-images at work. Even a carefully guided ASA cycle will do little to build a strong culture if employees do not have a voice in shaping organization identity.[39] Employees identify with an organization only if they can express their identities through the organization. Participation in management, job autonomy, and the opportunity to use valued skills at work appear to be factors in causing employees to act out an organization's culture.[40] Without the ability to shape organization identity, organization culture as an active force in the lives of employees disappears. This method is useful regardless of the objective of cultural management.

The final way of managing the culture-formation process is to allow and encourage symbols, ceremonies, observances, and myths that communicate culture. These are not meaningless rituals but the vehicles by which culture is communicated.[41] This method also is useful regardless of the objective of the process.

When a change in the culture is necessary, it should be possible to make changes easily if the change is minor—that is, if the change does not bring about an organization identity inconsistent with the favored possible selves of most current employees. What is called cultural change in organizations often is superficial. Such change may be brought about using the methods listed earlier.

Major changes in organization cultures, those that attempt to bring about an organization identity inconsistent with the favored possible selves of most current employees, will be extremely difficult to effect.[42] The methods discussed here may be used, but extensive effort may be required. For example, it probably will be necessary to replace many employees currently in the organization with employees suited to the new culture. Organizations considering such change should rethink their strategies first. Perhaps the strategies used should be changed to be compatible with the organization identity and the culture of the organization. Organizations should attempt major cultural change only if they are willing to expend the considerable time and money required to do it successfully.[43]

Financial Budgets

A financial budget is a plan for controlling the use of funds over a period of time. Budgets are used to authorize expenditures, to forecast resource requirements, and to motivate managers to control expenses.[44] A capital budget is a plan for investments; an appropriation budget is a plan for current expenses.[45] Budgeting becomes part of tactical planning when budgeting practices support the strategic plans of the organization.

Budget Process

In the budget process, budget proposals are submitted for approval to a budgetary review committee. When tactical planning is involved, the budgetary review committee and the tactical planning committee should have overlapping memberships. Four steps are especially important when budgeting for tactical purposes:

1. *Information.*[46] All persons who will be submitting budget proposals should be made aware of the strategic direction of the firm and should be provided with forecasts of conditions that are expected to exist during the budgeting period. Ideally, the information step is continuous. Providing the information needed to ensure that well-thought out budgets are submitted is not easy. Repeated use of various forms of communication will be required. If most persons in the organization understand clearly the strategic directions of the organization, constructive ideas for the use of financial resources will result and unrealistic proposals should be reduced to a minimum.

2. *Proposal.* Proposals usually are required of all managers, but special proposals may be submitted by the strategic planning committee, by the issue management team, or by employees throughout the organization. Standardized guides and forms should require information that will make clear the contribution of the activity to be financed to strategic objectives. Proposals for capital budgets should indi-

cate the consequences of financing a capital project. Proposals for appropriation budgets should indicate the consequences of financing alternative levels of expenditures. For example, a proposing unit would indicate the effect on strategic plans of expenditures 10, 15, or 20 percent more or less than the requested amount.[47]

3. *Selection.* Tactical planning is the allocation of resources to achieve strategic objectives and strategies. All members of the budget review committee must be intimately familiar with the organization's strategic plans. Each proposal must be weighed by comparing its strategic value with its cost. The committee should be able to to explain in tactical terms why each proposal is accepted or rejected.

4. *Monitoring.* Proposal effectiveness should be evaluated periodically to determine whether the projected contribution of the activity financed to strategic objectives actually is realized. The learning that occurs as a result of evaluation should be used to improve the budget formation process and should affect how each step of the process is carried out in the future.

Employee Participation in the Budget Process

Employees may or may not support and cooperate with the budget process. The key to getting employee cooperation appears to lie in selective participation in the process. This discussion will focus on department budgets because it is at the department level that employee cooperation is most critical.

Several levels of participation are possible:

- No participation—managers are told the budget limits for their departments.
- Participation by managers in establishing a budget process and/or in the setting of budget limits for their departments.
- Participation by both managerial and nonmanagerial employees in establishing a budget process and/or in the setting of budget limits for their departments.

Participation in the budget-setting process is worthwhile only if participating employees want to participate and have contributions to make to the process. Allowing participation solely as a way to get acceptance of decisions made by others usually is not effective.[48] For these reasons, planners may decide that there will be no participation by other employees in the budget-formation process.

When no participation is allowed in the budgeting process, consideration may be given to the use of incentives for managerial and nonmanagerial employees to improve budgetary performance. Managers are highly motivated to reach budgetary targets when significant rewards, such as salary bonuses, promotion prospects, and enhanced status, are attached to the achievement of budgetary targets.[49] However, if incentives are based only on managers staying within budget, managers may cut expenses in ways that reduce short-run costs but sacrifice long-term gains. Managers must be rewarded for outstanding contributions to the strategic plan for the money spent. Suggestion systems may be used to reward nonmanagerial employees for ideas that lead to better attainment of strategic objectives with less cost to the organization.[50]

Planners may choose to make managers part of the budget setting process.[51] This decision should be based on (1) whether managers want to participate, have worthwhile contributions to make, and have suitable attitudes,[52] motivations,[53] and personalities[54] and on (2) the managerial style used by the managers' superiors.[55] Used under the proper circumstances, participation by managers can help to ensure that budgets finally set by the process are realistic, improve managerial job performance, improve managerial budget performance, and create more favorable managerial attitudes toward budgeting for strategic objectives.[56]

In some instances, when nonmanagerial employees are able to make significant contributions, planners may include them in the budget-setting process. When these employees also work in departments that are especially significant to strategic objectives, it is even more strongly advisable to do so. Exact procedures for allowing participation will vary depending on the budgetary process and the authority structure of the department.

Departmental budgets in most large Japanese companies and in some U.S. firms are determined with extensive participation by employees in key departments. The setting of departmental budgets begins with studies by product development specialists to determine what features of the product are necessary if the company is to compete successfully in the market. A target selling price is established based on what it is believed the market will accept. From this target price a target profit margin is subtracted that reflects the company's strategic plans—the difference is the "allowable cost" of the product. Then production departments are asked to prepare a current estimated cost based on current technologies and practices. The current cost estimate typically is considerably above the allowable cost estimate. Management then selects a target cost figure somewhere in between the current cost and allowable cost estimates.[57]

During the design stage, the target cost figure becomes the focus for extensive collaboration within departments to see how the figure can be obtained without sacrificing product quality. For example, design engineers working on different parts of the product interact frequently with employees who will implement the final design. When an initial design is complete, cost estimates are prepared. These estimates are returned to product developers, who may revise the list of desired product features, and the cycle is repeated. The design cycle is complete with the approval of a final design that meets the target price.[58]

During the production stage, a similar process occurs. Each production department is given target cost figures for its part of the production process. These estimates include only costs controllable by worker effort and by process improvement activities.[59]

At the end of the entire budget process, a large number of employees have been allowed to take responsibility for the success of the company's strategic plans. When planned levels of usage of funds are modified during the budget process to reflect strategic plans of the organization, and when budgets are properly implemented, budgeting becomes a most important device by which the various parts of the organization can be brought together and directed toward strategic objectives.

Tactical Planning Process

The Tactical Planning Committee

Tactical structures are not discrete programs any one organization unit can initiate; they are not the concern of any one department. Rather, they are part of the organization's fabric and, as such, they must be designed at the organization level by a tactical planning committee with representation from the entire organization.[60]

The overall function of the tactical planning committee is to develop for approval by the total organization plans for the structures that will guide the deployment of resources to operations. Large amounts of tangible and intangible organization resources will be deployed on the basis of these plans. Therefore, committee members must be carefully chosen. The committee must include persons who have participated in both strategic and operational planning and who understand and can represent both processes. It should include persons who will be implementing the tactical plan, and it should include persons who understand the internal workings of the organization.

While meeting all these requirements, the committee should be as small as possible. About 18 members is ideal, for this allows the formation of three small subcommittees to spearhead the design effort regarding organization structure, organization culture, and budget systems. These subcommittees must be kept small since they will be required to perform intensive analysis of detailed data.

Guidelines for the Design of Tactical Structures

In carrying out its work, the committee should ensure that designs for the various tactical structures conform to seven guidelines:

1. Be Compatible with Each Other

The principle of systemic unity requires that distributive structures be compatible with each other. The tactical committee may ensure compatibility of the organization structure, the organization culture, and the budget system by having overlapping memberships on the subcommittees assigned to each of these design tasks and by reviewing the work of these subcommittees for compatibility.

2. Allocate Resources for Equal Incremental Return

Tactical planning is concerned with the effectiveness and efficiency of the allocation of resources. Managerial economics suggests that opportunity cost, not accounting costs, be considered in allocating resources. The true cost of using a resource is the net revenue that could be produced elsewhere with that resource. One way of ensuring that opportunity cost is considered is to employ incremental reasoning in allocating resources.[61] For all of the alternative uses for a resource (including standing idle), determine the *net* gain that would occur in each use.[62] That use of the resource should be chosen that will yield the greatest incremental gain to the organization. Through incremental reasoning, resources are allocated so as to achieve proper balance and emphasis in the organization.

3. Reflect the Complex and Iterative Relationship of Strategy to Structure

The overall structure of an organization, including the distributive structures under discussion here, is the result of a complex play of variables other than strategy. Technology(ies) available to an organization for producing its product or service, the nature of and variations in the environment, and the past history of the organization all influence the overall structure of an organization.

Although strategy affects overall structure, it is likely that strategy in turn is affected by overall structure. Certainly it has been demonstrated that, as an organization develops, its size and its organization structure begin to exert constraints on organization actions and, therefore, presumably on strategy.[63] There is no obvious reason to consider either strategy or structure as subordinate to the other. In practice there is a dependent relationship between the two, and one can accept that each follows the other.[64] Both strategy and structure should be under constant review so that change can be made as the need arises.

4. Conform to Organization Design and Identity

The organization, according to the systems theories presented in Chapter 1, is a combination of a rational design, constructed by organization leaders, and of an organization identity, achieved by the interplay of people, naturally occurring objects, and artifacts. Tactical structures must be consistent with rational decisions by management. They also must be consistent with the organization identity that exists collectively in the minds of organization members.

In order for these structures to reflect both organization design and organization identity, it is important, as suggested, that the tactical planning committee include not only persons familiar with strategic planning and operational planning but also those who understand and help to enact organization identity. The "right" decision will have a feeling or "rightness" to those persons because it is consistent with organization identity.

5. Leave Room for Subsequent Decision Making

The principle of system design called *equifinality* states that if systems are to avoid loss of the ability to adapt and to evolve, they must have flexible structures that allow choices among different courses of action to accomplish different end results. Another way of expressing this is that it is a choice between original design detail and later fleshing out of the basic design framework. This variance allows the expression and evolution of organization identity. While the correct balance between design detail and looseness of design will vary with the organization and its setting, every organization should make a conscious decision as to what the proper balance should be.

6. Make Provision for Their Own Revision

Guideline 5 speaks to decision making *within* the structure. Guideline 6 moves a step farther to revision of the structure itself.

Well-run companies change their tactical structures continuously.[65] This is necessary if strategy is to change in response to changing conditions in organization and environment. It is important for the structures to be designed not simply for efficient allocation of scarce resources at a given time but *for efficient change to different allocative solutions.* Change at a continuously more rapid pace seems to be an inevitable part of the human experience. Any structure currently designed with no provision for its own revision is shortsighted.

7. Produce the Desired Behavior

The major purpose of tactical structures is to shape the behavior of organization members so they are more likely to behave in a manner supportive of strategic objectives. Tactical planners must evaluate all tactical structures periodically to see that they are shaping behavior in appropriate ways.

The Human Resource Role in Tactical Planning

The human resource department supports tactical planning through the chief human resource executive and the various specialists in the human resource department.

The Human Resource Executive on the Tactical Planning Committee

The role of the human resource executive on the tactical planning committee is similar to the role of this executive on the strategic planning committee. The role includes contributing a general managerial knowledge and appreciation of the business and of the internal affairs of the organization and contributing HR knowledge for the development of the tactical structures.

The human resource executive must be able to make both of these contributions for two reasons. First, the committee must be small in order to be effective. This requirement does not permit the luxury of having narrow specialists on the committee whose ideas must be reworked by others before being practical. Second, the human resource executive will not be able to gauge trade-offs between human resource system impacts and organization performance impacts on the structural designs discussed unless he or she understands both the business of the organization and its human resource systems.

Human Resource Specialist Support for Tactical Planning

Human resource department support for tactical planning consists of helping to design the planning process to see that it is a personal growth experience for planners, helping to select and develop a cadre of persons who may serve as tactical planners, and helping to implement change required by the results of the planning process.

Designing the Planning Process for Behavioral Change

As with strategic planning, the more important part of tactical planning is the process, not the product, of planning. This is more so in the case of planning for organization culture and budgets, but it is also true for organization structure. In an age of rapid change, planning artifacts are outdated almost as soon as they are produced, but the personal growth that occurs in planning participants is of continuing value.

Davis said of the dramatic change in the culture of the First National Bank of Chicago:

> ...the process is...[what]...counts. It is a process of creating a culture appropriate to new internal and external demands. As a company goes through that process, there are many artifacts—concrete evidence of the intangible presence of culture. A formal and public commitment by the company's leadership is an important artifact. More important, however, is the behavior that was required for them to go through the process. This is the real culture that the words try to capture. The test of further success is measured by subsequent artifacts, but even more by the behavior that produces them—or does not.[66]

If the tactical planning process is to cause personal growth in the planning participants, it is of benefit to have a behavioral process consultant available to offer process advice. Most large and medium-sized companies will have a behavioral process consultant on their human resource staffs; smaller organizations will find it worthwhile to bring in an outside consultant. The consultant can advise the organization on how to structure the planning process; what behavioral change techniques to use and for what purposes; and what persons, positions, and units to have represented in the planning process.[67]

Selecting and Developing Tactical Planners

In many, perhaps most, U.S. firms it may be difficult or impossible to find 18 persons who, collectively, meet the experience requirements discussed here because we have allowed narrow specialization among employees. The human resource department of an organization must recognize this problem, know where it exists, and take steps to correct it. For the long run, organizations must develop employees with a broad outlook. These employees must be encouraged to accept promotions and transfers across functional[68] areas in the organization and to visit with employees in other locations of the organization when out of town on company business. This is not to say that everyone in an organization should be a generalist, only that the proportion of generalist employees is too low in many organizations for effective tactical planning.

Human resource departments should have information in their human resource information systems (HRISs) that will allow locating persons suitable for tactical planning. The system will identify persons intimately familiar with the internal workings of the organization—of the work done in the organization, of budgeting, of the organization structure, of the various parts of the organization, of the organization culture, of the organization technology—and with both operational and strategic planning. From this list staffing specialists will help to select those who are able and willing to participate in tactical planning and who possess the integrity needed to perform well the vital task.

Managing Planned Change

The discussion in Chapter 2, on the role of organization behavior specialists in helping to introduce change, can be applied to tactical planning and will not be repeated here.

An additional point is relevant. When tactical structures change, because these affect greatly the working lives of organization members, the change may be more traumatic than the change associated with the implementation of strategic plans. In order to manage change with as little trauma as possible, tactical planners should strive to preserve organization identity.[69] In terms of the distributive structures, organization culture has the most direct relationship with organization identity. The development of organization culture should be encouraged, but deliberate change of culture should be avoided whenever possible. As long as organization identity is preserved, other distributive structures may be changed as needed without serious effect on organization members.

OPERATIONAL PLANNING

In contrast to both strategic planning and tactical planning, which are done at the enterprise, functional, group, and business levels, operational planning, as its name implies, is done at the operational level only. Any operation that has an output with a primary impact on the achievement of strategic objectives and uses a large proportion of the resources of the organization must be included in the operational planning process. In a large manufacturing concern this normally would include manufacturing, human resources, marketing, finance, and research and development.

Operational planners formulate programs for the efficient use of resources assigned in tactical planning to produce outputs that realize strategic objectives.

Resources

People
Things
Money

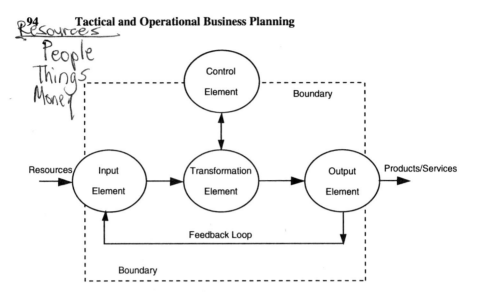

Exhibit 3-4.   Systems Diagram of an Operation

The resources they deal with may be finances, data, people, raw materials, and/or facilities and equipment.

Operational planning, unlike either strategic planning or tactical planning, involves work that is composed of repetitive cycles. These cycles may vary in length from a few months to many years. The work typically is much the same in consecutive cycles. These cyclical processes occur in settings protected from unplanned external influences.

Exhibit 3-4 illustrates a typical operation. As shown in the exhibit, resources are converted into products or services by a transformation element. The manner of transformation is regulated by a control element. Stored in the control element is information about the required characteristics of inputs and of outputs and the nature of the ways that inputs must be modified to produce outputs. Feedback is returned to the input element and is used to modify successive operations so that continual improvement is possible. The boundary shown in the exhibit prevents environmental intrusions that might infringe on the dedication of the process to continued improvements.

In this protected setting, changes in operations may be deliberately introduced and their effects observed and evaluated. Based on the learning that occurs as a result of the change introduced and its observed effects, further modifications may be made. This trial-and-error process continues until no further improvements in efficiency are possible.

Operational Planning Concepts

The trial-and-error process just described does occur in simple production processes with very short cycles, but it can become quite expensive in elaborate production processes and in processes with long cycles. Operational planning can

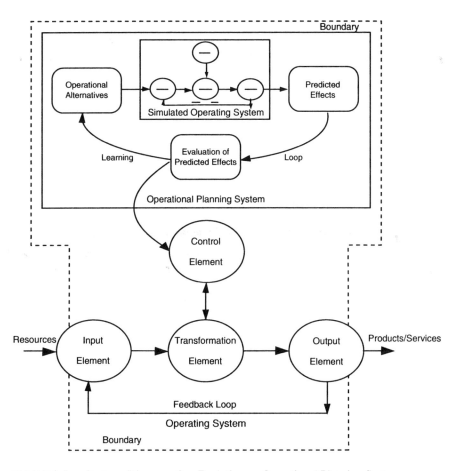

Exhibit 3-5.   Systems Diagram of an Evolutionary Operational Planning System

reduce sharply the time and expense of maximizing the efficiency of such operations by the use of a conceptual model. This model, very like a trial-and-error process, will achieve most of the improvements in efficiency that can be attained
through actual trial and error. It is shown in Exhibit 3-5.

During the planning phase of operations, alternatives, such as variations in
kinds of inputs, are tried in the simulated operating system. Based on the results of
the simulation, effects on the actual operating process are predicted. If these effects
appear to be favorable, they are tried out in the actual operating system. If feedback from output in actual production is favorable, permanent changes are made in
the way the product is produced.

The repetitive cycles of operations gives operational planning two of its most
distinctive features. Each cycle of work is an opportunity to use feedback for *continued incremental learning*. And operational planning is *action-oriented*: Learning
occurs while doing; planning and doing are contemporaneous.

The continued trial of new alternatives produces a continued succession of improvements in the efficiency of a given production process. At some point in this *evolutionary* progression, perhaps before or perhaps after maximum efficiency of the current production process has been reached, technological change may occur in the outside world and new production processes become available. At the point where other methods can produce the product or service at a lower cost, the present production process is obsolete. A new production process is then needed— a *revolutionary* change. The revolutionary change sets in motion a new cycle of evolutionary improvement in the efficiency of the new process.

As this discussion of evolutionary and revolutionary change suggests, operational planners, in their drive for efficiency, must achieve two results. They must use the current production process as efficiently as possible and they must introduce better processes as they become available and economically feasible.

Resources used, methods of operation, and outputs produced vary extensively among different operations in the same organization. Consider, for example, only the differences caused by variations in resources. If the primary resource of an operation is people, operations planners must be able to exercise conceptual skills with unusual adroitness as they relate to people. If the primary resource is raw materials, conceptual skills must be exercised with unusual adroitness as they relate to raw materials. The problems of predicting the performance of human resources in a given job have no counterpart in the use of the other resources; nor do the problems of predicting the way a given material will behave in a refiner. There is a complete body of knowledge necessary to the one problem that would be of no help with the other.

Because of these differences among operations, it is not feasible to plan at the organization level for all operations. Operational planning must focus narrowly on the particular kind of operation under scrutiny.

Operational Planning Process

The Operational Planning Committee

Persons who serve on the operational planning committee should have both generalist and specialist conceptual skills. Generalist conceptual skills are skills appropriate for all operations. Those most useful to operational planners are

- The ability to visualize alternative types of operations—that is, alternative ways to use resources to produce the product or service
- The ability to predict the effects of modifications in operations on the efficiency of operations
- The ability to evaluate the effectiveness of operations.[70]

Specialist conceptual skills are skills appropriate for a particular kind of operation. These skills must be appropriate to the resources used, the methods of operation employed, and the outputs produced.

Guidelines for Operational Planning

1. Before planning begins, objectives should be established for the planning process. Both process and product objectives should be considered.
2. Key participants should be identified to help with the planning. When selecting participants, organization leaders should consider objectively the viewpoints, skills, and representation of interests needed in the planning process and should structure the planning process to make possible the use of persons with those capabilities. They should think of persons who might:
   - Serve on an operational planning committee.
   - Review actions taken.
   - Serve as consultants at key points.
   - Serve on special task forces.
3. The operational planning committee should carry out the following steps of the planning process:
   - Decide those characteristics of the operation's output necessary to support organization objectives and strategies.
   - Assess realistically resources of all kinds available to the operation, given the tactical plans of the organization.
   - Evaluate the present product or service and the efficiency with which present operations produce these products or services.
   - Predict trends in future needs for levels and kinds of product or service.
   - Establish general operational objectives for levels and kinds of products or services to be produced and for efficiency of production of the products or services.
   - Establish operational policy guidelines for achieving these objectives.
4. Additional planning must be done when the current plan becomes out of date.
5. Provision should be made for continuing participant evaluation and periodic outside evaluation of the planning process.

The operational plans of different operations in an organization are coordinated by having overlapping membership on all operational planning committees. In addition, at least one member of each operational planning committee should participate in some way in the strategic and tactical planning processes of the organization.

The Human Resource Role in Operational Planning

The human resource department can support the operational planning process in several ways. Department members can help to design the planning process to achieve behavioral change, they can help to select persons who have the potential to be effective operational planners, they can provide programs to develop the operational planning skills of persons who do operational planning, and they can help to create an operating atmosphere conducive to the heuristic and experiential learning needed for effective operational planning.

The human resource department typically has a major responsibility for operational planning for the human resource function.

SUMMARY

This chapter discusses both tactical planning and operational planning. Tactical planning is done at the enterprise, group, business unit, and function levels. Tactical planners determine how to deploy the resources of the organization to particular uses within organization units and to job positions so as to implement the strategies and achieve the objectives of strategic planning. These resources are finances, data, people, raw materials, and/or facilities and equipment.

Deployment of resources at the enterprise, group, and business unit levels is accomplished through three distributive structures: organization structure, organization culture, and budgetary processes. Organization structure allocates authority and responsibility. By influencing the design of organization structure, tactical planners ensure that the kinds of authority and responsibility assigned to persons in the organization are appropriate for the carrying out of strategic plans. Organization culture allocates support. By influencing the formation of organization culture, tactical planners ensure that there is informal support for strategic objectives and strategies. Budgetary processes allocate finances. By their influence on budgetary processes, tactical planners ensure that strategic plans are properly financed. Deployment of resources at the function level is accomplished through policy statements and is discussed in Chapter 5.

The organization structure may be designed using either a retrospective or a prospective approach. The former probably has been used most often in the past; the latter is becoming increasingly common.

Organization culture has its origin in the attempt by individual employees to act out their self-image at work. If employees have sufficient autonomy in the workplace, and if they find reinforcement among other employees for the kind of organization identity they wish to establish, they will develop, over a period of time, a strong culture. Once the culture-formation process is established, it is difficult and expensive to make major changes in the culture. Changes can be avoided if the proper culture is established initially. This is done by hiring employees who have values consistent with the desired culture as required by the strategic plan and by otherwise encouraging the culture-formation process.

Budgetary processes may be rationally designed to direct financial resources as needed to achieve strategic objectives. But it is difficult in practice to place budgetary limits on people without negative behavioral results. The key appears to be the selective use of participation in the budgetary process by fund recipients.

The primary duty of the tactical planning committee is the design of distributive structures. The designs must conform to seven guidelines: They must be compatible with each other, they must allocate resources for equal incremental return, they must reflect the complex and iterative relationship of strategy to structure, they must conform both to organization design and organization identity, they must leave room for subsequent decision making, they must make provision for their own revision, and they must produce desired behavior.

The human resource department has a critical role to play in support of tactical planning. An organization development specialist from the human resource department can help design the planning process so that tactical planners experience personal growth as a result of their planning activities. Other specialists from the department can assist in the selection and development of employees who will do tactical planning. The primary concern here must be that sufficient numbers of generalist employees are available to provide the resource base from among whom persons with the proper knowledge, skills, and abilities may be selected. Finally, human resource specialists can help to introduce planned tactical change. The key here is to maintain organization identity in the face of continuing necessary change in tactical structures.

Operational planning is done separately for each operation of the organization. Operational planners determine how to obtain optimum efficiency in the use of the resources assigned to their operation by tactical planners. Operational planners simulate production processes and introduce changes. If these changes have desired effects, they may result in changes in the actual operations. Operational planners must recognize the point at which it is more economical to replace a production process than to try to further improve its efficiency.

Generalist conceptual skills useful to operational planners are the ability to visualize alternative types of operations, the ability to predict the effects of modifications in operations on efficiency, and the ability to evaluate the effectiveness of operations. Because operations differ so greatly in the kinds of resources used, the kinds of operations performed on these resources, and the kinds of outputs produced, specialist conceptual skills are unusually important to operational planners. Specialist conceptual skills are skills appropriate for a particular kind of operation.

The human resource department can assist in operational planning in the following areas: designing the operational planning process to achieve behavioral change, selecting persons who have the potential to be effective operational planners, providing programs to develop the operational planning skills of planners, and creating an operating atmosphere conducive to effective operational planning.

LEARNING EXERCISES

Case Analysis

If you have the opportunity for small-group discussion, you may use the procedure suggested for Case 1 in Chapter 1. If small-group discussion is used, you may wish to divide up the analysis, having some groups deal with questions 1, 2, and 3, and others with questions 4, 5, and 6. Each discussion group should report orally to the entire class or study group; these reports should be the basis for class or study group discussion of the case.

Assume that Mr. Shuckman, of Case 3, "Shuckman Interiors," initiated business planning in the organization. He assembled a strategic planning team and, after six months of deliberation, this team developed strategic plans for the organization at the enterprise level. This strategic plan established the following primary objectives for the organization:

- Long-term stability of the organization
- Employee quality of work life *NO HR*

The two major strategies for achieving these objectives were:

- Concentrate on marketing and product development
- Create new products and enter related lines of business.

Recommend to Mr. Shuckman the steps he should now take to initiate tactical and operational planing for the organization by answering the questions or taking the actions listed here:

1. Based on the information provided in the case, what tactical planning concepts appear immediately applicable to Shuckman Interiors? Explain your answer.
2. What persons in the organization should take part in tactical planning for the enterprise level? What can each contribute?
3. What should these persons do, and in what order should these actions be taken? For each action step recommended, be as specific in your recommendations as possible.
4. Considering the information provided in the case and the strategic objectives and strategies of Shuckman Interiors, what operations at Shuckman appear most in need of operational planning? Explain your answer.
5. What operational planning concepts appear most applicable to the operations chosen?
6. For any one of these operations chosen, decide what persons in the organization should take part in planning for these operations? Why do you suggest these persons participate?

Note: As an alternative to this assignment, some students may wish to continue with the "Bolling Laboratories" case begun in Chapter 2. This same analytical procedure may be used for "Bolling."

Discussion Question

1. Because tactical planning may involve change in the design of structures for allocation of scarce resources—authority, support, and finances—employee resistance to the change may occur. Assume that an organization that is beginning to do business planning does strategic planning first. Would those persons involved in both strategic and tactical planning efforts be more likely to accept needed changes in structure, culture, and budgetary processes than those persons who participate in tactical planning only? Why?

Endnotes

[1]Henn attributes this result to strategic planning alone. See William R. Henn, "What the Strategist Asks from Human Resources,"*Human Resource Planning*, 8, no. 4 (December 1985), 193–200.

[2]The guiding principles of tactical planning are primarily from economics, systems theory, organization theory, and accounting theory.

[3]A distributive structure is an expression of the principle of requisite variety of internal regulatory mechanisms. This important principle of systems theory calls for systems to have internal regulatory mechanisms as complex as the environment with which the systems deal. The consequence for a system of violation of this principle is isolation from the environment, atrophy of organization components, and consequent loss of complexity and identity. See Gareth Morgan, *Images of Organization* (Beverly Hills, CA: Sage Publications, 1986), p. 47.

[4]Sheridan suggests that the shelf life of any organization design is probably less than a year. See p. 16, John H. Sheridan, "Aligning Structure with Strategy," *Industry Week*, May 15, 1989, pp. 15–23.

[5]Note that distributive structure design is not a zero-sum game, except in the very short run. If additional resources are directed to uses that provide a net return on investment, and no investment should be made unless this condition is true, additional resources become available for allocation to other uses as well.

[6]Opportunities to specialize are a necessarily scarce resource in an organization because a higher level of integrative effort is required to coordinate the work of specialists than to coordinate the work of generalists.

[7]To the author's knowledge, not an actual company.

[8]Alfred D. Chandler, *Strategy and Structure: Chapters in the History of the Industrial Enterprise* (Cambridge, MA: MIT Press, 1962).

[9]Ibid., pp. 314–315.

[10]See pp. 150–151, David J. Hall and Maurice A. Saias, "Strategy Follows Structure!" *Strategic Management Journal*, 1, no. 2 (April/June 1980), 149–163.

[11]See pp. 575–576 of Barbara W. Keats and Michael A. Hitt, "A Causal Model of Linkages Among Environmental Dimensions, Macro Organizational Characteristics, and Performance," *Academy of Management Journal*, 31, no. 3 (September 1988), 570–598.

[12]Research suggests that structure may produce the organizational equivalent of "tunnel vision,"so that planners see an unduly constrained set of alternatives. See R. Pitts, "The Strategy-Structure Relationship: An Exploration into Causality," paper presented at the annual meeting of the Academy of Management, Detroit, 1980, cited in Keats and Hitt, "A Causal Model of Linkages,"p. 576. Neil W. Chamberlain called this effect "strategy set." See *Enterprise and Environment: The Firm in Time and Space* (New York: McGraw-Hill Book Co., 1968), pp. 48 and 204–205.

[13]This is a modified form of a procedure presented in Arnoldo C. Hax and Nicholas S. Majluf, "Organization Design: A Case Study of Matching Strategy and Structure," *Journal of Business Strategy*, 4, no. 2 (Fall 1983), 72–86. See also Leslie W. Rue and Phyllis G. Holland, *Strategic Management: Concepts and Experiences* (New York: McGraw-Hill Book Co., 1986), pp. 624–632; Arthur A. Thompson, Jr., and A. J. Strickland III, *Strategy Formulation and Implementation: Tasks of The General Manager*, 3rd ed. (Plano, TX: Business Publications, 1986), pp. 325–330; Henry Mintzberg, *The Structuring of Organizations* (Englewood Cliffs, NJ: Prentice Hall, 1979), pp. 104–133; Tana Pesso, "A Pathway to Change: The Honeywell Study

Model," *Personnel*, 61, no. 1 (January/February 1984), 75–80; Robert Drazin and Peter Howard, "Strategy Implementation: A Technique for Organizational Design," *The Columbia Journal of World Business*, 19, no. 4 (Summer 1984), 40–46; and John H. Sheridan, "Aligning Structure with Strategy."

[14]See the discussion of strategic objectives in Chapter 2.

[15]Bart presents evidence that, of the many contingencies that must be satisfied with organization structure, such as environment and size of the organization, contingencies arising out of strategic orientation can be isolated most effectively within a region of the organization structure. Christopher K. Bart, "Product Strategy and Formal Structure," *Strategic Management Journal*, 7, no. 4 (July-August 1986), 293–312.

[16]Mintzberg, p. 124.

[17]If geographic area or technological type is a basis of departmentation, business planning must be done for these units. See the discussion of levels of business planning in Chapter 1.

[18]Compare Hax and Majluf, "Organization Design," pp. 75–76.

[19]Bart, "Product Strategy and Formal Structure," p. 309.

[20]Hax and Majluf, "Organization Design," p. 84.

[21]For additional detail about these characteristics, see Andrew H. Van de Ven and Diane L. Ferry, *Measuring and Assessing Organizations* (New York: John Wiley, 1980). The modules and characteristics listed here are on pp. 10–13.

[22]Ibid., see especially pages 380–521.

[23]Robert Drazin and Peter Howard, "Strategy Implementation: A Technique for Organizational Design," *Columbia Journal of World Business*, 19, no. 2 (Summer 1984), 40–46.

[24]See Frances Gaither Tucker, Seymour M. Zivan, and Robert C. Camp, "How to Measure Yourself Against the Best," *Harvard Business Review*, 65, no. 1 (January/February 1987), 8–10.

[25]Sy Zivan, "Measure Yourself Against the Best," *Distribution*, 86, (August 1987), 68.

[26]Selznick calls this process by which organizations come to appreciate their distinctive nature and competence *institutionalization*. During the process, organizations are no longer simply organizations but become institutions. See Philip Selznick, *Leadership in Administration* (New York: Harper & Row, 1957), pp. 5–22.

[27]William G. Ouchi, *Theory Z: How American Business Can Meet the Japanese Challenge* (Reading, MA: Addison-Wesley, 1981), p. 41. Ouchi does not include observances as one of the means by which culture is transmitted.

[28]Gerald L. McManis and Michael S. Leibman, "Corporate Culture: What It Can and Cannot Do," *Personnel Administrator*, 33, no. 12 (December 1988), 24–29.

[29]Stanley M. Davis, *Managing Corporate Culture* (Cambridge, MA: Ballinger, 1984), p. 23.

[30]Anthropomorphism is used by people as a default mechanism to explain things they do not understand. See L. R. Caporael, "Anthropomorphism and Mechanomorphism: Two Faces of the Human Machine," *Computers in Human Behavior*, 2, no. 3 (1986), 215–234.

[31]See, for example, M. Cash Mathews, "How Society Whitewashes Corporate Crime," *Business and Society Review*, 6, no. 5 (Spring 1986), 48–50.

[32]Hazel Markus and Paula Nurius, "Possible Selves," *American Psychologist*, 41, no. 9 (September 1986), 954–969.

[33]There will, of course, be clusters of persons with similar self-images who have similar

ideas of what the organization should be and these cluster-specific organization identities will differ somewhat among clusters within the organization.

[34]Benjamin Schneider, "The People Make the Place," *Personnel Psychology*, 40, no. 3 (Autumn 1987), 437–453.

[35]The study was conducted by Jon. L. Pierce and was published as part of Commerce Clearing House's *Human Resources Management Service*, "1986 ASPA/CCH Survey," Chicago, June 13, 1986.

[36]Davis, *Managing Corporate Culture*, pp. 3–7.

[37]For example, Sparrow and Pettigrew report that management of culture is one of the major streams of human resource management activity that firms in the UK computer supplier industry are using to respond to strategic change. Paul R. Sparrow and Andrew M. Pettigrew, "Strategic Human Resource Management in the UK Computer Supplier Industry," *Journal of Occupational Psychology*, 61, no. 1 (March, 1988), 25–42.

[38]For a review of research about the effects of interviewer/interviewee similarity on hiring decisions, see p. 288 of R. D. Arvey and J. E. Campion, "The Employment Interview: A Summary and Review of Recent Research," *Personnel Psychology*, 35, no. 2 (Summer 1982), 281–322. Organizations should conduct tests of the validity of hiring decisions, including the validity of hiring decisions for employee groups traditionally subject to discrimination.

[39]Apparently employee loss of ability to shape organization identity is what caused the destruction of the original culture of the First National Bank of Chicago. A period of rapid growth and change between 1969 and 1981, under the chairmanship of Gaylord Freeman, culminated in several years of highly politicized competition among potential successors to Freeman. The race to succeed Freeman was one of the costliest in U.S. corporate history, with divisiveness, factionalism, and many casualties. Extreme tensions developed, employees became inward-looking, and uncertainty and confusion reigned. See Davis, *Managing Corporate Culture*, p. 22.

[40]Pierce, "1986 ASPA/CCH Survey."

[41]These vehicles of culture work well when they confirm, but not when they disconfirm, prior information and conceptions of organization members. See Joanne Martin and Melanie E. Powers, "Truth or Corporate Propaganda," pp. 93–107, in Louis R. Pondy, Peter J. Frost, Gareth Morgan, and Thomas C. Dandridge, *Organizational Symbolism* (Greenwich, CT: JAI Press, 1983).

[42]Carson K. Eoyang, "Symbolic Transformation of Belief Systems," pp. 109–205, in Pondy, Frost, Morgan, and Dandridge, *Organizational Symbolism*.

[43]See Davis, *Managing Corporate Culture*, pp. 47–48; McManis and Leibman, "Corporate Culture," p. 29; and Terrence E. Deal and Allan A. Kennedy, *Corporate Cultures: The Rites and Rituals of Corporate Life* (Reading, MA: Addison-Wesley, 1982), pp. 157–176.

[44]David T. Otley, "Budgets and Managerial Motivation," *Journal of General Management*, 8, no. 1 (Autumn, 1982), 26–42.

[45]A distinction must be made between an expenditure properly chargeable as an expense in the current accounting period and an expenditure made with the intention of providing benefits beyond the current accounting period and therefore properly amortized over the expected period of the benefits.

[46]Camillus calls this step the communication step. See p. 211 of John C. Camillus, *Strategic Planning and Management Control* (Lexington, MA: Lexington Books, 1986).

[47]For activities or units of major importance to strategic plans, this process of incremental

analysis may be carried one step farther and require justification for all spending levels—zero-base budgeting. See L. Allan Austin, *Zero-Base Budgeting: Organizational Impact and Effects* (New York: AMACOM, 1977).

[48]For a thorough consideration of the proper use of participation, see Edwin A. Locke, David M. Schweiger, and Gary F. Latham, "Participation in Decision Making: When Should It Be Used?" *Organizational Dynamics*, 14, no. 3 (Winter 1986), 65–79.

[49]Jerry D. Dermer, "Budgetary Motivation of Retail Store Managers and Buyers," *Journal of Retailing*, 50, no. 3 (Fall 1974), 23–32, 76.

[50]Frank G. Williams and Dwight C. Anderson, "Cost Control Incentive Programs—Appropriate for Nonprofits?" *Hospital Financial Management*, 32, no. 5 (May 1978), 14–17.

[51]For a discussion of approaches to managerial participation in the budget process, see Ian J. Campbell and W. G. Merriman, "Budgeting: Is It a Technical or Behavioural Process?" *Management Accounting*, 63, no. 2 (February, 1985), 66–70.

[52]Participation is less useful in instances where managers have unfavorable attitudes and motivation. See Lokman Mia, "Managerial Attitude, Motivation, and the Effectiveness of Budget Participation" *Accounting, Organizations and Society*, 13, no. 5 (1988), 465–475.

[53]Managers with an external locus of control benefit less from participation than do managers with an internal locus of control. Managers with an external locus of control attribute the results of their actions to chance, luck, or fate; managers with an internal locus of control feel they are in control of their own destinies. Peter Brownell, "A Field Study Examination of Budgetary Participation and Locus of Control," *Accounting Review*, 57, no. 4 (October, 1982), 766–777.

[54]Managers with authoritative, independent, and inflexible personalities appeared to prefer budgetary systems that did not allow participation. Robert E. Seiler and Roger W. Bartlett, "Personality Variables as Predictors of Budget System Characteristics," *Accounting, Organizations and Society*, 7, no. 4 (1982), 381–403.

[55]If the superior of the manager made little use of the managerial dimension initiating structure, participation was less effective. Peter Brownell, "Leadership Style, Budgetary Participation and Managerial Behavior," *Accounting, Organizations and Society*, 8, no. 4 (1983), 307–321. Consideration and Initiating Structure are two subscales of the Leader Behavior Description Questionnaire, developed at Ohio State University in the 1950s. These have no exact definition because they are names given factors representing items on the LBDQ, but they correspond approximately to a people orientation and a work-technology orientation by leaders. See Ralph M. Stogdill, *Handbook of Leadership* (New York: Free Press, 1974), pp. 128–134.

[56]Mia, "Managerial Attitude"; Brownell, "Leadership Style, Budgetary Participation and Managerial Behavior"; Brownell, "A Field Study Examination of Budgetary Participation and Locus of Control"; Seiler and Bartlett, "Personality Variables"; Steven D. Grossman and Richard Lindhe, "Important Considerations in the Budgeting Process," *Managerial Planning*, 31, no. 2 (September/October, 1982), 24–29; Marvin A. Feldbush, "Participative Budgeting in a Hospital Setting," *Management Accounting*, 63, no. 3 (September 1981), 43–46; Izzetin Kenis, "Effects of Budgetary Goal Characteristics on Managerial Attitudes and Performance," *Accounting Review*, 54, no. 4 (October 1979), 707–721.

[57]Toshiro Hiromoto, "Another Hidden Edge—Japanese Management Accounting," *Harvard Business Review*, 88, no. 4 (July–August 1988), 22–26.

[58]Ibid., 24.

[59]Ibid.

[60]Compare Gerald L. McManis and Michael S. Leibman, "Corporate Culture: What It Can and Cannot Do," p. 24.

[61]Many readers may be more familiar from their study of economics with the term *marginal analysis*. The principles of marginal analysis and incremental reasoning are the same. Incremental reasoning is preferable in managerial decision making because it applies to choices among discrete alternatives, whereas marginal analysis requires that choices be made among infinitely small units of change. See William R. Henry and W. Warren Haynes, *Managerial Economics: Analysis and Cases*, 4th ed. (Dallas, TX: Business Publications, 1978), pp. 20–21.

[62]That is, determine the profitability of the resource in each use by comparing the change in revenue that will occur with the change in cost that will occur. The time value of money must be considered, of course, where there are sizable differences among the alternatives in the time span over which the distribution of costs and revenues occurs.

[63]Keats and Hitt, "A Causal Model of Linkages."

[64]Hall and Saias, "Strategy Follows Structure!"

[65]Peters and Waterman found that the well-managed companies that they studied were continuously reorganizing. See Thomas J. Peters and Robert H. Waterman, Jr., *In Search of Excellence: Lessons from America's Best-Run Companies* (New York: Harper & Row, 1982), pp. 310–311.

[66]Davis, *Managing Corporate Culture*, p. 37.

[67]Much of what was said regarding the design of the strategic planning process in Chapter 2 also applies to tactical planning.

[68]If an organization is paying the relocation costs of an employee, it should consider transferring the employee not only between locations but also between functions for a greater return on its investment in the human resource.

[69]Chairman and CEO Richard Zimmerman, of Hershey Foods Corporation, said of the company approach to change: "What was needed was an anchor to windward—an identity, inspired by our founder, reflected in our sharing common values and goals....Sure, we'll get bigger and more diverse, and get new ideas and will have to change—but our values won't change. Instead, values will *guide* change." See p. 51 of Sally J. Blank, "Hershey: A Company Driven by Values," *Personnel*, 75, no. 11 (February 1987), 46–51.

[70]Compare these abilities with the elements of Buffa and Dyer's optimizing model; see Elwood S. Buffa and James S. Dyer, *Management Science/Operations Research* (New York: John Wiley, 1977), p. 16.

Part 2

Human Resource Planning:
Strategic and Tactical Stages

As we begin Part II, our focus shifts from business planning as a whole to business planning at the functional level. Human resource management is one of the most important functions in the organization. At least half of the financial resources of many organizations may be committed to human resources.

If an organization is to have truly effective human resource management, a sense of purpose and a direction for organization effort are necessary. This sense of purpose must be shared by employees throughout the organization. Clearly articulated strategic objectives for human resources and sound strategies for achieving those objectives will provide the sense of purpose. Policies that guide human resource decisions will provide the direction of organization effort to support these strategic plans.

Chapter 4

Strategic Planning for Human Resources

In the early 1970s, before Union Oil had introduced planning for human resources as part of business planning, the company was in the process of building a plant overseas. Planning for the construction and financing of the plant had been completed. Suddenly Union Oil realized that unless planning for human resources was begun immediately, it would be faced with two equally unsatisfactory alternatives for staffing the new plant when construction was completed. Either it would have to reassign a core of experienced employees already assigned to other projects, with concomitant disruption of employees' personal lives and of the company projects to which they had been assigned; or the company would have to hire an entire new work force, with concomitant excessive training costs and loss of cultural continuity.[1]

Today many organizations still carry on this form of planning for human resources.[2] Separate plans are prepared for such activities as staffing, performance appraisal, compensation, and development as a response to the business plans of the organization. There is no overarching plan to integrate the separate human resource activities into a cohesive, functional whole for the achievement of organization objectives.

Such an integrated plan can be achieved only when human resources are considered at the strategic and tactical planning stages of business planning. At the strategic planning stage, human resource planners influence the organization philosophy, develop objectives for the human resource function, and shape strategies for carrying out the organization philosophy and achieving the human resource objectives. At the tactical planning stage, human resource planners develop structures for the allocation of resources in accordance with strategic human resource objectives and strategies. Together, strategic and tactical planning for human resources provide guidance that will cause all members of an organization to manage the human resources in a unified manner. In this chapter ways for organizations to become proficient at strategic planning for human resources are considered. Ways for organizations to become proficient at tactical planning for human resources are discussed in Chapter 5.

NECESSARY CONDITIONS FOR STRATEGIC PLANNING FOR HUMAN RESOURCES

Strategic planning for human resources makes good business sense. Many organizations have at least half their financial resources continuously committed to the acquisition, development, maintenance, and use of human resources. Strategic planning in this area sets a direction for the organization to ensure that these encumbered finances yield a return.

Before an organization begins strategic planning for human resources, it should ensure that conditions are favorable for the process. Two of these conditions are directional stability for the organization and key people within the organization who will encourage and be able to do strategic planning for human resources.

Directional Stability of the Organization

Strategic planning for human resources is exceptionally complex and long-term. Considerable time is needed to install and perfect the process.[3] Indeed, Wickham Skinner has pointed out that resulting strategies may require a bare minimum of seven years to implement.[4]

The complex, long-term nature of strategic planning for human resources mandates that the planning have directional stability. To illustrate this requirement, assume that an organization, under chief executive officer Smith, establishes well-thought-out and coordinated strategic objectives and strategies. These objectives and strategies serve as a guide for investment in human resources for ten years under Smith. As the human resource plans are coming to fruition, Smith is replaced by Jones as chief executive officer. The business planning process begins anew under Jones, again producing well-thought-out strategic objectives and strategies—but objectives and strategies that are unrelated to those established under Smith's tenure as chief executive officer. The organization has lost most or all its investments in human resources of the preceding ten years.

Early in the life of an organization, stability of direction will depend on the longevity, the length of tenure, the influence on the choice of a successor, the rate of personal growth, and the personal sense of direction of the chief executive officer and/or on the influence and sense of direction of the board of directors. Good business planning can provide a clear sense of direction that unites the organization. Followed long enough, the plan helps to develop an organization identity that itself provides stability of direction.

Key People to Do Strategic Planning for Human Resources

Some persons in the organization will be more important than others to the process. The chief executive officer and staff, the chief human resource officer and staff, and line managers and staff form a critical triad in strategic planning for human resources.[5]

All members of this triad must be well informed about human resource management and the strategic planning process. But their roles differ. They bring different viewpoints to the process. They also have different symbolic importance. The chief executive officer and line managers are "the organization" to employees. In their day-to-day actions the strategic human resource plans are expressed. The chief human resource officer, in contrast, has little symbolic value. However, he or she has the best grasp of the three members of the entire process for planning for human resources. If all members of this triad perform their respective roles, strategic planning for human resources will succeed.

Chief Executive Officer and Staff

The best form of support a chief executive officer can give is personal involvement as a contributor to strategic planning for human resources. Because the job of the CEO requires a continual look at the organization as a whole and its dealings with the outside world, he or she brings a view of the total organization to planning that no one else can provide. Personal involvement allows him or her to have intimate knowledge in this area of planning.

The CEO, by personal involvement, serves as a role model and gains support of his or her staff and of the organization for human resource planning. The CEO must make clear that he or she supports the process, not any one group in the organization. This stricture does not rule out the CEO's granting of authority to the human resource department to take the lead in developing and implementing a *process* for planning. The *content* of planning , however, must be a collective decision of the entire organization, or at least of the critical triad. Care in how the CEO supports human resource planning can help to avoid political infighting that can vitiate the planning process.[6]

Chief Human Resource Officer and Staff

In organizations where human resource planning is a well integrated part of the business planning process, human resource departments are able to take the lead in planning for human resources[7] because they have

- A reputation for effective performance
- Integrated and unified professional personnel with a positive attitude toward the work of the department
- Professional personnel with very good interpersonal and political skills[8]

A *reputation for effective performance* gives credibility to a human resource department. It is especially important that the basic human resource functions, such as hiring, appraisal, compensation, and training, be performed well prior to initiation of a program of strategic planning for human resources. These functions become key elements in planning for a human resources program.[9] Not only must the department perform well, but it must show the contribution of departmental programs to organization success.[10] For example, a human resource department might collect and share with persons outside the department data showing increased benefits and reduced costs for the organization attributable to major activities of the department.

Integrated and unified human resource department personnel, with a positive mental attitude concerning the work of the department, are able to work cooperatively with one another and with persons outside the department. They are able to support planning for the human resource function as a whole, not just their areas of specialization.[11]

In the past, human resource administration, usually known as personnel administration, typically performed a maintenance role. In keeping with this role, the department was structured into clearly identified, very compartmentalized functional subunits, such as employment, compensation, and training. Professional employees in the subunits were respected for their knowledge within their functions but were not expected to transcend functional boundaries.[12] As a result, employees of the department had little sense of identification with, or allegiance to, the department as a whole.

The chief human resource executive officer needs to build a nucleus of persons who have proficiency in several areas of human resources and with specialists who see their role as part of the human resource whole. This will help to avoid the narrow specialization that results in a fragmented approach to human resources, and, further, it will allow the department to provide integrated and consistent support for strategic human resource planning.

Professional personnel with very good interpersonal and political skills are needed to participate in the strategic planning process at all levels, helping to formulate strategic business plans and serving as expert advisers to the business planning committee about human resources. As a member of a strategic planning committee, the chief human resource executive officer and/or other representatives of the department should

- Suggest to business planners business strategies that allow opportunities for capitalizing on human resource strengths and minimizing human resource weaknesses.

- Understand fully and be able to explain to other members of the human resource department the strategic plans of the business and their implications for human resources.
- Understand fully and be able to explain to other business planners the benefits of directional stability in terms of human resources and organization effectiveness.
- Counsel the strategic business planning committee about the effects of all objectives and strategies discussed on the human resource function.

Line Managers and Their Staffs

Line officers can bring a realistic and practical viewpoint to the human resource planning process. However, in many organizations, line managers are not prepared to participate effectively in strategic planning for human resources. Their human resource role is simply one of supervising employees.

Line managers must become full partners in the strategic planning for human resources, helping to shape and to execute the organization strategy. They must understand the principles and issues of planning for and managing the human resources of an organization. Line managers with this ability can be obtained by

Cross Training

- Hiring persons for line manager positions who are capable of, or can be trained for, the planning role
- Offering line managers short courses on planning
- Increasing contact between human resource professionals and line managers by assigning on a temporary basis line officers to human resource departments and human resource professionals to line departments

Every contact between human resource staff and line managers must be an occasion for learning. If line managers have basic human resource knowledge, the knowledge of the human resource staff can be shared fully and freely with line management.[13] The human resource staff who liaison with line managers must be generalists, able to deal with whole problems, not with problems segmented by human resource area of specialization. Whole problems have intrinsic interest for line managers. The objective of these contacts must be developing self-sufficiency on the part of line managers.

THE ELEMENTS OF STRATEGIC PLANNING FOR HUMAN RESOURCES

We now shift our attention from the setting of planning to the elements of planning for human resources. The elements are an organization philosophy, objectives of the human resource function, and human resource strategies. Each of these elements, in their generic form, was discussed in Chapter 2. The unique features of each for human resource planning will be considered here.

Organization Philosophy Respecting Human Resources

Need for a Human Resource Philosophy

An organization philosophy states the commitment of the organization toward its various stakeholders. One of those stakeholder groups is the employees of the organization. Employees, as the term is used here, includes all employees, managerial and nonmanagerial.

The extent of the commitment of an organization to its employees is revealed most clearly when employees are no longer needed by an organization. During the economic recession of 1981–83, when many organizations retrenched by separating employees from the company, Delta Airlines refused to do so and suffered staggering financial losses.[14] At Delta, employees are considered not only valued resources but members of the "Delta family" as well.

At the end of 1989, IBM announced that it would be cutting 10,000 jobs during the first quarter of 1990. An IBM spokesman said there would be no employee layoffs. The jobs would be eliminated through attrition, resignations, and early retirements. Each departing worker would be paid one week's pay for each six months of employment. "Full employment" is a tradition at IBM, begun by its founder, the spokesman said, but there is "no guarantee that it will always be that way." The tradition is based on a long-held practice of demonstrating respect for employees. The staff cuts and related streamlining steps were expected to cost the company nearly $2.3 billion in pre-tax dollars.[15]

Also in December 1989, AT&T announced plans to cut 8,500 jobs in 1990, after having cut about 25,000 jobs in 1989. Company officials said the job losses would be absorbed through normal turnover, early retirements, relocation within the company, and, as a last resort, layoffs.[16] In November 1989, Chrysler Corporation announced plans to reduce its work force by 4,000. This reduction was part of an overall plan to cut $1 billion in costs from its annual $26 billion budget by the end of 1990. The reductions were to be brought about through layoffs of employees, who would receive lump sum severance pay.[17]

As these examples illustrate, commitments to employees cost money. But the commitments often are considered good business practice by the firms adopting them. IBM contends that its full employment policy is "good resource management" that has helped the company maintain a high-quality, flexible, and dedicated work force.[18]

Some firms try to balance the interests of employees and the interests of the organization on an ad hoc basis as strategic decisions are made.[19] This practice is not satisfactory for two reasons. First, the practice provides no secure base for the planning of human resource systems and for the planning of individual employees. Second, when ad hoc decision making occurs, there is a pronounced tendency to make shallow assessments of the human resource implications of strategic decisions and to allow little or no input from employees.[20] Rational consideration of issues requiring sacrifice by employees is difficult when the sacrifice is imminent. Probably no issue is more potentially divisive of decision makers than the issue of how much responsibility the organization owes to its employees. With forethought, a sound, widely accepted human resource philosophy can be established to guide strategic decisions as the need occurs.

Substance of a Human Resource Philosophy

The part of an organization philosophy dealing with human resources provides a formula for reconciling the needs of the employees and the needs of the organization as a whole.[21] The philosophy provides an answer to the questions: How much sacrifice of employee well-being will be tolerated to enhance the well-being of the organization as a whole, and how much sacrifice of organization well-being will be tolerated to enhance the well-being of the employees? How much responsibility does the organization owe to its employees, and how much responsibility do employees owe to the organization?

An organization does not exist simply to provide employment. After a period of time, organizations become institutions, well entrenched in the fabric of a society and with extrinsic and intrinsic worth to many persons. The worth of the organization to nonemployees depends on the continuing vitality of the organization as an institution. An organization philosophy, therefore, must define the needs of an organization for its continued vitality. These needs will depend on the nature of the organization and its technology, its products or services, and its form of ownership. The needs may include, as a minimum, a well-maintained and healthy organization, a good product or service market reputation, and a good financial market reputation.

An organization philosophy also should define the work-related needs of its employees. These may include a need for

- Quality of work life
- Fulfillment
- Belonging to an organization one can be proud of
- Job and career security

These needs should be understood on a personal level and in as much depth as possible.

Finally, the organization philosophy should recognize the relationship of the needs of the organization to the needs of employees and should state the trade-offs to be made where these needs are in conflict. In some circumstances, what is good for employees also is good for the organization and what is good for the organization also is good for employees. In other circumstances, the needs are in conflict and a variety of trade-offs are possible, ranging all the way from the position that organization needs are paramount and are not sacrificed for employee needs to the position that employee needs are paramount and are not sacrificed for organization needs.

Objectives of the Human Resource Function

Must fit with strategic planning /objectives /Organ

Human resource management is done by many persons in the organization. As we indicated, the chief executive officer, the line managers, and the human resource department are especially critical to human resource management. To ensure that everyone acts in concert when managing human resources, it is necessary to define objectives for the function. To ensure that actions in the management of human resources are consistent with actions in other areas of organization work, human resource management objectives and the objectives of all other levels of planning must be mutually congruent and consistent with the organization philosophy.

Examples of human resource management objectives are: being a socially responsible employer of the nation's human resources, developing human resource competencies that provide a competitive advantage in the product market, making sound investments in human resources, respecting the rights of individual employees, being considered a good place to work, and managing human resources in a state-of-the-art manner.

Human Resource Management Strategies

A coordinated organization philosophy and statement of objectives respecting human resources set the stage for the selection of strategies for managing human resources. A philosophy and a statement of objectives are basic. They should not change except as the values of the organization and the roles of the organization members change. Strategies for managing human resources, on the other hand, will evolve over time with changing environmental conditions and with changes in human resource knowledge.

Discussed in this section are some strategies that organizations may consider for use in the management of their human resources. Addressing pressing needs confronting many organizations today, they allow the application of important recent advances in human resource knowledge.[22] The strategies deal with facilitating technological change, ensuring an adequate supply of employee talent, promoting the development of employees, promoting employee service to customers, improving the productivity of human resources, creating organization commitment, encouraging the participation and involvement of employees in organization affairs, keeping employees satisfied, and focusing on a key employee group—career employees. These strategies overlap, as all are based on the same set of human resource functions—the acquisition, development, maintenance, and use of human resources—but each establishes a different pattern of emphasis for the human resource functions.

We will not describe the strategies in detail because this would require a more extensive discussion than would be appropriate for this book. The description given for each strategy will allow planners to choose one or a small number of related strategies appropriate to their organization.

Managing Technological Change

The rate of development of new technologies is increasing. But older technologies are not being phased out immediately on the development of new technologies. In consequence, there are increasing numbers of technologies available. Often an organization has multiple technologies on which a given production process may be based.[23] Because organizations have both a wider choice of technologies and the need to choose a technology more often, they must learn to manage well the technologies of their organization. Organizations in an industry subject to rapid technological change will find the ability to manage technology especially valuable. So, too, will organizations that are technology-driven, that is, those organizations that depend for their survival on being masters of the technologies used in their industries.

As technological change becomes more frequent, organizations will have both a greater need to learn and more opportunities to learn how to accomplish this change effectively. An analogy may help to illustrate this point. When opening a new restaurant was an unusual occurrence for an organization in the restaurant industry, there was both little need and little opportunity for the organization to learn how to open a restaurant effectively. Today, some organizations, such as those in the fast food segment, open new restaurants at the rate of one a day. Thus, it is urgent that such organizations learn to open a new restaurant in the most effective manner possible. For the first time in known history, a single organization in the restaurant industry can learn from repetitive experience. In the same way, organizations that introduce technological change frequently can learn to introduce the new technologies in an effective and efficient manner. Those organizations that learn how to introduce technological change quickly and effectively will have a decided advantage over their competitors.

To introduce a new technology, organizations must learn to achieve compatibility between the technical and the human contents of the new technology.[24] A technology is a method of doing work,[25] and the technical content consists of the tools, equipment, and required activities of the work. The human content consists of the people and the organizations who will apply the technology. At present most organizations in the United States are technically proficient and humanly naive. They must achieve a better balance of expertise between the technical and human contents of technology.

When a technology is changed, the entire organization changes. The most important impacts of technologies fall on individual employees who work with the technology, on the human resource management systems of an organization, and on the organization identity.

Employees affected by technological change are likely to experience the obsolescence of valued skills, the disruption of established social relationships, the need to learn new jobs, and possible job loss.[26] Although they are intimately affected by the technological change, they have little or no control over, and cannot influence, the change. Employees believe that they are the least likely beneficiaries of improvements in productivity.[27] Under these circumstances, employees will resist the erosion of current skills that occurs with technological advance.[28]

Human resource management systems for the acquisition, development, maintenance, and utilization of human resources represent sizable investments of time and money. They include methods of supervision and programs for hiring, training, and compensating employees. The human resource management systems in many organizations become obsolete when technological change occurs. For instance, when new technologies are introduced, jobs of affected employees change and compensation rates no longer are appropriate for the jobs. New investments of time and money are necessary to institute new systems.

Secondary effects of technological change, that is, organization adjustments incidental to a new technology, sometimes are so pronounced that organization identity is threatened. This occurs when the relationships among people and other organization components—buildings, capital resources, equipment, holdings of land, and intangible assets of the organization—are changed in fundamental ways and on a widespread basis. Loss of organization identity will make impossible an integrated organization social system.

The introduction of new technologies must be managed by a team capable of integrating the technical and the human aspects of technology. This team should include system design engineers, human factors engineers,[29] and human resource professionals.[30] Assignment of human resource professionals to the technology management team will provide an opportunity for the human resource function to be represented in the use of technologies.[31] In organizations adopting a strategy of facilitating technological change, human resource professionals must be prepared to sit down with the engineers, in advance of the choice or design of technology, to ensure that human resource interests are considered before decisions about technologies become final. These considerations must be taken into account, along with technical considerations, to ensure that technology is managed for optimum value to the organization.

Human resource professionals, as members of the technology management team, have four primary responsibilities:

1. They must help to build an employee group capable of handling technological change.

They must earn the trust of employees and their willing, and perhaps enthusiastic, cooperation with technological change. This will require an ability to understand the concerns and aspirations of employees and to represent these aspirations to other technology team members.

Employees can be selected and oriented to adapt to change. At the time of hiring, an introduction such as the following helps employees to see the positive aspects of technological change:

> We stay in the forefront of technology in our industry so your job changes often. You will be able to try your hand at doing the job in different ways. You will help to make the changes and will suggest many of the changes yourself. We welcome your ideas. By continuing to progress in our ability to produce, we will remain competitive and you will benefit accordingly by an interesting and secure job with good wages and benefits.

Proficiency testing and, if necessary, job training can help all employees cope with technological change.[32] This training should include the following:

- Basic skills training, especially reading, writing, and arithmetic, where proficiency testing indicates a need
- Communication skills training[33]
- Group dynamics and problem solving skills, for the increasingly popular team-production work arrangements
- Listening training, to improve the ability of individual employees to learn and to perform with new technologies.[34]

2. They must advise other team members of the capabilities of human resource management systems. If human resource professionals know why human resource management systems function as they do, they will be able to advise system design engineers and human factors engineers about the design and choice of technologies that maintain the integrity of the systems.

3. They also must help to design human resource management systems with a greater capacity to absorb change.[35] Methods of supervision best suited to accept change often utilize self-managed teams. Such teams have fewer layers of authority relationships that must be adapted to the change. Employees can be selected, trained, and compensated not for the job being performed at a given time but for their ability to learn and adapt over time and to perform various jobs. To help employees learn new skills, training programs can be designed that use expert systems with generic tasks suitable, with slight modification, for training an employee to perform any of a large number of jobs.[36]

4. Whenever considerable technological change is expected, human resource professionals must act to preserve organization identity. They can do this by monitoring the organization change and its effect on organization identity and by taking action when needed to preserve organization identity. Monitoring the effect of technological change on organization identity should begin with a baseline measure of values held by employees,[37] of the meaning of the organization to employees,[38] and/or of the culture being enacted by employees.[39] Subsequent measures can be compared to the baseline measure to determine the effects of technological change on organization identity.

Another method of protecting organization identity is to encourage the formation of organization identity around the ability to cope with change; identity is sustained by change, not destroyed by it.

As human resource professionals become astute about the relationship of human resources and technology, the time may come when advances in human resource knowledge drive many of the changes in technology. A barometer of the adequacy of the influence of human resource professionals may be the ratio of the frequency of human-driven changes in technology to the frequency of technically driven changes.

Ensuring an Adequate Supply of Human Resource Talent

Hiring & developing people

Organizations replenish their supplies of human resources through staffing activities. Skinner contends that this function requires shrewder, wiser, longer-range planning than any other corporate endeavor.[40] A strategy emphasizing the staffing function often is given top priority among corporate activities.[41] Organization leaders recognize that if the quality of their human resources falls, the fortunes of the organization follow. This strategy may be especially attractive for labor-intensive organizations and for organizations that expect very long periods of reduced supply of labor in their labor markets or of continued increase in their own demand for labor.

Staffing is not simply hiring new employees from outside the organization. Rather, it is a combination of hiring new employees and of developing present employees for movement to other positions within the organization. The central concern of organizations adopting this strategy is to arrive at an optimal combination of the two.

To determine the optimal combination of hiring from outside and of developing present employees, organizations should first classify all positions in the organization as entry, dead-end, or nonentry. *Entry* positions are those that can be filled by hiring from the outside and that can serve as supply channels for nonentry positions. Entry positions are appropriate starting places in a developmental sequence of positions. *Dead-end* positions are those that can be filled by hiring from the outside but cannot serve as supply channels for nonentry positions. *Nonentry* positions are those that can be filled by transfer of employees from entry positions or other nonentry positions.

The determination as to whether each position is entry, dead-end, or nonentry can be done empirically or deductively. Empirical choice is possible if the organization has extensive past experience with hiring into, and movement among, most positions in the organization. Empirical choice uses past records of this hiring and movement among jobs to classify each position. In this method, an entry position is one in which employees hired directly into the position from outside do especially well both in the entry position and in other, subsequent positions as compared to employees hired directly from the outside.[42] A dead-end position is one in which employees hired directly into the position from outside do especially well in the dead-end position but not in other, subsequent positions as compared to employees hired directly from the outside. A nonentry position is one in which employees hired directly into the position from outside do poorly as compared to employees moved into the position from other positions in the organization.

Deductive choice uses logic to classify each position. In this method, an entry position is one that logic dictates would be a good introductory experience for new employees[43] and also would prepare these new employees well for service in other positions. A position may be a good entry position because

- All tasks of the position either are ones that employees already have learned to perform outside the organization or are ones that may be learned within the position itself.
- Some or all tasks of the position are challenging but can be mastered by most employees.[44]
- Tasks learned in the position are required in many other positions.
- The position is a good vantage point for learning about the entire organization.
- The position has supervisors and present incumbents who excel at the task of indoctrinating newcomers to the organization.

A dead-end position is one that logic suggests would allow a positive initial experience within the organization for a new employee but would not prepare the employee for movement to other positions. A nonentry position is one that logic dictates requires an introductory or developmental experience in other positions to prepare new employees for service in the position. A position may be a good nonentry position because it serves as a desirable promotional opportunity for employees in entry positions and most of its tasks can be learned readily in entry positions.

Whatever method or methods are used to make the initial choice of entry, dead-end, or nonentry positions, the choice should be continuously assessed and reconsidered.

When all positions in the organization have been classified as entry, dead-end, or nonentry, the firm develops proficiencies at hiring into the entry and dead-end positions and at managing the flow of resources within the organization in radial fashion away from the entry positions to nonentry positions in the organization. Persons hired should be those optimally suited either for an entry position and an associated sequence of nonentry positions or for a dead-end position. Support systems for the internal flows are evolved that maximize the developmental effects of moves among jobs and ensure that persons moved to nonentry positions are appropriate for these positions.

A strategy intended to ensure an adequate supply of human resource talent requires the artful integration of two functions, the hiring of employees into entry and dead-end positions and the management of flows of employees between entry and nonentry positions. This strategy can help to obtain, for the money invested in staffing, high-quality employees and consistently filled positions. These conditions can give organizations an important advantage over their competition.

✶ Promoting the Development of Employees

Employee development is the act of changing the capabilities of employees—their skills, knowledge, understanding, attitudes, and/or values. Economists term the accrued capabilities of human resources the human capital base of a nation. In the United States, this human capital base is increasingly inadequate for the needs of the economy.[45]

Jobs in the U.S. economy are changing. New technologies require progressively more cognitive skills and less physical skills. An estimated 60 percent of the new jobs in the the modern workplace need people with solid reading, writing, and arithmetic skills. Work is now being organized in Japanese-style work teams rather than assembly-line production. Employees who work in these teams must have good communication skills, the ability to efficiently convey and receive messages. The fastest growing occupational groups are those requiring the highest levels of skills.[46] As a result of these job changes, employers are placing demands on U.S. educational institutions as never before.

Taken as a whole, the response of educational institutions, particularly at the elementary and high school levels, has been a disappointment. Only about 80 percent of the adult population in the United States is functionally literate,[47] and an estimated 27 million adults lack the basic skills of arithmetic, reading, and writing. The number is increasing each year. An estimated additional 45 million are only marginally competent in the basic skills.[48] Not only are employees with inferior skills causing lower productivity, workplace accidents, and customer dissatisfaction, they also are unable to learn new technologies.[49] There is little indication that U.S. educational institutions will satisfy employer demands in the future.

The once pervasive family role in education is being seriously eroded as the family structure in the United States collapses. Forty-two percent of all children live in a single-parent household before they are 18 years of age. Further, large numbers of the new entrants to the labor force, an estimated 43 percent, will be minorities and immigrants, groups that have the highest school dropout rates and the lowest average test scores.[50]

Educational institutions, especially the graded schools, must respond to many needs, not simply to the needs of organizations for employees. As U.S. society becomes more complex, employer organizations must expect that educational institutions will have an even more diverse set of needs to satisfy and will find it even more difficult to respond to the particular needs of industry. The problem will not go away.

As a group, employers have done little to develop the nation's labor force. They are willing to operate with an insufficient number of qualified employees or with marginally qualified employees rather than to invest in long-term development programs. This point is illustrated by a December 1988, American Management Association survey. More than 1,000 human resources managers were questioned about the reactions of their organizations to the problem of illiteracy among American workers. Thirty-four percent of the organizations used basic skills proficiency testing and 89 percent of those that tested refused to hire candidates who failed the literacy test. Only 10 percent of the firms that tested, and less than 3 percent of the total sample, offered training in basic skills.[51]

Shortcomings in education and in training are causing a shortage of employees with the capabilities needed for the jobs of the economy. In particular, the lower half of the U.S. labor force is not competitive in the international economy. The nation is facing a monumental mismatch between jobs and the ability of Americans to do them.[52] Organizations that make employee development an integral part of their long-term investment programs can avoid the devastating inefficiencies many organizations will endure as the U.S. human capital base becomes overextended.

Organizations considering an emphasis on employee development must control employee turnover. This will be especially important if, as expected, serious shortages of employees in high-skill occupations occur. A long-term employment policy has been the typical answer to turnover. This policy is one that encourages employment continuity, often for a lifetime, although the lifetime relationship usually is not formally stated.[53]

A long-term employment policy can have two disadvantages. First, mismatches of employees with the firm, which will occur with even the most careful of selection procedures, cannot readily be corrected. Second, the invigorating effects of new employees with new ideas is reduced.[54] These disadvantages can be overcome. Mismatches of employees can be corrected by the selective use of outplacement, without abandoning the values of long-term employment guarantees.[55] Outplacement services help separated employees find alternative employment. To diminish stagnation, organizations with very low turnover tend to move employees frequently.into challenging new assignments.[56] And they manage the organization in ways that tend to break old habits—for example, they reorganize frequently.[57]

Once organizations have a known complement of employees to be developed, they must formulate strategies for the two major kinds of development: remedial development and continuing development. *Remedial development* is intended to bring employee capabilities up to minimum acceptable standards for a new job. *Continuing development* is intended to help employees to maintain or to improve on those minimum capabilities.

Decisions about remedial development may be approached in the same manner as "make-or-buy" decisions in managerial economics, where an organization must decide whether to make or buy the component parts used in the production of a product. In the normal course of hiring, employers follow the "buy" approach. They set minimum standards for the characteristics desired of employees in a position and screen job candidates until they find one who meets or exceeds all minimum standards. Such a procedure can be difficult and expensive. For example, Chemical Bank in New York City interviews an average of 40 applicants for each of its teller positions.[58] And New York Telephone Company had to administer basic proficiency tests to 60,000 applicants in order to hire 3,000 people.[59] In the "make" approach, employers accept candidates who lack some of the desired characteristics and develop those characteristics through training and development programs.

As in the managerial economics make-or-buy decision, organizations should choose the option with the highest present value of return on investment.[60] Also, organizations may consider which option will allow a better response to fluctuations in the organization's need for employees and which will allow better control over the quality of the persons hired.[61]

Continuing development is needed to help employees cope with changes—primarily technological changes and general advances in knowledge—and improve their capabilities beyond those minimum acceptable standards of their positions. Continuing development requires a blend of education and training. Education is the conscious effort of society to shape the physical, mental, emotional, and moral growth of the individual so that the person lives a socially effective and individually satisfying life.[62] Training is the conscious effort of an organization to shape the values, attitudes, understanding, knowledge, and skills of an employee so that the person becomes a more satisfactory employee of the organization.

Several studies suggest that employer sponsored courses or training programs alone are not effective in keeping employees up to date; education leading toward advanced degrees is needed.[63] The implications are clear: Keeping employees up to date will require that they continue their education.

In the past, high schools and colleges have provided continuing education courses for adults. These courses did not claim to keep the *degrees* of former students current; they kept former students current in selected areas of knowledge and in their major fields of learning only. The ability to learn requires that the foundations for knowledge are sound. Unfortunately, these foundations are being rapidly eroded by further advances in knowledge after students graduate. In the future, organizations may find it necessary not only to keep employees current in their fields of concentration but also, for at least some employees, to keep their degrees current.

Unless there are sharp increases in investments in human capital, the United States soon will experience severe shortages of labor to fill high-skilled occupations. Organizations that can control turnover and make effective decisions about remedial and continued development will prosper despite future shortages of human resources.

 Promoting Employee Service to Customers

In every industry, the opportunity exists for at least one firm to stand out for its ability to meet customer needs. This responsiveness to customer needs is an important distinctive competence for some organizations. In the supermarket industry, Giant Food, the country's twelfth largest supermarket chain, centered in the Washington, D.C., area, is a clear leader in providing customer service. The competitive advantage provided by Giant Food's leadership in customer service has helped to double its sales in the past eight years and to produce profits that far exceed the industry average.[64]

For organizations that wish to be leaders in responding to customer needs, the days of arm's-length relationships with customers, when customers were studied from afar through market research, are over. These organizations are continually in direct touch with their markets and respond quickly to the changing needs of the customer. Organizations that wish to be responsive to customer needs must promote service to the customer through its human resources. The human resource strategy of promoting employee service to customers requires

- Identifying the service aspect of employee performance and seeing that this aspect of performance is properly executed
- Deciding what occupations in the organization should be staffed with service-oriented employees

All employees are required to have certain technical skills and knowledge without which they cannot carry out their jobs. Many employees, in addition, are expected to understand customer or client needs and to carry out their jobs so that they meet those customer needs.[65] This is the service aspect of an employee's performance. Organizations have taken two approaches to get employees to carry out the service aspect of their jobs. First, they have established and enforced organization "feeling rules"—formal and informal norms that require employees to display emotions appropriate to their jobs.[66] Second, they have tried to hire people who are likely to carry out the service aspect of their jobs.

Adherence to feeling rules is a major requirement of some jobs:[67] While on the job, undertakers are to be somber and department store Santas are to be jolly. But feeling rules are found in nearly all public-contact jobs. Sales clerks are expected to smile frequently, to greet customers warmly, to establish eye contact with customers, and to thank customers for the sale. Organization feeling rules can be used with better effect by having employees wear identifiers, such as name tags or uniforms, that signify their employee status. Such identifiers may serve as reminders of their responsibilities as employees.[68]

The enforcement of feeling rules alone will not cause employees to provide good service. Some employees will not adhere to feeling rules;[69] others will adhere to the letter, but not the spirit, of feeling rules, displaying "conscripted clerk" behavior. The conscripted clerk is the public-contact employee who handles transactions by reciting mechanically lines learned in training. The service provided by the conscripted clerk is adequate for routine transactions but tends to deteriorate when customers behave in ways not anticipated in the training of the employee.

Because of these shortcomings of feeling rules alone, organizations have tried to predict at the time of hiring those candidates who will provide good customer service. Two characteristics appear related to the performance by employees of the service aspect of their jobs: good citizen characteristics and a service orientation.

Employees who display good citizen behavior—the tendency to be helpful to others and to be a good employee of the organization in general—probably will adhere both to the letter and to the spirit of feeling rules when serving customers.[70] Background checks and reference checks of previous experience in jobs and schools and behavior-based interviews[71] should be useful in determining good citizenship characteristics of job candidates.

Hiring people with a service orientation can help avoid the conscripted clerk problem. A service orientation is the predisposition to be helpful to customers.[72] Predispositions to be of service to customers can be predicted using a personality test called the Service Orientation Index[73] or by conducting behavior-based interviews[74] and performing background checks.

The good citizen employee and the service-oriented employee in consumer-contact positions may, in some instances, need more support or more kinds of support than the conscripted clerk employee. For example, the good citizen employee and the service-oriented employee in highly structured jobs in the service industry, such as the bank teller, may become frustrated because there is not enough scope to display their concern for others. These jobs might have to be redesigned to allow employees more autonomy. And the good-citizen employee and the service-oriented employee in jobs that require extremes of sacrifice and service, such as the hospital nurse, may experience burnout sooner than other employees because they exhaust their emotional reserves more rapidly. The good-citizen employee and the service-oriented employee in these positions may need more emotional support and more opportunities for respite than other employees.

Organizations need to determine which employees need to have a service orientation. In some cases, only those employees in direct contact with the customer will need to have a service orientation. In others, both direct-contact and nondirect-contact employees will need a service orientation.

Without proper selection and/or training, nondirect-contact employees may be reluctant to provide service to the customer. They may respond to what they consider to be more important competing demands, such as technical excellence, efficiency, or bureaucratic orderliness. If the support of these nondirect-contact employees is important to the success of delivering service to the customer, the organization must require that these employees have a service orientation as well.

There will be some instances where requiring a service orientation may compromise other primary job needs of the position. The work of John Holland suggests that persons with a service orientation tend to lack the realistic orientation needed for occupations such as mechanic and the investigative orientation needed for occupations such as biologist.[75] In such instances an organization must be aware of the trade-offs that will occur if a service orientation is required in the position.

Beginning from the point at which all direct-contact employees have a service orientation, organizations should decide on a department-by-department and an occupational-group-by-occupational-group basis whether other employees need a service orientation. In most cases all employees in management positions and all employees in departments and occupations that work closely with direct-contact employees should be required to have a service orientation. Then, the organization must establish management controls. These controls will ensure that departments and occupational groups not designated for a service orientation recognize that they, too, have a role in the provision of service to the customer.

Classically, organizations in the United States have followed the implicit practice that taking care of the customer is the marketing department's worry. For those organizations that feel that customer service is important, it would be wise to have a strategy that commits the entire organization to customer service. This commitment can be realized through the appropriate use of feeling rules and the hiring in selected positions of persons with a service orientation.

Improving the Productivity of Human Resources

The productivity of human resources can be defined as the number of units of a product or service produced per hour of labor used. For many years, the United States led the rest of the world in the productivity of its human resources. In recent years, although it still leads in productivity, the increases have slowed so that productivity is now increasing at a slower rate than in many other countries.

Traditionally, management in the United States has thought of technological advances, increasing mechanization, and methods improvement as ways to make gains in productivity. Innovative investment in human resources was seldom considered. This way of thinking has limited our gains in productivity. Now, many organizations are turning their attention to human resources as a significant way to improve productivity.[76]

The strategy of improving the productivity of human resources is especially attractive to U.S. organizations that compete with organizations in countries with lower cost labor. It is attractive to organizations in such industries as paper containers, where little product differentiation is possible and competition is based on product price. It is also attractive in industries where slowed growth has caused competition on the basis of price.[77]

Successful programs to improve productivity through innovative methods of human resource management depart from past practice in two ways: They focus on groups of employees, and they change basic features of organizations as necessary to accommodate human resources.

In the past, the few efforts to improve productivity through human resources were addressed to the individual employee, encouraging the employee to produce more. But, where work processes were interdependent, no one individual could improve output because that employee's work had to be coordinated with the work of other employees. Any attempt by one employee to act in a concerned and responsible manner was apt to disrupt the closely integrated production processes.

In those few cases where improvement in productivity could be accomplished through the individual employee, only isolated and superficial features of the organization were changed. For example, incentive plans were installed or jobs were enriched. A change in these isolated features seldom caused significant improvements in productivity because other features of the sociotechnical system did not provide support for the change. So many basic features of the facility were considered fixed by the technology that little could be done to improve productivity.

Noting the success of the group orientation to productivity improvement used by the Japanese, organizations in the United States have begun to adopt their own group approaches.[78] Although little hard data are available on the effectiveness of these approaches, reports show lower absenteeism, reduced employee turnover, lower production costs, and increased employee satisfaction.[79]

The focus of these successful programs is on groups of employees able to serve as vehicles for productivity improvement. The technology of an organization determines the group or groups where productivity improvement can be accomplished. These groups may vary from a small work group within a plant, to a department within a plant, up to and including all the employees in the plant. In each case the group must be capable of autonomous action to directly improve production. In addition, there must be an alignment of group interests and organization interests so that an improvement in group performance serves both group and organization interests.

The group approach has required organizations to change their basic features to support the group's functioning. Groups are complex and require a correspondingly complex support system. All important sociotechnical features of the workplace should be considered in designing a support system for the groups including planning and control systems, organization structure, plant design and layout, job and work-flow design, employee selection, employee training and team building, and compensation plans.[80]

General Motors is directing much of its productivity improvement strategy on its human resources. A major focus has been on individual plants. Because of increased foreign competition in the automobile industry, the company has had to close some of its plants and to lay off employees at other plants. GM has allowed management and labor at the plant level to take their own joint initiatives to improve productivity and enhance job security, without having to go through multiple layers of approvals.[81]

One of the many instances of local initiatives is the V-8 engine plant at Flint, Michigan.[82] In early 1986, labor and management at the plant recognized that their future was in jeopardy. Periodic reports of productivity at the various plants showed that the plant was falling behind other GM engine plants in quality and cost-effectiveness. Labor and management at the plant knew that there would have to be major changes if they wanted to ensure the future of the plant and their own jobs. In mid-1986, the local plant management and the union shop committee agreed to spend a week examining their future. Out of these meetings came a recognition that the battle between management and employees had resulted in lower quality output. Building on the trust and recognition of mutual interest that emerged during that week, the plant was able to transform itself.

A human resource center was established at the Flint plant in a converted area that was once part of the plant cafeteria, a sacrifice the people willingly accepted to have the opportunity for training. In less than a year, nearly every one of the 4,400 hourly and salaried employees had been through the center for some form of training or orientation. Each week, during the normal workday, 60 to 80 people take part in intensive job-related training in the center. In addition, about 340 plant employees, on their own initiative, take high school–level education courses. In the first 11 months of 1988, 27 learned to read, 14 received high school diplomas, and 45 received General Equivalency Diploma (GED) certificates. A slogan in use at the revitalized plant is, "If you think training is expensive, try ignorance."

Employees now have greater responsibility for quality. Each operator on the assembly line is empowered to shut down the line as soon as a problem is spotted rather than wait until later to make a fix. Some 90 inspection and repair points have been eliminated. As a result, scrappage rates and cost per unit have decreased, at the same time that quality and volume have increased.

The Flint plant has become one of GM's best engine plants. This was done by the people at the plant itself, not by corporate GM or the International United Automobile Workers.[83]

In contrast to General Motors, with its strategic focus on individual plants, Sherwin-Williams, the world's largest manufacturer and distributor of paints, has focused on small work teams within a plant.[84] The first plant designed with human resources in mind was the Richmond, Kentucky, plant, opened in 1976. This plant served as a pilot for the diffusion of benefits to other plants in the corporation. The plant was designed to conform to a set of sociotechnical requirements. These requirements were met even when they conflicted with usual design practice.

The company structured jobs at the plant to permit the 160 employees in three shifts to work in small work teams. These teams were relatively independent of each other. Each team was allowed responsibility for a work area and considerable discretion in how the team carried out its work. The plant layout and restructured jobs allowed considerable interaction among team members and among teams. Some of the benefits of the innovation to the organization included smaller work force size, reduced absenteeism, increased productivity, and better team coordination. Benefits to employees included high pay and high satisfaction with work.

The examples of General Motors and Sherwin-Williams illustrate the ingredients necessary for organizations to pursue a human resource strategy of productivity improvement—a focus on appropriate groups of employees and a willingness to change basic features of organizations as necessary to accommodate human resources. Both organizations chose employee groups appropriate to their needs.

General Motors focuses on the plant. Their plants are decentralized and many are old.[85] Closing down a plant is expensive. If local initiative can prevent the closing of a plant, both the organization and local employees benefit. Sherwin-Williams focuses on work teams. Its batch operation allows the organization to readily structure work into work teams. Since World War II, an extensive body of knowledge has been developed about small-group behavior, and Sherwin-Williams, with its small work teams, is able to take advantage of this body of knowledge.[86]

A readiness to make major changes to accommodate human resources also was apparent at both General Motors and Sherwin-Williams.[87] The decision to allow plants to take the initiatives required to revitalize their operations was no small matter for General Motors. And at the Flint plant, the decisions to eliminate inspection points on the assembly line, to allow operators to shut down the assembly line, and to train 4,400 employees during the course of a year were major departures from past practice. But the innovation at Sherwin-Williams was an even more radical departure from traditional practice. The new plant at Richmond, Kentucky, was designed specifically to accommodate human resources and required four years of planning and construction to complete. Features of the workplace, job designs, and human resource management practices were introduced that differed sharply from typical practice.

Of all the strategies described in this chapter, this strategy, improving the productivity of human resources, requires perhaps the greatest innovation in human resource management. Organizations in the United States are in the initial stages of implementing this strategy. Its full potential is yet to be realized.

Creating Employee Commitment to the Organization

Emotional & logic

Organization commitment is a linkage between the individual employee and the organization as a whole.[88] It is engendered by positive attitudes toward the organization by the individual, such that the individual is drawn toward, and is reluctant to leave, the organization. Organization commitment is characterized by

- A strong belief in and acceptance of an organization's goals and values
- A willingness to exert considerable effort on behalf of the organization
- A desire to maintain organization membership[89]

Organization commitment has been declining. Institutions in the United States have been under attack for a decade and a half. The media have researched and publicized numerous cases of government error and corporate scandal. Institutional pedestals have come crashing to the ground, those of organizations among them. Highly publicized corporate takeovers have erased corporate household names. Trust in organizations is at an all-time low.[90]

Commitment by employees is a valuable organization asset. Committed employees are more stable and consistent performers and are less likely to leave the organization than are uncommitted employees.[91] They will exert effort when motivational conditions are not ideal.[92] Committed employees support the organization with words and actions, even when they do not stand to benefit directly by the support, and perhaps even when they are dissatisfied with their work life.

Commitment will be especially valuable to organizations where employee loyalty to the organization is an asset to selling the product. For example, employee loyalty probably causes passengers on Delta Air to feel more secure. It will be especially valuable where loss of trade secrets is a threat because the organization depends on product innovation for its competitive edge and because the organization spends a high proportion of its revenue on product research. An example is IBM Corporation. More generally, commitment will be especially valuable in any organization where extensive and long-term investments in human resources are necessary. A return on these investments is possible only if these employees stay with the organization as supportive employees.

Organization commitment is fostered by two complementary mechanisms.[93] One mechanism operates almost entirely on an emotional level. The organization becomes, in many respects, a second family for the individual who identifies with the organization.[94] Identification with the organization satisfies needs that often are satisfied by the family, including mastery over the environment, nurturance, support, and affection.[95] With growing mobility of the labor force, organizations increasingly replace the family in the support system of individual employees.[96] The second mechanism operates on a cognitive level. Members of organizations engage in an evaluative process in which they assess the costs and benefits of maintaining membership in the organization. If the organization is felt to be sincerely concerned with the member's welfare and recognizes the member's contributions, then the member believes that the organization will provide a variety of symbolic and tangible rewards in exchange for effort and continued membership.[97]

Taken together, the psychological identification and exchange evaluation mechanisms for producing commitment suggest that organizations that wish to build commitment must provide a caring, supportive workplace for employees. The employee must be treated in a caring manner such that he or she is included within and integrated into the entire organization. This can be done by

- Exhibiting a concern not to lose employees
- Assisting employees undergoing organization transitions
- Making clear to the employee that he or she has an important place in the organization
- Acknowledging and reciprocating employee effort on behalf of the organization
- Providing caring, supportive supervisors

It is especially important to understand the relationship of employee turnover to commitment. Low turnover is both an effect and a cause of employee commitment. Developing commitment appears to take time;[98] both age and organization tenure of the employee have been shown to be related to organization commitment.[99] If an employee can be encouraged to stay, the opportunity exists to develop commitment in the employee.[100] In addition, when an organization tries to avoid losing an employee, it provides the most direct possible evidence of its care. A secure place in an organization is the quintessence of mastery over the environment for an employee.

Employees entering the organization for the first time or undergoing other organization transitions, such as relocation, transfer, or retirement, experience anxiety and look to inclusionary and support activities by others to help to reduce the anxiety. To the extent that the socialization processes of organizations provide mastery of a job and collective support,[101] employees will identify with the organization and feel committed to it.[102]

Employee identification with the organization appears to be enhanced by making clear to the employee how he or she fits into the organization. This may be done through thorough orientation processes, clear job descriptions, assignment of meaningful work, and participation in decision making.[103]

The efforts of employees on behalf of the organization must be acknowledged and reciprocated. Salary levels, pay equity, merit system accuracy, and performance-reward contingencies—that is, whether performance usually is recognized and rewarded—are related to commitment.[104] Opportunities for promotion and the perceived fairness of promotional processes also may be related to commitment.[105]

For all employees, supervisors are an important feature of the organization; for some employees, the supervisor is the organization. Supervisors' initiation of structure and consideration behavior furthers the commitment of subordinates.[106]

Organizations operating within a fiercely competitive product market often face times of testing where committed employees can mean the difference between survival and ruin. In a very real sense committed employees are reservoirs of goodwill to be drawn on in times of need.

Encouraging Participation

Studies based on opinion polls and in-depth interviews, and experiments in new forms of management indicate a significant shift in the values and attitudes of workers[107] and a decline in the overall job satisfaction of employees.[108] Graham Staines has suggested that the impetus for much of this shift in values and attitudes is a general and growing disaffection with the country's major institutions. Disaffection with nonemployment sectors of the lives of employees—political, economic, cultural, educational, and familial—is affecting the employment sector as well.[109]

These studies describe a new breed of workers who demand to be treated with respect as thinking, responsible people rather than as children or machine parts. The new-breed workers dislike taking orders without good reason and no longer are in awe of authority. They want to learn at work. They want to have a say in how the work is carried out, and they take advantage of opportunities to partici-pate in decision making.[110]

The place of these new-breed workers in the organization is changing.[111] The distinctions between office and factory are becoming blurred. New occupational groups are positioned in the information flow so as to be able to recognize needed changes in organizations more readily than could their predecessors.

For new-breed workers, hierarchical, policing-style management does not work. It can result in sabotage, costly absenteeism, and a negative attitude toward the organization. Living in an age of advanced education and enlightenment, and impatient because they see the real possibility of nuclear holocaust, these employ-ees "aren't going to take it any more." Resentment at not having a say in how work is performed is exacerbated when management makes errors that could have been avoided by listening to employees. When not treated as responsible adults, the new-breed workers become resentful and cynical game players who figure out ways of beating the system.

It is clear that firms have not asked enough of employees.[112] Employees want to contribute to their organizations; they especially want to contribute to the deci-sion-making effort of the organization. Management can allow employees to con-tribute to decision making by introducing participatory decision making in their organizations. Participatory decision making is the method typically used to allow nonmanagerial employees to contribute to decisions usually made by managers alone.[113]

There are possible advantages to the organization when employees con-tribute to decision making. The major advantage is that organizations can utilize the constructive ideas of employees. Over time, the continued flow of these ideas can have a significant cumulative effect on the direction and performance of the organization.[114] Allowing employees to contribute to decision making may pro-mote two-way communication, so that managers and employees better understand each other.[115] And it may improve the quality of work life for employees, an objec-tive of many organizations.[116]

The possible advantages of allowing participation will be especially apparent to organizations whose employees are positioned so that performing their jobs yields information of value in decision making. For example, salespeople in dynamic markets may note changes in customer needs long before those changes appear as sales trends. Or production employees may discover ways to modify pro-duction processes that would be known by management only after extensive engi-neering studies. These employees can be useful allies to the organization.

Use of a human resource strategy that allows employees to contribute to decision making requires that the organization decide what form of participation to use and what barriers need to be overcome to allow employee participation. Employee participation can assume many forms.[117] It can be temporary or long term. It can be formal or informal. It can be direct or indirect; that is, employees can participate directly in decisions or may have representatives who participate on their behalf.

A particular form of employee participation may allow employees much or little influence in the decision process. Peter Dachler and Bernhard Wilpert define levels of influence that employees may have over organization decisions. These range along a continuum from no advance information is given to employees about a decision, employees are informed about decisions in advance, employees are allowed to give their opinions about decisions to be made, employees' opinions are taken into account, employees can veto a decision, to the decision is made entirely by employees.[118]

Employee participation can concern many different kinds of content. Edwin Locke and David Schweiger suggest four content categories for employee participation:

1. Work itself, including task assignments, job design, and speed of work
2. Working conditions, including rest breaks, hours of work, placement of equipment, and lighting
3. Routine aspects of personnel functions, such as hiring, training, discipline, and performance evaluation
4. Company policies, such as layoffs, profit sharing, capital investments, and general company policies[119]

Organizations may choose a form of participation that incorporates any combination of these characteristics. Six combinations are well known in the literature. Exhibit 4-1 lists each of the 6 forms and presents the characteristics of each.[120]

Exhibit 4-1. Forms of Participation Most Often Discussed in the Literature and Their Characteristics
Source: Information presented in this table is from John L. Cotton et al., "Employee Participation: Diverse Forms and Different Outcomes," *Academy of Management Review*, 13, no. 1 (January 1988) 8–22.

CHARACTERISTIC / TYPE	Formality	Directness	Influence	Content	Duration
I. Making decisions about work	Formal	Direct	Complete	Work itself	Long term
II. Consultative participation about work	Formal	Direct	Opinion	Work itself	Long term
III. Short-term decisions about work	Formal	Direct	Complete	Work itself	Short term
IV. Informal decisions about work	Informal	Direct	Varies	Varies	Long term
V. Employee ownership	Formal	Indirect	Complete	All areas	Long term
VI. Representative participation	Formal	Indirect	Opinion or veto	All areas	Long term

The employee participation form, *making decisions about work*, is formal, direct, and long term. Employees either have a veto over or make the final decision. The participation focuses on decisions about the work itself, such as how it is organized, what is done, and who does what. In some instances, employees also participate in decisions about their pay. In studies of the outcomes of this form of participation, the immediate performance, productivity, and work satisfaction of employees were found to increase when this form of participation was introduced.[121]

Consultative participation about work refers to situations similar to the previous form in most respects except that employees do not make the decisions but only give their opinions. Participation is formal, direct, about the work itself, and long term.

Two types of participation are included in this form. First, there are Scanlon plans, where employees are given monetary bonuses for productivity-enhancing suggestions.[122] Because few studies of Scanlon plans have been done and these typically have not used control groups, evidence about the effects of the participation on employee performance and satisfaction is inconclusive. The few published studies indicate that employee performance is improved with the introduction of the Scanlon plan. Second, there are quality circles, where small groups of employees meet periodically to discuss and develop suggestions about the work but usually receive no monetary incentive.[123] Quality circles can help to solve specific problems in the organization. Their effect on overall employee performance and work satisfaction, if any, has not been demonstrated.[124]

Short-term decisions about work refers to participative efforts similar to the first form except that the effort is short term, normally two days or less. Participation is formal, direct, and about the work itself. Employees either have a veto about or make the final decision. Studies usually have not demonstrated gains in either performance or employee satisfaction with the use of short-term participation. This form of participation can be effective in solving work-related problems.[125]

Informal decisions about work refers to situations where employees and their supervisors behave in participative fashion within their work groups even though the organization may have no formal program to encourage participation. Participation is informal, direct, and long term. Its content and the amount of employee influence vary. Studies of this form of participation typically evidenced an improvement in both employee performance and productivity.[126]

In the *employee ownership* form of participation, employees typically are stockholders, with stockholder rights of ownership, and managers make day-to-day decisions. Employees can influence these decisions by electing the board of directors and by voicing their opinions at stockholder meetings. Some employees may serve on the board, but most do not. This form of participation, then, is formal, indirect, and long term. To the extent that employees choose to exercise their ownership rights, control may be complete and may extend to all areas of decision making.

In studies of employee ownership, both employee performance and employee satisfaction improve with employee ownership.[127] How much satisfaction improved depended on the proportion of ownership rights—the proportion of equi-ty—held by employees.[128]

In *representative participation*, employees do not own the organization, but do exercise control over it. Employees exercise this control through representatives elected to a governing council or through representatives to a board of directors. These representatives may have a vote or they may serve in an advisory capacity only. This form of participation, like employee ownership, is formal, indirect, and long term. Employee influence is low to medium and participation may deal with all areas of decision making.

The few studies of the effects of representative participation that have been conducted have not demonstrated an increase in employee performance and satis-faction with the introduction of this form of participation.[129] Available evidence suggests there is little effect on overall employee performance or satisfaction, though satisfaction of employees serving as representatives may increase.

The research evidence for the likely effects of the various forms of participa-tion may be used to decide which forms of participation to be tried out in an organ-ization. Such research evidence, however, should not be used as a substitute for program evaluation. Any participative program introduced in an organization should be carefully evaluated using before-and-after measures and control groups.

The primary requirement for successful use of participation is that the form of participation take effective advantage of employees' unique knowledge and viewpoints so that employees are able to make useful contributions to decision making. Employees who participate in management decision making must have the analytical, technical, and behavioral skills needed to analyze and to solve prob-lems. They should have access to adequate information and must have as much knowledge of the organization as possible. Having worked in several jobs and knowing how to do several jobs often is helpful. Employees may need interperson-al skills and team-building training in order to work cooperatively in problem-solv-ing groups.[130]

A second requirement is that if participative efforts are intended to have long-term effects, the programs must be both continuous and long term. When employees can make worthwhile contributions and the programs are long term, improvements in overall employee performance and satisfaction are likely to occur.

A third requirement for successful use of participation is that the method used be suited to its intended use. For example, employee ownership and informal participation seem consistently to produce both increased overall employee perfor-mance and satisfaction. Thus, they may reasonably be used for these purposes. On the other hand, the method short-term decisions about work typically does not pro-duce measurable effects on overall employee performance and satisfaction. This form of participation, however, may be used effectively to solve specific problems and to make specific improvements at work.[131]

A final requirement for successful use of participation is that the organiza-tion remove barriers to participation by traditional managerial hierarchies before attempting its use. Employee participation must achieve legitimacy within the organization decision-making structure and must receive the necessary support of managers.

Although managers typically have few doubts about the effectiveness of participation and its value to the overall organization, they see little personal gain to be derived from participation and seldom use it in their jobs.[132] Managerial concerns about loss of power, status, and authority to employees and about their abilities to manage the greater complexity of participative management often serve as an effective roadblock to participation.[133]

Studies show that managers' fears of power loss with employee participation are largely groundless; power expands so that more power is available and managerial power may actually increase.[134] An understanding must be promoted among managers that participation allows a necessary shift in emphasis from control of human resources to their development,[135] including the development of the managers themselves. Participation must be seen by managers as an important, worthwhile investment for the organization.[136]

Where possible, the management team should be selected in advance of the introduction of participatory decision making so that managers may participate in its introduction. It is important that the philosophy of the managers selected be consistent with participation. Managers must have necessary communication,[137] team-building, and interpersonal skills. They may need the assistance of a behavioral specialist to select and implement the kind of participation appropriate for the organization.

Keeping Employees Satisfied

Employee satisfaction is an overall feeling of satisfaction by an employee with his or her employment and employer.[138] Promoting employee satisfaction may be especially useful for organizations where managers wish to concentrate their attention on leading the organization along chosen paths. Such an organization may be one whose managers must deal with the problems and prospects of rapid growth. If employees are satisfied, they will be more likely to cooperate with management and less likely to divert managerial attention to employee problems. This strategy is also especially suited to organizations with relatively large numbers of noncareer employees. Noncareer employees are those more concerned with their present job in a particular organization than with their career work life experiences. For noncareer employees, immediate concerns of employment are a central consideration.[139]

Typically, satisfaction is promoted by causing employees to feel that the company is a good place to work. The following quote, from a top executive interviewed about the function of the human resource department of his organization, illustrates this point:

[Morale] is such a vital part of our organization and the human resource department should act as the extension of the president's arm and make the people feel like a vital part of this organization. In larger companies, this is even more important—to give that feeling to employees.[140]

Because many organizations emphasize feeling rather than substance, an element of subterfuge and manipulation may be involved. To counteract this tendency, promoting employee satisfaction should be direct and straightforward. The company should make an explicit promise to treat its employees well and expect in return willing cooperation with management's running of the organization.

The implementation of this strategy requires

- The selection of people as employees who are likely to be satisfied
- The encouragement of free and informed choice by job candidates of employment with the organization
- The treatment of employees in a manner that will produce satisfaction

The selection of employees is likely to be a more important influence on the satisfaction of employees than subsequent treatment of employees by the organization. Candidates can be selected who have a general predisposition to be satisfied at work. Such candidates usually have affective dispositions that predispose them to be generally satisfied with life,[141] or they have temperaments suited to the general conditions of modern-day employment.[142]

It should be possible to predict those persons who will display a predisposition to be satisfied at work. For persons with previous work experience, whether they were satisfied in previous employment should indicate whether they will tend to be satisfied in present employment.[143] Background checks and interviews, especially behavior-based interviews,[144] should be useful in determining whether employees were satisfied in previous employment.[145] Independent evidence should be gathered for each previous job and then combined for all jobs by averaging the separate ratings into an overall prediction.

For candidates with little or no previous work experience, satisfaction in other areas of their lives, such as school, family, and social/fraternal organizations, may be a predictor of satisfaction at work.[146] Background checks may be used to determine whether candidates generally were satisfied in these areas of their life. Each check should be made independently and the results combined to obtain an overall prediction of satisfaction.

Still another predictor of satisfaction is suggested by the work of Elaine Pulakos and Neal Schmitt. Candidates were asked what they expected of work. Those candidates who had an optimistic outlook about the expected outcomes of work were more likely to be satisfied at work.[147]

Selection on the basis of predispositions to be satisfied need not be perfect in order to create a satisfied work force. Studies show that employees take their cues from others as to whether or not to be satisfied at work.[148] If most employees are satisfied, other employees without a predisposition or reason to be satisfied may nevertheless be satisfied. The goal of selection should be to increase the likelihood of hiring persons who are predisposed to be satisfied.

Candidates who make a free and informed choice to work in an organization tend to be more satisfied than those who have little choice whether to accept employment.[149] Organizations can manage their selection process so that candidates hired have been able to select the organization as their place of work. Organizations can direct their attention to candidates who are likely to have more than one job offer. For example, they can recruit at heavily recruited college campuses and can compete for highly rated student prospects at less heavily recruited campuses. They can make sure that complete information about employment with the organization is available in readily usable form to the candidate.[150] They can avoid pressuring the candidate to make an early job decision. They can request that candidates not accept an employment offer with the organization until they have taken sufficient time and used sufficient information to be sure of their choice.

Once candidates have been hired, the organization may want to make changes in the organization environment to increase and maintain the level of employee satisfaction.[151] These may include changes in

- Job characteristics
- Role prescriptions
- Information flows
- Organization structure
- Distribution of organization power and authority
- Organization climate
- Organization culture
- Supervision
- Reward systems
- Internal equity
- Work group characteristics
- Employee support systems
- Physical working conditions[152]

The relationship between employment conditions and employee satisfaction is complex.[153] Both the objective reality of the above characteristics and the way employees interpret the conditions affect satisfaction. The same job, therefore, can be seen in quite different ways by different employees.[154]

Any one employment condition variable seldom has an independent effect on satisfaction. Employment condition variables typically interact to produce joint effects on satisfaction. These joint effects often cannot be anticipated by knowing the separate effects of the interacting variables. An example will illustrate this point. Job demands and decision latitude, both elements of employee role prescriptions, as separate employment condition variables have been shown to have an inconsistent relationship to satisfaction. However, the combination of heavy job demands and low decision latitude is consistently associated with job dissatisfaction.[155]

The satisfaction of different employees will be affected differently by different employment conditions. For example, power equalization between supervisor and employee, an element of the distribution of organization power and authority, contributes more to the satisfaction of employees with egalitarian values than for employees without egalitarian values.[156]

Because of the complexity of the relationship between employment conditions and employee satisfaction, in-house research is essential so that the organization does not misdirect its resources on changes inappropriate to its employment environment and to its employees. Four steps are involved in in-house research:[157]

- *Diagnosis*—used in the initial stages of a satisfaction improvement program to determine what specific improvements in components of satisfaction are needed.[158]
- *Conformance evaluation*—used in the middle stages of a satisfaction improvement program to determine whether projected sequences of changes are occurring as expected. This step is to determine if the program is conforming to its intended design.
- *Outcome evaluation*—used in the final stages of the program to determine whether expected outcomes were attained.[159]
- *Action research*—used in any stage of a satisfaction improvement program to discover the nature of relationship among employment condition variables and employee satisfaction and the interventions needed to achieve increased satisfaction.[160]

A selection process directed toward the acquisition of easily satisfied employees, informed candidate job choice, and a research-based satisfaction improvement program can result in a variety of benefits. Satisfaction at work is an important part of quality of life for employees. Satisfied employees are absent from work less often and are less likely to leave the organization.[161] Satisfied employees are not apt to engage in counterproductive behaviors, such as neglect, sabotage, refusal to cooperate with change efforts, drug use, theft, and dissent.[162] Dennis Organ has argued persuasively that satisfied people are more apt to cooperate, are more likely to support necessary change, are more willing to do little "extras" either spontaneously or when requested, and in general are easier to work with in a day-to-day relationship. He cites as evidence of the accuracy of his argument the nearly universal opinion of managers that satisfied people are more cooperative.[163]

Focusing on a Key Group: Career Employees

It may not be possible to satisfy some employees with rewards offered by the work environment alone. Career employees often fall into this category.[164] Career employees are those employees in an organization who feel a commitment to their careers as well as, or instead of, a commitment to the organization.[165] If they are to be managed effectively, special attention must be given to their career needs.

A career is a series of events meaningfully related to the success of an employee in the world of work. Included in career events are family life, schooling, social and recreational activities, career-planning activities, and work experience. The activities that employers engage in to satisfy the career needs of employees are called career management.

A strategy focusing attention on career employees will be especially attractive in organizations where there are many professional employees, such as a hospital or a management consulting firm, or where the relatively few career employees in the organization are unusually important to organization success, such as restaurant managers in a restaurant chain.

The most important influences on employee development occur on the job.[166] Organizations choosing to implement a strategy focusing on career employees must ensure that the work experience of these employees is appropriate for their optimum development. This can be accomplished by designing career paths that allow employees to develop career-relevant capabilities while performing useful work for the organization.

Design of Career Paths

A career path is a series of jobs and positions within a single organization that leads to one or more target positions to which the employee aspires. Career paths must be tailored to individual employees and designed and managed in such a way that they enhance the development of employees following the path.[167] Nine learning principles are especially applicable to career path design:[168]

1. Learning objectives should be established before the employee begins the learning process.

The employee normally works with a counselor to establish objectives, both for the overall career path and for the position currently being performed on a career path. Learning objectives are probably best developed using a goal-setting procedure.[169] The goals may deal with skills, knowledge, understanding, attitudes, and values that the employee wants to develop. Learning objectives must be realistic because they must be achieved at the same time that the employee is maintaining at least satisfactory performance in each job on the career path.

2. Participation in the planning of career paths may vary among employees.

Career path planning requires establishing the objectives, positions, sequences, time limits, and developmental support for the employee. Some employees will have little desire to plan their own career path, relying on the counselor to design it for them. Others, who have learned the career management system of the organization, may choose to manage their careers entirely on their own. Most employees will be informed users of the career counseling services, taking full advantage of the expertise of the counselor to help them to manage their careers. Organizations should provide both counselors and self-service career planning systems so that an employee can choose the system that best meets his or her needs.

3. Different kinds of learning require different times for completion.

Career counselors and career employees must have expectations reasonably related to the kind of change expected. For example, changes in employee values may require years of experience, whereas changes in employee skills may be achieved in a few hours of on-the-job experience.

    4. Learners must be motivated.

For employees to be motivated by a career path, they must "own" the career path. To own a career path, the employee should be able to

- Choose the target position or positions.
- Choose the jobs through which they move as they progress toward the target position or positions.
- Choose the rate at which they move among jobs.

These choices, of course, will be limited by organization constraints of what is reasonably possible.

Career paths typically are presented to employees as a series of jobs with progressively greater difficulty and status. In order to make an informed choice among career paths, an employee must understand in advance the developmental implications of each choice. Jobs can be understood in advance if they are described as complements of known duties.[170]

All professional/managerial jobs in the organization may be described in terms of a limited number of standardized duties. To illustrate how duties may be used to describe jobs and the differences among jobs, consider the following hypothetical discussion between a career counselor and a career employee:

Career counselor: In your present job you are performing seven duties. Three of these are career-critical duties, duties that will be performed in the target positions of your career path. You have indicated that you enjoy doing these three duties, so it looks as though your target positions are still reasonable choices.

        The position you have decided to go to next will require you to perform six duties. Four of these duties you have previously performed and feel comfortable in doing. Of the two new duties, one is career-critical. This duty is "to provide consulting/advisory help in a specialized area to persons outside the department." Are you satisfied with this position as your next career move? As you know, there are several other positions that we could consider now or within the next few months.

Career employee: Have you any information about how difficult it is to learn the consulting duty while performing the other duties contained in this job?

Career counselor: We have built up a good support system to help employees acquire the knowledge and skills needed to act as an internal consultant. There are several recommended readings, a seminar on consulting that we run periodically, and supervisors who are good at coaching novice consultants.

        A few employees have found it difficult to learn the internal consultant duty and do the remainder of this job at the same time. They had to put in several weekends to keep up their end of the work in the department. Most employees found this dual task challenging but were able to perform the job acceptably while learning the internal consultant duty. Most found that the recommended reading, the seminar on consulting, and the coaching by the supervisor must be attended to very carefully.

Career employee: I'm satisfied that this is the next move for me. The challenge is gone from the job I'm in now, although I do enjoy most parts of the job. I feel I've learned everything I can from the job and I'm anxious to move on. I want to try my hand at being a consultant as part of my job. Consulting is a key duty in all the target positions I have chosen, so this will tell me something about whether I really am cut out for those positions.

Notice that when jobs are seen as being composed of sets of duties common to other jobs in the organization, only those duties in a new job that are new to an employee need to be described.

5.   Career paths should be flexible to allow for employee growth and development.

As employees move along career paths, their skills and abilities and their awareness of their skills and abilities change. As illustrated in the dialogue between the employee and the counselor, each new job is an opportunity for the employee to learn about himself or herself, and each new career move is an opportunity to test this new knowledge. For this reason, career paths cannot remain fixed but must be subject to continual adaptation.

6.   Newly acquired skills and knowledge must be used or they deteriorate.

The use of skills and knowledge effectively prevents their deterioration. However, repetition that does not require new learning can cause boredom and lowered standards of performance. Repetition of career-critical duties should, therefore, not continue within any job beyond the point where new learning is occurring. Further repetition of these duties should occur in a different job. Performing a duty in a variety of job contexts tends to reveal weaknesses in the way an employee is performing the duty and broadens the employee's understanding of the way this duty relates to other work performed in the organization. In learning theory terms, performance of the same duty within a variety of job contexts requires generalization of learned material and thus new learning at a more fundamental level of understanding and value formation.

When the employee arrives at the target position, he or she will be thoroughly seasoned at performing all primary duties of the position.

7.   People learn more effectively when they are permitted to learn at their own pace.

The career path process must allow employees to decide how long to stay in a position before moving on to another position. As illustrated in the dialogue, the employee must announce a readiness to move to a new job once he or she is satisfied that the learning objectives of the current position have been accomplished.

8.   People learn more effectively when they receive feedback on performance.

Career employees receive feedback from three primary sources: from their own interpretations of how well they are performing, from their immediate supervisors, and from a career counselor. Employee assessments of their own performance are made easier if employees can compare their performance on career-critical duties with predetermined standards of performance established by the organization. These standards should be based on the performance of the same duties by incumbents in target positions.

Supervisory feedback on performance normally takes the form of performance appraisal. As typically done, performance appraisal provides an overall evaluation of job performance but does not measure performance by a career employee on those career-critical duties of the job of special interest to the employee. Organizations must provide a performance appraisal system that allows supervisors to appraise the performance of career employees on specific duties of the job. Performance appraisal systems based on management by objectives (MBO) and behaviorally anchored rating scales (BARS) are appropriate for measuring performance on specific duties.

Some employee characteristics are expected to develop as employees move along their career paths, not in connection with particular jobs. For example, the employee is expected to develop an understanding of the overall organization structure and its operations by seeing the organization from the viewpoint of a number of different positions in key locations of the organization. Or the employee is expected to develop communication skills, leadership/management techniques, or skills in diagnosing employee problems over the first few years he or she is with the organization.[171] Developments such as these are best monitored by the career counselor who sees the employee continuously during his or her career and therefore can observe changes in the employee and can provide feedback on those changes to the employee. Objective tests may be given to the employee periodically by the career counselor to measure changes in employee characteristics.[172]

9. Success is essential for proper development of employees.

Interest in a career comes from successful experiences. Personal feelings of success at a challenging task are the primary reinforcement for career employees. Social reinforcement, such as approval of others or status awards, can be effective if the organization culture and the norms of other persons significant to the employee value such rewards. Success causes a positive outlook for employees and more rapid learning. Although successful outcomes are necessary for learning, the *possibility* of failure also appears to be necessary. All learning theories support this conclusion.[173]

If career paths are carefully chosen and negotiated, and if support for employee growth and performance is adequate, success experiences will predominate in the careers of employees. Career counselors have extensive power to create success or failure in novice employees by helping them understand their preferences for and acceptance of risk in their decisions and by helping them use sound information and decisional approaches to career choices. The general rule for counselors to follow is that while failure must be possible, success must be probable. Where failure does occur, this failure may be turned into success by teaching employees to learn from their failures.

Career counselors must learn to recognize career plateaus and to explain to career employees what is happening so the employees do not become discouraged. Leveling off periods may be healthy for individual growth and development.[174] Internal organization and assimilation of previously-learned information occurs during plateaus that will enhance future learning.

Support for Career Path Experience

The organization should tailor its employee support activities to the needs of its employees. The following forms of employee support may be needed: assistance for employee career planning, organizational career counseling, mentoring, job coaching, career performance appraisal, and personal development aids.

Employer *support for career planning* may take the form of self-assessment tools, such as workshops, workbooks, and computer-assisted programs. Instead of, or in addition to, self-assessment tools, psychological assessment services may be provided. These offer interest and ability testing and relate the test scores to kinds of work in the economy. Both these services may be accompanied by information about career opportunities within the firm and in the world of work at large.

Organizational career counseling, conducted by professional, full-time counselors, helps employees to establish an optimal match between employee career aspirations and organizational career opportunities. Counselors usually prefer not to make career choices for employees but to assist employees to make their choices. Successful counseling requires a high level of interpersonal communication skill, knowledge of counseling theory, and extensive knowledge of career opportunities in the firm. Successful counseling also requires careful attention to the establishment of a counselor/client relationship appropriate to the exchange.[175] This last point in particular disqualifies most supervisors of career employees as counselors of their subordinates.

Mentors are important for many career employees. The mentor is usually a more experienced fellow employee who provides moral and other support for the career employee. A mentor may act as teacher, sponsor, host, guide, exemplar, counselor, and in general, a supporter and facilitator of one's dreams.[176]

Organizations should take two approaches to the provision of mentors for career employees. First, they should ensure that a sufficient number of employees capable of mentoring are available at strategic points in the organization so that all employees who want a mentor may have one. Second, organizations should encourage a helping relationship among employees so that employees may serve informally as mentors for each other.[177]

Job coaching, by the career employee's supervisor in each career path position, provides on-the-spot feedback, correction of errors, and reinforcement for appropriate behaviors. The objective of the coaching is to enable the career employee to reach quickly a satisfactory level of overall performance on the job and to learn carefully and thoroughly the career-critical duties of the job.

The best job development opportunities of organizations must be identified and those jobs must be designated for use in developing employees. Supervisors in these jobs, who are to have career employees assigned to them, should be carefully selected for their ability to coach employees, should receive special training for this task, and should be rewarded for successful development of employees.

Career performance appraisal consists of three elements: appraisal of overall job performance in each position on a career path, appraisal of performance on each career critical duty of each position, and appraisal of employee characteristics that are expected to develop as the employee moves along the career path. As discussed, the first and second of these elements should be appraised by the employee's immediate supervisor in each career path position. The third element should be appraised by the career counselor.

Personal development aids should be tailored for the individual employee.[178] Services may be purchased from outside the organization to allow a larger repertoire of aids to be available to meet a greater range of individual needs. Developmental requirements that recur in sufficient numbers can be provided by specialists within the firm.

A strategy focusing attention on career employees must provide carefully designed and managed career paths, tailored to the individual employee, and ready support for employee movement along these career paths. Attention to those requirements can both reduce sharply the time required to develop career employees and develop career employees to a much higher level of competence than is now being achieved.

STRATEGIC HUMAN RESOURCE PLANNING PROCESS

A process for strategic planning at the enterprise, function, group, and business unit levels was presented in Chapter 2. Planning for human resources is in many ways unique, and some aspects of the strategic planning process will be modified when applied to human resources. A discussion of the steps specific to human resource strategic planning will follow. The steps are

1. Initiate the process.
2. Set objectives for the human resource planning process.
3. Identify key participants.
4. Choose that part of the organization philosophy that concerns human resources.
5. Conduct a study of the setting of human resource planning.
6. Establish organization identity respecting human resources.
7. Select strategic objectives.

8. Formulate human resource strategies.
9. Implement the chosen strategies.
10. Evaluate the planning process.
11. Manage the issues arising under the strategic plan.

Step 1. Initiating the Process

For some organizations, a crisis or a dramatic event may precipitate the immediate introduction of strategic planning for human resources.[179] Examples are transitions in leadership, a class action lawsuit, emergence of new functions or purposes for the human resource department, significant growth in the organization, and dramatic changes in the external environment.[180] But in a typical situation, planning for human resources is being considered for introduction in an organization with a history of strategic business planning. The chief executive officer, the chief human resource executive, or other persons in the organization may have decided that the time has come for strategic planning for human resources. What obstacles will they face in initiating the strategic human resource planning process?

Many executives in the organization may have little appreciation of the need for strategic planning for human resources. The formula for past success in the organization was, in all likelihood, to perform well the financial and operating functions. It may be difficult for these executives to believe that strategic planning for human resources can be a formula for present and future success.

Strategic planning for human resources presents political risks and challenges for an organization. Its initiation may alter the distribution of power in the organization and may change the way people work with each other.[181] In such circumstances, management may be reluctant to disturb the status quo. In these cases, it may be easier to obtain acceptance for an embryonic program of strategic planning for human resources than for a fully developed program. Once it has begun, it can evolve into a full-fledged program of strategic planning for human resources.

Step 2. Setting Objectives for Planning

Although the objectives of strategic planning for human resources will vary depending on the needs of particular organizations,[182] the main objective must be to produce an integrated program of human resource management. As mentioned earlier, the principal collaborators in the management of human resources are the chief executive officer, the chief human resource officer and staff of human resource specialists, and line managers. If the planning process is properly designed, it will result in a team that will be in agreement about how to manage human resources. A strategic plan can provide a coordinative frame of reference for making decisions about human resources.

Another important objective of strategic human resource planning must be to help the participants as individuals to make better decisions about human resources in their day-to-day jobs. Dealing with people presents unique problems for decision makers that are not encountered when dealing with things. The planning process presents continuous opportunities for the display of good human resource decision making skills. These skills, when learned, may be taken back to the job.

Step 3. Identifying Key Participants

Past experience of the organization and the maturity of the strategic human resource planning process will determine who will be the key participants in strategic planning. The planning should begin with those participants who have played key roles in the management of human resources in the past, and the participants should change as it becomes clear the direction that strategic planning for human resources should take in the organization.[183] For many organizations, key participants in the initial stages of strategic planning for human resources will be the chief executive officer, the human resource specialists, and the line managers. As the planning process matures and specific human resource planning needs become apparent, some of these participants will be dropped and others, needed for their knowledge and skills, will be added.

Step 4. Drafting an Organization Philosophy Respecting Human Resources

Choice of an organization philosophy should be done at the enterprise level of strategic planning. It may or may not also be done at the group and business unit levels, depending on the amount of integration desired between enterprise strategic plans and group and business unit strategic plans.

If the organization philosophy was chosen prior to the initiation of strategic human resource planning, the portion of the philosophy dealing with the responsibility of the organization to its employees should be reconsidered. Strategic planning for human resources will develop a better awareness of the importance of the employees to the organization and may affect the terms of the trade-off between the commitment of the organization to its employees and to the other stakeholders of the organization.

Step 5. Studying the Setting

That part of the environment of importance to human resource management is termed the *human resource domain*. It is often erroneously assumed that the human resource domain is similar for all organizations. Such is not the case. Each organization must identify what is truly its human resource domain. As discussed in Chapter 2, an organization may identify its domain through a study of relationships and a study of sectors. It is the responsibility of the strategic human resource planning committee to ensure that all relationships and sectors relevant to human resources are examined. In the accompanying list are some variables of sectors of the environment that may be important for human resources.[184]

1. *Cultural Variables*
a) Educational Systems:
   Literacy rates, Educational levels, Educational orientation and characteristics, Educational trends, Institutional structure of educational system.
b) Local Geographic Area:
   Institutional structure, Levels of concentration of population and organizations, Modus operandi, Watching and reading levels, Types of organizations.
c) Family Practices:
   Living arrangements, Attitudes toward child rearing, Attitudes toward the world of work, Attitudes toward kinds of paid employment, Entertainment practices, Attitudes toward education and learning, Attitudes toward authority.

2. *Economic Variables*

a) GNP Growth Rate
b) Inflation Rate
c) Taxes
d) Income Distribution
e) Changes in Income Levels
f) Changes in Form of Income
g) Leisure/Income Preferences

3. *Technological Variables*
a) Methods for Dealing with People, Data, and Things
b) Capacities for Acquiring and Developing Technologies
c) Pace of Technological Change.

4. *Social Variables*
a) Structure of Each Economic and Social Segment of the Population:
   Percentage of population, Living conditions, Consumption structure, Life style trends, Value systems
b) Union Structure:
   Types of conflict, Levels of participation, Ideological characteristics
c) Political Structure:
   Types of organizations, Ideological characteristics, Organization characteristics, Types and degrees of participation

5. *Demographic Variables*
a) Population Density and Mobility
b) Birth and Death Rates and Relationships between the Rates
c) Immigration and Emigration Rates and Relationships between the Rates
d) Distribution of Population by Age, Sex, and Family Construction

6. *Political Variables*
a) Federal Legislative Changes and Trends
b) Federal Judicial Changes and Trends
c) Federal Executive Changes and Trends
d) Balance of Federal, State and Local Power and Control

Step 6. Establishing Organization Identity Respecting Human Resources

Different human resource strategies require expertise in carrying out different human resource functions. If an organization has the ability to perform a human resource function relatively well as compared to its competition, the organization has a distinctive competence in carrying out that function. Human resource planners should compare the abilities of their own organization to perform each of the functions with the abilities of competitors to perform the same functions.[185] This comparison will determine for which strategies the organization has distinctive competences in human resources.

Step 7. Selecting Strategic Objectives

Selection of the human resource strategic objectives should be done by the human resource planning committee, not by human resource department professionals alone. Too often human resource departments set their own objectives for the human resource function and end up working at cross-purposes to the rest of the organization.[186] It is important to confront any differences within the organization about how human resources should be managed at this planning step so that the human resource function is integrated smoothly with other activities of the organization.

Step 8. Formulating Human Resource Strategies

Strategies for the management of human resources should:

- Have the best possible fit with the organization philosophy.
- Yield the best possible characteristics of human resources for the time and money spent.
- Make the best possible use of human resource knowledge available to the organization.

The human resource segment of the organization philosophy provides an acceptable and agreed-on formula for the integration of organization needs and employee needs. Strategies that are consistent with the philosophy will have the widespread acceptance of, and will be carried out by, members of the organization. To ensure consistency of strategies with the organization philosophy, planners must anticipate the effects of various strategies on the needs of the organization and on the needs of its employees. They should adopt only those strategies that maintain the integrity of agreed-on terms of integration of these needs.

Human resource strategies can amplify desirable characteristics in human resources. If employers were asked to prepare a "wish list" of characteristics their employees should display, they would probably include

- Satisfied, happy, responsible, and loyal
- Energetic, motivated, and highly-skilled
- Highly productive in proportion to their cost
- Flexible, adaptive, and mobile

But human resources cannot be all things to the organization. Organizations must select those human resource characteristics that they wish to produce to an unusual degree. The strategies chosen must promote those characteristics.

Strategies must be selected with an eye to whether the strategies use knowledge available to effectuate the strategy. At times knowledge needed to effectuate a strategy may be available in some select circles but not be readily available to the firm. Under these circumstances, it may be inadvisable to adopt the strategy. However, the rate of advance of knowledge in the human resource field is increasing. What is not possible today may be possible tomorrow. Strategies may be selected, therefore, with an eye to whether trends in the advance of knowledge favor these strategies.[187]

Step 9. Implementing the Strategies

Implementation of human resource strategies presents a special challenge because these strategies require a long-term effort, carefully integrated by human resource professionals and line managers. The long-term effort is made difficult by the short-term nature of control systems in most organizations. Tony Hain has cautioned that control systems biased toward short-term results prevent the effective implementation of strategies and result in the "unconscious harvesting" of our industrial base.[188] Organizations must take steps to ensure that control systems applied to human resource strategy implementation are appropriate for the longer term.

Human resource specialists and line managers bring to the process of strategy implementation different values, viewpoints, and needs. If they are to work together effectively, each must learn to think more like the other. Few practices are as effective in helping human resource specialists and line managers to see each other's viewpoint as quality, cross-functional experience for both. Ways of accomplishing this are discussed earlier in the chapter.

Step 10. Evaluating the Planning Process

Strategic planning for human resources may be evaluated by direct and indirect outcomes.

A *direct outcome* of successful strategic planning may be that managers in the organization take a more strategic orientation toward human resource activities. They consistently make decisions with human resource strategies in mind, and their decisions are more purposive and informed. Another direct outcome may be that the managers are better able to evaluate how well they are managing the human resources and thus have a clearer idea of whether they are doing an effective job.

Indirect outcomes of successful strategic planning for human resources result from improved performance of human resource management. Arnoldo Hax suggests classifying these outcomes as organization and individual outcomes.[189] This is especially appropriate because human resource strategies seek to achieve a balance between organization and individual outcomes, as specified in the organization philosophy.

Organization outcomes are favorable changes in[190]

- Return on investment
- Market share
- Productivity
- Cost—unit cost, total cost, and life-cycle cost
- Delivery—percentage of on-time shipments, ability to predict delivery dates, and time required to respond to demand changes
- Quality—return rate, product reliability rates, cost and rate of field repairs, and cost of quality
- Flexibility—product options or variants, time required to respond to product or volume changes

Individual outcomes are favorable changes in[191]

- Job satisfaction
- Job performance
- Turnover
- Absenteeism
- Motivation
- Job security
- Career prospects
- Psychological stress
- Safety/health conditions
- Income
- Overall satisfaction with the organization[192]

Step 11. Managing Issues

In addition to evaluating strategic planning by observing both its direct and indirect outcomes, strategic planning may be evaluated by observing issues that arise under strategic plans. Issues should be used as feedback for improving the planning process and keeping it current. Issues management normally is more efficient if done for the human resource function as part of an organization-wide effort.

SUMMARY

Under ideal conditions, human resource planning should be a part of overall business planning from the inception of business planning. This ideal is not often realized in practice. Instead, human resource planning has been a response to business planning, serving in a supportive role only. This chapter describes how human resources can become a fully integrated part of the business planning process.

Before organizations begin strategic planning for human resources, they should ensure that conditions in the organization are favorable for the process. Two conditions crucial for planning are the directional stability of the organization and the presence of key people within the organization who are supportive of and able to do strategic planning for human resources. Directional stability of the organization is important because the complex and long-term nature of strategic planning for human resources mandates that it must have an assured and secure environment within which to mature.

Although everyone in the organization may take part in human resource planning, the key persons to planning success in most organizations are the chief executive officer, the chief human resource executive and professional staff, and line managers. The chief executive officer must become personally involved in human resource planning, serving as a role model to others in the organization. The CEO must provide support for the human resource function, not just for the human resource department. The chief human resource executive must ensure that the personnel of the human resource department are accomplished and unified so that the department will be able to carry out its part of human resource planning. The chief human resource executive must ensure that his or her involvement in the overall business planning process allows human resource planning to proceed in coordination with overall business planning. Line managers must be able to act as full partners in shaping and executing the organization strategy regarding human resources. This may require additional development of line managers and the selection of line managers who are able to think in strategic terms about human resources.

Before organizations begin strategic planning for human resources, they should have in mind a clear picture of the basic elements of strategic planning for human resources: an organization philosophy, human resource strategic objectives, and human resource strategies. An organization philosophy outlines the relative responsibilities of the organization toward its employees and toward the organization as a whole. Human resource strategic objectives state the purposes of the human resource management function. Human resource strategies state the manner in which these purposes are to be achieved.

Some strategies that allow the application of human resource knowledge to address pressing needs of many organizations today are facilitating technological change, ensuring an adequate supply of employee talent, promoting the development of employees, promoting employee service to customers, improving the productivity of human resources, creating organization commitment, encouraging the participation and involvement of employees in organization affairs, keeping employees satisfied, and focusing on a key employee group—career employees.

Once organizations have ensured that conditions in the organization are supportive of the strategic human resource planning process and have envisioned the basic elements of the process, they are ready to implement a process for strategic human resource planning. The process is similar in most respects to that used in other kinds of strategic business planning, but there are some important differences.

- Strategic human resource planning often will not have been part of the business planning process. Therefore, consideration should be given to how the process of strategic planning for human resources is to be integrated smoothly into business planning.
- The main objective of strategic human resource planning must be to produce an integrated program of human resource management.
- Studies of the environment of the organization will likely need to be modified to ensure that they scrutinize that part of the environment of concern to strategic human resource planning.
- Strategies for the management of human resources should be selected that have the best possible fit with the organization philosophy, yield the best possible characteristics of human resources for the time and money spent, and make the best possible use of the human resource knowledge available to the organization.
- Effective implementation of human resource strategies requires a long-run view of strategies and an effective integration of effort of human resource specialists and line managers.
- Important expected direct outcomes of the strategic human resource management process are that managers in the organization take a more strategic orientation toward human resource activities, that their decisions are purposive and better informed, and that they are better able to evaluate how well they are managing the human resources of the organization. Expected indirect outcomes of strategic planning for human resources include both organization outcomes and individual outcomes. It is appropriate that both outcomes be measured because human resource strategies seek to achieve a balance between organization outcomes and individual outcomes, as stipulated in the organization philosophy regarding human resources.

LEARNING EXERCISES

Case Analyses

If you have the opportunity for small-group discussion, you may use the procedure suggested for Case 1 in Chapter 1.

Bank of America

For Case 4, you are to draft that part of a statement of organization philosophy dealing with human resources. Answer the questions or take the following actions:

1. Based on the information given in this interview with Mr. Beck, what stakeholders would be considered in the statement of philosophy? How important do each of these stakeholders seem to be to Mr. Beck? Do you think his views of the various stakeholders will impair his ability to serve as a member of Bank of America's executive committee? Explain your answer carefully.

2. Draft a statement of philosophy that you feel would be consistent with the thinking of Mr. Beck. This statement should state the responsibilities of the organization to its employees and the responsibilities of the employees to the organization.

3. What human resource objectives and strategies would be consistent with the statements of Mr. Beck concerning his plans for Bank of America? Are there indications that he will urge the adoption of human resource strategies suited to Bank of America or does he appear to be copying strategies that worked at IBM?

Comparative Analysis

For this analysis you will need to use Case 4 and Case 9. If you are part of a class or study group, use the following procedure:

1. Establish discussion groups of three members each.

2. Assign to each discussion group the task of determining the human resource strategies being followed by either Bank of America or Chase Manhattan Bank. (This allows an independent, objective analysis of each organization.) Discussion groups may start with the generic strategies listed in this chapter but should not expect either organization to be following completely any one strategy or to be following one strategy only.

3. Each discussion group should report the results of its discussion to the class or group at large.

4. The class or group at large should answer the following questions or take the following actions:

a. Compare the strategies reported for the two banks. Are the differences greater or less than you expected? How do you account for any differences or similarities noted?

b. Based on information provided in the case and on your personal knowledge of these companies, which organization seems to be using a strategy or strategies that better fit the organization—its size, its history and traditions, its lines of business, its people, and its technologies?

c. Assume that you were offered a position with each of these companies as assistant to the chief HR executive officer. Based on answers to the first questions posed, with which company would you feel more comfortable working? Why?

Deft Research and Development, Inc.

Case 8, "Deft Research and Development," is a company that appears to be on the cusp of change. Karl Rhodes's invitation to the upcoming management committee meeting to discuss planning for the personnel function suggests that business planning for human resources is to begin. What changes would you anticipate between current conditions at DR&D and future conditions once human resource planning is fully integrated into the business planning process?

1. Is there an awareness at present of the responsibility of the various members of the organization for the human resource function? Whom do the vice presidents see as responsible for the function? Is part of the responsibility theirs?

2. Does Karl Rhodes seem to understand his role in planning? Once he begins to take part in business planning, can he continue to think of his role and that of his department as solely one of service and support for the business plans of line management? In what ways must his role in the organization change? Would he be able to fill this new role more easily if he were elevated to the position of vice president? Why or why not?

3. If you were Glenn Richards, new president of DR&D, and intended to initiate a complete business planning process to include human resource planning, how would you develop in your vice presidents and in Karl Rhodes the attitudes and understanding necessary for successful execution of the process? Can the planning process itself be designed to encourage their growth as mature members of the business planning team? Explain your answer carefully.

Northeast Data Resources, Inc.

Read Case 7, "Northeast Data Resources, Inc.," and answer the questions or take the actions listed here:

1. How would you describe the role that George Wellington is assuming in the business planning process of NDR? Describe this role as specifically as possible. What evidence is there of the nature of his role?

2. Is his present role in the best interests of the organization? What are the disadvantages to the organization, if any, in the way his role is defined at present?

3. Does George Wellington appear comfortable in his present role? Does Jack Logan appear satisfied with the role Mr. Wellington is assuming? What, if anything, might George Wellington do to modify the role?

Activity

For one or more organizations with which your are familiar, decide what, in your opinion, would constitute success for the organization. Now list the five stakeholders that, in your opinion, are most important to organization success. Establish a rank order of importance for each of these stakeholders.

What order of importance seems to be assigned by the organization you have chosen to its various stakeholders? Do those persons leading the organization have different objectives for the organization than you have? What factors may explain this difference of opinion about the relative importance to the organization of the various stakeholders?

A useful reference source for this activity is Thomas A. Falsey, *Corporate Philosophies and Mission Statements: A Survey and Guide for Corporate Communicators and Management* (New York: Quorum Books, 1989).

Endnotes

[1] See p. 81 of William E. Bright, "How One Company Manages Its Human Resources," *Harvard Business Review*, 54, no. 1 (January–February 1976), 81–93. For another excellent illustration of the dangers of failing to consider human resources at the strategic stage of business planning, see pp. 29–30 of Eddie C. Smith, "How to Tie Human Resource Planning to Strategic Business Planning," *Managerial Planning*, 32, no. 2 (September/October 1983), 29–34.

[2] See pp. 82–83 of Lee Dyer, "Linking Human Resource and Business Strategies," *Human Resource Planning*, 7, no. 2 (1984), 79–84. See also Joanne Marshall-Mies, Kerry Yarkin-Levin, and Marilyn K. Quaintance, "Human Resources Planning, Part 1: In the Public Sector," *Personnel*, 62, no. 8 (August 1985) 22–27; and Joanne Marshall-Mies, Kerry Yarkin-Levin, and Marilyn K. Quaintance, "Human Resources Planning, Part 2: In the Public Sector," *Personnel*, 62, no. 9 (September 1985), 38–44 .

[3] See p. 14 of Felix M. Lopez, "Toward a Better System of Human Resource Planning," *Academy of Management Journal*, 46, no. 2 (Spring 1981), 4–14.

[4]See p. 34 of Wickham Skinner, "Big Hat, No Cattle: Managing Human Resources," in Craig Eric Schneier, Richard W. Beatty, and Glenn M. McEvoy, *Personnel/Human Resource Management Today: Readings and Commentary*, 2nd ed. (Reading, MA: Addison-Wesley, 1986), pp. 26–35, reprinted from *Harvard Business Review* (September/October 1981). Mirvis contends that studies of HRM show that it can take ten years or more for a new strategy and HR orientation to take hold in a firm. See p. 385 of Philip H. Mirvis, "Formulating and Implementing Human Resource Strategy: A Model of How to Do It, Two Examples of How It's Done," *Human Resource Management*, 24, no. 4 (Winter 1985), 385–412.

[5]If employees are organized, union leaders will also be important influences on strategic planning for human resources.

[6]Chief executives sometimes exacerbate political problems of strategic planning for human resources by giving too much authority to the human resource department to carry out the planning task. This is done because chief executive officers tend to equate the granting of authority with the giving of support. Giving the human resource department more power than is politically acceptable can block the initiation of strategic planning for human resources. See p. 60 of Robert H. Schwartz, "Practitioners' Perception of Factors Associated with Human Resource Planning Success," *Human Resource Planning*, 8, no. 2 (1985), 55–66.

[7]The chief executive officer typically expects his or her chief human resource officer and staff to take the lead in strategic human resource planning. See pp. 50–52 of James W. Walker and Gregory Moorhead, "CEO's: What They Want from HRM," *Personnel Administrator*, 32, no. 12 (December 1987), 50–59.

[8]Evidence for these characteristics was found in a survey of human resource planners, reported in Schwartz, "Practitioners' Perception," pp. 55–66.

[9] See the discussion in the next section of this chapter.

[10]Schwartz, "Practitioners' Perception," p. 60.

[11]In the survey of human resource planners mentioned above, 48 percent of respondents who had been unable to establish a state of the art human resource planning program in their organizations indicated that they had problems with intradepartmental relationships. Ibid., p. 62. Strategic human resource planning requires using a human resource plan as a rational framework for organizing and conducting the entire range of human resource management activities; firms seldom are able to do this. For a group of midwestern firms studied, none used HRP as a rational framework or basis for organizing and conducting their entire range of human resource management activities. Kendrith M. Rowland and Scott L. Summers, "Human Resource Planning: A Second Look," *Personnel Administrator*, 26, no. 12 (December 1981), 73–80.

[12]See, for example the description of the personnel function at 3M Corporation during the 1950s and 1960s, on pp. 58–59 of Harold L. Angle, Charles C. Manz, and Andrew H. Van de Ven, "Integrating Human Resource Management and Corporate Strategy: A Preview of the 3M Story," *Human Resource Management*, 24, no. 1 (Spring 1985), 51–68.

[13]Ibid., p. 63.

[14]See p. 265 of Lee Dyer, "Bringing Human Resources into the Strategy Formulation Process," *Human Resource Management*, 22, no. 3 (Fall 1983), 257–271.

[15]See p. 1 of Dan Huntley, "50, 000 Workers Laid Off Last Quarter of 1989," *HRNews*, 8, no. 1 (January 1990), 1, 13.

[16] Ibid.

[17] Ibid., p. 1.

[18] Ibid.

[19]See, for example, the report of strategic planning for two of the divisions of Dun and Bradstreet in Julia Reid Galosy, "Meshing Human Resources Planning with Strategic Business Planning: One Company's Experience," *Personnel*, 60, no. 5 (September/October 1983), 26–35. HRP was a one-way process—that is, business planning affected HRP but not the other way around, and there appeared to be no mechanism for gauging the acceptability of trade-offs between organization welfare and the welfare of human resources.

[20]M. F. Mandl, "Influencing Corporate Strategy Through Human Resource Planning—A Practical Solution," *Optimum* (Canada), 13, no. 2 (1982), 74–77.

[21]Compare Mirvis, "Formulating and Implementing Human Resource Strategy," p. 395: "[Caterpillar Corporation] undertook a world-wide human resource strategy conference in 1980 to define the needs of employees and the business and to chart a course for integrating them in the next decade."

[22]The strategies chosen are based on a review of the literature. Especially helpful were the following articles: Mirvis, "Formulating and Implementing Human Resource Strategy"; Robert A. Bolda, "Utility: A Productivity Planning Tool," *Human Resource Planning*, 8, no. 3 (1985), 111–132; Luis R. Gomez-Mejia, "Dimensions and Correlates of the Personnel Audit as an Organizational Assessment Tool," *Personnel Psychology*, 38, no. 2 (Summer 1985), 293–308; Paul A. L. Evans, "The Strategic Outcomes of Human Resource Management," *Human Resource Management*, 25, no. 1 (Spring 1986), 149–167; Paul R. Sparrow and Andrew M. Pettigrew, "Britain's Training Problems: The Search for a Strategic Human Resources Management Approach," *Human Resource Management*, 26, no. 1 (Spring 1987), 109–127; George S. Odiorne, "Human Resource Strategies for the '80s," *Training*, 22, no. 1 (January 1985), 47–51; Gerald R. Ferris and Dan Curtin, "Shaping Strategy: Tie Personnel Functions to Company Goals," *Management World*, 14, no. 1 (January 1985), 32–33, 38; Roy Foltz, Karn Rosenberg, and Julie Foehrenbach, "Senior Management Views the Human Resource Function," *Personnel Administrator*, 27, no. 9 (September 1982), 37–51; Arnoldo C. Hax, "A New Competitive Weapon: The Human Resource Strategy," *Training and Development Journal*, 89, no. 5 (May 1985), 76, 77–82; Mary Anne Devanna, Charles Fombrun, and Noel Tichy, "Human Resources Management: A Strategic Perspective," *Organizational Dynamics*, 9, no. 3 (Winter 1981), 51–67; Frederick E. Schuster, "A Tool for Evaluating and Controlling the Management of Human Resources," *Personnel Administrator*, 27, no. 10 (October 1982), 63–69.

[23]David A. Aaker, *Developing Business Strategies* (New York: John Wiley, 1984), p. 48.

[24]Pelz and Munson distinguish between a change in the technical content of a technology and a change in the embedding content of a technology. D. C. Pelz and D. Munson, "The Innovating Process: A Conceptual Framework," Working Paper, Center for Research on Utilization of Scientific Knowledge, University of Michigan, 1980, cited in Louis G. Tornatzky et al., *The Process of Technological Innovation: Reviewing The Literature* (Washington, DC: National Science Foundation, May 1983), p. 5.

[25]Technology is "any tool or technique, any product or process, any physical equipment or method of doing or making, by which human capability is extended." Donald A. Schon, *Technology and Change: The New Heraclitus* (New York: Delacorte Press, 1967), p. 1.

[26]For an excellent discussion of the effects of technological change on the employees using the technology, see p. 71 of Michael Maccoby, "A New Way of Managing," *IEEE Spectrum*, 21, no. 6 (June 1984), 69–72.

[27]In one nationwide survey of workers, only 9 percent thought that workers were the most

likely beneficiaries of productivity gains. See Ronald H. Clarke and James R. Morris, *Workers' Attitudes Toward Productivity* (Washington, DC: Chamber of Commerce of the United States, 1980), p. 13.

[28]Michael Maccoby has pointed out that workers in the typical bureaucratic-industrial organization protect themselves against arbitrary authority by becoming experts in their jobs and using this expertise to control their turf. They resist technological change because the change threatens to make obsolete their skills and their only defense against arbitrary authority. See p. 71, Maccoby, "A New Way of Managing."

[29]Human factors engineers are responsible for anticipating human physiological and psychological characteristics and for ensuring that these characteristics are considered in the design of technical systems. See Carl Heyel, *The Encyclopedia of Management*, 2nd ed. (New York: Van Nostrand Reinhold, 1973), pp. 307–309; and Harold P. Van Cott and Robert G. Kinkade, editors, *Human Engineering Guide to Equipment Design*, rev. ed. (Washington, D.C.: U.S. Government Printing Office, 1972). The human resource representative, in contrast, must represent the needs of the specific employees using the technology and of the human resource systems involved.

[30]Compare Steve W. J. Kozlowski, "Technological Innovation and Strategic HRM: Facing the Challenge of Change," *Human Resource Planning*, 10, no. 2 (1987), 69–79.

[31]Human resource professionals in most organizations have little authority for the choice and introduction of new technologies. See Andrew Templer, "Managers Downplay the Role of the HR Function in Introducing New Technology," *Personnel Administrator*, 30, no. 7 (July 1985), 88–96.

[32]When General Motors opened its new Fort Wayne, Indiana, truck plant, it provided an average of 633 hours of training for each of its 3,000 employees. See pp. 105 and 108 of Aaron Bernstein, "Special Report; Where the Jobs Are Is Where the Skills Aren't," *Business Week*, September 19, 1988, pp. 104–105, 108.

[33]Gene Remoff, vice president of human resources for ARA Corporation, has pointed out to the author that one of the most critical needs his organization experiences is for employees in all occupational categories to be able to state or write a point concisely. Personal conversation, August 16, 1989.

[34]Michael J. Papa and Ethel C. Glenn, "Listening Ability and Performance with New Technology: A Case Study," *Journal of Business Communication*, 25, no. 4 (Fall 1988), 5–15.

[35]Gene Remoff, vice president of human resources for ARA Corporation, has pointed out to the author that, because of the complexity of human resource systems, professionals must work in the field for a number of years before they begin to understand these systems. Personal conversation, August 16, 1989.

[36]Dean Leib, vice president of human resources for North American Operations, Rohm and Haas Company, observed, in personal conversation with the author on November 15, 1989, that the experience of Rohm and Haas with task teams demonstrates that turnover must be kept at low levels if task teams are to progressively develop greater skills at introducing change.

[37]See Sally J. Blank, "Hershey: A Company Driven by Values," *Management Review*, 75, no. 11 (November 1986), 46–51, for an example of the identification of a base line identity measured by values.

[38]See Chapter 2.

[39]See Chapter 2.

[40] See p. 31 of Skinner, "Big Hat: No Cattle."

[41]In a survey of 203 members of four affiliates of the Human Resource Planning Society,

Robert Schwartz found that those members with sophisticated planning approaches cited the most important factor contributing to the growth of their HRP programs as: "A recognition that not having critical talent available to meet organizational needs represents a threat to the well-being of the organization." See Schwartz, "Practitioners' Perception," p. 56. A survey of senior managers revealed that "recruiting professional/technical talent" was the human resource activity most in need of increase. Foltz, Rosenberg, and Foehrenbach, "Senior Management Views the Human Resource Function," p. 38.

[42]Criteria of effectiveness of employees hired from a recruitment source may include average cost of hiring a new employee for the position, average time required of the new employee to reach standard performance, average level of performance of the new employee at the completion of a break-in period, percentage of candidates who file discrimination complaints, and percentage of new employees who quit the position within the break-in period.

[43]A new employee's first position in the organization should be a positive experience in every respect for everyone concerned. For a discussion of the importance of first jobs in the later careers of employees, see Joseph A. Raelin, "First-Job Effects on Career Development," *Personnel Administrator*, 28, no. 8 (August 1983), 71–92.

[44]For a discussion of the importance of a challenging first job in the organization, see H. G. Kaufman, *Obsolescence and Professional Career Development* (New York: American Management Association, 1974).

[45]Bruce Nussbaum, "Special Report; Needed: Human Capital," *Business Week*, September 19, 1988, pp. 100–103.

[46]Dale Feuer, "The Skill Gap: America's Crisis of Competence," *Training*, 24, no. 12 (December 1987), 27–35; Bernstein, "Where the Jobs Are," pp. 104–105.

[47]Nussbaum, "Needed: Human Capital," p. 101.

[48]Eric Rolfe Greenberg, "Corporate Testing for the Three 'Rs,'" *Management Review*, 78, no. 4 (April 1989), 56–58; Harold W. McGraw, Jr., "Adult Functional Illiteracy: What to Do About It," *Personnel*, 64, no. 10 (October 1987), 38–42.

[49]McGraw, "Adult Functional Illiteracy." During the balance of the twentieth century, severe shortages of employees are expected in jobs at the upper end of the occupational tier.

[50]Nussbaum, "Needed: Human Capital," p. 103.

[51]Greenberg, "Corporate Testing."

[52]Bernstein, "Where the Jobs Are," p. 104.

[53]William G. Ouchi, *Theory Z: How American Business Can Meet the Japanese Challenge* (Reading, MA: Addison-Wesley, 1981), p. 71.

[54]For a discussion of the disadvantages of an unqualified lifetime employment policy, see Sparrow and Pettigrew, "Britain's Training Problems," p. 41.

[55]Today some organizations with a long-standing practice of lifetime employment are reevaluating this policy in light of the current availability of outplacement services. These organizations believe that a modified lifetime employment guarantee, with selective use of outplacement is a more enlightened policy than an unqualified lifetime employment policy. Helping unneeded or improperly placed employees to find employment elsewhere is felt to be "tough love" in action, and to be better for both the employees who are relocated and the employees who remain.

[56]Ouchi, *Theory Z*, p. 72. See also Rosemary Stewart, "Developing Managers by Radical Job Moves," *Journal of Management Development*, 3, no. 2 (1984), 48–55. Kaufman found that giving engineers challenging work had an important ancillary effect—

engineers who worked at challenging work participated in more graduate-level courses of study. H. G. Kaufman, *Work Environment, Personal Characteristics, and Obsolescence of Engineers*, Grant No. 91-34-69-23, Clearinghouse for Federal Scientific
and Technical Information Report No. P B 192273 (Washington, DC: U.S. Department of Labor, Office of Manpower Management, June 1970).

[57]Thomas J. Peters and Robert H. Waterman, Jr., *In Search of Excellence: Lessons from
America's Best-Run Companies*, (New York: Harper & Row, 1982), pp. 316–317.

[58]Nussbaum, "Needed: Human Capital," p. 102.

[59]Bernstein, "Where the Jobs Are," p. 105.

[60]See Lawrence Southwick, Jr., *Managerial Economics* (Plano, TX: Business Publications,
1985), pp. 539–540. In the classic make-or-buy decision, a comparison of present
value of costs can be used because it is reasonable to assume that the component is
comparable in quality whether made by the organization or purchased outside. In
applications to staffing, the quality of employees obtained using the buy-and-make
approach is likely to differ. If quality differs, the options must be compared in terms
of present value of net return on money invested.

[61]Ibid., p. 540.

[62]Arthur J. Jones, *Principles of Guidance*, 5th ed. (New York: McGraw-Hill Book Co.,
1963), cited in William F. Hopke, ed., *Dictionary of Personnel and Guidance Terms*
(Chicago: Ferguson, 1968), p. 122.

[63]Richard Kopelman, Paul Thompson, and Paul Dalton, "Factors Contributing to the Effec-
tiveness of the Older Engineer," pp. 18–36, in Samuel S. Dubin, Howard Shelton, and
Joan McConnell, *Maintaining Professional and Technical Competence of the Older
Engineer—Engineering and Psychological Aspects* (Washington, DC: American
Society for Engineering Education, 1974), see pp. 23–30, 35; J. K. Hemphill, ed., *The
Engineering Study* (Princeton, NJ: Educational Testing Service, 1963); Kaufman,
Work Environment, 1970; H. G. Kaufman, "A Comparative Analysis of University
versus In-Company Continuing Education for Engineers," pp. 179–186, in Dubin,
Shelton, and McConnell, *Maintaining Professional and Technical Competence*.

[64]"Supermarket V.P. Has Consumer's Welfare in Mind," *Times Herald* (Norristown, PA),
September 1, 1988, p. 21.

[65]See p. 167 of Joyce Hogan, Robert Hogan, and Catherine M. Busch, "How to Measure
Service Orientation," *Journal of Applied Psychology*, 69, no. 1 (February 1984),
167–173.

[66]A. R. Hochschild, *The Managed Heart* (Berkeley: University of California Press, 1983).

[67]Jobs such as flight attendant, where adherence to feeling rules is the dominant requirement, have been termed *emotional labor*. Such jobs are not physical or intellectual;
they are emotional. See Arlie Hochschild, "Emotional Labor in the Friendly Skies,"
Psychology Today, 16 (June 1982), 13–15.

[68]See pp. 386, 389–390 of Anat Rafaeli, "When Clerk Meets Customer: A Test of Variables
Related to Emotional Expressions on the Job," *Journal of Applied Psychology*, 74,
no.3 (August 1989), 385–393.

[69]Hogan, Hogan, and Busch, "How to Measure Service Orientation," note that employees on
the same job differ greatly in the extent to which they carry out the service aspect of
their positions (p. 167).

[70]C. Ann Smith, Dennis W. Organ, and Janet P. Near, "Organizational Citizenship Behavior:
Its Nature and Antecedents," *Journal of Applied Psychology*, 68, no. 4 (November
1983), 653–663.

[71]Christopher Orpen, "Patterned Behavior Description Interviews versus Unstructured Inter-

views: A Comparative Validity Study," *Journal of Applied Psychology* (November 1985), 774–776.

[72]Hogan, Hogan, and Busch, "How to Measure Service Orientation."

[73]Ibid.

[74]Orpen, "Patterned Behavior Description Interviews."

[75]John L. Holland, *Making Vocational Choices: A Theory of Careers* (Englewood Cliffs, NJ: Prentice Hall, 1973); Duane Brown, Linda Brooks, and Associates, *Career Choice and Development* (San Francisco: Jossey-Bass, 1986), pp. 61–93.

[76]Senior managers of organizations, surveyed in 1982, reported they want the human resource function "heavily involved" in productivity improvement efforts. See Foltz, Rosenberg, and Foehrenbach, "Senior Management Views," p. 45.

[77]The paint industry is an example where slowed growth has caused the industry to become price competitive. See p. 10 of Ernesto J. Poza and Lynne M. Markus, "Success Story: The Team Approach to Work Restructuring," *Organizational Dynamics*, 8, no. 3 (Winter 1980), 2–25.

[78]Ikujiro Nonaka, "Self-Renewal of the Japanese Firm and the Human Resource Strategy," *Human Resource Management*, 27, no. 1 (Spring 1988), 45–62.

[79]Edward E. Lawler III, "The New Plant Revolution," *Organizational Dynamics*, 6, no. 3 (Winter 1978), 3–12.

[80]Lawler, cited in Poza and Markus, "Success Story," p. 12.

[81]General Motors, in negotiations in 1982 with the United Automobile Workers union, granted more generous economic terms than those negotiated by the UAW at Ford Motor Company. In return, GM asked for and obtained a promise that was considered by GM to be the core of the agreement: the union would consider at the local union level work-rule changes "necessary to effectively utilize the services of employees." This agreement sent a message to the local unions that work-rule changes must be addressed if the plant represented by the union was to stay off the list of plant closings. See "The Work-Rule Changes GM Is Counting On," *Business Week*, April 5, 1982, pp. 30–31.

[82]Alan Smith, "The 'People Factor' in Competitiveness," an address presented at the University Club of Chicago, Chicago, December 6, 1988. Copies of these remarks were mailed by John W. McNulty, vice president of public relations, to university faculty across the United States. See also the discussion of the role of people in the new GM strategy in Roy S. Roberts, "Remarks on Getting Back to the Basics of Competition: People," *Executive Speeches*, 2, no. 11 (June 1988), 17–21.

[83]Having the participation of the United Auto Workers may help GM overcome pessimism among its employees about the benefits to be gained for workers by helping to improve productivity of the organization. Less than 10 percent of the U.S. work force believes productivity gains will be of benefit to workers. D.Yankelovich and J. Immerwahr, *Putting the Work Ethic to Work* (New York: Public Agenda Foundation, 1983). For an interesting contrast to improving productivity at the plant level in a company with a union, see the discussion of improving productivity in a nonunion plant using self-managed work teams in William H. Wagel, "Working (and Managing) Without Supervisors," *Personnel*, 64 (September 1987), 8–11.

[84]See Poza and Markus, "Success Story," pp. 5 and 12.

[85]Industrial Relations Research Association, *Collective Bargaining and Productivity* (Madison, WI, 1975), p. 29.

[86]Poza and Markus, "Success Story," pp. 11–12.

[87]There seems to be little doubt that General Motors is still a technology-driven, not a peo-

ple-driven, organization, in spite of its rhetoric. It is instructive that Roy Roberts, an executive at GM, lists "to forge new partnerships with employees" as the fifth point in a five-point strategy for improving the competitiveness of the company. Human resources appear to be a necessary adjustment to allow technology to function well. Roberts, "Remarks on Getting Back to the Basics."

[88]Organization commitment is distinctly different, in the minds of employees, from career commitment and job commitment. See Ted Howard Shore, "The Distinctiveness of Three Work Attitudes: Job, Career, and Organizational Commitment," Ph.D. dissertation, Colorado State University, 1985.

[89]Richard T. Mowday, Lyman W. Porter, and Richard M. Steers, *Employee-Organization Linkages: The Psychology of Commitment, Absenteeism, and Turnover* (New York: Academic Press, 1982), p. 27.

[90]Robert Lawrence Kuhn and George Thomas Geis, *The Firm Bond: Linking Meaning and Mission in Business and Religion* (New York: Praeger, 1984), p. 101; T. F. O'Boyle, "Loyalty Ebbs at Many Companies as Employees Grow Disillusioned," *The Wall Street Journal*, July 11, 1985, p. 27.

[91]For a review of this research, see Harold L. Angle and James L. Perry, "An Empirical Assessment of Organizational Commitment and Organizational Effectiveness," *Administrative Science Quarterly*, 26, no. 1 (March 1981), 1–14. Wing also found that number of previous jobs was negatively correlated with organizational commitment; this suggests that persons who are unlikely to become committed to the organization can sometimes be screened out at time of hiring. See Donald Sherman Wing, "Organizational and Structural Antecedents of Organizational Commitment," Ph.D. dissertation, California School of Professional Psychology, 1985.

[92]R. W. Scholl, "Differentiating Commitment from Expectancy as a Motivating Force," *Academy Of Management Review*, 6, no. 4 (October 1981), 589–599.

[93]See p. 338 of John R. Ogilvie, "The Role of Human Resource Management Practices in Predicting Organizational Commitment," *Group and Organization Studies*, 11, no. 4 (December 1986), 335–359.

[94]Wing, "Organizational and Structural Antecedents," found that primary relationships were a significant predictor of organizational commitment.

[95]For a discussion of the various contributions to the psychological identification view of commitment, see J. H. Morris and J. D. Sherman, "Generalizability of an Organizational Commitment Model," *Academy of Management Journal*, 24, no. 3 (September 1981), 512–526. See especially R. T. Mowday, R. M. Steers, and L. W. Porter, "The Measurement of Organizational Commitment," *Journal of Vocational Behavior*, 14, (1979), 224–247; J. Kagan, "The Concept of Identification," *Psychological Review*, 65, no. 5 (1958), 296–305; and Harry Levinson, "Reciprocation: The Relationship Between Man and Organization," *Administrative Science Quarterly*, 9 (1964/1965), 370–390.

[96] Harry Levinson, "Reciprocation," p. 372–374.

[97]For a discussion of the various contributors to the exchange evaluation view of commitment, see Robert Eisenberger, Robin Huntington, Steven Hutchinson, and Debora Sowa, "Perceived Organizational Support," *Journal of Applied Psychology*, 71, no. 3 (August 1986), 500–507. See especially Howard S. Becker, "Notes on the Concept of Commitment," *American Journal of Sociology*, 66, no. 1 (July 1960), 32–40; Lawrence G. Hrebiniak and Joseph A. Alutto, "Personal and Role-Related Factors in the Development of Organizational commitment," *Administrative Science Quarterly*, 17, no. 4 (December 1972), 555–573; and Scholl, "Differentiating Commitment from Expectancy as a Motivating Force."

[98]T. S. Bateman and S. Strasser, "A Longitudinal Analysis of the Antecedents of Organizational Commitment," *Academy of Management Journal*, 27, no. 1 (March 1984), 95–112.

[99]Ogilvie, "The Role of Human Resource Management Practices"; Hrebiniak and Alutto, "Personal and Role-Related Factors"; Morris and Sherman, "Generalizability of an Organizational Commitment Model"; J. M. Stevens, J. M. Beyer, and H. M. Trice, "Assessing Personal, Role, and Organizational Predictors of Managerial Commitment," *Academy of Management Journal*, 21, no. 3 (1978), 380–396; Mary E. Sheldon, "Investments and Involvements as Mechanisms Producing Commitments to the Organization," *Administrative Science Quarterly*, 16 (1971), 143–150; R. M. Steers, "Antecedents and Outcomes of Organizational Commitment," *Administrative Science Quarterly*, 22, no. 1 (March 1977), 46–56; Wing, "Organizational and Structural Antecedents."

[100]A word of caution is necessary. "Golden handcuffs" alone—the use by organizations of narrowly focused rewards to bind employees to the organization, as through rapid promotion, nonvested pension plans, and organization-specific skills training—may prevent employees from leaving but also may cause employees to resent their entrapment and to perform at a minimum level. See John P. Meyer et al., "Organizational Commitment and Job Performance: It's the Nature of the Commitment That Counts," *Journal of Applied Psychology*, 74, no. 1 (February 1989), 152–156. Encouraging commitment of employees must be a comprehensive plan incorporating all elements of the strategy outlined above.

[101]Thomas Rotondi, Jr., "Organizational Identification and Group Involvement," *Academy of Management Journal*, 18, no. 4 (December 1975), 892–896; Sheldon, "Investments and Involvements"; Steers, "Antecedents and Outcomes."

[102]John Van Maanen and Edgar H. Schein, "Toward a Theory of Organizational Socialization," in Barry M. Staw, ed., *Research in Organizational Behavior*, vol.1 (Greenwich, CT: JAI Press, 1979), pp. 209–264.

[103]Ogilvie, "The Role of Human Resource Management Practices"; Susan R. Rhodes and Richard M. Steers, "Conventional versus Worker-Owned Organizations," *Human Relations*, 34, no. 12 (December 1981), 1013–1035; Bruce Buchanan II, "Building Organizational Commitment: The Socialization of Managers in Work Organizations," *Administrative Science Quarterly*, 19 (1974), 533–546; Steers, "Antecedents and Outcomes"; Hrebiniak and Alutto, "Personal and Role-Related Factors"; Natalie Jean Allen, "Organizational Commitment: A Three-Component Model," Ph.D. dissertation, The University of Western Ontario, Canada, 1985.

[104]George Ritzer and Harrison M. Trice, "An Empirical Study of Howard Becker's Side-Bet Theory," *Social Forces*, 47 (1969), 475–479; Rhodes and Steers, "Conventional versus Worker-Owned Organizations"; Sang M. Lee, "An Empirical Analysis of Organizational Identification," *Academy of Management Journal*, 14, no. 2 (June 1971), 213–226; Stevens, Beyer, and Trice, "Assessing Personal, Role, and Organizational Predictors"; Ogilvie, "The Role of Human Resource Management Practices."

[105]R. M. Kanter, *Men and Women of the Corporation* (New York: Basic Books,1977).

[106]Morris and Sherman, "Generalizability of an Organizational Commitment Model."

[107]See Michael Maccoby, "Human Factors Affecting Innovation and Productivity," in Sven B. Lundstedt and E. William Colglazier,Jr., eds., *Managing Innovation: The Social Dimensions of Creativity Invention and Technology* (New York: Pergamon Press, 1982), pp. 207–214. See also Chris Lee, "The New Employment Contract," *Training*, 24, no. 12 (December 1987), 45–56.

[108]One of the most significant studies of job satisfaction is the University of Michigan Sur-

vey Research Center's surveys of employee job and life satisfaction in 1969, 1973, and 1977. See Graham L. Staines, "Is Worker Disaffection Rising?" *Challenge*, 22, no. 2 (May/June 1979), 38–45. Chelte, Wright, and Tausky have argued that the University of Michigan findings that worker discontent is rising are in error; see Anthony F. Chelte, James Wright, and Curt Tausky, "Did Job Satisfaction Really Drop During the 1970's," *Monthly Labor Review*, 105, no. 11 (November 1982), 33–36. Most longitudinal studies suggest that job satisfaction has been declining. See, for example, Frank J. Smith, Kenneth D. Scott, and others, "Trends in Job-Related Attitudes of Managerial and Professional Employees," *Academy of Management Journal*, 20, no. 3 (September 1977), 454–460; Frank Smith, Karlene H. Roberts, and others, "Ten-Year Job Satisfaction Trends in a Stable Organization," *Academy of Management Journal*, 19, no. 3 (September 1976), 462–469; Jack L. Rettig and Robert F. McCain, "Job Satisfaction of Personnel Managers," *Personnel Administrator*, 23, no. 9 (September 1978), 23–26; Dorothy F. Murray, "A Picture Is Worth a Thousand Words," *Managers Magazine*, 57, no. 1 (January 1982), 14–16; M. R. Cooper, B. S. Morgan, P. M. Foley, and others, "Changing Employee Values: Deepening Discontent?" *Harvard Business Review*, 57, no. 1 (January-February 1979), 117–125; Richard R. Cooper, Peter A. Gelfond, and Patricia M. Foley, "Early Warning Signals—Growing Discontent Among Managers," *Business*, 30, no. 1 (January-February 1980), 117–125.

[109]Staines, "Is Worker Disaffection Rising?" pp. 45–46. See also Thomas L. Keon and Bill McDonald, "Job Satisfaction and Life Satisfaction: An Empirical Evaluation of Their Interrelationship," *Human Relations*, 35, no. 3 (March 1982), 167–180; Charles N. Weaver, "Job Satisfaction as a Component of Happiness Among Males and Females," *Personnel Psychology*, 31, no. 4 (Winter 1978), 831–840; and Vida Scarpello and John F. Campbell, "Job Satisfaction and the Fit Between Individual Needs and Organizational Rewards," *Journal of Occupational Psychology*, 56, no. 4 (December 1983), 315–328.

[110]Marcy Pollock and Nina L. Colwill, "Participatory Decision Making in Review," *Leadership & Organization Development Journal* (UK), 8, no. 2 (1987), 7–10; John Richard, Gary Mauser, and Richard Holmes, "What Do Workers Want? Attitudes Toward Collective Bargaining and Participation in Management," *Industrial Relations* (Canada), 43, no. 1 (Winter 1988), 133–150.

[111]See p. 32 of Gayle J. Yaverbaum and Oya Culpan, "Human Resource Planning," *Journal of Systems Management*, 37, no. 12 (December 1986), 32–35.

[112]A key finding of a study by 3M Corporation of the expectations of its employees was that the company simply was not asking enough of its people. Mirvis, "Formulating and Implementing Human Resource Strategy," p. 400.

[113]Pollock and Colwill, "Participatory Decision Making in Review."

[114]The Japanese refer to this effect as the cumulative impact of "little brains" in the form of the opinions of the salespeople, dealers, and production workers of the organization. See p. 116 of Richard T. Pascale, "Our Curious Addiction to Grand Strategy," *Fortune*, January 25, 1982, pp. 115–116.

[115]John W. Dickson, "Values and Rationales of Key Organisational Members for Participation," *Personnel Review* (U.K.), 8, no. 2 (Spring 1979), 5–13.

[116]See Marshall Sashkin, "Participative Management Remains an Ethical Imperative," *Organizational Dynamics*, 14, no. 4 (Spring 1986), 62–75; and Pollock and Colwill, "Participatory Decision Making in Review."

[117]John L. Cotton, David A. Vollrath, Kirk L. Froggatt, Mark L. Lengnick-Hall, and Ken-

neth R. Jennings, "Employee Participation: Diverse Forms and Different Outcomes," *Academy of Management Review*, 13, no. 1 (January 1988), 8–22.

[118]Peter H. Dachler and Bernhard Wilpert, "Conceptual Dimensions and Boundaries of Participation in Organizations: A Critical Evaluation," *Administrative Science Quarterly*, 23, no. 1 (March 1978), 1–39, cited in Cotton et al., "Employee Participation."

[119]This list, slightly modified, is from Edwin A. Locke and David M. Schweiger, "Participation in Decision-Making: One More Look," in Barry M. Staw, ed., *Research in Organizational Behavior*, vol. 1, (Greenwich, CT: JAI Press, 1979), pp. 265–339.

[120]This classification follows Cotton et al, "Employee Participation," p. 10.

[121]Ibid., p. 11.

[122]For a discussion of the history and operation of Scanlon plans, see J. Kenneth White, "The Scanlon Plan: Causes and Correlates of Success," *Academy of Management Journal*, 22, no. 2 (June 1979), 292–312. Similar in operation to the Scanlon plan are the Rucker and Improshare plans. For a discussion of all three plans, see Michael Schuster and Donald DeSalvia, "Productivity Improvement Programs for Smaller Firms," *Journal of Small Business Management*, 21, no. 1 (January 1983), 14–20.

[123]"IW Study Team Visits Japan: Quality Control Circles Pay Off Big," *Industry Week*, October 29, 1979, pp. 17–19.

[124]Cotton et al., "Employee Participation," p. 12. It appears that quality circles in the United States may be de facto short-term decisions about work, the next classification discussed above. This is indicated by the high mortality rate of such groups after some initial success in solving specific problems. See Rober Drago, "Quality Circle Survival: An Exploratory Analysis," *Industrial Relations*, 27, no. 3 (Fall 1988), 336–351. In Japan, quality circles appear to have a much broader, long-term purpose than in the United States. See, "IW Study Team Visits Japan."

[125]In the Materials Management Division of Los Alamos National Laboratory, for example, temporary task forces are used successfully to solve specific problems, after which they disband until needed again. These task forces have resulted in sizable cost savings and the elimination of unnecessary tasks. See, "Employee Participation: Key to Success," *Modern Office Procedures*, 27, no. 5 (May 1982), 92–94.

[126]Cotton et al., "Employee Participation," p. 14.

[127]Ibid., p. 15.

[128]R. J. Long, "Job Attitudes and Organizational Performance Under Employee Ownership," *Academy of Management Journal*, 23 (1980), 726–737.

[129]Cotton et al., "Employee Participation," p. 15.

[130]Edwin A. Locke, David M. Schweiger, and Gary P. Latham, "Participation in Decision Making: When Should It Be Used?" *Organizational Dynamics*, 14, no. 3 (Winter 1986), 65–79.

[131]See, "Employee Participation: Key to Success."

[132]See Janice A. Klein, "Why Supervisors Resist Employee Involvement," *Harvard Business Review*, 62, no. 5 (September/October 1984), 87–95.

[133]Ibid.; Pollock and Colwill, "Participatory Decision Making in Review."

[134]Pollock and Colwill, "Participatory Decision Making in Review."

[135]Bhabatosh Sahu, "Participatory Management: A Conceptual Framework and Review of Literature," *ASCI Journal of Management* (India), 12, nos. 1 and 2 (September 1982/March 1983), 1–18.

[136]Susan Albers Mohrman and Gerald E. Ledford, Jr., "The Design and Use of Effective

Employee Participation Groups: Implications for Human Resource Management," *Human Resource Management*, 24, no. 4 (Winter 1985), 413–429.

[137]One study suggests that quantity and quality of superior-subordinate communication may be a necessary precondition for effective participative decision making. See Teresa M. Harrison, "Communication and Participative Decision Making: An Exploratory Study," *Personnel Psychology*, 38, no. 1 (Spring 1985), 93–116.

[138]As defined here, employee satisfaction includes both organization satisfaction and job satisfaction and is distinguished from organization commitment and job commitment. See Lynn Ann McFarlane, "A Comparison of Two Work Attitudes: Satisfaction versus Commitment," Ph.D. dissertation, Colorado State University, 1985.

[139]In contrast, immediate concerns of employment for career employees are a secondary consideration; meeting these immediate needs does not necessarily produce satisfaction.The correlation between need/reward match and job satisfaction is not high for career employees. See Scarpello and Campbell, "Job Satisfaction." For career employees, it is best to follow a strategy of promoting their career interests. This strategy is discussed in the next section of this chapter.

[140]Foltz, Rosenberg, and Foehrenbach, "Senior Management Views the Human Resource Function," p. 20.

[141]The research of Staw et al. support the "life-is-fun" explanation of the predisposition to be satisfied at work. See, for example, Barry M. Staw, Nancy E. Bell, and John A. Clauson, "The Dispositional Approach to Job Attitudes: A Lifetime Longitudinal Test," *Administrative Science Quarterly*, 31, no. 1 (March 1986), 56–77.

[142]The research of Pulakos and Schmitt supports the "work-is-fun" explanation of the predisposition to be satisfied at work. Elaine D. Pulakos and Neal Schmitt, "A Longitudinal Study of a Valence Model Approach for The Prediction of Job Satisfaction of New Employees," *Journal of Applied Psychology*, 68, no. 2 (May 1983), 307–312.

[143]Staw and Ross found a correlation of 0.33 between satisfaction ratings measured in 1969 and satisfaction ratings measured in 1971 for employees who had changed both employer and occupation during the two-year period. See p. 474 of Barry M. Staw and Jerry Ross, "Stability in the Midst of Change: A Dispositional Approach to Job Attitudes," *Journal of Applied Psychology*, 70, no. 3 (1985), 469–480.

[144]Orpen, "Patterned Behavior Description Interview."

[145]However, Bem and Allen have observed that persons who described themselves as highly consistent had more stable satisfaction levels across jobs than did persons who described themselves as not consistent. Daryl J. Bem and Andrea Allen, "On Predicting Some of the People Some of the Time: The Search for Cross-Situational Consistencies in Behavior," *Psychological Review*, 81, no. 6 (November 1974), 506–520.

[146]A number of studies have shown that life satisfaction is correlated with job satisfaction. See Keon and McDonald, "Job Satisfaction and Life Satisfaction." They contend that this correlation exists because life satisfaction and job satisfaction are jointly determined, perhaps in part by predispositions of persons toward satisfaction. See also Weaver, "Job Satisfaction." Using data drawn from four national surveys of the U.S. population, Weaver demonstrated that happiness is a generalized phenomena, such that employees are either generally satisfied or generally dissatisfied with most areas of their lives.

[147]Pulakos and Schmitt, "A Longitudinal Study," p. 310.

[148]Sam E. White and Terence R. Mitchell, "Job Enrichment versus Social Cues: A Comparison and Competitive Test," *Journal of Applied Psychology*, 64, no. 1 (February 1979), 1–9.

[149]O'Reilly and Caldwell found in a study of newly employed MBAs that those who freely

chose their employer from among a number of job offers, who had sufficient justification for choosing their employer, and who saw the choice as irrevocable were more
satisfied than those who had no other job offers, had little justification in their own
mind for accepting work with the employer, and considered their job choice to be
conditional. Charles A. O'Reilly and David F. Caldwell, "The Commitment and Job
Tenure of New Employees: Some Evidence of Postdecisional Justification," *Administrative Science Quarterly*, 26, no. 4 (1981), 597–616.

[150]Realistic job previews, in which all pertinent information about working in the organization is presented without distortion to job candidates, do not by themselves consistently produce greater job satisfaction. Wanous reports that studies of the effect of
realistic job previews on subsequent job attitudes of candidates were evenly divided
between those who found attitudes to be more positive and those who found attitudes
to be unchanged. John P. Wanous, *Organizational Entry: Recruitment, Selection, and
Socialization of Newcomers* (Reading, MA: Addison-Wesley, 1980), p. 70.

[151]Bonjean et al. have demonstrated through carefully documented developmental research
that a program of organizational change can improve the job satisfaction of employees. Charles H. Bonjean, Billye J. Brown, Burke D. Grandjean, and Patrick G. Mack-
en, "Increasing Work Satisfaction Through Organizational Change: A Longitudinal
Study of Nursing Educators," *Journal of Applied Behavioral Science*, 18, no. 3
(1982), 357–369.

[152]This list of treatment variables affecting job satisfaction is based on a literature search.
The following articles, presenting causal models of job satisfaction and commitment,
were especially helpful: John E. Mathieu and Karin Hamel, "A Causal Model of the
Antecedents of Organizational Commitment Among Professionals and Nonprofes-
sionals," *Journal of Vocational Behavior*, 34, no. 3 (June 1989), 299–231; John E.
Mathieu, "A Causal Model of Organizational Commitment in a Military Training
Environment," *Journal of Vocational Behavior*, 32, no. 3 (June 1988), 321–335;
Thomas A. DeCotiis and Timothy P. Summers, "A Path Analysis of a Model of the
Antecedents and Consequences of Organizational Commitment," *Human Relations*,
40, no 7 (July 1987), 445–470; Larry J. Williams and John T. Hazer, "Antecedents
and Consequences of Satisfaction and Commitment in Turnover Models: A Reanaly-
sis Using Latent Variable Structural Equation Methods," *Journal of Applied Psychology*, 71, no. 2 (1986), 219–231.

[153]The models presented in the following articles help to clarify the relationship of job satisfaction to some very general causal variables: Mathieu and Hamel, "A Causal Model
of the Antecedents"; Mathieu, "A Causal Model of Organizational
Commitment";DeCotiis and Summers, "A Path Analysis"; and Williams and Hazer,
"Antecedents and Consequences." Unfortunately, the causal variables are so general
as to be useful only in forming initial assumptions about operational models for satisfaction improvement programs.

[154]See, for example, Charles A. O'Reilly, G. Nicholas Parlette, and Joan R. Bloom, "Percep-
tual Measures of Task Characteristics: The Biasing Effects of Differing Frames of
Reference and Job Attitudes," *Academy of Management Journal*, 23 (1980), 118–131.

[155]Robert A. Karasek, Jr., "Job Demands, Job Decision Latitude, and Mental Strain: Implications for Job Redesign," *Administrative Science Quarterly*, 24, no. 2 (June 1979),
285–308. For other examples of interactive effects of employment condition variables, see Thomas S. Bateman and Stephen Strasser, "A Cross-Lagged Regression
Test of the Relationships Between Job Tension and Employee Satisfaction," *Journal
of Applied Psychology*, 68, no. 3 (August 1983), 439–445; William F. Joyce, John W.
Slocum, Jr., and Michael Abelson, "A Causal Analysis of Psychological Climate and
Leader Behavior Relationships," *Journal of Business Research*, 5, no. 3 (September

1977), 261–273; William E. Souder, "Autonomy, Gratification, and R&D Outputs—A Small-Sample Field Study," *Management Science*, 20, no. 8 (April 1974), 1147–1156; Mathieu and Hamel, "A Causal Model of the Antecedents"; Mathieu, "A Causal Model of Organizational Commitment"; DeCotiis and Summers, "A Path Analysis"; and Williams and Hazer, "Antecedents and Consequences."

[156]Halim Ahmed A. Abdel, "Interaction Effects of Power Equalization and Subordinate Personality on Job Satisfaction and Performance," *Human Relations*, 32, no. 6 (June 1979), 489–502. For other examples of the differential effects of employment condition variables among employees, see Philip E. Varca, Garnett S. Shaffer, and Cynthia D. McCauley, "Sex Differences in Job Satisfaction Revisited," *Academy of Management Journal*, 26, no. 2 (June 1983), 348–353; Paul R. Jackson, Lucy J. Paul, and Toby D. Wall, "Individual Differences as Moderators of Reactions to Job Characteristics," *Journal of Occupational Psychology*, 54, no. 1 (March 1981), 1–8; Mathieu and Hamel, "A Causal Model of the Antecedents"; Mathieu, "A Causal Model of Organizational Commitment"; DeCotiis and Summers, "A Path Analysis"; and Williams and Hazer, "Antecedents and Consequences."

[157]These types of research are adapted from Allan Williams, "Researching Personnel," *Management Today*, September 1980, pp. 43–48.

[158]A number of standard scales are widely used to measure satisfaction, both overall and satisfaction with separate features of employment. Means and standard deviations of satisfaction scores are available for different employee groups allowing a comparison of satisfaction in the organization with other employee groups in other organizations. See John D. Cook, Sue J. Hepworth, Toby D. Wall, and Peter B. Warr, *The Experience of Work: A Compendium and Review of 249 Measures and Their Use* (London: Academic Press, 1981), pp. 12–74. Measures should be administered to both experimental and control groups.

[159] The standard scales used in the diagnostic research phase may be repeated for experimental and control groups to determine what changes, if any, have occurred. Several forms of some scales are available for this purpose. See Cook et al., *The Experience of Work*.

[160]Taylor, referenced above, has questioned whether current measures of job satisfaction are accurate enough for use in programs to improve the quality of working life; see James C. Taylor, "Job Satisfaction and Quality of Working Life: A Reassessment," *Journal of Occupational Psychology*, 50, no. 4 (December 1977), 243–252. He urges that employees themselves be more involved in change programs to overcome flaws in the measurement of satisfaction. Action research is a way of bringing employees into the change process and is an additional reason why action research should be part of every satisfaction improvement program.

[161]Scott and Taylor conducted a meta-analysis of 23 research studies of the relationship between job satisfaction and absenteeism. They concluded that inconsistent findings in the studies were the result of research shortcomings and that job satisfaction is associated with both the frequency and duration of employee absence. K. Dow Scott and G. Stephen Taylor, "An Examination of Conflicting Findings on the Relationship Between Job Satisfaction and Absenteeism: A Meta-analysis," *Academy of Management Journal* (September 1985), 599–612. Cotton and Tuttle conducted a meta-analysis of research studies of the relationship between job satisfaction and employee turnover. They confirmed that job satisfaction has a stable, reliable correlation with turnover. John L. Cotton and Jeffrey M. Tuttle, "Employee Turnover: A Meta-analysis and Review with Implications for Research," *Academy of Management Review*, 11, no. 1 (January 1986), 55–70.

[162]T. W. Mangione and R. P. Quinn, "Job Satisfaction, Counter-productive Behavior, and

Drug Use at Work," *Journal of Applied Psychology*, 60 (1975), 114–116; and Caryl E. Rusbult, Dan Farrell, Glen Rogers, and Arch G. Mainous, "Impact of Exchange Variables on Exit, Voice, Loyalty, and Neglect," *Academy of Management Journal*, 31, no. 3 (September 1988), 599–627. See also B. M. Staw, "Organizational Behavior: A Review and Reformation of the Field's Outcome Variables," *Annual Review of Psychology*, 35 (1984), 627–666.

[163]Dennis W. Organ, "A Reappraisal and Reinterpretation of the Satisfaction-Causes-Performance Hypothesis," *Academy of Management Review*, 2, no. 1 (January 1977), 46–53. See also Dennis W. Organ, *Organizational Citizenship Behavior: The Good Soldier Syndrome* (Lexington, MA: D.C. Heath and Co., 1988), p. 50. In this later publication, Organ again restates his earlier position that satisfied employees are more cooperative. For further evidence of the relationship of satisfaction and cooperative behavior, see Rusbult, Farrell, Rogers, and Mainous, "Impact of Exchange Variables on Exit, Voice, Loyalty, and Neglect." See also Michael M. Gruneberg, *Understanding Job Satisfaction* (New York, NY: John Wiley, 1979), pp. 118–120.

[164]Scarpello and Campbell, "Job Satisfaction," have shown that individual differences in aspiration level and different views of career progression help to explain job satisfaction over and above the match of individual needs and organization rewards. Shore, "The Distinctiveness of Three Work Attitudes," has shown that organizational commitment and career commitment are separate concepts in the minds of employees.

[165]Bearse has shown that organization commitment and professional commitment are separable constructs with differential relationships to employee performance. Linda M. Bearse, "A Development of Measures of Job, Organizational, and Professional Commitment, and an Evaluation of Their Relationships with Performance," Ph.D. dissertation, Bowling Green University, 1985. See also Shore, "The Distinctiveness of Three Work Attitudes."

[166]Harry L. Wellbank et al., "Planning Job Progression for Effective Career Development and Human Resource Management," *Personnel*, 55, no. 2 (March-April 1978), 54–64.

[167]A recent study of 1,300 MIT graduates from the 1950s revealed a surprising amount of dissatisfaction at all levels of the organizational pyramid. A common factor in this dissatisfaction of employees in the various organizations was the failure of the organizations to treat employees according to their individual needs and interests. See Lotte Bailyn, "Ready, Set and No Place to Go," *Wharton Magazine*, 4, no. 2 (Winter 1980), 58–63.

[168]For a more complete discussion of learning principles and employee development, see Craig Eric Schneier, "Training and Development Programs: What Learning Theory and Research Have to Offer," *Personnel Journal*, 53, no. 4 (April 1974), 288–293, 300.

[169]For a discussion of goal-setting procedure, see Michael F. Wolff, "To Motivate, Set Goals," *Research Management*, 28, no. 6 (November/December 1985), 9–12; Ron Zemke, "Goal Setting Is the First Step in Any Performance Program," *Training*, 17, no. 7 (July 1980), A5, A7; Edwin A. Locke, Gary P. Latham, and Miriam Erez, "The Determinants of Goal Commitment," *Academy of Management Review*, 13, no. 1 (January 1988), 23–39; Gary P. Latham, Miriam Erez, and Edwin A. Locke, "Resolving Scientific Disputes by the Joint Design of Crucial Experiments by the Antagonists: Application to the Erez-Latham Dispute Regarding Participation in Goal Setting," *Journal of Applied Psychology*, 73, no.4 (November 1988), 753–772.

[170]The task inventory approach to job analysis allows jobs to be described as complements of duties. See Chapter 6 for a description of the task-inventory method of job analysis. Research by the Personnel Research Laboratory of the U.S. Air Force has shown

that employees can estimate the difficulty of tasks but not the difficulty of jobs. See Joseph M. Madden, "What Makes Work Difficult?" *Personnel Journal*, 41, no. 7 (July-August, 1962), 341–344.

[171] A recent study found that communication skills were significant predictors of the progress of female career employees. See Zalabak Pamela Shockley, Constance Courtney Staley, and Donald Dean Morley, "The Female Professional: Perceived Communication Proficiencies as Predictors of Organizational Advancement," *Human Relations*, 41, no. 7 (July 1988), 553–567.

[172] Employee career evaluations are invaluable for the refinement of career paths and career support systems.

[173] See p. 143 of Russell W. Burris, "Human Learning," pp. 131–146, in Marvin D. Dunnette, ed., *Handbook of Industrial and Organizational Psychology* (Chicago, IL: Rand McNally, 1976).

[174] See D. J. Levinson, "A Concept of Adult Development," *American Psychologist*, 41 (1986), 3–13.

[175] See "Counseling for Career Decisions," pp. 41–67 in David J. Srebalus, Robert P. Marinelli, and Jeffrey K. Messing, *Career Development: Concepts and Procedures* (Monterey, CA: Brooks/Cole, 1982).

[176] Daniel J. Levinson, *The Seasons of a Man's Life* (New York: Alfred A. Knopf, 1978), pp. 98–99.

[177] Recent research has shown that the mentor functions for many employees are performed by fellow employees and not by an organizationally appointed mentor. See James G. Clawson, "Is Mentoring Necessary?" *Training and Development Journal*, 39, no. 4 (April 1985), 36–39.

[178] A recent study of MIT graduates revealed a surprising amount of dissatisfaction caused by the failure of organizations to treat employees according to their individual needs and interests. Bailyn, "Ready, Set and No Place to Go."

[179] Gradually deteriorating situations tend not to trigger action or attention thresholds. The environmental trends that are combining to make planning for human resources necessary are insidious and are less effective than a dramatic event in helping to bring about strategic planning for human resources. See Angle et al., "Integrating Human Resource Management and Corporate Strategy," p. 64.

[180] See Pesso, pp. 76–77.

[181] Mirvis, "Formulating and Implementing Human Resource Management," p. 402.

[182] To illustrate the diversity of reasons organizations initiate human resource planning, at Lockheed Corporation, HRP was designed to (1) create dialogue between HR and general management, (2) create an appreciation of the interrelationship between planned business activities and support requirements, and (3) evaluate functional plans against strategic directions. At the American Hospital Supply Corporation, HRP was instituted to address management-succession issues resulting from expansive growth, such as personnel needs and career ladders. See Marshall-Mies, Yarkin-Levin, and Quaintance, "Human Resource Planning, Part 2." Further diversity is found, of course, if one looks at HRP in the public sector; see Marshall-Mies, Levin-Yarkin, and Quaintance, "Human Resource Planning, Part 1."

[183] It may seem to some readers that this approach depends too much on the statesmanship of key participants in an organization to recognize that additional participants need to be brought into the process. This, in the opinion of the author, is a reality of organization life. Organizations can never succeed beyond the capacities of their key participants.

[184] This list is an extension and revision of a listing of environmental variables by de Vas-

concellos Filho. See pp. 25–26 of Paulo de Vasconcellos Filho, "Environmental Analysis for Strategic Planning," *Managerial Planning*, 33, no. 4 (January-February 1985), 23–30, 36.

[185]Warren E. Clarke, "Long-Range Planning: The Need for Strategic Skills," *Journal of Business Strategy*, 5, no. 2 (Fall 1984), 101–102.

[186]A case in point occurred during 1980, in Caterpillar Corporation. Caterpillar was facing a corporate crisis brought on by stagnation within the company and by increased foreign competition. Personnel department representatives conducted a study and reported to top management a deep discontent among employees, with consequent sharp declines in motivation and morale. Top management reacted to the report by stigmatizing the personnel representatives as "choir boys" and issued a pamphlet complaining of the loss of the work ethic among employees, and stressing the need for more training for these employees and more investment in labor-saving equipment. Mirvis, "Formulating and Implementing Human Resource Management," p. 397.

[187]Hyatt Hotels Corporation uses employee opinion surveys to track the relationship between employee satisfaction and customer satisfaction. The surveys were found to be one of the best indexes of customer satisfaction, much better than customer comment cards left in guests' rooms. See page 34 of Tim R. Davis, "Two Conference Reports: Internal Markets–Part I: Satisfying Internal Customers: The Link to External Customer Satisfaction," *Planning Review*, 20, no. 1 (January/February, 1992), 34–37.

[188]See p. 272 of Tony Hain, "Commentary on Dyer," *Human Resource Management*, 22, no. 3 (Fall 1983), 272–273. Tony Hain, in 1983, was director of Plans Consolidation, Corporate Strategic Planning, General Motors Technical Center, General Motors Corporation.

[189]Hax, "A New Competitive Weapon," p. 78.

[190]This list is adapted from Hax, "A New Competitive Weapon," p. 78. An alternate approach to measuring the indirect outcomes of organization strategies is an audit procedure to measure the extent to which the HR department contributes to the carrying out of organization strategies. See John A. Hooper, "A Strategy for Increasing the Human Resource Department's Effectiveness," *Personnel Administrator*, 29, no. 6 (June 1984), 141–146, 148.

[191]This list is adapted from Hax, "A New Competitive Weapon," p. 78

[192]Cross-organizational exchange of data on employee satisfaction with the organization has been done by the Mayflower Group, which consists of 24 companies, including Xerox, GE, and Prudential Insurance. Employees in each company are asked to indicate level of agreement with 64 positive statements about the organization. These items are scored and reported individually and also as part of a composite score on each of 15 factors. See Schuster, "A Tool for Evaluating and Controlling," p. 81.

Chapter 5

Needs more info to give Hum R planning comp.

more problems ①

Tactical Planning for Human Resources

There is no organization unit that can be assigned the sole responsibility for carrying out the human resource function. Rather, this function is performed by a diverse group of persons scattered throughout the organization—from the chief executive officer to line managers and personnel who work in the human resource department. How can all these persons be persuaded to act in concert to achieve human resource strategies? The development of tactical policies will coordinate the activities of these diverse persons to accomplish strategic human resource objectives with minimal organization effort.

TACTICAL HUMAN RESOURCE PLANNING CONCEPTS

We have said that tactical planning is the allocation of an organization's resources to particular uses within organization units and job positions. At the functional level of planning, tactical planning becomes an allocation of human effort. Planners must choose the areas where they wish to direct effort on behalf of organization strategies and objectives. Then tactical policies are developed for these areas to ensure that the effort is directed throughout the entire organization. These tactical policies must take precedence over other, nontactical policies.

Two concepts are central to tactical planning for human resources, activity areas and policy set. *Activity areas* are clusters of activities that may be controlled by a common policy statement. A *policy set* is a group of policies that, together, control all tactical activity areas.

Activity Areas

Identification of activity areas is key to tactical planning for the human resource function. By selecting those areas that are important to the strategic plan, the tactical human resource planning committee concentrates control in those areas and helps to ensure that the intent of the strategic plan is realized.

Activity areas that may be of importance to strategic human resource plans of the organization include the following:

Appeal systems	Human resource flows
Benefits and services	Individual development
Career management	Organization development
Career counseling	Orientation
Compensation/rewards	Performance appraisal
Design of work	Placement
Discipline	Recruitment
Employee communications	Research
Employee influence	Scheduling of work
Employee relations	Selection
Employee support systems	Supervision
Employment planning	Training
Employment security	Union relations
Health and safety	

Selecting Tactical Activity Areas

There are two methods for identifying activity areas. One is judgmental selection and the other is empirical selection. *Judgmental selection* bases the choice of activity areas on contribution to human resource *strategies*. *Empirical selection* bases the choice on contribution to human resource *objectives*. Small organizations with operations at one or a few locations may use the judgmental selection method. Larger organizations with operations at many locations may use both the judgmental and the empirical selection methods.

Judgmental Selection

In judgmental selection, the committee prepares a list of human resource management activity areas believed to include all activities performed in the organization. (The list of activities given previously in this section may be used as a starting point for this task.) The committee then evaluates each area for its importance in carrying out the human resource strategies of the organization. This process uses a specially structured meeting, or series of meetings, designed to reduce the tendency of individual participants to conform thoughtlessly to group or leader opinions.[1] The structure of the meeting will allow committee members to develop a common and thorough understanding of both the activity areas and the human resource strategies; it will supply the information needed to select activity areas; and it will encourage the objective use of this information.

The meeting should make use of an outside facilitator who will facilitate the work of the group, not lead the group. This avoids another common tendency of meeting participants, to shift responsibility for results to the leader. The facilitator does the following[2]:

1. Prepares for the meeting by decomposing the task for the group. Decomposition of complex tasks into simple tasks greatly improves the accuracy of decisions made by allowing the use of information in a more efficient manner.[3]

The overall task of the committee is to answer the question: How important to our human resource strategies is each activity area, as compared to other activity areas?" The facilitator may break this question into a series of simpler questions, such as:

- What results does each activity area achieve?

    Persons involved in the activity may be asked to suggest results that they observe while performing the activity. For example, an observed result of the activity area "appeal systems" might be "equitable treatment of employees."
- How important is each of these results for each human resource strategy of the organization?

    Human resource theoreticians or practitioners may be asked to brief committee members on whether the outcomes of each activity area are preconditions for the carrying out of each strategy. Continuing the example, human resource theoreticians or practitioners may advise committee members that "equitable treatment of employees" is a precondition for the achievement of the strategy "creating organizational commitment" but would not likely be an important enabling condition for the strategy "ensuring an adequate supply of employee talent."
- On a scale of 1 to 10, how important is each activity area for each strategy?

    Answering this question requires the information gained by answering the preceding two questions.
- Now, on a scale of 1 to 10, how important to our human resource strategies is each activity area as compared to all other activity areas?

    An answer to this question is obtained by using the results of all of the preceding questions.

2. Provides an opportunity for all members to participate and especially encourages the expression of minority opinions.

3. Encourages the group to suspend evaluation until the analysis is complete.

4. Avoids introducing his or her own ideas to the group.

5. Provides for the preparation of a written report outlining the group consensus of

- The relative importance of activity areas
- The activity areas to be used as tactical areas
- Why each selected activity area is important to each strategy

Exhibit 5-1 gives examples of the kinds of activity areas that might be selected by tactical committees for the strategies outlined in Chapter 4. Not all committees will select the same activity areas for similar strategies. Special circumstances will affect activity areas selected. For example, for a firm in a continuous-process industry, where the organization must be open 24 hours a day, 7 days a week, such as a hospital, "scheduling of work" may be an important activity area for most strategies pursued by the organization. For a firm in a discontinuous-process industry, where the organization need be open only limited hours and days of the week, such as a commercial bank, "scheduling of work" may be an unimportant activity area for all strategies pursued by the organization.

Empirical Selection

The empirical selection method takes advantage of the fact that different operating locations of an organization tend to emphasize different human resource management activities. The locations are studied to determine the amount to which those activities they emphasize contribute to successful achievement of human resource objectives. The activity areas found to contribute most are targeted for tactical use.

Activity areas may be identified by the following steps:[4]

1. Conduct an audit of human resource activities in each location.

For the audit, measures are selected or developed to determine the extent and effectiveness of activities in the various locations. These measures are based on objective indexes[5] or on opinions of recipients of human resource services. Data for the objective measures are found in company records of location operations. Opinions are obtained by surveying employees, managerial and nonmanagerial, in each company location.[6]

2. Perform a factor analysis to group the activites into activity areas and to determine the extent and effectiveness of activities in each activity area.

This analysis will yield factor scores that will be used in step 4. A discussion of factor analysis may be found in most basic statistical texts and will not be discussed here.[7]

3. Develop measures of the contribution of each location to the achievement of organization human resource objectives. These measures will be applied to the human resource activities of the various locations.

Measures may be based on objective indexes available in organization records or on opinions of outside observers and organization employees, especially higher level executives. The exact measures used by an organization will depend on the particular objectives established in strategic planning.

Following is a list of strategic human resource objectives taken from Chapter 4 and an example of a possible objective measure for each:

STRATEGIES	ACTIVITY AREAS	
Managing technological change	Compensation/rewards Organization development Research	Selection Supervision Training
Ensuring adequate supply of HR talent	Design of work Employment planning	Human resource flows Training
Promoting employee development	Human resource flows Individual development	Training
Promoting customer service	Design of work Employee support systems Research	Selection Supervision
Improving human resource productivity	Design of work Employee influence Employee support systems Organization development	Research Training Union relations
Creating organization commitment	Appeal systems Compensation/rewards Employee support systems Employment security	Human resource flows Orientation Performance appraisal Supervision
Encouraging participation	Design of work Employee communication Employee influence	Supervision Training
Keeping employees satisfied	Employee communication Employee relations Employee support systems	Recruitment Research Selection
Focusing on career employees	Career counseling Career management Design of work	Employment planning Individual development

Exhibit 5-1.   Tactical Activity Areas for Selected Human Resource Strategies

Being a socially responsible employer—number of equal employment opportunity complaints filed by job applicants and employees at a location

Developing human resource competencies for competitive advantage—number of invited presentations by employees at meetings of professional associations

Making sound investments in human resources—provision for human capital budgeting at each location

Respecting the rights of individual employees—existence of a sound grievance procedure for nonunion employees

Being considered a good place to work—employee responses at each location on quality-of-work-life surveys

Managing human resources in a state-of-the-art manner—average amount of time between the first publication of a new idea for human resource management and its consideration for use in a location

4. Perform a regression analysis to establish relationships between extent and effectiveness of activity areas and achievement of organization human resource objectives. The analysis will reveal those activity areas that are very important to the achievement of strategic objectives.[8]

Comparison of the Selection Methods

The judgmental method and the empirical method are effective tools for selecting activity areas important to strategic plans. The judgmental focuses on strategies; the empirical on strategic objectives. A company with just one or two locations is limited to the judgmental method, but companies with multiple locations may realize the advantages of the independent use of both methods.

Because each method provides separate evidence about topics that should be covered in the policies for the activity areas, a comprehensive analysis is achieved. The independent results of the two methods act as a check on the accuracy of the strategic planning. There should be considerable overlap in the tactical areas designated by the different methods. If little overlap exists, the committee should question whether the strategies chosen are appropriate for the organization's strategic objectives.

Policy Set

Developing Policies within Tactical Activity Areas

Once activity areas have been selected to serve as tactical activity areas, policies must be developed for these areas. Policies adopted must be consistent with the organization philosophy respecting human resources and with the human resource objectives and strategies. At least some policies are likely to exist already for each area. These policies must be revised to serve tactical purposes.

The analyses done to select activity areas will suggest specific topics and even specific wording for policy statements. If activity areas are chosen using the judgmental method, members of the tactical planning committee will have prepared a report stating the reasons they feel the carrying out of strategies will involve each activity area selected. These reasons will likely point out important decisions that should be controlled by policy. For example, the activity area concerned with "compensation/rewards" would likely be chosen if one of the strategies was "creating organizational commitment." It has been shown that equitable treatment in compensation is important for building employee commitment. Reasoning suggests that a policy statement should be drafted as follows: "In determining wage and salary structures, internal equity will be given priority over other considerations."

If activity areas are chosen by the empirical method, attention to the measures included in each factor (activity area) will provide clues to important decisions that should be controlled by policy. Those measures more heavily loaded on a factor should be given greater emphasis in policy development. To illustrate this point, assume that the most important measure included in an activity area concerned with "compensation/rewards" is the "extent to which positions are evaluated in such a way that equity is maintained throughout the plant." A secondary measure associated with a less important activity area, "staffing/EEO," is "average time required to fill vacancies."[9] These results suggest a policy as follows, "In determining wage and salary structures, internal equity of individual wages and salaries will be given priority over external equity."

In practice, some differences in policies suggested by the two methods will occur, and judgment must be used by the tactical planning committee to reconcile those differences.

TACTICAL HUMAN RESOURCE PLANNING PROCESS

Chapter 3 contains a general discussion of the tactical planning process. That discussion concerns the makeup of the tactical business planning committee and of guidelines for the design of tactical structures. That discussion is, for the most part, relevant to tactical planning for the human resource function and will not be repeated here.

The Tactical Human Resource Planning Committee

The tactical human resource planning committee may not need to be as large as the tactical planning committee for enterprise, group, and business unit level planning because there is less work to do. Whereas enterprise, group, and business unit tactical committees must design organization structure, organization culture, and budgetary processes, the tactical human resource planning committee must design a set of tactical policies.

However, it is essential that the tactical human resource planning committee be representative of the entire organization. As mentioned previously, a diverse group of persons scattered throughout the organization must carry out tactical policies. If all these persons are to be persuaded to act in concert to achieve human resource strategies, there must be a high level of agreement with, and acceptance of, these policies.

The committee should be as small as possible, consistent with the requirement that the various facets of the organization be well represented.

Guidelines for the Design of a Tactical Policy Set

The guidelines for the design of distributive structures discussed in Chapter 3 apply to the distributive structure tactical policy set. These guidelines, applied to tactical policy set, are the following:

- The tactical policy set must be compatible with the other distributive structures—organization structure, organization culture, and financial budgets. To further this compatibility, the committee that designs the human resource tactical policy set and the subcommittees that design each of the other distributive structures should have overlapping memberships.
- The tactical policy set must allocate human resource management effort for equal incremental return.
- The tactical policy set must function as an integrated whole to implement strategic plans. Tactical policy set and human resource strategies must be in a mutually interactive relationship such that each is adjusted for optimum effectiveness of the relationship.
- The tactical policy set must conform both to organization design and organization identity.
- The tactical policy set must leave room for subsequent decision making by line managers and human resource department personnel in day-to-day operations.
- The tactical policy set must include a policy statement requiring review periodically and whenever strategic plans are changed.
- The tactical policy set must produce desired behavior.

SUMMARY

Tactical planning for the human resource function consists of designing a set of policies that drive the daily operations of human resource management toward human resource strategies and objectives. The key to good tactical planning is the careful selection from among the many possible activity areas those areas for which tactical policies are to be developed. Attempting to control all activity areas tends to dissipate effort and is uneconomical control.

Activity areas of importance to strategic plans may be chosen by the judgmental method or by the empirical method. In the judgmental method, activity areas are chosen by considering a comprehensive list of standard activity areas and weighing each for its importance to the carrying out of human resource strategies of the organization. This can be done only if planners are objective and understand thoroughly both the activity areas and the strategies. Proper structure of their task is important here.

In the empirical method, activity areas are chosen that are important to strategic human resource objectives. An audit is conducted of the extent and effectiveness with which human resource activities are carried out in the organization. A factor analysis of the audit measures is conducted. The factor analysis surfaces from among the activities clusters of activities performed as a unit. Factor scores—representing the extent and effectiveness with which activities in each activity area are carried out in each location—are regressed against measures of the extent to which each location contributes to organization strategic human resource objectives. The regression formula provides a basis for choice of activity areas of prime importance to strategic human resource objectives. This method is possible only in multilocation organizations.

In organizations with a number of operating locations, it is wise to use both methods to determine activity areas because each method provides different but, in the main, complementary information about policies needed in the organization. Using this information, organizations may draft specific policies that constitute a tactical policy set to drive the organization toward its strategic objectives for human resources.

LEARNING EXERCISES

Case Analysis

If you have the opportunity for small-group discussion, you may use the procedure suggested for Case 1 in Chapter 1.

In Case 5, "Westview Company, Inc.," John Stoltz, human resource manager, is faced with another important challenge in his very exciting career at the fast-growing company. He must guide the committee that is to choose the policies that will direct human resource management in support of human resource objectives.

Develop a work plan for John that will enable him and the committee to work well together and to do a thorough and complete job of considering all possible policy alternatives as they arrive at a set of key policy choices. You should develop recommendations for the following parts of John's task:

1. Preparation of information. Has John enough information for the initial meeting of the committee? What additional information, if any, should he collect during the two weeks before the meeting is held? Give examples of the types of information he must collect.

2. Opening remarks to the committee. Develop a background statement describing the task of the committee and the importance of the task. Be sure the statement distinguishes tactical policies from other nontactical policies.

3. Proposed work plan. Develop a step-by-step plan for the work of the committee. John will present this plan for discussion at the first meeting. If the plan holds up under committee review, it will provide a framework for the group's planning.

Activity

Secure a recent issue of several business newspapers or business journals, such as the *Wall Street Journal, Business Week, Fortune*, or *Forbes*. (Most libraries hold these.) Scan several issues for examples of planning. How much attention is given to function-level planning for human resources as compared to planning at enterprise, group (strategic business unit), and business level? As compared to other functional areas, such as marketing and finance? Collect representative samples for each of these levels and functional areas. If your findings are typical of business news reporting generally, what are the implications, if any, for human resource planning?

Discussion Question

1. What are the advantages of having as many people as possible involved in human resource planning? Are there instances when human resource planning should be done by a small group? Explain your answers carefully.

Endnotes

[1] Research shows repeatedly that the typical meeting does little to improve the decisions of individual participants. See J. Scott Armstrong, *Long-Range Forecasting: From Crystal Ball to Computer*, 2nd ed. (New York: John Wiley, 1985), pp. 120–121.

[2] This procedure is adapted from one developed by Maier and Maier. They found their method could increase accuracy in decision making from less than 50 percent to 84 percent. Step 5 was not part of their procedure. See Norman R. F. Maier and Richard A. Maier, "An Experimental Test of the Effects of 'Developmental' vs 'Free' Discussions on the Quality of Group Decisions," *Journal of Applied Psychology*, 41, no. 5 (December 1957), 320–323; see p. 121.

[3] Armstrong, *Long-Range Forecasting*, pp. 57–64.

[4] Gomez-Mejia devised a method for relating audit measures to criteria for organization success. This method has been adapted to identify activity areas that contribute to human resource objectives. Luis R. Gomez-Mejia, "Dimensions and Correlates of the Personnel Audit as an Organizational Assessment Tool," *Personnel Psychology*, 38, no. 2 (Summer 1985), 293–308.

[5] An index measure does not directly measure effectiveness or extent of an activity, but it does *indicate* or *suggest* that the activity is extensively carried out or is effectively carried out.

[6] For an example of measures used in an audit, see the section "Human Resource Audit" in Chapter 8.

[7]See, for example, Joseph F. Hair, Rolph E. Anderson, Ronald L. Tatham, and Bernie J. Grablowsky, *Multivariate Data Analysis,* 2nd ed., (Tulsa, OK: Petroleum Publishing Co., 1987).

[8]It is possible that activities within a policy area are not causes of the associated performance. This can be tested through further statistical analysis. In most instances members of the tactical planning committee who are intimately familiar with the organization will know whether a lack of causal relationship is a possibility. Where there is a lack of causal relationship, policy cannot be used as a tool to direct organization effort toward strategic objectives.

[9]These examples occurred in a factor analysis conducted by Gomez-Mejia. See Gomez-Mejia, "Dimensions and Correlates of the Personnel Audit," p. 297.

Part 3

Operational Planning
for Human Resources

Operational planning deals with work composed of repetitive cycles. These cycles may vary from a few months to years in length. The work is much the same in consecutive cycles. Repetitive cycles give operational planning its distinctive features. Each cycle presents opportunities to use feedback for continued incremental learning. And operational planning is action-oriented; learning occurs while doing—planning and doing are contemporaneous.

Part III begins with a discussion of topics important to all planning—meeting information needs, defining the future, and evaluating. They will be discussed in the context of operational planning for human resources because this level of planning allows constant use of information, future definition, and evaluation as operations proceeds through the cycles.

The latter part of Part III is devoted to operational planning as it is applied to human resource flows. People enter organizations. People move among jobs within organizations. People leave organizations. These human resource flows are the underlying events around which the entire human resource management activity is structured. Planning for the strategic use of these flows at the operational level ensures that the overall human resource plans for the organization are carried out in day-to-day operations.

Chapter 6

Meeting the Information Needs of Human Resource Planning

Information is the raw material of planning. Planning requires more information and more kinds of information than other forms of decision making.[1] If information becomes inadequate for the planning task, the quality of the planning rapidly deteriorates.

AN INFORMATION SYSTEM FOR HUMAN RESOURCES

An information system is an interrelated set of procedures and processes to provide information for decisions. Information is data that have been processed so that they are meaningful. It adds to the representation of an idea. It corrects or confirms previous information. It has surprise value. It tells us something we did not know.[2] Many organizations have computer-assisted information systems, but this is not a definitive feature of an information system.

An information system especially developed for human resource management is referred to as an HRIS—a human resource information system. Human resource management, when it does not include the human resource planning function, requires only a basic HRIS. It typically includes only information needed to support the work of the human resource department in carrying out staffing, training and development, appraisal, compensation, and safety and health functions. If this basic HRIS is computer-supported, it is likely to include a transaction processing system or a management information system. Typically, the sole or primary user of this system will be the human resource department.[3]

Functions of an Information System

An information system provides for the accumulation, maintenance, and delivery of information. Information is *accumulated* by gathering, processing, and storing information. Consider, for example, the accumulation of information about a job. Suitable information is gathered through interviews with experts about the job and with current job holders. The information is then processed by deleting extraneous information, deciding among divergent information, and putting the information in a logical arrangement that promotes its understanding. Finally, the information is stored in a readily accessible configuration, such as labeled data in a data base or as a job description.

Information is *maintained* by ensuring its security and by updating it. For example, the security of a job description is ensured in part by giving it an official stamp of approval. The integrity of this particular description of the job is then protected. Other descriptions of the job are not allowed to serve as the official description. If the way the job is actually performed changes, either the official description must be changed to maintain its accuracy or the way the job is performed must be brought into conformity with the official job description.

Information is *delivered* to potential users in a configuration and at a time most suited for its use. For example, it is inefficient for all employees in an organization to maintain continuously descriptions of all jobs, either in their human memories or in their personal files. But when an employee is offered an opportunity to move to another job, he or she will want a description of that job.

Repositories of Information

Information is accumulated in three major kinds of repositories: employees of an organization, technologies used in the organization, and subsidiary information storage devices.

Highly motivated and committed employees are efficient repositories of large stores of information. They store in short-term memory large amounts of specific information that they use on a daily basis. They store in long-term memory specific information organized around such concepts as organization history. Employees may be classified according to the kinds of information they store, as professionals, including professional managers; as technicians; as craftsmen; as clerical workers; and as operative employees. Each stores a different kind of information useful for doing the work of the organization. Occupations listed first, such as professionals, tend to be repositories for information acquired principally outside the organization; occupations listed last, such as operative employees, tend to be repositories for information acquired principally inside the organization.

Technologies are methods for doing work. Technologies accumulate information in the designs of methods for doing work. As technologies are used, people discover ways to improve them and this information is built into the technologies.

This continual use, discovery, and integration of the information continues. The technologies used to perform human resource management functions, such as the training of employees, represents large amounts of accumulated information.

Stores of information accumulated in people and in technologies are supplemented by information accumulated in subsidiary storage devices. These devices include computer and paper files and data bases.

Employees, technologies, and subsidiary storage devices are necessary stores of information in the modern organization. Each is a part of an HRIS. A deficiency in the information stored in any one of these repositories can threaten the effective operation of the human resource management function.

Official and Unofficial Information

An information system consists of both official and unofficial stores of information. By "official" is meant those work-related stores of information that employees are directed to accumulate. By "unofficial" is meant those work-related stores of information that are accumulated at the discretion of employees or that are accumulated unintentionally as a by-product of doing work. Stores of information may be public or private. Examples of typically official and unofficial stores of information, both public and private, are shown in Exhibit 6-1.

Unofficial Stores of Information

      Manager's recall of personal information about subordinates
      Unscheduled study by new employee of jobs other than own
      Plan by employee for proper sequencing of assignments for day
      Supervisor's recall of work assignment preferences of subordinates
      Personal career plan by individual employee
      Employee's personal record of work performance during month

Official Stores of Information

      Recall by interviewer of training for conduct of interview
      Supervisor recall of employee performance during year
      Required procedures for considering employee leave request
      Assessment center procedures for screening candidates
      Policy statement regarding compensation practices
      Data on numbers of employees hired per job candidate screened

---

Exhibit 6-1. Examples of Official and Unofficial Stores of Information in People, Technologies, and Subsidiary Storage Devices.

AN INFORMATION SYSTEM FOR HUMAN RESOURCE PLANNING

When an organization begins human resource planning, the HRIS must become more complex and information-rich. Human resource planning requires much more information and different kinds of information than does human resource management alone. Human resource planners in the early stages of planning must look at the HRIS of their organization to determine the changes necessary to support the human resource planning process.

Kinds of Information

Planning decisions, as compared to management decisions, are concerned with effectiveness rather than efficiency. Efficiency is achieved by performing a given task as well as possible in relation to some predefined performance criteria. Effectiveness is achieved by identifying what tasks should be done and establishing criteria for determining whether the proper tasks are being done.[4] Planning, then, must consider both a broader range and a greater number of alternatives. Data must encompass the external environment, the entire organization, and the past and future of the environment and of the organization. Qualitative information must be included also to allow choices among alternatives.

The information needs of an organization will depend on the comprehensiveness of the approach to human resource planning. As an organization attempts to achieve additional human resource objectives and to utilize additional human resource strategies, it must do more comprehensive planning and will need more and better information. Exhibit 6-2 lists the kinds of information that a firm engaging in comprehensive HRP is likely to need.

The Role of the Computer

Computers, because of their ability to process large amounts of data, are almost indispensable to an information system. They contribute much to the creation of an information-rich environment.

Linkages of Repositories

Advances in computer-based information technologies are allowing the accumulation, maintenance, and delivery of large amounts of information at a low cost per unit. This potential for manipulating information has made feasible dramatic advances in information system capabilities through better linkages of people, technologies, and subsidiary information storage devices. These linkages take the form of computer-aided management and artificial intelligence.[5]

Enterprise/group/business objectives and strategies
HR objectives and strategies
Data for evaluating HR planning
Characteristics of CEO
   Attitudes/values regarding HR
   HR skills and knowledge
Characteristics of line managers
   Attitudes/values regarding HR
   HR skills and knowledge
Characteristics of HR specialists
   Attitudes/values regarding HR
   HR skills and knowledge
Characteristics, human resources
   Work classifications
     Job titles—numbers, distribution
   Personal: age, dependents
   Education/training
     Levels of achievement
     Specialties developed
   Capabilities
     Experience (jobs and tasks)
     Performances
     Key abilities and attributes
   Career plans
     Target positions
     Training, education goals
     Career path preferences
Characteristics, work to be done
   Jobs
     Complements of tasks
     Motivating potential
     Reward opportunities
   Tasks
     Expected changes, rates of change
     Key requirements
       Results, behaviors

Characteristics of organization
   Organization philosophy
   Organization structure
     Number and mix of units
       Companies, groups, divisions, departments, sections
       Strategic units/support units
     Number and mix of levels
       Institutional, entrepreneurial, policy, operational
     Number and mix of locations
       Domestic/foreign, headquarters, region, plant, office
     Number and mix of jobs, positions
       Generalist/specialist, staff/line, managers/nonmanagers
   Organization culture
     Behaviors reinforced
     Influence of staffing process
     Employee influence on culture-formation process
   Budgetary processes
     Influence of budgets on strategic plans
Characteristics of HR domain
   Sectoral environment
     Cultural, economic, social, political, technological, demographic
   Relationships environment
     Outside relationships—types, objects of exchange
Value of human resources
   Employees—manager/nonmanager, professional/nonprofessional
   Human resource systems—acquisition, development, maintenance, compensation

Exhibit 6-2.   Information Needs for a Firm Doing Comprehensive HRP

Computer-aided management includes three kinds of systems: transaction processing systems, management information systems, and decision support systems. The degree of structure of the tasks to be performed by the managers determines which system is used. Transaction processing systems are used for highly structured tasks, such as handling hourly payroll. Management information systems are used for moderately structured tasks, such as preparing reports about trends in the use of overtime. Decision support systems are used for unstructured tasks, such as planning to ensure the optimal balancing of overtime costs and the costs of hiring temporary employees.

Artificial intelligence is the use of computers to perform tasks that normally require human intelligence. Artificial intelligence consists of expert systems and policy-capturing models. Expert systems are computer applications that guide the performance of less knowledgeable employees in tasks that usually require experience and specialized knowledge of a subject matter expert.[6] Policy-capturing models are similar to expert systems; they are computer applications that guide the performance of less knowledgeable employees in tasks that usually require experience and extensive knowledge of organization policy.

Decision Support System

Computer ask questions

Of the various kinds of computer-based systems, the one most extensively used to support the planning function is a decision support system.[7] A decision support system (DSS) is, in itself, a complete information system, as it performs all three information system functions of accumulating, maintaining, and delivering information. Formally defined, a DSS is a computer-based system to allow the integrated use of computer, manager, and decision environment in support of management decision making.[8] The term *support* in decision support system is a key to using a DSS appropriately. A DSS supports the decision-making process. It should not make decisions for the participants.

Managers differ widely in their decision-making styles, skills, and knowledge.[9] A DSS supports decision making by individual managers but does not necessarily endorse fully the decision-making style of an individual manager. On the one hand, a DSS allows managers to exercise direct, personal control over the support system;[10] on the other hand, a DSS assists managers to move toward a more effective decision process.[11] The end objective of a DSS is to help decision makers develop and use more effectively their unique styles, skills, and knowledge.[12]

Planning tends to be an iterative and evolutionary activity within an organization. Planners learn as they plan and, as a result, change the way they plan. As planners are exposed to more information relevant to the planning task, their understanding of planning itself, and of what they wish planning to accomplish for the organization, changes. For these reasons, it is difficult to decide in advance what kinds of support and how much support to provide for human resource planning.

Given the nature of planning, a DSS to support the function must have available generalized system capabilities with reserved "as-needed" capabilities.[13] Four basic components of a DSS that support and enhance individual decision-making skills are[14]   → graphs & tables

- Specific *representations* of continuously updated information, such as graphs, tables, and pictures, to provide planners with more accurate conceptualizations of current conditions and, therefore, of decision problems.
- *Operations* on data to support the decision-making activities. For example, the computer may
  - Allow queries of data bases to support intelligence
  - Allow "what-if" analyses of data bases to support design
  - Allow comparison of differences among alternative solutions to support choice
- *Memory aids* to support the use of the representations and operations. Examples are
  - Prompter messages to advise decision makers of logical next steps in decision making   Exp. Do you really want to delete this
  - Automatic reminder messages to warn decision makers of common errors in decision making
  - Computer "remembering" of decision steps previously used by a decision maker, combined with prompter messages to allow the development of progressively more complete decision processes tailored to specific decision makers
- *Control aids* to help the decision maker to control the way these representations, operations, and memory aids are used. Examples are allowing the decision maker to customize the representation used by choosing among optional features of the representations, providing readily understood explanations of what each operation does, and allowing the decision maker to introduce his or her own prompter messages into a preformatted decision sequence.   help msg. Tutorial

Once the DSS is introduced, both planners and DSS designers must resist the inherent tendency for migration from thinking of planning as an unstructured task toward thinking of it as a narrowly defined task. This change in thinking may be caused by changes in the ability of planners to use, and their preferences for, computer support. As they see the rapidity with which the computer can handle the structured subtasks of planning, it is tempting to turn the planning function as a whole into a structured task that can be performed by the computer. Planners may come to make simplistic assumptions about planning. They may no longer be satisfied with the "soft," generalized system capabilities of the DSS and may instead demand "hard," streamlined, powerful operators.[15]

Simplistic assumptions about planning and hard system capabilities allow highly efficient planning with apparently well-supported decisions that are valid only in the short run and within the assumptions made. The DSS thus developed is an efficiency-improving information system appropriate for relatively structured administrative problems, rather than the originally envisioned planning system appropriate for improving decision effectiveness.[16]

A DSS is a decision support system, not a planning system in itself. The migration effect can be avoided if planners as a group insist on using the DSS to help evolve a sound planning approach, an approach in which they continually grow in their ability to produce effective, long-term planning decisions.

MANAGING AN HRIS FOR HUMAN RESOURCE PLANNING

Determining the Kinds of Information Needed

The information system must support the planning needs of everyone who participates in the planning process. Human resource planning is done for the organization as a whole by persons drawn from and representing the entire organization. Frequently, planners will wish to include in some way every person in the organization, as well as some persons from outside the organization. The decisions about whom to include in the planning and the role these persons will play are basic to the design of an information system for planning.

The information provided must support the planning process as a whole and each of the stages of planning—strategic, tactical, and operational. For the planning process itself, information will be needed about the people available to assist with the planning. For strategic planning, information will be needed about the environment. Strategic planning, along with tactical and operational planning, will need information about the organization—its structure, culture, and budgetary processes. For operational planning, information about the movements of employees through the organization and about key persons and systems that support those movements will be needed. All three stages of planning require information to allow a definition of the future and an evaluation of the present status.

Because planning tends to be iterative and evolutionary, it is not possible for planners to determine in advance all the information needed for planning. However, with an awareness of the importance of complete information for planning and of the kinds of information that may be useful, they can build an initial information base for planning and can modify the system as planning evolves and as their needs for information become apparent.

Choosing Repositories

When deciding on the storage of information, information specialists should consider the combination of repositories that will allow storage and retrieval of the most useful information in a cost-efficient manner.

People can store vast amounts of information useful for planning, and can adapt and update this information, particularly when motivated by their work and when committed to the organization. People are especially important repositories for storing abstract concepts and ideas that are difficult to describe and measure.

Organizations can inexpensively enhance the storage of information in their employees by arranging work experiences appropriately and by sharing widely the available information. Somewhat more expensive approaches to storing information in people are the hiring of educated and/or experienced people, and keeping the information stored in them current through training and development. The cost of storing information can escalate sharply if turnover of employees is high.

A technology can be a highly efficient repository for the storage of information to be used for very specific purposes. Of the relatively few technologies that have been developed for human resource planning, the most important are those that give basic guidelines on how to do the planning process. Organizations develop their own technologies as they learn how to plan. Quite sophisticated technologies can be built around decision support systems. These systems can be used, for example, to track and plan for the management of human resource flows in an organization. Technologies allow the efficient storage and use of information about how to perform the planning function and allow the accumulation of additional information as it is developed. Technologies can be expensive to acquire, and the information contained in the technology can become obsolete if not maintained.

Subsidiary storage devices are superior passive stores of information. They store information over a long period of time that can be stored by people only in short-term memory. It is relatively easy to update the information stored in files and data bases.

At times the use of outside repositories should be considered as an alternative to storing information within the organization's HRIS. Some examples would be

- Using information, as needed, in the subsidiary storage devices of other organizations—for example, accessing outside computer data bases of information useful for human resource planning
- Hiring consultants for short-term work that recurs infrequently rather than retaining an equivalent employee on a full-time basis
- Purchasing computer software with prepackaged technologies

Promoting Effectiveness

Vast amounts of information are available to planners. Unless information is delivered in usable form, planners will be overwhelmed and their information needs will not be met. The information delivered to planners must be timely, current, accurate, reliable, and suited to their special planning needs.

Human resource planners may examine the effectiveness of the HRIS in their organization by considering the following questions:

- Do we usually have the information needed to make decisions?
- How frequently are sound decisions made because information was correct and available? How frequently are poor decisions made because information was incorrect, lacking, or out of date?

- What were the monetary effects of those sound or poor decisions?
- Was information available at an economical cost that could have helped to avoid the poor decision?
- Are people involved in planning aware of the need to consider the costs and benefits of all information uses?
- How frequently is information made available to or used by planners in a wasteful manner?

While asking these questions, human resource planners, who also may be operating managers, must remember that an information system intended for planning must be subjected to a different kind of evaluation than is a system for other parts of the management function. Because human resource planning includes many more unstructured and nonroutine activities, an information system requires much more redundancy and allowance for trial and error.[17]

SUGGESTED IMPROVEMENTS FOR HRISs

Two important information areas that are not well supported in most organizations and offer great potential for improving human resource planning are information about the work done in the organization and accounting information about investments in the human resources of the organization.

Information About Work

Information about work is basic to the human resource planning function. Human resource specialists have tended to leave the study of the work people do in an organization to industrial engineers and human factors engineers. The information derived from such studies often is of little use for human resource planning.

Work analysis is a study of the work that must be done by employees to use the technologies adopted by the organization. A number of well-established methods of work analysis now exist.[18] Of these methods, the one uniquely suited for the planning function is the task inventory method, developed by the U.S. Air Force Human Resources Research Laboratory to study the work performed in a wide range of civilian and military jobs.[19] A task inventory consists of a detailed list of all tasks, perhaps 500 or more, that may be performed in a job family, occupation, group of occupations, or all jobs in the organization. Collection of data about the tasks performed in these jobs allows the identification of all tasks carried out in every job and allows an analysis of the distribution of those tasks among jobs. An example may illustrate how this information can be helpful in planning.

Assume that all the tasks performed in all exempt positions in an organization have been identified and that a factor analysis[20] to group these tasks reveals a group of tasks (a factor) that might be termed "interfaces with a government regulatory body."[21] When the factor scores of individual jobs are examined, it is found that a number of jobs in different parts of the organization have, as part of the job, the duty "interfaces with a government regulatory body." Furthermore, this duty is fairly standard throughout the organization; it includes much the same tasks, whether it occurs in the finance, marketing, or human resource department. Now that this duty has been identified, planners deal with such questions as

> How much does successful performance of this duty contribute to competitive advantage?
> Is performance of this duty important to the carrying out of our human resource strategies?
> Is this duty likely to be performed more frequently in the future? Should the duty be added to additional jobs?
> Will employees need additional training for this duty in the future?

Breaking work down into basic units such as a task reveals commonalities of work across jobs and allows the identification of units of work with strategic importance. More studies of work by human resource specialists are needed. Information gained from such studies may be used to further the human resource planning process by enhancing planners' understanding of the work that must be done by the organization and its human resources.

Information about the Value of Human Resources

As early as 1922, it was recognized that organizations in the United States lacked systematic, reliable methods for valuing their human resources, and that this shortcoming was hampering the ability of organizations to manage their human resources responsibly.[22] In the 1960s, interest in human resource valuation among academicians blossomed with the writings of Rensis Likert.[23] At the same time, human resource valuation achieved notice among practitioners by attention given to the practice of human resource accounting at the R. G. Barry Corporation.[24] As human resource planning becomes more important to the success of an organization, attention should be given to human resource accounting.

Most professionally managed organizations that do human resource planning appear to have adopted some method for valuing their human resources. These methods usually are tailor-made by organizations for their own needs.[25] Typical of these methods, and one of the most practical that has been published, was that used in the Upjohn Company during the 1980s.[26] As shown in Exhibit 6-3, Upjohn tracked measures of employee costs as a percentage of total costs, expected expenditures required for each new hire, return on expenditures for human resources, and return on combined expenditures for human resources and capital. These measures were developed at the enterprise, company, division, and business levels.

Methods of human resource valuation such as the one used in the Upjohn Company allow the tracking of expenditures on human resources and a comparison

	1978	1983	Used as a Measure of
Cost of human resources[1] expressed as a percentage of total expenses[2]	38%	Up significantly; figure not reported	Employee costs as a percentage of total costs
Ratio of expected total future cost of a new hire[3] to current starting salary[4]	117	134	Expected investment for each new hire approved
Pretax earnings[5] expressed as a percentage of the cost of human resources	52% (1977)	Down significantly: figure not reported.	Return on investment in human resources
Pretax earnings expressed as a percentage of value added[6]	36%	32%	Return on investment in human resources and capital

Notes:
[1]Total cost of payroll, benefits and employee taxes.
[2]Total sales less pretax earnings.
[3]Total expenditures expected for typical current new hire, now to normal retirement.
[4]Annual salary at time of hire.
[5]Earnings before payment of required taxes.
[6]Total sales less purchased goods and services.

Exhibit 6-3.   Measures Used for Human Resource Valuation at Upjohn Company
Source: Henry L. Dahl, Jr., "Measuring the Human ROI," *Retail Control*, 51, No. 5 (January 1983), pp. 9–19.

of trends in expenditures on human resources with trends in expenditures on capital resources. Although this accumulation of information is a step in the right direction, it does not allow placing a value on an organization's investments in human resources, nor does it allow a distinction between investments and current expenses.[27]

    Imagine that you are on the human resource planning committee of a service organization. You are considering whether to adopt a strategy that will require sending 1,000 key managers to a training program during the coming year at a direct cost of $3,500 each. The total cost of training is 1,000 × $3,500 = $3,500,000. This training and the strategy it supports are expected to improve organization performance over a period of at least ten years before the strategy becomes fully obsolete. Because some of the return from this training will be received after the current accounting period (assumed to be one year) has passed, the expenditure can be considered an investment. Viewed as an investment, and assuming that straight-line depreciation is used, only $350,000 of the total cost of $3.5 million would be charged against this year's income; the balance of $3.15 million would be charged over the remainder of the ten-year depreciation period at a rate of $350,000 per year. Viewed as a current expense, as would be typical in most organizations, a cost of $3.5 million would be charged against this year's income. Studies suggest that you will be more likely to adopt the strategy when the expenditure is presented as an investment than when it is presented as a current expense.[28]

Organizations need to strike a balance between spending for today and spending for tomorrow. To strike this balance, information is needed about how much they are spending for today, how much they are spending for tomorrow, and the rate at which they are accumulating value in their human resources.

SUMMARY

Information is the raw material of planning. A quality planning effort cannot be accomplished without sound and adequate information. Information is provided in an organization by an interrelated set of procedures and processes known as an information system. An information system accumulates, maintains, and delivers information.

An information system especially developed for the human resource management function is called an HRIS—a human resource information system. Organizations accumulate information needed for the human resource management function in official and unofficial repositories, both public and private. Three major information repositories are employees of an organization, technologies used in the organization, and subsidiary storage devices.

Employees may be classified according to the kinds of information they store as professionals, including professional managers; technicians; craftsmen; clerical workers; and operative employees. Occupations listed first, such as professionals, tend to be repositories for knowledge acquired outside the organization; occupations listed last, such as operative employees, tend to be repositories for knowledge acquired inside the organization. In larger organizations of the U.S economy, human resource technologies are highly developed. The designs of the technologies represent progressive accumulations of information developed over many years. Stores of information accumulated in people and technologies are supplemented by information accumulated in subsidiary storage devices. These devices include computer and paper files and data bases.

When an organization begins human resource planning, the HRIS must become more complex and information-rich. Computers allow extensive storage and retrieval of information and linkages of repositories. For planning, decision support systems are especially helpful.

The proportions of information stored in employees, technologies, and subsidiary storage devices are not fixed. Choices are possible, and it is necessary, therefore, for planners to appreciate the advantages and disadvantages of storing information in each of these kinds of repositories so that their choices are informed. Technologies, employees, and subsidiary storage devices differ in the kinds of information they are suited to store, in their capacity to serve as active and as passive stores of information, and in the cost of storing and updating the information.

Two important information areas that are not well supported in most organizations and offer great potential for improving human resource planning are information about the work done in the organization and accounting information about investments in the human resources of the organization. Information about work is basic to the human resource planning function. Human resource specialists need to perform more studies of the work people do in the organization. A method of work analysis uniquely suited for the planning function is the task inventory method. Most professionally managed organizations have some way for valuing their human resources. Development of such methods is a step in the right direction, but most do not allow placing a value on an organization's investments in human resources, nor do they allow distinguishing between investments and current expenses. This information is needed to allow planners to strike a balance between spending for today and spending for tomorrow.

LEARNING EXERCISES

Case Analysis

If you have the opportunity for small-group discussion, you may use the procedure suggested for Case 1 in Chapter 1.

Bill Linden, president and general manager of Apex Manufacturing Company, Inc., Case 6, has developed a six-point plan for the modernization of his company. He has asked senior managers to comment on his recommendations in 20 days. Jayne Mico, director of human resource management, has asked key people in her department to assemble the best information possible to support any changes the department will recommend for the plan. Assume that you are Jeff Gilby, assistant personnel manager and director of human resource development, and you are to return your recommendation to Ms. Mico in five days. Answer the questions listed here:

1. What kinds of information are needed to plan for the immediate future of the human resources in Apex? Develop as complete a listing of information as possible.

2. What of this information does Mr. Linden seem to be using at present? What information has he not used?
3. In what kinds of repositories is the information Mr. Linden lacks likely to be stored? What problems do you anticipate he may have getting this information? Could personnel in your department obtain this information for him? How?

Activity

Consider the relative impact to the human resource planning function of most organizations if there were a sudden loss of all information about human resources contained in any one of the information repositories—people, technologies, or subsidiary storage devices. For example, if almost everyone in an organization decided to quit their employment at once, requiring their replacement by new employees, how useful would the information be in the existing technologies and subsidiary storage devices of the organization? Take an example of an organization unit (to simplify the analysis), such as an office, section, department, or location, that you know well. List the major kinds of information contained in the organization about human resources of the unit. In what kinds of repositories is this information stored? If the information contained in any one repository were lost, how useful would the remaining information be?

Endnotes

[1]G. Anthony Gorry and Michael S. Scott Morton, "A Framework for Management Information Systems," *Sloan Management Review*, 13, no. 1 (Fall 1971), 55–70.

[2]Gordon B. Davis and Margrethe H. Olson, *Management Information Systems: Conceptual Foundations, Structure, and Development*, 2nd ed. (New York: McGraw-Hill Book Co., 1985), p. 200.

[3]See, for example, the discussion in Alfred S. Walker, *HRIS Development: A Project Team Guide to Building an Effective Personnel Information System* (New York: Van Nostrand Reinhold, 1982), pp. 9–10, 13.

[4]Peter G. W. Keen and Michael S. Scott Morton, *Decision Support Systems: An Organizational Perspective* (Reading, MA: Addison-Wesley, 1978), p. 7.

[5]Other kinds of linkages are computer-aided manufacturing and computer-aided design. Neither has applications at the moment in human resource planning.

[6]Davis and Olson, *Management Information Systems*, p. 375.

[7]See pp. 20–23 of Eric D. Carlson, "An Approach for Designing Decision Support Systems," in John L. Bennett, ed., *Building Decision Support Systems* (Reading, MA: Addison-Wesley, 1983), pp. 15–39. A decision support system is one of three kinds of computer-based information systems. The other two are transaction processing systems and management information systems. See p. 178 in Jeffrey H. Moore and Michael G. Chang, "Meta-Design Considerations in Building DSS," in John L. Bennett, ed., *Building Decision Support Systems* (Reading, MA: Addison-Wesley, 1983), pp. 173–204.

[8]See Moore and Chang, "Meta-Design Considerations," p. 175.

[9]James L. McKenney and Peter G. W. Keen, "How Managers' Minds Work," *Harvard Business Review*, 52, no. 3 (May/June 1974), 79–90.

[10]Carlson, "An Approach for Designing Decision Support Systems," p. 19.

[11]See p. 221 of Charles B. Stabell, "A Decision-Oriented Approach to Building DSS," in John L. Bennett, ed., *Building Decision Support Systems*, pp. 221–260.

[12]Carlson, "An Approach for Designing Decision Support Systems," p. 19.

[13]Moore and Chang, "Meta-Design Considerations," p. 179.

[14]Carlson, "An Approach for Designing Decision Support Systems," p. 21.

[15]Moore and Chang, "Meta-Design Considerations," p. 174.

[16]Ibid., pp. 184–185.

[17]Keen and Scott Morton, *Decision Support Systems*, p. 7, state: "Effectiveness requires adaptation and learning, at the risk of redundancy and false starts."

[18]For a survey of the ten most widely used methods of work analysis, see Stephen E. Bemis, Ann Holt Belenky, and Dee Ann Soder, *Job Analysis: An Effective Management Tool* (Washington, DC: Bureau of National Affairs, 1983), pp. 13–58. For a more complete discussion of the theory and research of work analysis, see Ernest J. McCornick, *Job Analysis: Methods and Applications* (New York: AMACOM, 1979). For an analysis of the uses for eight of the most commonly used methods of job analysis, see Patrick M. Wright and Kenneth N. Wexley, "How to Choose the Kind of Job Analysis You Really Need," in Kendrith M. Rowland and Gerald R. Ferris, *Current Issues in Personnel Management*, 3rd ed. (Boston: Allyn and Bacon, 1986), pp. 72–76, reprinted from *Personnel*, 62, (May 1985).

[19]See Kathleen E. Donohue, Aurora Medellin, and Kay Loup, eds., *Bibliography: Occupation and Manpower Research Division, Air Force Human Resources Laboratory (1957–1979), Final Report* (Brooks Air Force Base, TX: Air Force Human Resources Laboratory, December 1979).

[20]Factor analysis permits finding those tasks that often occur together in the same job.

[21]This example is based on an actual study. See Frank Krzystofiak, Jerry M. Newman, and Gary Anderson, "A Quantified Approach to Measurement of Job Content: Procedures and Payoffs," *Personnel Psychology*, 32, no. 2 (Summer 1979), 341–357.

[22]W.A. Paton, *Accounting Theory* (New York: Ronald Press, 1922), pp. 486–487, quoted in R. Lee Brummet, William C. Pyle, and Eric G. Flamholtz, "Human Resource Accounting in Industry," *Personnel Administrator*, 32, no. 4 (July-August 1969), 34–46.

[23] Rensis Likert, *New Patterns of Management* (New York: McGraw-Hill Book Co., 1961), ch. 5, pp. 61–76; and *The Human Organization: Its Management and Value* (New York: McGraw-Hill Book Co., 1967).

[24]See "An ASTD Feature—Human Resource Accounting: An Exclusive Journal Interview with HRS Pioneer, Robert L. Woodruff, Jr.," *Training and Development Journal*, 27, no. 11 (November 1973), 3–8. Woodruff was vice president of human resources and management services of R. G. Barry Corporation.

[25]For the viewpoints of executives in four different organizations about what systems for valuing human resources should include, see Adrienne L. Gall, comp. and ed., "Four by Four: What Should Human Resource Accounting Systems Count?" *Training and Development Journal*, 42 (July 1988), 20–25.

[26]Henry L. Dahl, Jr., "Measuring the Human ROI," *Retail Control*, 51, no. 5 (January 1983), 9–19.

[27]Dahl believes this distinction is unnecessary. Ibid., pp. 10–12.

[28]See "Human Resource Accounting and Personnel Decisions," pp. 57–101, in Eric G. Flamholtz and John M. Lacey, *Personnel Management, Human Capital Theory, and Human Resource Accounting,* (Los Angeles: Institute of Industrial Relations, University of California, 1981). See also p. 35 of Thomas W. McRae, "Human Resource Accounting as a Management Tool," *The Journal of Accountancy,* 138, no. 2 (August 1974), 32–38.

Chapter 7

Defining the Future

As knowledge increases and the pace of change quickens in the information age, organizations face both new opportunities and new threats in increasing numbers. Dealing forthrightly with these opportunities and threats requires a plan. But to plan effectively, planners must have a set of assumptions about the future on which to base their plan. They must set the boundaries and trace the outlines of the future in order to deal with it. They must define the future. Defining the future allows planners to make assumptions about the future. It allows realistic planning for the future.

The methods used for defining the future are universal. They are much the same, whether done in the context of strategic, tactical, or operational planning. Most of the discussion of this chapter involves human resource planning at the operational stage.

FUTURES ANALYSIS

Determining the future state of a variable alone, such as future supplies of labor, usually means little. It must be studied in the context of other variables. If labor is in short supply while there is little demand for the products or services of the organization, the tight labor market may not be of concern. But if labor is in short supply during a time of great demand for the products or services, opportunities for increased market share may be lost. The future state of every variable that may present an opportunity or threat must be anticipated in the present.

Futures analysis seeks to predict the states of the future of those variables that are part of the organization's future domain. To define the future of the organization, a futures committee should be established. The members of the futures committee must be well informed about the present, for unless the committee

Host· ⊃ Ability to work shifts
X credit
↓ Pg. ~~146~~ e 149   2) 3rd Party Payers

Type of Variable	Identified Variable
Environmental—Relationships	Relationships of local units with placement offices of university schools of nursing
	Relationships with national unions representing employees in local units
	Reputation with public at large for quality care
Environmental—Sector	Physical fitness and health of senior citizens (expanding the number available for employment by the organization)
	State legislative support for stiffer penalties for those found guilty of abuse of the elderly
	Technological change allowing better patient care with lower staff/patient ratios
Organizational—Coping	Organization success at recruiting nurses from nursing schools
	Competence level of nurses and nurses aides employed at E. C. Corporation
	Quality of teams available for on-site inspections and development of quality improvement programs
Organizational—Core Identification	Currency of techniques for care of the elderly
	Extent to which organization culture promotes a caring environment
	Extent of employee pride and commitment to E. C. Corporation

Exhibit 7-1.   Human Resource Planning Variables for E. C. Corporation

understands present conditions, there is little chance it will be able to handle the more complex task of anticipating future conditions.[1] To ensure that the futures committee is well informed, its members should be chosen from the memberships of the strategic, tactical, and operational human resource planning committees.

Several methods of futures analysis are available, but currently only one appears to be practical for human resource planning.[2] It makes use of a nominal group meeting. A nominal group meeting is a procedure for allowing the stimulative effect of interaction among members of a group without the loss of individual objectivity or individual responsibility for group outcomes that usually occurs in traditional group meetings.[3] It does not require that the group meet face to face. A futures committee using this procedure will need the help of a management analyst to assist with the surveys and the reports required by the procedure.

For the discussion that follows, a hypothetical organization, E. C. Corporation, will be used as illustration. E. C. Corporation is an elder care organization.
Headquartered in Atlanta, Georgia, it has 887 nursing homes and 21 regional
offices located across the United States.[4]

The first step in futures analysis is to determine what variables are to be used
to define the future domain of the organization. These future domain variables will
have emerged from a study of the environment and the organization, as discussed
in Chapters 2 and 4. For E. C. Corporation, its organization study and environmental scan yielded 26 variables of importance in the future of the organization.[5] A
partial list of these variables is shown in Exhibit 7-1.

Second, each member of the committee completes a questionnaire asking
him or her to predict the future state, the direction of change, and major causes of
change of each of the variables.[6] They are asked to indicate whether each cause of
change is important or very important. Members are asked to extend their predictions as many years into the future as they feel would allow at least an even chance
of being correct regarding the direction of change.

For the environmental relationship variable "reputation with the public at
large for quality care," members of E. C. Corporation's futures committee were
asked to state whether the organization's reputation would improve or worsen at
five-year intervals, as compared to its reputation during the previous five-year period; by how much its reputation would change (in percentage terms); and the reasons for the change. They were asked to continue to make predictions as far into
the future as they felt their prediction had at least a 50/50 chance of being correct
with respect to the direction of change.

Third, the responses of the committee are analyzed and a summary report of
the analysis is given to each committee member. This report shows the distribution
of direction of change, the amounts of change expected, and a list of all causes of
change given by members. The causes are classified as important and very important. The outcome of the analysis may reveal other variables that will need to be
taken into consideration in the future. These should be added to the list of original
variables. In E. C. Corporation, these summaries were given for a ten-year period
in the future only, as that was the longest period of time that most persons were
able to predict with assurance the direction of change of most variables. A new
variable, "court receptiveness to negligent hiring suits,"[7] emerged from the analysis and was added to the list of future domain variables.

Fourth, after reviewing the report, members of the committee are asked to
complete another questionnaire to make a new set of predictions using the original
and any added variables. Steps 3 and 4 are repeated until no significant new information is generated for consideration by committee members. In E. C. Corporation, the questionnaire used in the second round asked committee members to predict changes in 27 variables for a ten-year period only, and a second summary
report was prepared. Three full rounds were completed.

Fifth, when steps 3 and 4 are completed, a final summary report of the analysis is prepared by the analyst. The report consists of two parts. The first part lists

all future domain variables and identifies the expected future states of those variables at selected intervals. The second part identifies major causes of variables. In E. C. Corporation's report, public attitudes toward senior citizens was seen as staying the same or improving slightly and was identified as an important cause of change of several future domain variables, including organization success at recruiting nurses. Success at recruitment of nurses was seen as a very important cause of a number of other variables, such as the competence level of nurses and nurses aides employed by the corporation.

Sixth, an order of importance is established for the future domain variables. To establish an order of importance, each member of the committee is asked to rank all variables on the basis of two criteria:

- The extent to which they directly present significant opportunities or threats for the organization
- The extent to which they tend to cause future states of other variables that themselves present significant opportunities or threats for the organization

They are instructed to rank first all variables on the basis of the first criterion. Next they are instructed to reconsider for possible advance in rank any variable ranked below another variable for which it is an important or a very important cause. The median value of the individual member rankings is taken as the overall measure of importance of the variables.

Seventh, each of three to five members of the committee are asked to use the most important of the ranked variables to write a scenario describing a possible future domain for the organization.[8] Each scenario is circulated to the committee to critique for consistency with committee findings, credibility, and usefulness[9] and for suggested refinements of the scenarios. Scenarios are modified by the scenario writers and again are critiqued by the committee. This process continues until all scenarios are judged to be acceptable. At E. C. Corporation a task force composed of four members of the committee was asked to write a scenario of approximately ten pages describing a possible future domain for the corporation at the end of ten years. They were instructed that the scenario should meet the following requirements:

- It should be built around the ten most important variables in the corporation's future domain.
- It should reflect as accurately and as completely as possible the final report of the committee. All justification of details were required to be stated in terms of committee findings.

Eighth, other committee members independently compare the scenarios and consider the implications of each scenario for the organization. At E. C. Corporation, four committee members independently compared the four scenarios, identifying common elements and major points of divergence. Each then took one of the four scenarios and identified the significance for the corporation of that scenario.

The findings were summarized and reported to the full committee, which suggested revisions. The revised findings made up the final scenarios analysis report.

The futures analysis report, the scenarios, and the scenarios analysis report are the primary information base for assumptions about the future to be used in carrying out the planning process. They also are the basis for recommendations for further definition of specific variables.

FURTHER DEFINITION OF SPECIFIC VARIABLES

Futures analysis encourages the futures committee to think about possible futures and extends the members' awareness of the range of possible future states. Once the larger picture has been defined, planners should decide whether additional attention needs to be paid to some of the variables. Variables may be further defined by

1. Controlling the variable
2. Altering the relationship between the organization and a variable so that the organization is less dependent on or is no longer dependent on the particular variable
3. Forecasting possible future states of the variable

Controlling Variables

An organization controls a variable by taking direct action that will regulate or determine the state of that variable in the future. Planning then can be done based on assumptions that the state of the variable is assured for the future. For example, an electronics firm wants to ensure that at least 25 percent of its product engineers previously have been technicians. The firm takes steps to ensure that this will happen by

- Hiring technicians who are likely to continue their education to obtain an engineering degree[10]
- Removing the major obstacles that prevent technicians from continuing their education, such as the cost and fear of failure, by establishing appropriate support programs
- Enticing technicians to continue their education and become engineers by offering clearly defined career advancement opportunities

The firm found that the proportion of its engineers who previously had been technicians soon rose to 28 percent and continued at that level.

Variables differ in the degree to which they are subject to control. In general, organizations have considerable control over organizational variables, less control over environmental relationship variables, and least control over environmental sector variables.

An organization may decide to control a variable when it becomes necessary to have a known future value for the variable. For example, computer literacy of job candidates in labor markets of the future is critical to the plans of some organizations. These organizations often seek to control this variable by making gifts of computer equipment or by giving restricted grants for the purchase of computers to schools expected to supply their future employees.

Conditions may occur that allow an organization to control a variable that it previously was unable to control. An organization may have more resources at its disposal, or knowledge about the variable may increase. For example, employee commitment and employee turnover are variables critical to the plans of some organizations. Both variables are much more within the control of organizations because of increased knowledge that has resulted from research done in recent years.

Neutralizing Variables

An organization may take direct action to counteract or deter the effects of a variable. In this case the variable no longer poses a threat and can be ignored. In many cases both organizational and environmental variables may be neutralized. An organization may neutralize variables important for human resource planning by promoting organization agility, developing the ability to manage surprises, buffering and insulating the organization from the environment, and insuring the organization against risk.

Promoting Organization Agility

Organization agility is the ability of an organization to absorb the effects of a broad range of future states of a variable with little or no loss of operational efficiency.[11] Organization agility may be improved by developing flexibility and alertness within an organization.[12]

Organizations may take a number of actions to improve flexibility, allowing their human resource systems to adjust to changes in technologies and in product markets. They may target for hiring persons who can adapt more readily to changing demands of their jobs, who have aptitudes across a wide range of job-related skill areas, and/or who can adjust the amount of hours they work. Organizations can develop multiskilled work forces. They can create human resource systems that allow the smooth transfer of employees among jobs as needed, that develop additional employee skills on short notice, that allow a smooth adjustment of hours of work, and that allow the smooth influx and outflow of employees as needed.

Organizations that wish to react quickly to rapidly changing circumstances cannot depend on control mechanisms that operate through periodic assessments, reporting procedures, and chain of command. Organization alertness requires that many parts of the organization serve as sensory and response mechanisms and that these parts be authorized to respond to changing conditions. In order to avoid the mixed messages that may occur when local autonomy is permitted, a spirit of inter-dependence and close communication must be maintained among the units.[13] Key employees in various parts of the organization must be aware of, and committed to, the achievement of organization strategic objectives and the strategies for achieving those objectives.

Managing Surprises When They Occur

Managing surprises—unexpected opportunities or unexpected threats—may be equated with crisis management, often considered the bane of planners. However, if an organization is adept at crisis management, it probably is rational to rely on this strength in selected instances. If an organization can handle well the surprises that the future holds, some aspects of the future need not be defined at all or at least less precisely.

The job positions most often assigned the task of managing surprises are boundary agents, internal consultants, and issues management teams. Boundary agents are those whose job it is to interact with the environment on behalf of the organization.[14] For example, public relations personnel help the organization to take advantage of last-minute opportunities for publicity and help provide damage control for gaffes in the human resource area. And staffing personnel are experts at building up or reducing work forces on short notice. Internal consultants are highly adept generalists who serve as internal human resource consultants on call as needed. Issues management teams handle those surprises that have implications for the planning effort of an organization.

Buffering and Insulating the Organization

Buffering absorbs the shock or softens the impact of an environmental variable. Insulation shields the organization against the effects of an environmental variable.

Professional employees assigned to the human resource department and line managers often perform buffering and insulating functions. They handle the entry of employees into the organization and the exit of employees from the organization. They represent the organization in its dealings with unions. And they represent the organization in its relations with government regulatory agencies. Because buffering and insulating tasks are scattered among a large number of persons, standing plans of various kinds—policies, procedures, standard methods, and rules—are necessary. Examples of such standing plans abound.

Buffering for the hiring function may be accomplished by five-year-average hiring. Each year's hiring is based on average hiring needs of the organization for a five-year period centered on the current year. For instance, at the end of 1992, to determine the actual new hires for 1993, the number of new hires in 1991 and 1992 are averaged with the estimated new hires needed for 1993, 1994, and 1995. If the new hires in 1991 and 1992 were 90 and 90, respectively, and the estimated new hires for 1993, 1994, and 1995 are 93, 96, and 100, respectively, the actual number of new hires for 1993 would be set at 94. This practice has the effect of creating surplus stocks of employees in years when organization needs are low to buffer the firm from effects of years when organization needs are high.

The same effect is achieved by the use of internal labor markets. Promotions, in promotion chains, are delayed in years when there is little need for employees in higher level positions, allowing the storage of employees until needed.

Insulation for the development function may be accomplished by erecting firm boundaries and highly efficient input/output mechanisms. Organizations that restrict entry to a relatively few port-of-entry positions are able to insulate the organization from the effects of external labor markets. This practice allows the formation of stable internal labor markets within which turnover is managed and employees can be developed at leisure for higher level jobs as they move through promotion chains.

Insuring the Organization Against Risk   *Insure your key people*

Insurance lessens the need to predict the future state of a variable because the risk associated with fluctuations in the variable is transferred to a professional risk carrier, usually an insurance organization. Such insurance allows a pooling of risks among organizations.[15] Insurance is used when the likelihood of loss for each insured organization is low but the amount of loss may be quite large. Pooling of risks allows all organizations to be protected with a much smaller reserve to cover the loss than would be required if each organization had to set aside its own reserve.

Organizations use insurance in the human resource area primarily to protect themselves against catastrophic loss of human resource assets. For example, a sports team may insure the lives of their key players. In the event of an accident resulting in the loss of part of the team, insurance would cover the monetary loss until a new team could be assembled. As organizations make more investments in human resources, the magnitude of their exposure to loss will increase and insurance will become a more important way to deal with these losses.

Forecasting Variables   *Predict better decision about future*

Forecasting is an attempt to predict the range of possible future states of one or several variables and the likelihood of occurrence of these future states. Forecasting is done when

- It is necessary to know the state of a variable in the future so that a decision can be made in the present and control or neutralization alone is not sufficient
- Prior forecasts become outmoded because the basic conditions underlying the forecast have changed
- A surge in the number of issues arising under planning signals that a method of defining the future has failed and that better or more complete predictions are needed

- Actions taken by the organization require forecast—for example, the start-up of a new plant requires forecasts of personnel needed.

Forecasting Methods

The method used for a forecast is determined by the kind of information that will yield the best prediction of the future state of a variable. If people are the most likely source of information, the advice of people—either their intentions or their opinions—may be sought. If the best information is the past behavior of a variable or related variables, these variables may be extrapolated into the future. If the best source of information is the way the variable is produced, a model of the process that produces the variable may be constructed and examined.

Measuring Intentions and Opinions

People often have information that will permit the forecasting of a variable. This information is elicited through the collection of intentions and opinions. An intention is a conjecture about what the respondent plans to do in the future. Intentions are used to forecast variables over which the respondent has substantial control. An opinion is a conjecture about what the respondent feels will happen in the future. Opinions are used to forecast variables over which the respondent has little or no control.

Intentions tend to be a valid source of information about the future state of a variable when the respondent has made an investment of time or money in carrying out the stated intention.[16] Thus an estimate by managers of the numbers of people they will hire during the coming year will be more accurate if they have autonomy over their operations and if they have planned their operations for the coming year.

Opinions tend to be a valid source of information about the future state of a variable when the respondents have expert knowledge or personal insight that allows an informed opinion. For example, managers may be able to estimate staffing needs five years in the future if they know

- Expected changes in demand for service
- The career plans and/or the retirement plans of employees
- Expected changes in the technology by which service is delivered

This information may enable them to estimate staffing needs more closely than would be possible without this information.

Intentions and opinions may be gathered in a number of ways: interview, mail questionnaire, nominal group meeting, personal interview, telephone interview, and focus group. The choice of method depends largely on how many people need to be surveyed, where these persons are located, and how much cooperation can be expected with the survey.

A proper approach to the measurement of intentions and opinions is critical because proper use can increase immeasurably the accuracy of the forecast. The following actions may be taken to improve accuracy:

- Ensure, through selection or training, that those to be surveyed have knowledge of the *current* state of the variable to be predicted. To illustrate the importance of this point, ask yourself if you would be able to predict more accurately the number of employees who will use day-care facilities ten years in the future if you knew how many use day care now. Research shows that you will.[17]
- Structure the forecast problem posed to respondents by breaking complex predictions into several simpler, more direct predictions. For example, rather than ask persons the proportion of employees who will use day-care facilities ten years from now, break the forecast problem down into three (or more) questions: What proportion of employees will be in the childbearing age group ten years from now? What proportion of these employees will have children? What proportion of these employees will use day-care facilities? Again, research suggests that properly structured questions elicit more accurate judgments about future changes in the variable.[18]
- Enhance the realism of the prediction. Realistic forecasts may be encouraged by asking respondents to imagine the setting of the forecast. Assume that managers are asked to forecast the impact of a procedure for handling customer complaints on customer satisfaction. Managers can be asked to describe the chain of events that lead to an increase or decrease in satisfaction. Or managers may be asked to role-play a typical customer with a complaint while another manager plays an employee trying to resolve the complaint using the procedure.[19]
- Provide forecast skills training for respondents. Respondents who are called on repeatedly to make predictions may be trained to structure and analyze the forecast problem and to recognize and deal with common causes of bias in forecasts.
- Provide feedback on performance for respondents. For persons used repeatedly in similar forecast situations, giving personalized feedback on the accuracy of their forecasts tends to improve performance.[20]

Extrapolation   *Taking data look at patterns*

Extrapolation is the extension of a data series into the future based on information about the past behavior of the variable. Because human resource data often display stable patterns of change over long periods of time, extrapolation is quite useful for forecasting in the human resource area.

Extrapolation methods that base the prediction on information about the past behavior of the variable may range from simple to complex, depending on how much information about the past behavior of the variable is used. Extrapolations based on moving averages use little of the information about past behavior of the variable. When moving averages can be adjusted to give more weight in the calculation of the average to recent data, somewhat more information is used.[21] Extrapolations based on underlying trends of change in the data taking into consideration the effects of seasonal and cyclical influences use even more of the information contained in a data series.[22] Newer methods of extrapolation allow very extensive use of the information contained in a data series. These methods employ computer analysis of the data series to determine relationships between each data point and all previous data points. A method of extrapolation is then custom-designed to take into account patterns peculiar to the particular data series.[23]

Complex methods tend to be much more costly than simple methods. This causes the expectation that forecasts based on complex methods will be much more accurate than those based on simple methods. This expectation is not justified. In practice, simple procedures that use relatively little of the information from a data series often are as effective as more complex procedures.[24] This occurs because extracting additional information from a data series has practical limits. The data series contains information about past behavior of the data series only. At best the information can accurately predict future values only if there is no change in the basic conditions causing change.

At times a data series does not seem to display a stable pattern. Expressing the variable as a ratio of another variable may result in a data series that displays a stable pattern of change. For example, the total number of employees leaving an organization each year is likely to be less stable from year to year than will be the number of employees leaving per 100 employees.

Forecast Models

A model is a simplified representation of an actual process. A good model includes all important aspects of the actual process but no additional information to obscure cause-and-effect relationships. A forecast model is one that models the process that produces the variable.

Forecast models may be either qualitative or quantitative. A qualitative model explains how a process works, but its causes and effects have not been measured. Qualitative models are frequently used in human resource planning because many of the variables are difficult to measure. Exhibit 7-2 is a qualitative model used to predict the future performance of newly-hired employees in an organization. The model directs the attention of planners to many of the important causes of good and poor employee performance and of the interrelationships among these causes. If the model has included only the important causes of performance, it should allow accurate predictions of job performance.

A quantitative model explains how a process works, and its causes and effects have been measured. The typical quantitative model uses a regression equation or a set of equations to express the relationships among variables of the model.

Assume, for example, that a model is to be used to predict turnover of employees in a particular job in XYZ Corporation. Theory suggests that turnover from the position will be determined by economic factors represented by differences in wage rates between XYZ Corporation and other organizations, by levels of business activity, and by the number of new entrants into the labor force. All these factors, plus past data for turnover in XYZ Corporation, are used to build a formula in which turnover is regressed against the related variables. This formula

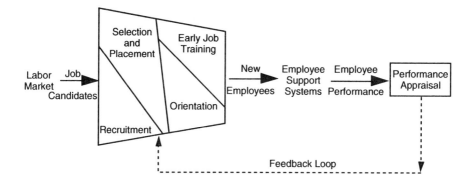

Exhibit 7-2.   Qualitative Model of an Organization Staffing Process

is used to estimate future values for the forecast variable using expected values of the related variables.[25] Expected values for the related variables can be obtained in several ways. A related variable may be controlled by the employer or by someone else and therefore can be known in advance. In our example, the wage rate paid by the organization is known in advance and wage rates in other organizations are established under union agreements for the next three years. Forecasts of expected future changes in levels of business activity and numbers of new entrants into the labor force are conducted and published by the U.S. government. Use of the formula allows a prediction of expected future turnover.

When building a forecast model, organizations frequently can use either a qualitative or quantitative model for the same purpose. Because human resource variables often are difficult to measure, quantitative models are used infrequently. A quantitative model should be considered when the gain in forecast accuracy justifies the added cost.[26]

Guidelines for Using Forecast Methods

Before carrying out a forecast, a search should be done to determine whether a similar forecast already has been conducted. Many environmental variables in the human resource area are forecast and are available for public use.[27] When a decision has been made that a forecast is needed, the choice of the method should be based on the kind of information available, the cost of using the method, and the reliability of the method. The reliability of a forecast method may be determined by looking at the past track record of the method in similar forecast situations.

Where possible, multiple, independent forecasts should be conducted, using different methods. If two or three independent forecasts all predict similar future events, the reliability of the combined forecast increases markedly.[28]

When evaluating a forecast method, remember it may have two benefits. First, there is the obvious benefit—it may yield an accurate forecast allowing the organization to take timely action based on the expected future value of a variable.

A less obvious benefit is learning that occurs through the use of the forecast method. Some methods, such as forecast models, contribute much to our understanding of why and how a variable changes. Other methods, such as extrapolation, contribute less. For planners, learning may be as important as accuracy of prediction.

SUMMARY

Organizations in the modern world face new opportunities and new threats in increasing numbers. Dealing forthrightly with these opportunities and threats requires a plan. But to plan effectively, planners must define the future. The methods used for defining the future are much the same, whether done in the context of strategic, tactical, or operational planning. The discussion of this chapter primarily involves human resource planning at the operational stage.

Determining the future state of a variable alone usually means little. It must be studied in the context of other variables. Futures analysis seeks to predict the future states of all variables of interest to planners—the organization's future domain. The method of futures analysis recommended makes use of a nominal group meeting procedure.

The results of the futures analysis are a primary information base for carrying out the planning process. They also are the basis for recommendations for further definition of specific variables. Variables may be further defined by controlling the variables, neutralizing the variables, or forecasting the variables. An organization controls a variable by taking direct action that will regulate or determine the state of that variable in the future. Planning then can be done based on assumptions that the state of the variable is assured for the future.

An organization may neutralize a variable by taking direct action to counteract or deter the effects of a variable. In this case the variable no longer poses a threat to the planning of the organization and can be ignored. An organization may neutralize variables important for human resource planning by promoting organization agility, developing the ability to manage surprises, buffering and insulating the organization from the environment, and insuring the organization against risk.

Forecasting is an attempt to predict the range of possible future states of one or several variables and the likelihood of occurrence of these future states. The method used for a forecast is determined by the kinds of information available to predict the future state of a variable. If people are the most likely source of information, the intentions or opinions of people may be sought. If the best information is the past behavior of a variable or related variables, these variables may be extrapolated into the future. If the best source of information is the way the variable is produced, a model of the process that produces the variable may be constructed and examined.

LEARNING EXERCISES

Case Analysis

If you have the opportunity for small-group discussion, you may use the procedure suggested for Case 1 in Chapter 1.

At the time the case was written, George Wellington saw the problem facing "Northeast Data Resources, Inc.," Case 7, as one of handling the layoffs of a sizable number of employees. After setting in motion a procedure for handling the layoffs, Mr. Wellington saw that a more important issue was the avoidance of future, unpleasant surprises such as those now confronting the company. Mr. Wellington began to prepare a report for Jack Logan, briefing him on the role of futures definition in planning and recommending an approach to futures definition suited to NDR.

Assume that you are George Wellington and answer the questions or take the actions listed here:

1. Which of the various ways of defining the future (futures analysis, controlling, neutralizing, forecasting) was Jack Logan using? Did he appear to make good use of the method(s) used? Based on your knowledge of futures definition, how close to state of the art was the approach Jack Logan took to futures definition?

2. What specific problems facing the organization might have been avoided with better futures definition in 1977 (when George Wellington first became adviser to Jack Logan)? With the benefit of hindsight, what methods of futures definition would have worked best with each problem? Is it likely that opportunities as well as problems are being overlooked by a failure to better define the future? What do the inroads competitors are making suggest in this regard?

3. Would you advise Jack Logan to initiate futures definition in the organization? If so, how should futures definition be integrated into the ongoing system of business planning? Should Jack Logan become his own expert at futures definition, develop a futures definition specialist internally, develop the expertise of his entire planning committee, and/or seek professional help from outside the organization?

Activities

1. For an organization with which you are familiar, list at least ten variables important to the future human resource domain of the organization. Recom-
⮑ HR setting

Just #1

mend an approach to defining the future human resource domain of the organization in terms of these variables, discussing the role, if any, of futures analysis and further definition of specific variables. Make tentative recommendations for the use of controlling, neutralizing, and forecasting for specific variables.   *Pg 205*

2. Challenge your current ideas about futures analysis and forecasting. Check out of your local library (or ask that it be borrowed for you on interlibrary loan) Michael Godet, *Scenarios and Strategic Management* (London: Butterworths, 1987). See especially his discussion of the prospective approach and how it differs from forecasting.

Endnotes

[1] Research shows that the judgment of people about future states is considerably less accurate when they lack knowledge of current states. This is because systematic error in estimation of current status is reflected in the estimates of future changes in status. See J. Scott Armstrong, *Long-Range Forecasting: From Crystal Ball to Computer* (New York: John Wiley, 1985), pp. 236–237.

[2] See Michel Godet, *Scenarios and Strategic Management* (London: Butterworths, 1987); Jay S. Mendell, ed., *Nonextrapolative Methods in Business Forecasting: Scenarios, Vision, and Issues Management* (Westport, CT: Quorum Books, 1985); Olaf Helmer, *Looking Forward: A Guide to Futures Research* (Beverly Hills, CA: Sage Publications, 1983); H. Jones, "The State of the Art: Futures Techniques and Economic Forecasting," in D. E. Hussey, ed., *The Corporate Planners' Yearbook, 1978–79* (New York: Pergamon Press, 1978), pp. 45–70; Jib Fowles, ed., *Handbook of Futures Research* (Westport, CT: Greenwood Press, 1978).

[3] The nominal group meeting is defined in the appendix to Chapter 2.

[4] To the author's knowledge this is not an actual company.

[5] Sears, in its strategic planning, surfaced 25 variables ("issues") for consideration in planning. See p. 127 of William C. Ashley, "Strategic Issues Forecasting and Monitoring at Sears," in Jay S. Mendell, ed., *Nonextrapolative Methods in Business Forecasting*, pp. 125–132

[6] Some future domain variables may themselves be causes of other future domain variables.

[7] A negligent hiring suit is a court action, usually by a customer or client of the organization, claiming injury or harm resulting from improper service or treatment attributable to the failure of the organization to screen its employees properly.

[8] Three to five scenarios seem to be all that a futures committee can critique effectively. See p. 238 of Ian H. Wilson, "Scenarios," in Fowles, ed., *Handbook of Futures Research*, pp. 224–247.

[9] Credibility and usefulness are suggested as criteria by Zentner, who also suggests intelligibility as a criterion. See p. 30 of Rene D. Zentner, "Scenarios in Forecasting," *Chemical and Engineering News*, October 6, 1975, pp. 22–34, cited in Wilson, "Scenarios," p. 233.

[10] A biographical data predictor may be used for this purpose.

[11] See p. 29 of John L. Brown and Neil McK. Agnew, "Corporate Agility," *Business Horizons*, 25, no. 2 (March/April 1982), 29–33.

[12]Ibid., p. 29.

[13]Rosabeth Moss Kanter, "Frontiers for Strategic Human Resource Planning and Management," *Human Resource Management*, 22, nos. 1/2 (Spring/Summer 1982), 9–21.

[14]See p. 322 of J. Stacy Adams, "Interorganizational Processes and Organization Boundary Activities," in Barry M. Staw and Larry L. Cummings, *Research in Organizational Behavior*, vol. 2 (Greenwich, CT: JAI Press, 1980), pp. 321–355.

[15]When organizations purchase insurance for employees as an employee benefit, such as employee medical insurance, the insurance serves to pool risks among individual employees. The individual employee risks pooled by this type of insurance normally are not part of business planning and this type of insurance therefore does not serve to define the future domain of the organization.

[16]For evidence of the importance of investments for the interpretation of intentions, see Meni Koslowsky, Avraham Natan Kluger, and Yoel Yinon, "Predicting Behavior: Combining Intention with Investment," *Journal of Applied Psychology*, 73, no. 1 (1988), 102–106.

[17]Armstrong, "Long-Range Forecasting," pp. 59–61.

[18]See Howard Raiffa, *Decision Analysis: Introductory Lectures on Choices Under Uncertainty* (Menlo Park, CA: Addison-Wesley, 1968), p. 258. See also J. Scott Armstrong, William B. Denniston, Jr., and Matt M. Gordon, "The Use of the Decomposition Principle in Making Judgments," *Organizational Behavior and Human Performance*, 14 (1975), 257–263; Edwin T. Cornelius III and Karen S. Lyness, "A Comparison of Holistic and Decomposed Judgment Strategies in Job Analyses by Job Incumbents," *Journal of Applied Psychology*, 65, no. 2 (1980), 155–163.

[19]For evidence of the value of role playing in enhancing the accuracy of a forecast, see Armstrong, "Long-Range Forecasting," pp. 124–132.

[20]Ibid., p. 119.

[21]This process is termed exponential smoothing. See James R. McGuigan and R. Charles Moyer, *Managerial Economics* (St. Paul, MI: West, 1986), pp. 202–204.

[22]The process of separating patterns of change into types based on underlying causes of change is called decomposition or adjustment of the data. Data may be adjusted for secular, cyclical, seasonal, and random influences. See ibid., pp. 196–200.

[23]The best known methods are the autoregressive/moving average methods. See Steven C. Wheelwright and Spyros Makridakis, *Forecasting Methods for Management*, 3rd ed. (New York: John Wiley, 1980), pp. 171–198. For a discussion of the place of the autoregressive/moving average methods in forecasting, see Elwood S. Buffa and James S. Dyer, *Management Science/Operations Research: Model Formulation and Solution Methods* (Santa Barbara, CA: John Wiley, 1977), pp. 149–184.

[24]See Wheelwright and Makridakis, *Forecasting Methods for Management*, pp. 43–45; Armstrong, "Long-Range Forecasting," pp. 178–179.

[25]Sometimes related variables have a lagged relationship to the variable to be forecast. When this is so, the value for the related variable used in the regression formula may be a current actual value.

[26]It appears that quantitative models are seldom cost-effective. A survey of forecast practice by Feuer, Niehaus, and Sheridan indicates that quantitative models are little used in human resource forecasting. See Michael J. Feuer, Richard J. Niehaus, and James A. Sheridan, "Human Resource Forecasting: A Survey of Practice and Potential," *Human Resource Planning*, 7, no. 2 (1984), 85–97. Fiorito, Stone, and Greer conclude, based on another survey of forecasting practice, that choice of forecasting technique is a function of perceived costs and benefits. See pp. 8–10 of Jack Fiorito,

Thomas H. Stone, and Charles R. Greer, "Factors Affecting Choice of Human Resource Forecasting Techniques," *Human Resource Planning*, 8, no. 1 (1985), 1–17.

[27]An especially good source for forecasts is the U. S. Department of Labor.

[28]See James A. Craft, "A Critical Perspective on Human Resource Planning," *Human Resource Planning*, 3, no. 2 (1980), 39–52.

Chapter 8

Evaluating Human Resources

THE ROLE OF EVALUATION IN PLANNING

Evaluation is necessary in all stages of business planning—strategic, tactical, and operational. Of the three, operational planning offers the most opportunities to evaluate. The repetitive nature of the work allows changes to be made from cycle to cycle, and through evaluation, operations are continuously refined.

Research shows that many organizations feel that they do not need to evaluate, that they "know how they are doing."[1] This is a shortsighted view for two reasons: First, waiting until there are obvious signs of deterioration in the condition of human resources is wasteful. Opportunities for wise investment in human resources are missed, and major overhauls of human resource systems—often inefficient and disruptive—become necessary. Second, and even more important, this viewpoint has severely and unduly restricted the human resource function. Evaluation has its greatest potential when used to guide planning-based, proactive programs that build on current successes.

If evaluation is to achieve its full potential in operational planning for human resources, organizations must depart from much of current practice. Two points of departure especially are necessary:

- Organizations need to evaluate in support of the planning function.
- Organizations need to evaluate the work of the entire organization in managing human resources, not the work of the human resource department alone.

Evaluation in Support of Planning

In operational planning, three human resource activities will be evaluated:

- *Procedure*—a sequence of steps to be followed in carrying out a process
- *Program*—a coordinated set of actions to be taken to solve a problem or accomplish a result
- *Accumulation of stocks*—an accumulation of stores of people within the organization capable of filling job positions inside the organization as the need arises

Evaluation has been used almost exclusively for control of the human resource function rather than for planning. Evaluation for control is modeled after financial audits and sets a value on an activity according to its contribution to organization success. Evaluation for control asks: What is the value of this particular procedure, program, or stock?[2] Is it worth keeping in the organization?

Evaluation for planning is done to determine how and why activities have value. It asks, first and foremost: Why does this procedure, program, or stock have value to the organization? How and where can it be most effectively utilized? The value of an activity is used as a tool to answer these questions.

Both evaluation in support of the control function and evaluation in support of planning are needed in organizations. However, the two should not be combined. Evaluation in support of control provides limited information for the planning function. Often, it is threatening to people. It discourages information sharing and critical analysis.[3] Evaluation in support of planning requires a spirit of inquiry among organization members. It searches for cause-and-effect relationships and determines whether these relationships can be generalized to other activities and settings. In other words, will the relationships still exist when conditions change or when an attempt is made to reproduce the relationship in a different setting with different conditions? This learning becomes an important input to operational plans.

Evaluation of the Human Resource Function

Traditionally, evaluations of the human resource function have been largely limited to evaluations of the work of human resource departments.[4] This practice continues[5] in spite of the recognition that human resource departments alone do not carry out the human resource function.[6]

Evaluating the work of the human resource department alone sends a signal to the organization that only the department is responsible for human resource management. As has been pointed out in previous chapters, the entire organization must be involved in human resource management. Evaluations should involve everyone in the organization both as evaluators and as those whose work is evaluated. In this way, a large number of employees, including the chief executive officer, the line managers, and the professionals in the human resource department, become informed on the workings of the human resource function and can give input into the planning process.

A SUPPORTIVE SETTING FOR EVALUATION

Effective evaluation in support of planning is a natural outgrowth of a supportive organization setting. This setting is one in which

- Evaluation is a planned and integral part of every activity.
- Managers at all levels and in all functional areas demonstrate their belief in the evaluation process.
- Honesty in evaluation is encouraged.
- Learning through evaluation is encouraged.

When evaluation is included as a part of an activity at the design stage, people who are responsible for carrying out the activity are encouraged to see evaluation as a normal part of the work. Features of an original design tend to shape the way people see an activity. Further, these persons have time to become accustomed to the idea of evaluation and to accommodate their work schedules to include evaluation.[7]

Managers demonstrate their belief in the human resource evaluation process by speaking out in support of evaluation; by using evaluation in their own work, thus serving as evaluation models; and by insisting that others use evaluation. The central idea that managers must champion, both by their words and by their deeds, is the idea that no one in the organization has the right to use organization resources without a legitimate effort to learn how to use these resources to best advantage.

Honesty in evaluation is important, otherwise evaluation becomes a political tool and cannot fulfill its function of promoting learning. Managers can encourage honesty by modeling honesty in their own behavior.[8] A critical place for honesty in evaluation is in performance appraisals. Performance appraisals are by far the most prevalent form of evaluation.[9] And they touch almost everyone in an organization. Unless honesty is encouraged here, it is unlikely to occur in other forms of evaluation.

In many organizations the opportunity to encourage honesty in evaluation through the appraisal process is lost. For example, Bank of America, in a study of its corporate culture in 1984, found that employees felt that managers "lied like hell" when it came to performance appraisals.[10] Dishonesty in evaluation must be confronted. When presented with hard evidence of the extent of dishonesty in its performance appraisal process, Bank of America decided the problem was important enough to merit the attention of the chief executive officer. In 1984, all 100 top executives at the bank, who were required to appraise their own performance, gave themselves ratings of "far exceeded" or "consistently exceeded" job requirements. These appraisals followed three consecutive years when the bank had missed its business goals by a considerable margin.

> The CEO assembled all 100 executives in one room and said, "I don't understand this—all of you said your bonuses should be paid at the 100–130 percent level. Am I really the only one in this room who didn't meet his goals?" You could have heard a pin drop in the room.[11]

When the top executive models honesty, the effect can spread rapidly throughout the organization.[12]

Learning through evaluation may be encouraged through modeling by managers who show by example that they are learners. Learners keep abreast of new ideas about human resources, they introduce the new ideas at work, and they seek candid feedback on how well the new ideas work.

An evaluation shouldnt be a end to itself

A PHILOSOPHY OF EVALUATION

A supportive setting for evaluation will allow the development of a meaningful philosophy of evaluation for planning. Developing a philosophy is basic, and should be done before any formal evaluations begin. The discussion that follows suggests a number of principles that should be included in such a philosophy. It is understood that these principles should be tailored to be consistent with the organization's overall philosophy and with the organization's approach to human resource management.

Each formal evaluation effort should be justified. We have said that evaluation is vital for learning about human resource activities. However, it is important to recognize when an evaluation is worth doing and when it is not worth doing. The costs of evaluation, including the disruptions to day-to-day operations, should not exceed the gains expected to be achieved through use of the evaluation results.

Specific objectives should be established for each evaluation effort. There are multiple users and multiple purposes for most evaluations. Before an evaluation is begun, the reasons for the evaluation and the intended uses of the evaluation should be clearly understood.[13] It is likely that some trade-offs among legitimate objectives will be necessary.

Political factors are inimical to an objective evaluation process, and should be accommodated in an evaluation only if the benefits justify the costs of doing so. Alternative means for achieving the political ends should be considered.

Persons who will be expected to support and assist in an evaluation should help to plan the study. If evaluations are to serve a learning purpose, the active assistance and willing cooperation of many persons will be required. In addition, support is necessary from those who must approve or finance the study and from those with access to information needed for the evaluation. These persons can better understand the importance of their support and can be of more assistance if they or their representatives are involved in planning and conducting the study.[14]

Evaluations should be done in a straightforward and open manner. There are no "one-time" evaluations. The people and organizations involved in an evaluation effort at any one time will be involved in later evaluations. If they are treated in a forthright manner, they will cooperate with future evaluations.

No evaluation should be considered as a final answer, but rather as an additional source of information to supplement an ongoing process of evaluation. Every evaluation effort takes a skeletal view of the procedure, program, or stock to be evaluated and evaluates the procedure, program, or stock only from that perspective.

The results of an evaluation should be disseminated very carefully. The rights to privacy of persons and organizations whose products and activities are evaluated must be respected. Results should be disseminated only to persons and to organizations who will respect these rights to privacy and who can and will make constructive use of the results.

AN APPROACH TO EVALUATION

Think about the objectives you're trying to achieve.

Once a philosophy of evaluation for planning has been developed, an organization may choose an approach or a combination of approaches appropriate to its planning needs. Choice of approach should be predicated on obtaining as much useful information as possible for the time, money, and effort expended.

Approaches differ, depending on the focus of the evaluation:

- An evaluation may focus on a human resource activity (the activity-specific approach).[15] Or the evaluation may focus on the activity as part of a larger system (the systems approach).
- An evaluation may focus on a predetermined set of goals (the goal-constrained approach) or be goal-free (the goal-free approach).[16]
- An evaluation may focus on the evaluation itself (the classical approach)[17] or on the use of the evaluation (the planned-change approach).[18]

An *activity-specific approach* tends to focus narrowly on the human resource activity being evaluated. Causal analysis is done by comparing inputs to outputs, explaining changes that occur in terms of characteristics of the activity. For example, an evaluation of a training program to familiarize new employees with company policies might compare employee knowledge of company policies at the beginning and at the end of the program. Changes in knowledge would be explained in terms of such characteristics of the training program as expertise of the trainer and techniques used in the training.

A *systems approach* to evaluation takes into account not only those causes and effects observable by focusing on the human resource activity being evaluated but also on causes and effects attributable to the surroundings. For example, if the training program were evaluated using a systems approach, it would consider the possibility that much of the learning about company policy might be acquired outside the classroom itself, during on-the-job experience of trainees.

The activity-specific approach and the systems approach offer a continuum of choice for planners ranging from an activity-specific approach through ever more comprehensive systems approaches. For example, an evaluation may consider only the human resource activity and its constituents. Or an evaluation might consider the activity, its constituents, and the organization. Or an evaluation might consider the activity, its constituents, the organization, and the external labor market. Extending the area of investigation may add considerable complexity and cost to a study, but it also may add considerably to planners' understanding of why the activity has its effects and whether the activity is likely to be effective in other settings of the organization. At some point a decision must be made that the added cost of further extension of the area of investigation will not be justified by the additional explanatory value associated with the extension. Exactly where to limit the study is a critical consideration in choosing an approach.

Where organizations have clearly in mind the goals of a human resource activity, use of a *goal-constrained approach* to evaluation is appropriate. Goals of the procedure, program, or stock may be used to set strict guidelines of what and how to evaluate. In contrast, the use of a *goal-free approach* should be considered when a firm set of goals for an activity cannot be established because the full potential of a human resource activity is not well understood. This might occur when radically new designs are being introduced. Or the goal-free approach may be used when the organization wants to learn more about an already established activity being used in radically new settings. As the first step in the evaluation, a broad list of possible effects of an activity may be developed to guide the evaluation so that unnecessary search for very unlikely effects is avoided.[19] Such a list could be prepared based on interviews with administrators, field personnel, and clients who have experience with the type of activity being evaluated.

Both the goal-constrained and the goal-free approaches have potential weaknesses. In the goal-constrained approach, preconceived goals may cause the evaluator to see goal-related effects and to overlook even more important, unintended effects. The goal-free evaluation may do an incomplete job of measuring the extent to which the activity achieves goals important to those who designed them.

In the *classical approach* to evaluation, an evaluator (or evaluators) gathers the best evidence possible, without regard to the possible effects of the evidence on the outcome of the evaluation and presents the evidence in as fair and as open a manner as possible. Infrequently, an evaluator also draws conclusions from the findings and recommends action.[20] This approach works best in organizations where evaluation and learning are accepted as a routine part of day-to-day life.

When evaluation is likely to be resisted and is not valued as a part of the learning process, the organization may have to resort to a *planned-change approach*. In this approach, field personnel perform the evaluation as part of a larger change effort. The change effort is assisted by a change agent who helps to design a process that opens communication, helps field personnel to recognize and to work through problems, and helps to generate internal acceptance for change.

What are your objectives?

Approach Type	May Be Combined with These Other Approaches
Activity-specific	Goal-constrained, classical, and planned-change
Systems	Goal-free and classical
Goal-constrained	Activity-specific and classical
Goal-free	Systems, classical, and planned-change
Classical	Activity-specific, systems, goal-constrained, goal-free
Planned-change	Activity-specific and goal-free

Exhibit 8-1. Logical Combinations of Approaches to Evaluation

Though the three approach choices have been discussed separately, they may be combined. Logical combinations of the approaches are shown in Exhibit 8-1.

WHAT TO MEASURE

Human resource procedures, programs, and stocks have value to the extent that their attributes contribute, directly or indirectly, to the carrying out of human resource strategies and to the achievement of human resource objectives. Attributes of individual employees, of groups of employees, or of both are used to measure the value of stocks. Effects on employee attributes are used to measure the value of procedures and programs. Following are some attributes of individual employees that have been used to measure human resource value:

> abilities, attitudes, behaviors and traits, beliefs, cost-benefit effects measured in dollars, capitalized value, character or integrity, citizenship, commitment, condition and health, contribution to profit, energy level, job performance, job satisfaction, knowledge and understanding, personality, productivity, skills, service orientation, tenure, values, and work ethic.

Most of the attributes listed here are useful to measure the value of groups of employees.[21] In some instances, however, synergistic effects tend to occur when many persons in a group have an attribute. It is useful in these instances to use a different term for the group attribute. The attributes most likely to have synergistic effects in groups are listed below. The most closely related individual employee attribute is shown in parentheses following each term.

> culture (behaviors and traits)
> loyalty (commitment)
> morale (job satisfaction)
> social character (character or integrity)[22]

It is not feasible to measure all attributes of a procedure, program, or stock. People can only pay attention to a limited number of measures, and organizations can only afford a limited number of measures (such measurements can be expensive). Therefore, planners must encourage the selective use of measures that will promote learning about attributes critical to human resource strategies and objectives.

Both intermediate and final measures of value are likely to be useful. Intermediate measures of value are those that measure attributes of a procedure, program, or stock that contribute indirectly to the realization of strategies or objectives. Final measures of value are those that measure attributes that contribute directly to the realization of strategies or objectives.

If profitability is a human resource objective, health and physical conditioning of employees may be an intermediate measure of value because we may assume that healthy employees will have higher energy level, fewer absences, and more alertness on the job and, in the long run, contribute to the profitability of the organization.[23] If health and physical conditioning of employees is a human resource objective, then health and physical conditioning is a final measure of value.

Intermediate measures of value are useful supplements to final measures of value in two ways. First, when not enough precise final measures of value are available, intermediate measures may help to meet the need for more indicators of value. Second, intermediate measures often are essential for understanding why human resource activities have final value. For example, some plants in a multi-plant manufacturing organization may be more profitable than other plants. This difference may not be understood until it is noticed that employees in these same plants are more productive, have higher energy levels, are absent less often, and are more alert on the job.

STANDARDS FOR THE EVALUATION

Evaluators, set adrift without the guidance of standards, become captive to their own or other persons' biases. This is true whether evaluators are evaluating their own work or the work of others. It is essential that standards to guide the decisions of evaluators be established in advance.

A *standard* is a measure selected to serve as a basis for judging other similar measures. The purpose of the standard is to call attention to deviations from the standard. Such deviations should trigger a search for cause. Standards may be comparative or absolute. Comparative standards are based on what is actually possible. The standard is determined by looking at what others are doing. Comparative standards are valid only when the activities being evaluated are similar to the activities on which the standards are based. Absolute standards are based on what is theoretically possible. The standard is determined by looking at some ideal of what can be done. Both comparative and absolute standards are available for organization-wide activities, for activities of organization units, and for specific procedures, programs, and stocks.

Comparative standards for organization-wide activities may be based on survey reports of such activities in other organizations. These reports are published by government agencies, educational or research institutions, professional societies, and cooperating groups of employers.[24] For example, the Society for Human Resource Management and the Saratoga (California) Institute for Human Resource Measurement Standards annually conduct and publish the results of a survey of several hundred companies from a number of industries. Measures reported are employee productivity, revenues, expenses, and profits, and the contribution of human resource functions, such as staffing and compensation, to productivity, revenues, expenses, and profits. Results are published as part of a software program and in a hard copy survey report. The software program is personal computer-operated and allows an organization to collect, calculate, and analyze its own operating data and to compare its data with those for surveyed organizations of similar size, industry, region, and revenue growth rate.[25]

Comparative standards for the human resource activities of an organization unit or for a specific procedure, program, or stock may be based on comparisons with similar activities within the organization. Occasional outside comparisons also are advisable to determine how activities are being performed as compared to similar activities in other organizations. For this purpose, benchmarking is helpful. (As discussed in an earlier chapter, a benchmark is a standard of performance based on data from outside organizations.[26])

Absolute standards may be based on the judgment of subject matter experts, managerial personnel, and/or operating employees. Subject matter experts will tend to set standards in terms of achievement of state of the art. Managers will tend to set standards based on optimum achievement of objectives or optimum efficiency of use of resources. Operating employees will tend to set standards based on what can be achieved with given resources.

The kind of standard used, whether comparative or absolute, will depend on what the organization hopes to learn. If it is important to an organization to know how its activities compare to each other or to other organizations, comparative standards are used. If it is important to an organization to know how closely the value of its activities approximate the ideal, absolute standards are used.

METHODS OF EVALUATION

Most information derived from evaluation can and should be generated through informal means as a by-product of daily activities. Informal evaluation occurs when managers at all levels and human resource specialists keep up to date about human resource matters, introduce new ideas at the workplace, objectively evaluate their own activities, and serve as effective models of self-evaluation. If these managers and specialists are involved in planning, the planning will be both up to date and practical.

Formal evaluation—a more rigorous application of the principles applied in informal evaluation—may be necessary when new human resource activities are introduced, when it is obvious that informal evaluation is not generating enough information to allow the intelligent use of a human resource activity, or when an organization is unsure whether informal evaluation is adequate.

A wide variety of formal methods of evaluation are available for use in operational planning for human resources. Some of the methods discussed here will be more suited to the evaluation of a human resource activity that is organization-wide or organization unit-wide; other methods will be more suited to an evaluation that is less comprehensive in scope. Methods more suited for organization-wide or organization unit-wide activities are discussed first. Where a method is best suited to measure one or a limited number of attributes, this fact will be pointed out.

At one time or another, organizations will use most of these methods, and in many cases a combination of methods will be used at the same time. Where more than one method of evaluation is employed, they should be used so that each complements the other to promote optimum learning. The combination arrived at will be dictated by the planning needs of the organization.

Performance Appraisal

A performance appraisal evaluates the performance of an employee in his or her current job. Typically, a performance appraisal is conducted by the employee's immediate supervisor.[27] Most appraisals are intended for control purposes—to determine whether an employee will be promoted or to determine the amount of compensation an employee is to receive.[28] To meet these control needs, performance appraisals must measure with precision the level of performance.

Organizations should carry out appraisals dedicated to the planning process in which control needs are not a consideration.[29] Performance appraisals in support of the planning function need to provide information that not only tells organizations how well employees are performing but, even more important, how employees may be of more value to the organization. Two methods of performance appraisal, behaviorally anchored ratings and objective-determined ratings, are especially suited to meet the informational needs of planning.

Behaviorally anchored rating scales are developed through the use of a job analysis process. This process requires supervisors and employees familiar with the job to think carefully about the job—what the various duties of the job are, how important to total job performance each duty is, what behaviors are displayed in carrying out each duty, and differences in behaviors displayed by employees who carry out a duty effectively and those who do so poorly.[30] A scale is developed for each duty of a job position.

Exhibit 8-2 illustrates the type of rating scale that might be developed for the duty "handling customer complaints" for the job position "retail clerk." As the example shows, a behaviorally anchored rating scale typically has seven performance rating points, each point associated with a given level of performance. For

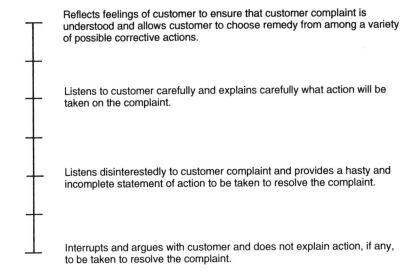

Reflects feelings of customer to ensure that customer complaint is understood and allows customer to choose remedy from among a variety of possible corrective actions.

Listens to customer carefully and explains carefully what action will be taken on the complaint.

Listens disinterestedly to customer complaint and provides a hasty and incomplete statement of action to be taken to resolve the complaint.

Interrupts and argues with customer and does not explain action, if any, to be taken to resolve the complaint.

Exhibit 8-2. Behaviorally Anchored Rating Scale for Retail Clerk Performing the Duty "Handling Customer Complaints"

example, the highest point on the scale might be defined as a level of performance that would be achieved by only the top 5 percent of employees performing the duty. Certain points on the scale are defined by, "anchored by," statements describing job behavior that, according to those familiar with the job, are descriptive of behavior displayed only by employees performing at that level. Only those points are defined for which there is an appropriate behavioral statement. In Exhibit 8-2 only four points are defined.

The employee's performance on the job is evaluated by an appraiser who uses the set of behaviorally anchored rating scales developed for the employee's job position. The appraiser selects a statement from each scale that most nearly describes a behavior displayed by the employee. Overall job performance is determined by combining the ratings of performance of the various duties of the job.

Objective-determined ratings are used by organizations as part of a management-by-objectives approach to performance management. Objectives are set jointly by the employee to be rated and his or her supervisor. At the time of evaluation, the employee's performance rating is based on progress in achieving the objectives. The expected length of the project(s) and/or the expected timing of events in the job assigned to the employee determine how often employee performance is evaluated.[31]

The objective-determined rating method, when used in support of planning, may need to be adapted so that it promotes learning about cause and effect. If control is no longer the major focus, more general objectives can be set. Narrow objectives probably restrict rather than promote learning.

These two rating methods, especially when used together, provide two kinds of information helpful for human resource planning. First, because each method is both developed and implemented through a team effort by line managers, job analysts, and/or by employees who are evaluated, they create a large pool of people in the organization who are well informed about the work being done in the organization—about what people are doing and how successful these efforts are. These people constitute a knowledgeable pool of persons who may be drawn on to assist in operational planning for human resources.

Second, behaviorally anchored ratings and objective-determined ratings provide a central bank of data that allow an organization to determine how related behaviors are related to the achievement of objectives. This information may be used to develop hypotheses about how performance may be improved.

If a number of employees in various jobs are not achieving the objectives of their jobs and if these employees also display particular kinds of behavior, such as an inability to distinguish between important and unimportant problems, a hypothesis may be formulated that: "changing the behavior through better selection or training of employees would improve performance."[32] Programs are implemented for training present employees to improve their ability to prioritize problems and for selecting as employees those candidates that have displayed relevant focusing behavior in previous work experience. A follow-up study can determine whether behavior has been changed by the improved training and selection and, if so, whether this behavioral change is accompanied by better performance.

Assessment Center

Assessment centers have been used to predict the expected performance of employees in a position or family of positions markedly different from the job they currently hold, to screen job candidates recruited from outside sources, and to assess developmental needs of current employees. An assessment center is a carefully coordinated, comprehensive battery of selection techniques. The most important of these techniques are simulation instruments in which candidates are evaluated while carrying out exercises that require skills similar to those required in the target position(s). Organization managers on temporary rotational assignment serve as assessors.

An assessment center can assist the operational planning process for human resources in three ways. First, the center, through early identification of viable candidates for positions in the organization, allows the organization to determine whether present employees are suitable for future positions. Organizations thus receive early warning of problems with the quantity or quality of their future work force.

Second, an assessment center allows the testing of hypotheses about cause and effect. For example, an organization may foresee the problem of not having enough managerial candidates for future positions in the organization. They may test the hypothesis that some nontraditional candidates or employees previously bypassed for managerial positions might be suitable. This could be accomplished by

- Assessing the nontraditional or previously bypassed employees
- Identifying those with remedial deficiencies
- Providing training to these persons to overcome the deficiencies
- Reassessing both the trained and untrained (untrained employees serving as a control group) employees

Finally, an assessment center can develop widespread understanding among organization members of the requirements of the work and of the capabilities of the employees. Various studies have been conducted to determine the learning effects of assessment centers on organization members.[33] Among the effects on managers who served as assessors were

- Better understanding of the duties, scope, and requirements for success in the target positions
- Better understanding of why certain performances and behaviors of subordinates are of value to the organization
- Better understanding of the nature of potential in subordinates
- Better appreciation of the variety of possible solutions to problems in the target position
- Better appreciation of the variety of skills applicable to the target position

Among the effects on employees who were assessed were

- Insight into their own strengths and weaknesses
- Insight into the nature of the target position.

An assessment center will better assist the planning process if it is modified to mirror more accurately the work of the organization and to serve as a vehicle for learning by all participants.

- Assessment center ratings should be based on exercises, such as in-baskets, role plays, or leaderless group discussions.[34] Exercises approximate the divisions of work used within organizations—tasks, duties, and jobs. Ratings of exercises, therefore, are likely to mirror performance in the career development process and to cause the transfer of learning in the center back to the job.[35]
- An assessment center should focus less on the simulation of work done in particular positions, such as managerial or sales positions, and more on the simulation of common features of work in a broad range of positions in the organization.
- An assessment center should involve a broad range of persons as assessors and assessees, including all persons who can contribute to, or benefit from, the learning opportunities available in the center.[36]
- An assessment center should be used to do long-term studies of individuals and their jobs through repeated assessments of the same persons, while observing the effects of job changes and developmental experiences.[37]

The potential impact of assessment centers on planning is great because many persons in the organization can be affected in some way by the activities of a center, either through helping to develop the job simulations and other selection techniques or through serving as participants in center activities. These persons become a pool of informed collaborators who will be able to assist with the planning for human resources.

Human Resource Audit

The human resource audit is used to evaluate the overall human resource function of an organization and its organization units, as well as such major functional areas as training or staffing. The audit follows systematic procedures and uses checklists containing a large number of measures. These measures include both indexes—key objective measures of extent and effectiveness of the activity—and perceptions—key subjective measures of how extensively and how well people think the function is being performed.[38]

To aid in the selection of measures, organizations should consult standard lists of measures.[39] To illustrate the nature of such lists, we show here audit measures for activities within the training area.[40] The first four measures are objective measures; the following four are subjective.

1. Percentage of employees participating in training programs
2. Percentage of employees receiving tuition refunds
3. Training hours per employee
4. Training dollars spent per employee

1. Extent to which trainees feel training programs meet their job needs
2. Extent to which managers feel they are assisted in identifying employee training needs and in developing programs to meet these needs
3. Extent to which managers feel training programs are cost-beneficial
4. Extent to which employees are aware of available training opportunities

The standard lists may be supplemented with measures that organization members feel are key in their particular organization, or measures that do not apply to the organization may be deleted. For example, audit measures of the extent and effectiveness of union relations activities will be meaningless in an organization in which the employees are unorganized.

Once the measures have been selected, data for the measures are collected. The primary sources of data are organization files and information from interviews and questionnaires administered to key persons in the organization.

Traditionally, the information gathered through audits has been used to determine how extensively and how well the human resource function is being performed through

- Internal comparisons of audit results about similar activities carried out in different parts of the organization. For example, comparisons of audit measures of the extent and effectiveness of the organization entry and exit functions in various plants of a manufacturing organization.
- Comparisons of audit results for human resource activities of the organization or of parts of the organization with absolute standards of performance. For example, comparisons of audit measures of the extent and effectiveness of equal employment activities in various individual stores of a retail chain as compared with the obligations of stores under equal employment opportunity legislation.
- External comparisons of audit results for human resource activities of the organization or of parts of the organization with results of audits of other organizations; the use of standardized measures allows this comparison. For example, comparisons of audit measures of the extent and effectiveness of training activities in the organization with similar measures in other organizations in the industry.

In each of these instances, the audit has been used to determine how extensively and how well the human resource function is performed but not to learn how to perform the function better. A more extensive analysis of the audit results is needed.

Luis Gomez-Mejia devised a method for relating audit measures to criteria for organization success.[41] His method contained four steps.

1. Select audit measures from published lists and collect data for the measures.
2. Factor analyze the data.
3. Collect data about criteria of organization success.
4. Regress the factors obtained in step 2 against data for criteria of organization success.

These steps may be used to discover how to further the realization of strategic objectives and strategies. The details of the Gomez-Mejia study will be followed as an example of this use. Assume that a strategic human resource objective of the organization was per-employee profitability.

1. An audit was conducted in a manufacturing organization with 26 plants. Thirty-seven audit measures appropriate for the operations were selected from published lists.
2. The information gathered for the selected measures was factor analyzed and summarized using nine dimensions (factors).
3. The per-employee profitability of each plant was determined by dividing actual profits by number of employees at each plant.
4. These nine dimensions were regressed against plant profitability and it was found that three of the nine were significantly related to per-employee profitability of each plant. These three dimensions were
   - How well each plant performed the *organization entry and exit* functions
   - How well each plant performed the *compensation and reward* functions
   - The extent of employee satisfaction in each plant with the implementation of *policies and procedures*.[42]

For the most effective use of the audit, both the traditional analysis and the extended analysis are necessary. In our example the study suggests that the performance of the organization might be improved with increased emphasis on the functional areas corresponding to the three audit dimensions. Assume that the traditional analysis revealed that several of the plants were giving little emphasis to these areas as compared to other plants, and, moreover, that the organization at corporate level was devoting little attention to these areas as compared to other similar organizations in the industry. The combined results of the two studies suggest that more attention to the three functional areas would be an effective use of organization resources to achieve its strategic objective.[43]

Reputation Assessment and External Peer Review

Reputation assessment and external peer review are related methods. Both use as sources of information outside persons not especially trained as evaluators but possessing knowledge useful to an evaluation. And both are applicable either to the overall human resource management function or to major functional areas, such as training and development or staffing.

Reputation assessment bases the evaluation on information obtained from objective outsiders who have knowledge about the overall characteristics of the human resource function in the organization.[44] The outsiders may have some, usually limited, direct experience with the human resource function being evaluated and typically have talked to others and have read widely about the function. The basic assumption of this method is that these outsiders will have some insights that insiders may not have. They may have these insights because they know only the essential characteristics of the function; their minds are not encumbered by knowledge of countless details as well. Or they may look at the function in a different way or compare it with different other organizations than do insiders. Because the persons relied on are not trained evaluators, information must be gathered from them using good questioning techniques[45] and careful listening.

The success of this method depends on the availability of knowledgeable but objective outsiders who can and will give an opinion about human resources of the organization. Such outsiders may be

- Former employees of an organization—especially human resource professionals and managers—who have worked for a number of other organizations
- Human resource professionals from other organizations who are active in professional circles
- Past clients or suppliers of the organization—human resource consultants, university placement officers, and employment agencies
- Other—university faculty members teaching human resource subjects, upper-level officials of unions with members from the organization or the industry

Reputation assessment lends itself well to both informal and formal use. Informally, it relies on people in the organization who have day-to-day contacts with outsiders from whom they may solicit insights about the human resource function. Formally, the method is best accomplished through focus groups. In either case, the method is inexpensive and is easily used. It can provide insights about strengths and weaknesses of human resources, as well as creative ideas for improving the function.

External peer review is a formal examination to determine the extent to which practitioners in an organization are adhering to professional standards of practice; it is conducted by a team of widely respected, independent practitioners. External peer review is used for the overall human resource area and for any of the highly developed specialties within human resource management such as compensation and benefits, organization development, staffing, and training and development.[46] Standards used in the evaluation have included nearness to state of the art appropriate for the given organization, adherence to standards of ethical practice, and displayed competence in making human resource applications.

External peer review should not be used simply to learn how well the organization is doing. Rather, it should be used to discover specific ways to improve the human resource function. It is particularly useful for discovering whether the organization has an appropriate balance of effort in each of the following areas and which area, if any, needs additional attention:

Keeping abreast of advances in knowledge
Maintaining ethical standards of practice
Applying the knowledge already obtained.

External peer review may also provide specific examples of ways to improve practice in each of these areas.

Analysis of Data in Organization and External Files ~~From records~~

This method makes use of data found in various organization documents and records, and often in files of outside agencies. It usually serves as an adjunct to other evaluation methods.

Data analysis is only as good as the available data. The quantity and quality of the data must be determined before analysis begins. To determine value, the analyst should examine

- The reason or reasons for collecting and storing the data
- How the data were collected
- Where possible, the accuracy of the data

Shortcomings of either quantity or quality of data can be overcome to some extent by using data from a number of independent sources—those that have different motives for collecting the data, those that use different methods to collect the data, and those that collect the data from different primary sources.[47] Data from independent sources may supplement each other, may be useful as a cross-check of accuracy, and may have offsetting errors.

Depending on the amount and the quality of data, the information may be analyzed using time-series analysis, factor analysis, correlation analysis, regression analysis, and/or canonical correlation analysis. Descriptions of these methods of analysis, using both metric and nonmetric data, may be found in basic statistical texts.[48] The most important contribution of these analyses is to suggest possible causal relationships.[49] These relationships, in turn, can be tested by causal analysis,[50] by formulation and application of theory, and by other evaluation methods to confirm or refute the hypotheses of relationships.

Attitude and Opinion Survey

Traditionally, attitude and opinion surveys, using interviews and questionnaires, have been conducted by human resource specialists to measure how well human resource activities are working in an organization. These surveys have evaluated activities ranging from the overall human resource management function to specific procedures, programs, or stocks.

Surveys usually have been "owned" by human resource specialists who decide to whom the survey instrument is addressed, what is to be asked in the survey, and how the survey results are to be used. Such limited ownership severely restricts the learning possibilities.

When surveys are used as part of the planning process, they should be designed and conducted by a committee that includes not only a human resource specialist but also other managerial and nonmanagerial employees. Involvement of employees from throughout the organization allows for a broader exchange of ideas. A representative committee is likely to have a better feel for what should be asked, for the way certain questions will be received, and for whether respondents will be able and willing to provide honest answers.

The learning objectives of the survey will determine which employees to survey. When the intent of the survey is to learn the attitudes of employees about human resource activities, all employees in the organization or a representative sample of all employees may be surveyed. When opinions are required, only those who are in a position to have informed opinions should be surveyed. If the same employees will be asked repeatedly for their opinion, these employees may be recognized as an advisory panel. Such a select group of employees may offer well-formed opinions about which human resource activities have value and why they have value. They may know, for example, why turnover is high in their unit or why the performance of their unit is high. And employees often will be astute observers of the effects of human resource activities.

Not only should the survey promote learning through the use of the information obtained from respondents, but the survey itself should promote learning by its effects on respondents. For example, firms with fixed benefit plans may promote learning by employees about benefits through the use of surveys. Employees typically have little knowledge of benefits and can recall few of the benefits to which they are entitled.[51] A survey may overcome this problem by asking employees to express their preferences among various benefits offered, or proposed to be offered, by the organization. A cost is attached to each benefit and the employee may choose no more than the total value of benefits to which he or she is entitled.[52] The effect of the survey is to help employees become more knowledgeable about their benefits and the cost of the benefits. They are then able to make informed inputs in planning a benefit program that provides maximum value to employees for the money expended.

⟶ give comparison decision
more accuracy

Cost-Benefit Analysis and Utility Analysis

Cost-benefit analysis and utility analysis are used most often to evaluate new or existing human resource procedures and programs. Utility analysis combines cost-benefit analysis with research-based knowledge about human resources to obtain more precise estimates of human resource costs and benefits than are possible using cost-benefit analysis alone.

Cost-benefit analysis usually is carried out as a managerial economy study; it evaluates an activity by expressing both the costs and the benefits of the activity in dollar terms and compares costs to benefits.[53] Using cost-benefit analysis alone, it is difficult to obtain precise estimates of human resource costs and usually impossible to obtain precise estimates of human resource benefits. However, it is important to recognize that precise estimates of costs and benefits are not always necessary where the evaluation is intended to support the planning process. Cost-benefit analyses that yield only approximate estimates of costs and benefits may be useful to planners by

- Allowing a *comparison* of the approximate costs and benefits of several alternative procedures or programs and, where cost-benefit differences among programs are great, indicating which of the alternatives is best.
- Increasing planners' awareness of the *kinds* of costs and of benefits associated with a procedure or program. Awareness of the kinds of costs and benefits associated with an activity allows more astute observations of the effects of procedures and programs on costs and benefits.
- Revealing *hidden* cost and benefit items and improving the ability of planners to judge value. Both benefits and costs tend to be elusive but because benefits typically are less visible and less measurable than costs, worthwhile human resource activities are seen mistakenly as unnecessary "overhead," contributing little to revenues and much to costs.[54]

If more precise estimates of the costs and benefits of a human resource procedure or program seem to be warranted, utility analysis may be employed. Utility analysis makes use of specialized knowledge about human resources to help to overcome and to compensate for the difficulties of measuring the costs and benefits of human resource activities.

Several formulas have been developed to calculate utility.[55] One of the most often used is that which calculates the utility of a human resource procedure or program designed to improve employee performance

$$\Delta U = (N)\,(T)\,(d_t)\,(SD_y) - (C)$$

where

ΔU = the expected increase in utility resulting from treating one group of employees

N = number of employees processed

T = expected duration of effects of the activity

d_t = the difference in average job performance between the employees processed through the activity and similar employees not processed, in standard deviation units

SD_y = the standard deviation of dollar-valued job performance among the incumbent employees

C = cost of processing N employees.[56]

For example, this formula could be used to determine the monetary value of an employee selection technique or the monetary value of a training method.[57]

Until recently, extensive studies were required to determine values for some of the variables used in the formula, notably the terms d_t and SD_y. Recent research has shown that the variables for particular kinds of procedures and programs do not vary greatly among organization settings. Appropriate estimates for these variables may be based on data developed through extensive studies already done in other organizations. The estimation methods and tables of values are presented in the human resource literature.[58]

Utility analysis allows estimates of value that are accurate enough for virtually all uses. However, it should be kept in mind in using cost-benefit analysis and utility analysis that the objective of evaluation is to learn why and how to produce value. The added cost of the additional precision allowed by utility analysis may not be warranted for most evaluation studies. Selective use of either cost-benefit analysis or utility analysis can help planners understand the causal relationships of costs and benefits and to consider in a rational manner the contribution of human resources to the profitability of the organization.

Experiment   *Great benefit to organization if you can set it up.*

An experiment is an attempt to produce and measure the effect of a causal agent on an object by introducing the causal agent while controlling all other possible causes. An experiment often is thought of as occurring only within a laboratory setting, but the field experiment, an experiment conducted within an operating environment, is much more common. An operating environment offers continual opportunities for experimentation. Every new activity or modification to an existing activity is an opportunity to experiment. The most useful human resource experiments are those that reveal the effects of new procedures or programs or the effects of changes in existing procedures and programs.

An experiment provides useful information about a human resource activity to the extent that the results are both interpretable and generalizable. These terms are defined as follows:

- *Interpretable*—From the results it can be determined whether the observed effects (if any) are attributable to the activity and not to other possible causal agents.
- *Generalizable*—From the results it can be determined whether the observed effects (if any) can be applied in other settings of this or other operating environments.[59]

Exhibit 8-3 shows an experimenter introducing a causal agent (the human resource activity) into a setting (the human resource operation) located at a particular time and space in an (operating) environment. The environment, acting through the medium of the setting, both influences and is influenced by the experimenter and by the participants, apparatus, and activities of the experiment. The experimenter conducts and charts the experiment and, in doing so, influences in various ways the agent, object, and response. The experimenter, in turn, is influenced by the experiment and by the agent, object, and response. The causal agent influences an object and the resulting effects may, in turn, influence the causal agent.

Of this large number of influences, many are unintended and may affect the outcome of the experiment, masking the intended effects and making the results of

Exhibit 8-3.   The Experiment in an Operating Environment

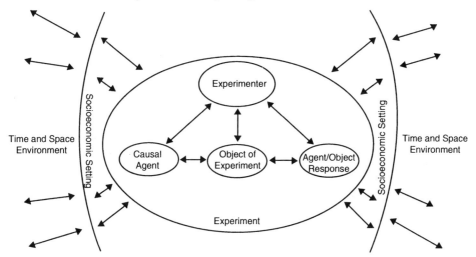

the experiment neither interpretable nor generalizable. These unwanted influences may be controlled either by isolating them or by eliminating them. This may be done by the use of randomly assigned or matched experimental and control groups, by the use of repeated measures of effectiveness, by standardization of experimental activities, and by after-the-fact separation of effects through statistical or judgmental techniques.

Assume that an organization is considering the use of a new training method and wishes to conduct an experiment to measure the effects of training on the job performance of individual employees receiving training. A randomly selected equal number of employees are assigned to a training group and to a control group. Random selection allows the assumption that both groups are representative of the larger employee group. Because both groups are influenced similarly by the setting, space-related influences are controlled and no longer are a cause of difference between the two groups.

If random assignment of employees is impossible, matched training and control groups can be formed; employees in each group are matched on the basis of characteristics, such as age or work experience, that may cause the training to be more or less effective. Compared to random sampling, matched groups allow the control of only a small number of known or suspected unwanted influences.

Control groups also allow the control of some influences caused by the conduct of the experiment itself but not attributable to training. The more important of these effects, especially for new activities that receive considerable publicity, are Hawthorne and Pygmalion effects. Hawthorne effect is the name used to describe the change in individual or group behavior of employees that often occurs when employees receive special attention. Pygmalion effect is used to describe the change in individual behavior that often occurs when employees do well on their jobs because they are expected to do well. To allow separation of these effects from the effects of the training itself, the control group is treated in all respects possible like the experimental group so that Hawthorne and Pygmalion effects, if any, will be produced in both training group and control group alike.

To identify and control time-related influences, measurements of the effectiveness of the employees in the training group and in the control group are taken just prior to the experiment, immediately after the experiment, and some time after the experiment. The comparison of job performance just after the training with that just before the training measures the effects that occur during the training and removes all influences on job performance that occurred prior to the training. The comparison of job performance some time after training with job performance just after training measures influences on job performance, such as atrophy or enhancement of training effects, that occur after training.

To identify and control unintended influences caused by the actual conduct of the experiment, the experimenter should take pains to maintain an unimpaired relationship with the experimental group, make all measurements carefully, record all pertinent information, and avoid the creation of an artificial environment in which people taking part in the experiment behave in contrived and uncharacteristic ways.

If the organization intends to compare the results of the experiment in more than one location, the way the experiment is conducted must be standardized across the locations. Standardization may be accomplished through the establishment of standing plans of various kinds and by training of experimenters used in the various locations.

To identify and control unintended influences remaining after other control measures have been taken, the organization may use either statistical techniques or judgmental techniques. Statistical techniques (metric or nonmetric) may be used for all influences for which quantitative measures are available. Factor analysis is used to reduce the number of unintended influences that must be considered. Correlation analysis is used to indicate how one characteristic, such as whether an employee was a member of a training group or a control group, is related to a second characteristic, such as employee performance, when a third characteristic, such as the job tenure of an employee, is held constant. Time-series analysis may be used to study the pattern of changes in employee performance over time in the training group and to compare this pattern with that of employees in the control group. Regression analysis may be used to determine the nature of the joint relationship of two or more characteristics, such as employee participation in training and employee growth needs, to a third characteristic, such as job performance.[60] Canonical correlation analysis may be used to determine the nature of the joint relationship of two or more characteristics, such as employee participation in training and employee job tenure, to two or more other characteristics, such as quantity of work done and supervisory evaluation of overall performance. None of these techniques in themselves establish causation. Further causal analysis will be necessary to establish causal relationships.

Judgmental techniques may be used for all unintended influences, whether or not quantitative measures are available. They bring to bear opinions about cause-and-effect relationships of persons familiar with the experiment. Participants in the experiment may be assembled and asked to help develop a verbal model of cause-and-effect relationships that lead to job performance and of the place of training in this model. Nominal group techniques can help to enhance the contribution of individual participants to the model.[61] Judgmental techniques are particularly supportive of planning because of the learning that occurs as a by-product of their use.

If judgmental techniques are kept separate from statistical techniques—for example, by making sure that no members of a nominal group have knowledge of any results of statistical analyses—statistical and judgmental techniques may serve as independent checks on each other.

The field experiment is one of the most powerful of the evaluation methods. When the experiment is planned prior to the introduction of an activity, minor modifications often can be made in the way that an activity is introduced that add markedly to the value of the information obtained about an activity and the consequent learning that occurs. With ingenuity, the experimental method may be fit comfortably into ongoing activities and still meet the requirements of producing interpretable and generalizable results.

THE EVALUATOR(S)

Evaluation is an opportunity to learn how human resource activities produce value. This learning produces a knowledge base so that planning can be more effective. The choice of evaluator must further this learning process.

The learning process is simplified when those who need to understand a human resource activity in order to help with planning also do the evaluation. These persons may be individuals or teams. Every individual needs to understand his or her job and should evaluate his or her own work. A unit supervisor needs to understand the work of the unit and should evaluate the work of subordinates. Or a committee of supervisors who have some knowledge of each other's subordinates may occasionally conduct performance appraisals jointly to allow a sharing of viewpoints about how particular employees may be of more value to the organization. Employees responsible for a human resource activity, such as the staffing function for an organization unit, should evaluate the activity; they may evaluate as a team or the evaluator mantle may be passed among them. In each of these instances, organization knowledge about human resources is furthered directly by the evaluation process.

Learning becomes more complex when evaluation is done by a third party—someone from outside the organization or an employee with a full-time position as evaluator. Examples of full-time evaluator positions are internal auditor of human resources and employees of an organization unit responsible for human resource evaluation. What the third party evaluator learns must be transferred to planning participants and integrated with what the participants already know to form a meaningful body of knowledge. This complication in the learning process is warranted when the learning opportunities justify the added complexity and cost of the evaluation.

Third party evaluation should be the exception, not the rule. But the evaluation system, like other organization subsystems, may benefit from deliberate interaction with its environment. For example, human resource audits might normally be done by persons who are part of the process being evaluated. From time to time, an evaluator from outside the organization might be asked to perform an audit using different audit forms and procedures. This affords a different perspective for the audit examination to allow additional learning and to allow a comparison of audit measures at points where there is agreement in the audit approaches. And performance appraisal might normally be done by the supervisor and subordinate alone, but might be done on occasion with the help of a clinical psychologist to allow added insights on how the superior/subordinate team may be strengthened.

As a general rule, having employees who serve as full-time evaluators will make more sense when evaluations are done for control purposes. Here, it is advantageous to maintain an arm's-length relationship between the evaluator and the persons responsible for the activity being evaluated. For planning purposes, full-time evaluators should be used only when the persons in the position are suited for a facilitator role, helping persons in the organization to learn about human resource activities.

The choice of a specific person or persons to carry out the evaluation function will depend on the approach to evaluation, the method of evaluation, and the personal characteristics of the evaluator(s). The approach to evaluation and the method of evaluation will dictate the competencies required of the evaluator(s). For example, activity-specific approaches to evaluation favor narrow technical skills and knowledge about the design and measurement of specific human resource procedures, programs, and stocks. Planned change approaches require skills and knowledge about sociotechnical systems, organization change, and group processes. The cost-benefit method of evaluation requires skills and knowledge about principles of human resource accounting and managerial economics. The experimental method requires skills and knowledge about scientific method and the design of experiments.

The organization can acquire the competencies needed by employing specialists qualified in some of the more useful approaches and methods of evaluation. Or an organization may expand the pool of qualified evaluators in an organization by offering training to all employees in approaches and methods of evaluation.

The most important personal characteristics of an evaluator are acceptability and objectivity. Acceptability is a special concern when there is a third party evaluator. For others to learn from the evaluation, the evaluator must be one whom they respect and trust. Objectivity is important to both participant and third party evaluators. Evaluators must have integrity, be willing to form an opinion without regard to what may be expected, and have the courage of their convictions. Little can be learned if evaluators are not forthright.

USING THE EVALUATION

Most evaluation for planning takes place because it is built into the jobs of persons in the organization and is supported by the culture of the organization. It is continuous and is applied through incremental change. Such evaluation is a normal part of operations and provision for its use is not an issue.

Nonroutine evaluations may require special attention to ensure that they are used. This will be especially likely where an organization does not have a culture that supports evaluation as an important part of the learning process. Some suggestions may help to ensure that use is made of nonroutine evaluations:

1. Make sure that the plan for the evaluation provides for use of the evaluation. A 1983 government-wide audit of program evaluation in Canada carried out by the Canadian Office of the Auditor General found that careful attention to planning of the study is the most critical factor for ensuring evaluation use.[62]
2. Build a base for acceptance of the evaluation report by allowing those who must use the report to take part in planning and conducting the evaluation.
3. Choose an evaluator, or evaluators, who can remain objective without maintaining extremes of social distance or abrasive approaches that offend those who must use the evaluation results.

4. Appoint a liaison within the organization to ensure that the report is complete and understandable to those who are to use the report.
5. Remember that people who are to use the report will normally be doing this in addition to their usual day-to-day activities. Finding time for this extra work may not be easy even if people accept the need for evaluation. Making specific assignments, setting deadlines, asking for reports of follow-through on the evaluation, and providing special help to handle the extra work load can help to ensure that the report is used.

SUMMARY

Evaluation is an essential tool in all stages of the human resource planning process, allowing the organization to learn how and why human resource activities have value. Organizations need to evaluate not only the work of the human resource department but also the human resource activities throughout the entire organization.

Effective evaluation in support of planning requires a supportive organization setting in which evaluation is a planned and integral part of every activity, managers at all levels and in all functional areas demonstrate their belief in the evaluation process, honesty in evaluation is encouraged, and learning through evaluation is encouraged. A supportive setting for evaluation will allow the development of a meaningful philosophy of evaluation for planning. Developing a philosophy is a basic decision and should be done before any formal evaluations begin.

Once a philosophy of evaluation for planning has been developed, an organization may choose an approach or a combination of approaches to evaluation. Approaches differ, depending on the focus of the evaluation. An evaluation may focus on a human resource activity (the activity-specific approach) or on a larger system (the systems approach), on a predetermined set of goals (the goal-constrained approach) or be goal-free (the goal-free approach), on the evaluation itself (the classical approach) or the use of the evaluation (the planned-change approach). Approaches may be used alone or in combination. Choice of approach should be predicated on obtaining as much useful information as possible for the time, money, and effort expended.

Attributes of individual employees, of groups of employees, or of both are used to measure the value of human resource stocks. Effects on employee attributes are used to measure the value of procedures and programs. These attributes and effects are compared to standards—measures selected to serve as a basis for judgment of value. The standards serve to call attention to deviations from expected value. Such deviations should trigger a search for cause.

A number of methods of evaluation may be used either alone or in appropriate combinations. These methods are performance appraisal, assessment center, human resource audit, reputation assessment and external peer review, analysis of data in organizational and external files, attitude and opinion survey, cost-benefit analysis and utility analysis, and experiment.

The learning process is simplified when those who need to understand a human resource activity in order to help with planning also do the evaluation. Learning becomes more complex when evaluation is done by a third party evaluator—someone from outside the organization or an employee with a full-time position as evaluator. This complication is warranted when the learning opportunities justify the added complexity and cost of the evaluation.

The choice of a person or persons to carry out the evaluation function will depend on the approach to evaluation, the method of evaluation, and the personal characteristics of the evaluator(s).

Most evaluation for planning should be built into the jobs of persons in the organization. This evaluation is continuous and its application is routine. Nonroutine evaluations may require special attention to ensure that they are used.

LEARNING EXERCISES

Case Analyses

If you have the opportunity for small-group discussion, you may use the procedure suggested for Case 1 in Chapter 1.

Deft Research and Development, Inc.

Case 8, "Deft Research and Development," was chosen to illustrate an audit of the work of a personnel department. The consultants have presented their report, outlined in Exhibits 4 and 5 of the case, to Karl Rhodes, manager of personnel. Assume that you are Mr. Rhodes. You intend to meet with your 11 subordinates to debrief them on what you feel was learned, both directly and indirectly, as a result of the audit. You are especially concerned with whether your overall approach to evaluation is sound and whether evaluation is being used as a constructive planning tool. In making this determination, consider the following points:

1. Is there agreement within the personnel department and within DR&D as to what the role of the department should be? How many different views are there? Is an evaluation likely to be helpful under these circumstances? Why or why not?
2. Is the setting of DR&D supportive of evaluation? Why or why not?
3. What changes would you recommend to allow evaluation to play a constructive role in DR&D? Be as specific as possible in your recommendations.

Apex Manufacturing Company, Inc.   *Case 6, 337*

Bill Linden, president and general manager of Apex, Case 6, has directed that a promote-from-within program be established within four months. Jayne Mico, director of human resource management, has assigned Jeff Gilby, assistant personnel manager and director of human resource development, the responsibility for establishing this program. Assume that you are Jeff Gilby. Design a promote-from-within program for this organization. For example, in the first two steps of your design you might

- State the objectives of the program.
- List the jobs or families of jobs to be included in the program.

As you carry out the design, pay careful attention to how the program is to be evaluated. Following are specific points relevant to evaluation that you should consider in your design:

1. Will you list only the objectives implied in Mr. Linden's remarks at the meeting of senior managers, or will you incorporate other objectives that seem reasonable expectations of a promote-from-within program? What implicit human resource objectives or strategies does Mr. Linden appear to have in mind that will be furthered by this program? Is it likely that he would accept other objectives as well? Why is it important to know the objectives of a program before carrying out an evaluation?
2. Can you think of ways that evaluation may be built into the design? What are the advantages of doing so?
3. What approach to evaluation do you recommend for this program? Why? What should be measured and what standards should be used for those measures? What method or methods of evaluation should be used?

4. How can you ensure that evaluation will be used as feedback to maintain and improve the promote-from-within program? Be specific here, relating your answer carefully to specific steps of your design and to other features of evaluation.

Activity

Observe the various human resource activities that take place in an organization with which you are familiar. Select one of these activities and choose both an approach to evaluation and a method of evaluation appropriate for this activity. Explain why the approach and the method you chose are appropriate.

Discussion Question

1. What activities would you include in an evaluation of the work of the organization as a whole in carrying out the human resource function that would not be included in an evaluation of the work of a human resource department alone? For what different purposes would each evaluation be carried out?

APPENDIX
GLOSSARY OF EMPLOYEE ATTRIBUTES

Individual

Abilities. Proficiencies to perform tasks, either physical or mental, without additional training and development.

Attitudes and Values. Affective inclinations by employees that tend to be reflected in the thoughts, feelings, and/or actions of employees. Attitudes are displayed by consistent tendencies to think, feel, and behave either positively or negatively toward specific people, institutions, or events. Values are manifested by consistent tendencies to feel positively or negatively toward specific social goals or ends. Values, because they attach to more abstract concepts than do attitudes, less frequently cause value-specific thoughts and behaviors but do create tendencies toward both thought and action.

Behaviors and Traits. Employee behaviors and traits of interest in human resource management usually are observable or have observable effects. Traits are groups of related behaviors that tend to persist in an individual and are work-related—for example, behaviors that might collectively be termed "meticulous."

Beliefs and Opinions. The acceptance of something as true. Opinion often is used to denote readily measurable and specific beliefs.

Cost-Benefit Effects. The value of the work of employees, measured in dollars and arrived at through a cost-benefit analysis.

Capitalized Value. The equivalent net present value of future streams of revenues and costs associated with the work of an employee.

Character or Integrity. A consistent or enduring aspect of the personality that serves to identify a person's ethical or moral point of view.

Citizenship. The tendency of employees to be helpful to fellow employees and/or to the organization and to organization units.

Commitment. A feeling of attachment by employees to an employer, a psychological "casting of their lot" with the employer.

Condition and Health. Condition is a measure of employee fitness for work. Health is a measure of the extent to which employees are free of physical or emotional illness or of predispositions toward physical or mental illness.

Contribution to Profit. The amount by which the profit of an organization is increased over a period of time as a direct result of the work of an employee.

Energy Level. The capacity and predisposition of an employee to expend psychic (mental) and physical energies to accomplish work.

Job Performance. The extent to which an employee achieves desired end results or objectives of a job.

Job Satisfaction. The extent to which an employee enjoys being an employee of an organization.

Knowledge and Understanding. Knowledge is information learned by an employee about a topic. Understanding is the act of combining information learned in ways that give meaning beyond that intrinsic to each discrete bit of information.

Personality. The unique pattern of qualities that serve to define each individual employee.

Productivity. The number of units of output produced for each unit of input. Expressed in terms of labor inputs only, productivity is the number of units of product or service produced for each unit of labor used.

Skills. Acquired abilities of employees to deal with people, to manipulate data, and/or to use things.

Service Orientation. The predisposition of an employee to want to provide, or to find pleasure in providing, service to a client or customer.

Tenure. The length of time an employee has worked in a particular job, organization unit, or organization.

Work Ethic. The set of beliefs of an individual about work, especially about paid employment.

Group

Culture. A socially approved set of norms for the behavior of members of an organization or of units of the organization that serve to routinize and to lend predictability to social behaviors.

Loyalty. The social display of commitment to an organization (or group) that may occur when social awareness develops within an organization that a significant number of employees are committed to the organization as an employer. Loyalty tends to occur only if social needs are met by the display of commitment.

Morale. A feeling shared by most members of a group, and reinforced in individual members through social exchanges, of confidence and of desire to continue an activity or set of activities (high morale) or of lack of confidence and unwillingness to continue an activity (low morale).

Social Character. The social display of character traits that may occur when a mature social group realizes that a significant number of its members share similar character traits.[63] It differs from culture in that culture is expressed through the policing effect of behavior norms, whereas social character is expressed because people as a group enjoy expressing shared traits.

Endnotes

[1] See pp. 1-204–1-207 of Anne S. Tsui and Luis R. Gomez-Mejia, "Evaluating Human Resource Effectiveness," in Lee Dyer, ed., *Human Resource Management: Evolving Roles and Responsibilities* (Washington, DC: Bureau of National Affairs, 1988), pp. 1-187–1-227.

[2] The term *stock* is defined in Chapter 9. Stock refers to supplies of human resources.

[3] See p. 435 of Robert A. Snyder, Charles S. Raben, and James L. Farr, "A Model for the Systemic Evaluation of Human Resource Development Programs," *Academy of Management Review,* 5, no. 3 (July 1980), 431–444.

[4] See Alfred H. Lievertz, "Developing Your Functional Fingerprint," *Personnel Administrator,* 32, no. 1 (January 1987), 61–65, for an example of a report of an audit of the operations of the human resource department of an organization assumed to be equivalent to an audit of the human resource function. For a different view of the human resource function and of the associated audit, see George E. Biles, "Auditing HRM Practices," *Personnel Administrator,* 31, no. 2 (December 1986), 89–94.

[5] One of the recommendations made by Tsui and Gomez-Mejia, "Evaluating Human

Resource Effectiveness," p. 1-222, is to emphasize the "operating HR department" in an evaluation.

[6]Compare pp. 1-187–1-189 and pp. 1-209–1-212 of Tsui and Gomez-Mejia, "Evaluating Human Resource Effectiveness."

[7]For an example of an approach to the design of training programs that incorporates evaluation into the programs, see Barbara Bennett and David F. Griswold, "Proving Our Worth: The Training Value Model," *Training and Development Journal*, 38, no. 10 (October 1984), 81–83.

[8]The social learning through which behavior tendencies such as honesty in evaluation are learned is termed identificatory learning. Identificatory learning causes the imitation of values, attitudes, and beliefs in others and is an especially important learning method for persons in the early years of work life. See Chapter 9.

[9]Tsui and Gomez-Mejia, "Evaluating Human Resource Effectiveness," p. 1–199.

[10]See p. 179 of Robert N. Beck, "Adding Value: The Accountability of Human Resources for Impacting Business Results," *Human Resource Planning*, 8, no. 4 (December 1985), 173–191.

[11]Ibid., p. 180.

[12]See pp. 241–247 of Albert Bandura, " Social-Learning Theory of Identificatory Processes," in David A. Goslin, ed., *Handbook of Socialization Theory and Research* (Chicago: Rand McNally, 1969), pp. 213–262.

[13]See Carol H. Weiss, *Evaluation Research* (Englewood Cliffs, NJ: Prentice Hall, 1972), pp. 18, 117.

[14]Ibid., p. 117.

[15]See Samuel Messick, "Medical Model of Evaluation," in Scarvia B. Anderson, Samuel Ball, Richard T. Murphy and Associates, *Encyclopedia of Educational Evaluation* (San Francisco: Jossey-Bass, 1975), pp. 136–140. Messick refers to these approaches as the "engineering model of evaluation" and the "medical model of evaluation."

[16]See Samuel Messick, "Goal-Free Evaluation," in Scarvia B. Anderson et al., *Encyclopedia of Educational Evaluation*, pp. 178–179. The idea of "goal-free" evaluation is attributed to Michael Scriven, "Pros and Cons About Goal-Free Evaluation," *Evaluation Comment*, 3, no. 4 (December 1972), 3–4.

[17]For a description of the classical approach to evaluation, see p. 21 of Samuel Ball, "Adversarial Model of Evaluation," in Scarvia B. Anderson et al., *Encyclopedia of Educational Evaluation*, pp. 21–22.

[18]Weiss, *Evaluation Research*, pp. 112–113, 117–118.

[19]Scriven apparently feels that the experienced evaluator will be able to recognize an effect worth considering in the evaluation without benefit of a list. See Scriven, "Pros and Cons," pp. 2–3.

[20]Weiss, *Evaluation Research*, p. 111.

[21]Care must be taken in aggregating attributes of individual employees to describe groups. For an excellent discussion of this topic, see Irving H. Siegel, *Aggregation and Averaging, Methods for Manpower Analysis No. 1* (Kalamazoo, MI: W. E. Upjohn Institute for Employment Research, May 1968).

[22]Most of the individual and group attributes listed here will be understood by readers; all attributes are defined in an appendix at the end of this chapter.

[23]For a more comprehensive view of the possible impact of health and fitness programs, see Russell W. Driver and Ronald A. Ratliff, "Employers' Perceptions of Benefits Accrued from Physical Fitness Programs," *Personnel Administrator*, 29, no. 8

(August 1982), 21–26; Richard P. Sloan, Jessie C. Gruman, and John P. Allegrante, *Investing in Employee Health* (San Francisco: Jossey-Bass, 1987).

[24] A group of 24 companies, calling themselves the Mayflower Group, exchanged data from attitude surveys of their employees. Employees in each company were asked to indicate level of agreement with 64 positive statements about the organization. These items were scored and reported individually and also as part of a composite score on each of 15 factors. See Frederick E. Schuster, "A Tool for Evaluating and Controlling the Management of Human Resources," *Personnel Administrator*, 27, no. 10 (October 1982), 63–69.

[25] See "Survey Measures Effectiveness of Human Resource Operations," *Resource* (December 1988), 10.

[26] Benchmarking is described in Chapter 3.

[27] Appraisals prepared by the supervisor often are supplemented by objective data indicating quantity or quality of performance. Where supervisors have limited opportunity to observe employee performance, evaluations by other persons such as clients or peers also may be used.

[28] See, for example, Charles J. Fombrun and Robert L. Laud, "Strategic Issues in Performance Appraisal: Theory and Practice," *Personnel*, 60, no. 6 (November–December 1983), 23–31.

[29] A classical study of performance appraisal at General Electric Company led to the conclusion that appraisal is ineffective when appraisals for different purposes are combined. See Herbert H. Meyer, Emanuel Kay, and John R. P. French, Jr., "Split Roles in Performance Appraisal," *Harvard Business Review*, 43, no. 1 (January–February 1965), 123–129.

[30] For a description of the job analysis methodology used to develop behaviorally anchored rating scales, see Donald P. Schwab, Herbert G. Heneman, and Thomas A. DeCotiis, "Behaviorally Anchored Rating Scales: A Review of the Literature," *Personnel Psychology*, 28, no. 4 (Winter 1975), 549–562; and Frank J. Landy, James L. Farr, Frank E. Sall, and Walter R. Freytag, "Behaviorally Anchored Scales for Rating the Performance of Police Officers," *Journal of Applied Psychology*, 61, no. 1 (December 1976), 750–758.

[31] Proper use of objective-determined ratings is especially critical for their success. For an excellent review of the points to consider in installing or modifying a management-by-objectives (MBO) program—the more popular of the various approaches to objective-determined ratings—see Robert W. Hollmann, "Applying MBO Research to Practice," *Human Resource Management*, 15, no. 4 (Winter 1976), 28–36.

[32] This example is based on the experience of Corning Glass Works with the joint use of behaviorally anchored rating systems and objective-determined rating systems. See p. 62 of Michael Beer and Robert A. Ruh, "Employee Growth through Performance Management," *Harvard Business Review*, 54, no. 4 (July–August 1976), 59–66.

[33] Reviews of the literature concerning the effects of assessment centers on managers who served as assessors and on employees who were assessed have been done by Howard and by Boehm. See pp. 127–129 of Ann Howard, "An Assessment of Assessment Centers," *Academy of Management Journal*, 17, no. 1 (March 1974), 115–134; and pp. 46–50 of Virginia R. Boehm, "Using Assessment Centers for Management Development—Five Applications," *Journal of Management Development*, 4, no. 4 (1985), 40–53. Only a small number of studies present hard evidence of the learning effects of assessment centers. However, there is considerable anecdotal evidence, as well as considerable logic, to support the conclusion that assessment centers have important

developmental effects on all persons involved with the center, even when no developmental effect is intended.

[34]Ratings typically have been based on dimensions, such as organizing or decision making. Paul R. Sackett and George F. Dreher, "Situation Specificity of Behavior and Assessment Center Validation Strategies: A Rejoinder to Neidig and Neidig," *Journal of Applied Psychology*, 69, no. 1 (February 1984), 187–190. See also Ivan Robertson, Lynda Gratton, and David Sharpley, "The Psychometric Properties and Design of Managerial Assessment Centres: Dimensions into Exercises Won't Go," *Journal of Occupational Psychology*, 60, no. 3 (1987), 187–195.

[35]For a discussion of the effect of rating method on the way assessors organize the information assembled in an assessment center, see William H. Silverman, Anthony Dalessio, Steven B. Woods, and Rudolph L. Johnson, "Influence of Assessment Center Methods on Assessors' Ratings," *Personnel Psychology*, 39, no. 3 (Fall 1986), 565–578.

[36]Douglas W. Bray, "Fifty Years of Assessment Centres: A Retrospective and Prospective View," *Journal of Management Development*, 4, no. 4 (1985), 4–12, believes the current success of the assessment center is largely due to its facility for teaching nonpsychologists to use valid psychological knowledge and techniques to the benefit of themselves and the organization. He suggests principles useful to accomplish this teaching.

[37]See Douglas Bray, "The Assessment Center and the Study of Lives," *American Psychologist*, 37, no. 2 (February 1982), 180–189, for a description of the classical longitudinal study of managers within AT & T.

[38]See Tsui and Gomez-Mejia, "Evaluating Human Resource Effectiveness," pp. 1-189–1-195.

[39]The best single source of information about audits of the human resource function is George E. Biles and Randall S. Schuler, *Audit Handbook of Human Resource Management Practices* (Alexandria, VA: American Society for Personnel Administration, 1986). See also Tsui and Gomez-Mejia, "Evaluating Human Resource Effectiveness."

[40]This list is adapted from p. 1-192 of Tsui and Gomez-Mejia, "Evaluating Human Resource Effectiveness."

[41]See ibid., p. 295, for a partial list of sources of these published checklists.

[42]Ibid., p. 304.

[43]If these audit dimensions are different from the dimensions that contribute to employee satisfaction, it might be questioned if "keeping employees satisfied" was an appropriate strategy to achieve the profitability objective. Causal analysis could be used to determine whether employee satisfaction appeared to be an important intervening variable in the chain of variables causing profitability.

[44]Tsui would base reputation assessment of a personnel department on its reputation for effectiveness among all its constituencies, both within and outside the organization. See Anne S. Tsui, "Personnel Department Effectiveness: A Tripartite Approach," *Industrial Relations*, 23, no. 2 (Spring 1984), 184–197.

[45]The standard for this area continues to be Stanley Payne, *The Art of Asking Questions* (Princeton, NJ: Princeton University Press, 1951).

[46]For an example of external peer review of an employee assistance program, see Dale A. Masi and Michelle E. Goff, "The Evaluation of Employee Assistance Programs," *Public Personnel Management*, 16, no. 4 (Winter 1987), 323–327.

[47]See p. 307 of Scarvia B. Anderson, "Quasi-Experimental Design," in Anderson et al., *Encyclopedia of Educational Evaluation*, pp. 301–310.

[48]For example, Morris Hamburg, *Statistical Analysis for Decision Making*, 4th ed. (New

York: Harcourt Brace Jovanovich, 1988); Sidney Siegel, *Nonparametric Statistics for the Behavioral Sciences* (New York: Mcgraw-Hill Book Co., 1956); Joseph F. Hair, Rolph E. Anderson, Ronald L. Tatham, and Bernie J. Grablowsky, *Multivariate Data Analysis*, 2nd ed. (Tulsa, OK: Petroleum Publishing Co., 1987).

[49]See p. 49 of Richard T. Murphy, "Causality," in Anderson et al., *Encyclopedia of Educational Evaluation*, pp. 48–50.

[50]See, for example, chap. 9, pp. 258–279, of James E. Rosenbaum, *Career Mobility in a Corporate Hierarchy* (Orlando, FL: Academic Press, 1984). For an explanation of causal analysis concepts and techniques, see Herbert B. Asher, *Causal Modeling* (Beverly Hills, CA: Sage Publications, 1976); Lawrence R. James, Stanley A. Mulaik, and Jeanne M. Brett, *Causal Analysis: Assumptions, Models, and Data* (Beverly Hills, CA: Sage Publications, 1982); David R. Heise, *Causal Analysis* (New York: John Wiley and Sons, 1975).

[51]W. B. Werther, "A New Direction in Rethinking Fringe Benefits," *MSU Business Topics*, 22, no. 2 (Winter 1974), 35–40, cited on p. 30 of Randall B. Dunham and Roger A. Formisano, "Designing and Evaluating Employee Benefit Systems," *Personnel Administrator*, 27, no. 4 (April 1982), 29–35.

[52]Dunham and Formisano, "Designing and Evaluating Employee Benefit Systems," p. 32, used this procedure in an exercise with selected employees to validate the model used to design a benefit plan.

[53]For a general discussion of cost-benefit analysis in management, see chap. 14, pp. 608–653, of Lawrence Southwick, Jr., *Managerial Economics* (Plano, TX: Business Publications, 1985). For a discussion of the application of cost-benefit analysis in human resource management, see Wayne F. Cascio, *Costing Human Resources: The Financial Impact of Behavior in Organizations*, 2nd ed. (Boston: PWS-Kent Publishing, 1987); and Jac Fitz-Enz, *How to Measure Human Resource Management* (New York: McGraw-Hill Book Co., 1984).

[54]See pp. 1-125–1-126 of John W. Boudreau, "Utility Analysis," in Dyer, *Human Resource Management*, pp. 1-125–1-186.

[55]See John W. Boudreau, "Decision Theory Contributions to HRM Research and Practice," *Industrial Relations*, 23, no. 2 (Spring 1984), 198–217.

[56]Ibid., pp. 199–200.

[57]This formula is used to determine the value of a procedure or program with current employees. Boudreau has extended utility analysis to include not only a current employee group (cohort) but any number of future employee groups. See John W. Boudreau, "Effects of Employee Flows on Utility Analysis of Human Resource Productivity Programs," *Journal of Applied Psychology*, 68, no. 3 (August 1983), 396–406.

[58]Boudreau, "Decision Theory Contributions to HRM Research and Practice," pp. 200–201. See also Robert A. Bolda, "Utility: A Productivity Planning Tool," *Human Resource Planning*, 8, no. 3 (1985), 111–132. See, however, the recommendations of Nambury S. Raju, Michael J. Burke, and Jacques Normand, "A New Approach for Utility Analysis," *Journal of Applied Psychology*, 75, no. 1 (February 1990), 3–12. Whichever method is used, an experimental design should be used to validate the utility estimates. See p. 133 of Robert J. Vance and Adrienne Colella, "The Utility of Utility Analysis," *Human Performance*, 3, no. 2 (1990), 123–139.

[59]For a discussion of interpretability and generalizability as considerations in the design of an evaluation, see Scarvia B. Anderson, "Design of Evaluation," in Anderson et al., *Encyclopedia of Educational Evaluation*, pp. 122–126.

[60]For nonmetric data, either multiple analysis of variance or multiple discriminant analysis may be used.

[61]The nominal group technique is defined in the appendix to Chapter 2 and is discussed in more detail in Chapter 7.

[62]Nancy Soper, Kathleen Petersen, Neil Maxwell, and Rona Shaffran, "Facilitating Use: The Canadian Experience," *Optimum*, 15, no. 4 (1984), 64–75. This same study also found that a broad definition of "use" was advisable in planning the use of an evaluation.

[63]See Benjamin B. Wolman, comp. and ed., *Dictionary of Behavioral Science* (New York: Van Nostrand Reinhold, 1973), p. 350; this definition is attributed to Erich Fromm, collaborator.

Chapter 9

Determining Flows
of Human Resources

As we learned in the discussion of organization identity in Chapters 2 and 4, organizations are complex phenomena—difficult to see and difficult to conceptualize. It is correspondingly difficult to see patterns and underlying logic in the many disparate activities concerned with human resources that occur daily in the organization.

These activities begin to make sense, though, when we view the flows of persons within organizations. People enter the organization as new employees, move from position to position within the organization, and eventually leave the organization. The process then begins anew with replacement employees.

Human resource flows are continuous. They supply the stocks for the organization. Stocks are stores of people within the system with actual or potential skills or abilities to fill job positions within the organization as the need arises. For example, people hired as stockroom employees in a department store may later become sales clerks, and college graduates hired into the training program of a bank may become managers of the bank's operations.

There is increasing evidence that job positions in the human resource flows do not simply employ and hold employees for later use, but the very process of being in the positions changes the people involved. Their perceptions, their feelings, their values are changed. They gain knowledge, skills, and abilities that may be used in other positions.[1] For example, the stockroom employee gains knowledge about the merchandise that can be applied later as a salesperson. And the college graduate in the training program of the bank will be exposed to a variety of experiences that may someday make him or her a more sensitive, effective bank executive.

VIEWS OF HUMAN RESOURCE FLOWS

There are several ways to view the flows of human resources in an organization: as movements of people through economic systems, as movements of people through social systems, and as movements of people along career paths. Each view contributes to our understanding of what is happening as human resources flow through the organization and each view helps us to plan for these flows.

Movements Through Economic Systems

Human resources are allocated to different uses in an organization through external and internal labor markets. External labor markets are those where an organization competes with other organizations for services of available job candidates. Effective external labor markets improve the efficiency of an economy by helping to ensure that labor resources are allocated to their best possible uses. But what may improve the efficiency of an economy as a whole may prove inefficient or inconvenient for a specific organization. For example, there may not be enough persons of good quality available for hire at wage rates and at times the organization needs to hire.

In order not to be subject to the vagaries of external labor markets, organizations establish internal labor markets as sources of labor for many jobs within the organizations. These internal markets are protected by organization boundaries against the economic forces of external labor markets. Formally defined, internal labor markets are clusters of jobs within organizations for which interrelated decisions about hiring can be made.[2] These intraorganizational job clusters are characterized by

- Hierarchical arrangement of the jobs by level of difficulty and pay[3]
- Linkages of the jobs to external labor markets by a few port-of-entry jobs and to other internal labor markets through a few port-of-entry and port-of-exit jobs
- Hiring from within as the main way of filling vacancies within jobs
- Formal, often elaborate, procedures for hiring, firing, and transfer among jobs within the cluster
- Progress along job ladders mostly determined by demonstrated ability through on-the-job experience and by accumulation of training and development credits

Seldom, if ever, does an entire organization constitute a single internal labor market. More often, an organization includes a number of internal labor markets that, together, incorporate a large proportion of the organization's employees.

Some jobs do not fall into job clusters. They stand independent, and the labor supply for these will need to be handled through the external market.

A word of caution is necessary about the internal labor market. Internal labor markets are more complex than are external labor markets.[4] Both markets perform pricing and allocation functions, but because internal markets take place within, and as a subset of, sociotechnical economic systems, they are concerned not only with bargains struck over money but with bargains struck over power and status as well. Further, internal labor markets are concerned not simply with the purchase of knowledge, skills, abilities, and other desirable employee characteristics but also with the development of these characteristics. They are concerned with the accumulation and sale of human capital.

Human Capital and Internal Labor Markets

The theory of human capital states that how well individuals fare in the labor market depends not only on their innate characteristics of value to potential employers but also on how well they maintain these innate characteristics and on the extent to which they acquire new characteristics.

Characteristics of value in the labor market are maintained and acquired by the expenditures of both time and money. For example, individual employees invest in education, training,[5] and work experience. Families of employees may provide emotional support, and society at large may provide child care and physical health care. These expenditures are termed investments and the resulting accretion in the value of individuals as employees is termed human capital.[6]

Employers enter external labor markets to obtain employees and often are required to pay premium wages to employees with accrued human capital. But employees with appropriate characteristics may not be available or may not be willing to work at wages that employers are willing to pay at that time. In part to avoid the uncertainties of market fluctuations, employers may choose to invest in the human capital of their own employees. The internal labor market is the vehicle employers typically use to make decisions about these investments.

Employees are hired through port-of-entry jobs and are moved into other positions through predetermined other jobs and according to normatively approved procedures. Advancement through these other jobs may occur over a period of years. While employees are thus held in the "pipeline," they are available for investments.

Internal labor markets allow much of the human capital in employees to be accrued with no corresponding cost, direct or indirect, to the organization beyond that of the normal employee support system. Because employees are in the vicinity of the jobs they eventually will occupy, they learn about the jobs through observation, through informal conversations at lunch hour and on work breaks, and through filling in for each other during temporary absences.[7]

Employers may take advantage of the availability of employees in the pipeline to make sizable planned investments in human capital, such as paying for employees' advanced education, providing training opportunities, providing developmental work experiences, and providing programs that encourage physical and emotional well-being.

On-the-job training is a particularly good investment, especially for blue-collar workers. This training takes advantage of the physical proximity of employees to the organization and to the jobs for which they are being trained. Employees are readily available and need not travel to the training. Marginally productive or slack times, when employees, facilities, and/or equipment are partly or fully idle, can be used for the training. Excess training is avoided because training is tailored to the exact needs of the specific job or job family.[8]

If employers are to make the investments in human capital, turnover of employees must be sufficiently low so that employers can recover their investments.[9] The internal labor market contributes to low turnover rates. It affords job security and chances for advancement.[10] Organization-specific training increases the worth of the employees to the employer but not usually to other employers; this affords the employer a competitive advantage when competing for the services of its own employees in the marketplace. Employers may gain additional competitive advantage by returning part of the returns on the training investment to participating employees through increased compensation and benefits.[11]

Movements Through Social Systems

Networks of Interlocking Roles

In formal organizations people construct elaborate, well-defined expectations about the ways people in specific jobs should behave. The behavior expected of an employee filling a specific job is called a "role." Those persons who have expectations about the behavior of the employee are part of the employee's "role set."[12] The social roles developed within an organization reflect the norms and values of people in the organization and the organization identity that organization members are enacting.

In a highly developed organization, roles are appropriately interrelated so as to yield predictable and favorable outcomes. The set of interrelated roles comprises a social system, a stable collective pattern in which people play their parts.[13] As people move among jobs within the organization, they move within a network of interlocking roles. They must continually learn to fulfill new role requirements. The process of adjustment for the employee moving to a new position may be seen as a transition cycle consisting of four stages (see Exhibit 9-1).[14] The stages are interdependent. How well an employee does in each stage depends on how well he or she performed in the previous stage.[15]

The first stage, preparation, is primarily concerned with psychological readiness to move. It involves expectations one has for the new position and the feelings and motives aroused by the expected change. The second stage, encounter, involves the first few days and weeks in a new job. The task of making sense of all that is happening is of primary importance in this stage. Pronounced "reality shock" and dysfunctional amounts of surprise may occur if the preparation stage was not properly performed. Once any shock and surprise of the encounter stage has been dealt with, and an initial relationship with tasks and people in the new job has been formed, the real work of adjustment begins. In the adjustment stage a

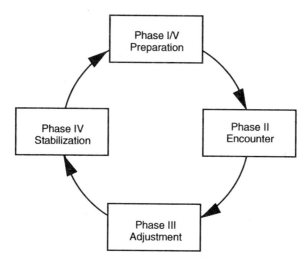

Exhibit 9-1. The Transition Cycle of Employee Adjustment to a New Work Role
Source: Nigel Nicholson and Michael West, *Managerial Job Change: Men and Women in Transition* (Cambridge: Cambridge University Press, 1988), p. 9.

resocialization process takes place. This involves accommodation on three levels—with one's work, with the people with whom one interacts, and with the culture of the new environment. The adjustment process may require drastic changes that affect the lifespan development of the individual, perhaps resulting in changes in focus and direction of his or her life. The final stage of the cycle is stabilization. Where adjustment is allowed to run its course, the stabilization stage sees the individual striving to maintain valued elements of the role, making fine-tuning adjustments to experience and action, and enjoying or suffering the fruits of success or failure. Stabilization becomes preparation as the employee begins to think of the next job. For stabilization to flow effectively into preparation, appraisal functions need to be allied with forward-looking review activities.

The movement of employees among jobs presents challenges and opportunities for both those employees moving and those employees affected by the move. At any given time, most employees in an organization are not moving among jobs. Most of these employees will be in the stabilization stage of their adjustment cycle. While there, they will be affected by new employees moving into their role set. They must adjust to these new persons. They take part in their socialization process. And they have an opportunity to learn from the new ideas introduced by these new persons.

Social Learning Theory

Social learning is learning from other people. It determines to a great extent the behavior of people in organizations. As the transition cycle illustrates, employees moving through organizations both experience, and cause in other people, considerable social learning. A move to a new social grouping is an important learning opportunity.

Social learning theory suggests that social learning occurs in two primary ways. First there is instrumental training.[16,17] In *instrumental training*, reinforcing agents with particular socialization goals in mind explicitly attempt to shape a learner's responses by differential reinforcement.[18] An example is the attempt by a supervisor (the reinforcing agent) to reduce the number of times that certain monthly reports are submitted by his or her subordinates after the report due date (the socialization goal). As each report is submitted, the supervisor responds positively if the report is on time, negatively if the report is late (differential reinforcement). The percentage of times subordinates submit late reports drops (behavior is shaped). In modern organizations many persons serve as instrumental trainers for another person, attempting to shape that persons behavior through differential reinforcement.

Little instrumental training is needed in many role networks. Roles are established, the status quo built around these roles is reasonably satisfactory, and little attempt is made to bring about new behavior. Instrumental training is used on occasion only to maintain current behavior patterns. However, when something happens to disturb this status quo, such as a new person moving into one of the roles in a role network, attempts to shape behavior may occupy for an interval much of the time and attention of persons in the network. This will continue until a reasonably satisfactory new status quo develops.

Instrumental training is an important force for building and maintaining roles in organizations. It tends to stabilize behavior and retain continuity of roles. It is one of the important ways of building a well-defined organization identity and culture.

A second type of social learning is observational learning.[19] *Observational learning* refers to behavioral changes that occur in one person, the observer, as a result of observing the behavior of another, the model. It is pervasive and often occurs without conscious awareness. It is the vehicle for most social learning in modern society.[20]

Observational learning takes one of three different forms: imitation, identification, or simple observation. *Imitation* is learning through patterning behavior after that of a model. It requires that the environment positively reinforce such learning.[21] Most persons carry from their childhood imitative skills, and those skills can be improved by conscious effort and practice. In the beginning stages of learning a new job or in the early stages of learning any new task, imitation is an especially valuable tool for learning.

In *identification* learning, imitation is focused on one or a few others who model through their behavior a self-identity that seems desirable to the observer. The driving force in identification learning is the search for identity; instrumental training has little effect on the process. Identifying with another typically causes emulation not only of a wide range of overt behaviors but also such general dispositional behaviors as values, attitudes, and beliefs.[22] Identification may promote very rapid self-development. This form of learning may occur at any stage of work life but is especially important during the early years of work life.

When the observer has established a repertoire of basic social behaviors and a basic identity, *simple observation* learning begins to take the place of other forms of observational learning. The observer adopts some of the behaviors of a few others when those behaviors are thought likely to produce more favorable outcomes than does his or her own behaviors.[23] In addition, the observer looks for cues to guide the choice of behaviors from his or her repertoire to use in specific situations. Instrumental training has relatively little effect on this form of behavior.

As the individual establishes a well-developed social identity and begins to enact this identity using a complete and carefully selected repertoire of social behaviors, he or she becomes more often the model rather than the observer.

Movements Along Career Paths

As discussed in Chapter 4, a career is the entire set of work-related experiences of a person over his or her lifetime. Career employees are those employees who feel a commitment to their careers as well as, or instead of, a commitment to the organization. The time an employee spends within any one organization often is but one leg on a career path journey. Organizations that wish to have a mutually successful relationship with career employees need to devote attention to the concepts of career decision making and career success.

Career Decision Theory

Careers tend to be vividly marked by career decisions. Career decisions are recognized as important by career-oriented employees and, for these employees, career decisions tend to occupy much of their attention for relatively brief, but recurrent, periods during their work lives.

According to the widely accepted Miller-Tiedeman model of career decision making, people make career decisions in a highly experiential fashion.[24] As Exhibit 9-2 shows, the career decision-making process begins when a person learns about an opportunity and/or a problem in his or her career. This "learning-about-an-opportunity/problem-discovery event" may initiate a thinking stage in which the person explores the available opportunity and/or defines the problem. He or she then considers the advantages and disadvantages of the present situation as compared to other opportunities, or looks at alternative approaches to solving the problem. This thinking stage is followed by doing stages in which the decision is implemented; these stages are "problem solving/beginning to act," and "solution using/carrying out."[25] The final stage is one in which the decision has been implemented and the person is in the early stages of "living with" the decision, and still is reflective about the decision. This is a doing with awareness stage in which the person "reviews/thinks about" the decision.

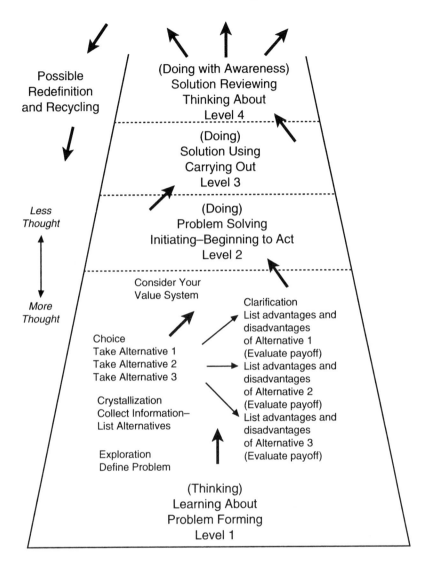

Exhibit 9-2.   The Miller-Tiedeman Pyramidal Model of Career Decision Making
Source: Adapted from A. L. Miller-Tiedeman, *Individual Career Exploration, Picture Form: Manual of Directions* (Bensenville, IL: Scholastic Testing Service, 1977), p. 141, reprinted in David V. Tiedeman and Anna Miller-Tiedeman, "Career Decision Making: An Individualistic Perspective," in Duane Brown, Linda Brooks, and Associates, *Career Choice and Development* (San Francisco: Jossey-Bass, 1984), pp. 281–310.

The doing with awareness stage may be followed by a career stage during which the person is relatively little concerned with career decision making but is simply involved in the day-to-day implementation of a career step, such as pursuing a degree or working at a particular job.

Dynamics of Career Success

If career decisions are carefully considered, people have expectations that their opportunities for career success are improved. And career success may be important not only as an end in itself but also as a key ingredient in a cyclical process that tends to produce better career decisions.[26] This process is shown in Exhibit 9-3.

The cycle shown in Exhibit 9-3 is continuous. Starting at the left of the exhibit, we see that feelings of career success cause an expanded career identity.[27] Expansion in career identity is a specific kind of personal growth defined as a greater awareness of one's career competencies. Expansion in career identity, together with feelings of career success, leads to more realistic aspiration levels.[28] Expansion in career identity alone causes increased career involvement[29] and improved self-esteem.[30] Career involvement is a measure of the strength of one's motivation to work in a given career field, as distinguished from commitment to an organization or a job.[31] More realistic aspiration levels,[32] increased career involvement,[33] and improved self-esteem[34] cause the choice of a challenging but appropriate goal. Choice of a challenging but appropriate goal leads to greater effort to achieve the goal and to an increased likelihood of goal attainment.[35] Achieving a challenging personal goal causes feelings of success, and the cycle is ratcheted to a higher level to begin anew.[36]

A Career Path

In a complex and constantly changing world, detailed planning at any one time for a lifetime of work is neither practical nor possible. Rather, people who plan their careers tend to plan at any given time for the opportunities known to them at that time. They then seize the best of the available opportunities. There fol-

Exhibit 9-3. The Career Success Process.
Source: Adapted from Douglas T. Hall, *Careers in Organizations* (Pacific Palisades, CA: Goodyear Publishing Co., 1976), p. 32.

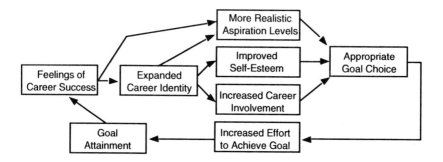

lows a relatively long period of day-to-day career experience and personal growth. This in turn is followed by a relatively brief, and possibly metamorphic, period of concentrated decision making. This decision making may be brought on by an outside event, such as availability of additional career information or the emergence of additional career opportunities, or by an event within the individual such as a change in the individual's picture of self brought about by the achievement of one or more career goals. Major events tend to be followed by major changes in career direction, minor events by minor changes in career direction. And so the process continues. Exhibit 9-4 shows a model of a career path.

Exhibit 9-4.   Unfolding Paths Model of a Career

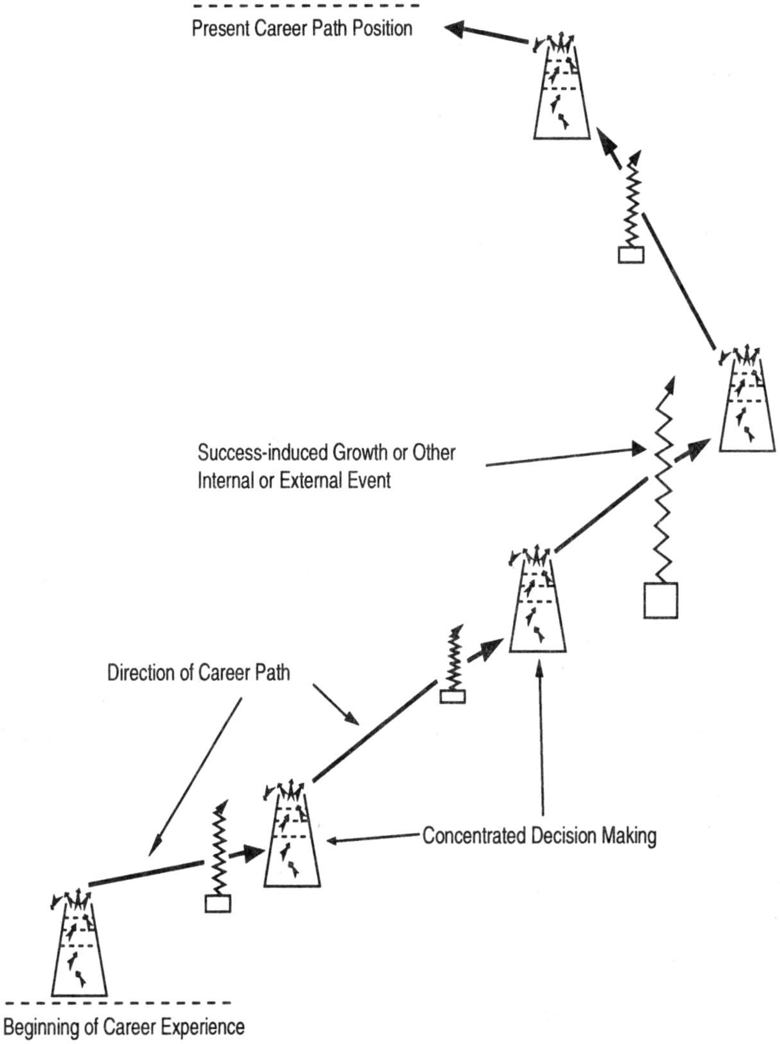

To career-oriented employees, career paths are continuously unfolding conceptual maps marked by periods of experience and growth and periods of career decision. They see organizations as possible legs on their career paths—as periods of experience and growth, and/or as settings for career decision making. At various times in their careers, employees may see different organizations as appropriate to their careers. Organizations aware of the needs of career-oriented employees can provide a set of career management activities that induce employees to choose their organization as a place to work, to work effectively while they are there, and, when appropriate, to leave with amicable ties that will be of benefit to both the employee and the organization.

Comparison of Perspectives

All three views of human resource flows are of use to the organization. The strategic objectives and strategies of the organization may cause the organization to rely more heavily on one view than another. The economic view offers the opportunity to develop human capital, the social view offers the opportunity to build a well-defined organization identity and culture, and the career path view offers the opportunity to provide a mutually beneficial relationship between the organization and the career employee.

The application of these views of human resource flows is discussed in Chapter 10.

IDENTIFYING HUMAN RESOURCE FLOWS AND THEIR EFFECTS

A researcher had just completed a study of the flows of human resources in a large corporation, when he happened to overhear a senior personnel manager telling young recruits about the promotion opportunities within the organization. The general thrust of the talk was that the firm offered opportunities for all lower level managers. When the researcher presented his research findings, it was clear that the personnel official's information was incorrect. Though managers in some departments had considerable opportunity, those in other departments had little opportunity. Company officials were shocked. The researcher felt that the official genuinely believed what he was saying, for soon after learning the results of the research, this manager was instrumental in getting the company to change its practices.[37]

If organizations are to plan for human resource flows, they must identify with reasonable precision present flows and their effects. It is unwise to assume that these flows are known with sufficient precision.

Collecting the Data

Ideally, the data about human resource flows should include information about all job changes, for every employee, including when each job change occurred, the previous job, what the employee did in the new job, and how the employee was affected by the job change(s). In practice, organizations must decide where to focus their data collection efforts.

The views of human resource flows presented in the preceding section can help organization planners to focus their data collection efforts on flows of more importance to the strategic plans of the organization. In the final analysis, the data collected depend on what problems the organization is experiencing and which human resource flows present the most opportunities for strategic advantage.

Assembling and Presenting Flow Data

The numerical data collected about human resource flows can be assembled initially through the use of a transitional matrix. This tool is suitable for almost every organization. The data can be further assembled in flow tables and.complement ratio tables. This will allow other factors, such as quality of employee performance or employee opportunity to move among jobs, to be presented for analysis.

Transitional Matrices

A transitional matrix shows either the numbers or proportions of employees in an organization in corresponding states (jobs, positions, classifications, or grades) at different times. It usually focuses on all employees in given states at an earlier time period and is used to show the numbers or the proportions of employees who moved at a later time period from these states to one or more other states. Less often, the matrix focuses on all employees in given states in a later time period and is used to show the numbers or the proportions of employees in these states who came from one or more other states.[38]

Transitional matrices are flexible. They can be used to show the movements of all employees in the organization or the movements of selected groups of employees. They can be used to show the movements of the selected employees over a time period of one year or many years. With computer assistance, the possibilities of data accumulation and manipulation are numerous.

Exhibit 9-5 is an illustration of a basic transitional matrix. It shows the entry-level jobs of all employees hired by Organization XYZ in 1985 and the jobs they held in 1992. For example, of the 1,000 persons hired in 1985 and placed initially in job A, 290 are still in job A in 1992, 250 have moved to job B, 200 to job C, 50 to job D, and 210 have left the organization.[39]

	A 290	B 475	C 488	D 275	Out 472
A 1,000	290	250	200	50	210
B 500	0	225	120	90	65
C 350	0	0	168	42	140
D 150	0	0	0	93	57

Exhibit 9-5. Transitional Matrix Showing Numbers of Employees Hired in 1985 into Jobs A, B, C, and D in Organization XYZ Who Were in Jobs A, B, C, and D and Outside the Organization in 1992

Flow Tables

A flow table takes the information assembled through a transitional matrix and presents it in a concise form. A basic flow table is illustrated in Exhibit 9-6. The exhibit shows a more complete version of the information presented in Exhibit 9-5 for Organization XYZ. All positions occupied by the employees between 1985 and 1992 are shown, not simply their positions in 1985 and in 1992.

When information about all moves is provided for the employees hired in 1985 into jobs A, B, C, and D, as in Exhibit 9-6, the data acquire additional meaning. It becomes clear that there is a significant hiring chain A → B → C → D; persons hired into job A often are moved consecutively to job B, job C, and job D. Of the 475 persons in job B in 1992, 250 were hired initially into job A; of the 488 persons in job C in 1992, 190 were hired initially into job A and moved through job B; of the 275 persons in job D in 1992, 50 were hired initially into job A and moved through jobs B and C. The pertinent numbers for this hiring chain are shown in boldface in the exhibit.

Another observation is now possible: There is one point in this hiring chain where people are moved in the opposite direction from the normal flow. On ten occasions, persons initially hired into job A were moved to job B and later returned to job A. This is a corrective flow that is little used in the United States.[40]

Exhibit 9-7 shows the same data as were shown in Exhibit 9-6, except that quality indexes have been included. A quality index is a measure of the value of a group of employees as an organization resource. When quality indexes are added to the flow table, it becomes possible to evaluate each human resource flow for its

Entry Job	Intermediate Job(s)	Present Position					Grand Total
		Job A	Job B	Job C	Job D	Out	
A	--	280	**250**	10	0	80	--
A	B	10	0	**190**	0	65	--
A	B, C	0	0	0	**50**	45	--
A	B, C, D	0	0	0	0	20	--
Total	--	290	250	200	50	210	1,000
B	--	0	225	120	0	0	--
B	C	0	0	0	90	0	--
B	C, D	0	0	0	0	65	--
Total	--	0	225	120	90	65	500
C	--	0	0	168	42	0	--
C	C	0	0	0	0	140	--
Total	--	0	0	168	42	140	350
D	--	0	0	0	93	57	--
Total	--	0	0	0	93	57	150
Grand total		290	475	488	275	472	2,000

Exhibit 9-6. Flow Table Showing Numbers of Employees Hired by Organization XYZ into Jobs A, B, C, and D in 1985, Who Moved by Various Routes to Jobs A, B, C, and D and Outside the Organization in 1992

apparent contribution to the building of human capital, to the building of social structure, and to the enhancement of employee development. The quality index used in Exhibit 9-7 is the median[41] value of the most recent performance appraisals of individual members of the group.[42] The levels of performance range from I, the best performance, to IV, the poorest performance.

Flow A → B → C → D, the human resource flow considered in Exhibit 9-6, shows that the internal hiring sequence A → B → C → D appears not only to provide large numbers of employees but also employees of excellent quality. This sequence is shown in boldface in Exhibit 9-7. Similarly, the internal hiring sequence A → B → A—ten employees moved to job B and subsequently returned to job A—appears to provide excellent employees.

Measures of behavior, knowledge, skills, abilities, understanding, attitudes, values, commitment, creativity, job satisfaction, career success, effort level, quality of work life, and performance of employees all may be used as quality indexes in a

Entry Job	Intermediate Job(s)	Present Position					Grand Total
		Job A	Job B	Job C	Job D	Out	
A	--	280 II	250 I	10 III	0	80 IV	--
A	B	10 I	0	190 I	0	65 III	--
A	B, C	0	0	0	50 I	45 I	--
A	B, C, D	0	0	0	0	20 I	--
Total	--	290 II	250 I	200 I	50 I	210 III	1,000 I
B	--	0	225 II	120 III	0	0	--
B	C	0	0	0	90 III	0	--
B	C, D	0	0	0	0	65 II	--
Total	--	0	225 II	120 III	90 III	65 II	500 III
C	--	0	0	168 II	42 III	0	--
C	C	0	0	0	0	140 III	--
Total	--	0	0	168 II	42 III	140 III	350 II
D	--	0	0	0	93 II	57 III	--
Total	--	0	0	0	93 II	57 III	150 II
Grand total		290 II	475 I	488 II	275 II	472 III	2,000 II

Exhibit 9-7. Flow Table Showing Numbers of Those Employees Hired by Organization XYZ into Jobs A, B, C, and D in 1985, Who Moved by Various Routes to Jobs A, B, C, and D in 1992, with Quality Indexes for The Resulting Employee Groups.

flow table. The apparent effects of flows observed using flow tables should be tested for statistical significance and otherwise validated. Then each flow should be evaluated to determine if it is a worthwhile investment of organization resources. Procedures for conducting an evaluation are discussed in Chapter 8.

Complement Ratio Tables

A complement ratio table shows the ratios of numbers of employees in adjacent positions or job families. The table provides a measure of the opportunities for employees to move within an organization. Complement ratio tables are especially useful for studying opportunities for movement of employees between positions in vacancy chains. A vacancy chain is a sequence of jobs arranged sequentially so that a vacancy at the end of the chain initiates a chain reaction of vacancies and job movements throughout the length of the chain.

To illustrate the use of a complement ratio table, assume that most research employees in the XYZ Organization are moved through the job sequence A → B → C → D → E → F as they progress through the organization. The numbers of employees in jobs A, B, C, D, E, and F are as follows:[43]

F	215
E	265
D	756
C	1,075
B	2,475
A	5,450
Total	10,236

The numbers of employees in successive positions A through F steadily decline, displaying the typical pyramidal structure of jobs in organization hierarchies. Because the numbers of employees in successive positions decline, opportunities to move between jobs also appear to decline as employees move toward the top of the pyramid. This view of advancement opportunity is incomplete.

Another view of opportunities to advance is given by complement ratios.[44] The complement ratios for this same group of jobs are shown in the third column of Exhibit 9-8. The complement ratio of job A is obtained by dividing the complements of all jobs above job A in the vacancy chain by the complement of job A. If a vacancy occurs in any of jobs B, C, D, E, or F, a sequence of promotions begins that eventually creates a promotion opportunity for someone in job A.

F/E	215/265	0.81
(E-F)/D	480/756	0.63
(D-F)/C	1,236/1,075	1.15
(C-F)/B	2,311/2,475	0.93
(B-F)/A	4,786/5,450	0.88

Exhibit 9-8. Complement Ratios for Gateways Among Jobs of the Vacancy Chain A → B → C → D → E → F Within Organization XYZ

The complement ratio is a measure of the width of the "gateway" out of a job position. Exhibit 9-8 shows that the gateway from job A is narrow as compared to the gateways from jobs B and C, but is wider than the gateways from jobs D and E. Obviously, advancement opportunities do not steadily decline with advancement along the vacancy chain A → B → C → D → E → F. It is more accurate to say that advancement opportunities along this job sequence change markedly with advancement but display no consistent trend toward either increase or decrease.[45]

There are factors that influence probability of movement for the individual employee other than complement ratios. These include

- Employee's current position and selection-related characteristics of the employee
- Turnover rates and where the turnover occurs
- Growth in numbers of positions needed and where the growth occurs
- Criteria used by the organization to decide those employees who will be offered job opportunities

These factors can be considered when calculating the probability of movement for the individual employee. For example, given an 8 percent annual turnover rate and a 5 percent organization growth rate, the combined effect of turnover and growth produces a 13 percent vacancy rate. Assuming that the vacancy rate is the same for all jobs, multiply 13 percent by the complement ratio of the different job levels to yield the probabilities of promotion listed in column four of Exhibit 9-9. Similar calculations can include the factors dealing with employee characteristics and selection criteria used by the organization.

F/E	215/265	0.81	0.11
(E-F)/D	480/756	0.63	0.08
(D-F)/C	1,236/1,075	1.15	0.15
(C-F)/B	2,311/2,475	0.93	0.12
(B-F)/A	4,786/5,450	0.88	0.11

Exhibit 9-9.   Complement Ratios and Probability of Promotion for Employees Waiting at Gateways of the Vacancy Chain A → B → C → D → E → F

Analyzing Flows

Kinds of Flows

For purposes of analysis, flows may be grouped according to their similarities or differences.

Flows may be similar in the kind of change in state involved. For example, all flows from specialist to generalist positions or all flows across an organization boundary may be studied as a group.

Flows may be similar in their point of origin or in their point of destination. For example, the later job performance of all employees transferred out of an organization unit with a particularly strong developmental emphasis might be compared with the later job performance of employees transferred out of other organization units.

Flows may differ in direction of flow. Some flows may run counter to the usual direction of flow—such as job rotation programs in which trainees are started in positions at the top of the organization hierarchy and are moved to progressively lower levels of the hierarchy. And some corrective flows may occur, in which persons moving within a flow are returned to prior positions when it is discovered that the move was ill-advised. These flows may be studied as a group to determine whether problems are caused by the novelty of the flows and whether there are offsetting advantages.

Flows may differ in the rate of flow. For example, employees who differ in the frequency they have moved among job states may be compared to determine whether there are optimum rates of movement for maximum social bonding between persons who move and others in the organization.

Flows may differ in the volume of flow. For example, transfers in which several persons at a time, or entire task teams, are transferred from one organization unit to another may be compared with transfers in which only one person is transferred to determine whether multiple transfers tend to hasten or to retard the rate of adjustment of those who move to the new positions.

Effects of Flows

Flows affect a variety of people and units of the organization. A list would include the following:

Persons moving	Receiving career cohorts
Sending role sets	Sending work group
Receiving role sets	Receiving work group
Sending internal labor markets	Sending organization unit
Receiving internal labor markets	Receiving organization unit
Sending career cohorts[46]	Organization as a whole

Possible effects on people or units might be changes in

Behavior	Morale
Knowledge, skills, abilities	Human resource stocks
Understanding	Quantities
Attitudes, values	Qualities
Commitment	Varieties
Creativity	Complementarities
Job satisfaction	Rates of accumulations of HR
Work load	stocks
Interpersonal relationships and compatibilities	Synergy/fit
	Innovation rates
Career success	Organization learning and
Chances of career success	forgetting rates
Efforts to achieve career goals	Renewal and decay rates
	Unit productivity and
Quality of work life	performance
Individual performance	Organization productivity and
Group performance	performance

Any and all of these items—people and units affected and kinds of changes—can be subjects of analysis. Those chosen should be ones considered important for human resource strategic objectives and strategies.

Where effects are expected to occur immediately after an employee has moved from one job state to another, analysis is straightforward. However, effects may not occur in this timely fashion. Some effects of flows may occur prior to a job state change. For instance, in a transition cycle, there is a preparatory stage that occurs in advance of the job move. In this stage, employees prepare themselves psychologically for the new position by anticipating conditions of the new job. This anticipation will affect both the employee and those working with him or her. Many effects of the job state change may not occur, or at least not be observable, until some time after a job state move. For example, social learning that occurs at the time of a move may not be exhibited in behavior until long after a move has occurred.[47]

Analysis should cover a period long enough to observe all likely effects of a move.

Extent of Flows

Organizations differ markedly in the number and use of human resource flows. They may be thought of as aligned on a continuum from those organizations that have very low turnover, that hire from within almost exclusively to fill vacant positions, and that make direct investments in the development of their human resources to those organizations that have very high turnover, that rely heavily on external labor markets to fill vacancies, that make only required direct investments in the development of their human resource systems, and that invest heavily in hiring from the outside.

Organizations should determine the extensiveness of their human resource flows. Measures of the extensiveness of flows may be determined for groups of employees by calculating the average tenure of employees in a job state or the proportions of employees in the group who change job states each year. The extensiveness of flows for a family of jobs (or other states) may be determined by calculating for each family the average length of time that the typical employee remains in a job or the proportions of jobs that experience a given percentage of employee turnover in a year.

Organizations with extensive flows but few beneficial effects of flows should question their planning. Organizations with few flows should question whether more extensive use is warranted.

SUMMARY

Human resource flows constitute movements of persons within organizations. People enter the organization as new employees, they move from position to position within the organization, and they eventually leave the organization. There is increasing evidence that the path a person follows in an organization has much to do with the kind of person one becomes. Perceptions, feelings, and values are changed by experiences within organizations. So too are knowledge, skills, and abilities.

Movements of people within an organization may be seen from three viewpoints—as movements through economic systems, as movements through social systems, and as movements along career paths.

From an economic point of view, the organization is composed of internal labor markets—clusters of jobs within the organization for which interrelated decisions about hiring can be made. Movements of people into and through internal labor markets allow the accelerated development of human capital.

Within each organization are networks of interlocking social roles. In the modern organization, these social roles are appropriately interrelated so as to yield predictable and favorable outcomes. Because social roles differ, movements among these roles require the individual to undergo a complex adjustment process to meet expectations of new roles. Learning new roles occurs in two primary ways—instrumental training and observational learning. Observational learning, in turn, takes one of three different forms: imitation, identification, or simple observation.

Organizations often are seen by career employees as one leg on a career path journey. If organizations are aware of the key role of career success in employee career development and of the nature of the career decision-making process, the career drives of these employees may be harnessed to allow a mutually successful relationship between the organization and its career employees.

If organizations are to plan for human resource flows, they must identify with reasonable precision present flows and their effects. Identification of flows is best accomplished by accumulating information about movements of employees among job states. Numerical data collected about these movements can be assembled initially through the use of a transitional matrix. which shows either the numbers or proportions of employees in an organization in corresponding states (jobs, positions, classifications, or grades) at different times.

Data from a transitional matrix may be presented for analysis in flow tables and in complement ratio tables. Flow tables allow the identification of all states occupied by an employee over any time period of interest. When quality indexes—a measure of the value of a group of employees as an organization resource—are added to the flow table, it becomes possible to evaluate each human resource flow for its apparent contribution to the building of human capital, to the building of social structure, and to the enhancement of employee development. A complement ratio table shows the ratios of numbers of employees in adjacent positions or job families. The table provides a measure of the opportunities for employees to move within an organization.

Analysis of human resource flows should begin by classifying the flows based on their similarities or differences. Effects of each type of flow on a variety of people and units of the organization, including the organization itself, may be studied. Some effects of flows may occur prior to a job state change; other effects may occur long after the job state change occurred. Extensiveness of flows for each employee group and for each job family in the organization also should be considered. Organizations with extensive flows but few beneficial effects of flows should question their planning. Organizations with few flows should question whether more extensive use of flows is warranted.

LEARNING EXERCISES

Case Analysis

If you have the opportunity for small-group discussion, you may use the procedure suggested for Case 1 in Chapter 1.

Case 9, "Chase Manhattan Bank," is a wide-ranging interview with Alan F. Lafley, executive vice president of corporate human resources. Analyze the remarks of Mr. Lafley by answering the questions or taking the actions listed here:

1. How does the management of flows of human resources fit into Mr. Lafley's overall approach to managing the human resources at Chase? Explain your answer carefully.

2. As Mr. Lafley discusses flows of human resources within his organization, is he thinking of these flows primarily as movements of people through economic systems, as movements of people through social systems, or as movements of people along career paths? If he seems to be using one of these views more that another, why, in your opinion, is he doing so? Explain your answer carefully.

3. There is little direct evidence in the case itself of the methods used within Chase to identify the flows of human resources. Does Mr. Lafley seem knowledgeable about these flows and their effects? Explain your answer carefully.

Activity

If possible, conduct a follow-up study of the human resource function at Chase after 1984. You may do this by reading career literature at your current university or alma mater, by interviewing someone you know who is or has been employed at Chase, or by conducting a search of the human resource professional literature. Has Chase's approach to human resource management changed since Mr. Lafley retired in 1984? In what respects? Is there still as much emphasis on management of the flows of human resources. Is Chase still respected for its management of human resources?

Discussion Question

1. To what extent could the identification and analysis of the effects of flows of human resources be done by computer? Would it be cost-effective to do so? Be specific in your answer.

Endnotes

[1]See, for example, Melvin L. Kohn, *Class and Conformity: A Study in Values*, 2nd ed. (Chicago: University of Chicago Press, 1977); Melvin L. Kohn and Carmi Schooler, *Work and Personality: An Inquiry into the Impact of Social Stratification* (Norwood, NJ: Ablex, 1983); Rosabeth Moss Kanter, *Men and Women of the Corporation* (New York: Basic Books, 1977); and Nigel Nicholson and Michael West, *Managerial Job Change: Men and Women in Transition* (Cambridge: Cambridge University Press, 1988).

[2]For further discussion of the internal labor market concept, see James N. Baron, Alison Davis-Blake, and William T. Bielby, "The Structure of Opportunity: How Promotion Ladders Vary Within and Among Organizations," *Administrative Science Quarterly*, 31, no. 2 (June 1986), 248–273; David B. Bills, "Costs, Commitment, and Rewards: Factors Influencing the Design and Implementation of Internal Labor Markets," *Administrative Science Quarterly*, 32, no. 2 (June 1987), 202–221; and James E. Rosenbaum, *Career Mobility in a Corporate Hierarchy* (Orlando, FL: Harcourt Brace Jovanovich, 1984), pp. 20–23.

[3]In some internal labor markets there is not a hierarchical arrangement of jobs but a serial arrangement of jobs. As an employee moves from one job to another, the employee accumulates knowledge and skills and receives additional pay for this accumulation.

[4]Dugger argues that internal labor markets are not markets in the strict sense at all. Therefore wage differentials are determined by institutional factors, not economic ones. See William M. Dugger, "The Administered Labor Market: An Institutional Analysis," *Journal of Economic Issues*, 15, no. 2 (June 1981), 397–407.

[5]Most human capital theorists believe that "general" training, training that produces skills of value to other employers, when provided by employers, is subsidized, if not paid for outright, by workers who must accept lower current earnings to induce employers to provide the training. See Mark Blaug, "The Empirical Status of Human Capital Theory," *Journal of Economic Literature*, 14, no. 3 (September 1976), 827–855.

[6]See Gary Becker, *Human Capital: A Theoretical and Empirical Analysis with Special Reference to Education*, 2nd ed. (New York: National Bureau of Economic Research, 1975), especially chap. II, pp. 15–44; Jacob Mincer, *Schooling, Experience, and Earnings* (New York: National Bureau of Economic Research, 1974), pp. 128–144.

[7]Peter B. Doeringer and Michael J. Piore, *Internal Labor Markets and Manpower Analysis* (Lexington, MA: Heath Lexington Books, 1971), pp. 18–19.

[8]Rosenbaum, *Career Mobility*, p. 21.

[9]Employers using internal labor markets often have been able to obtain low turnover rates. Doeringer and Piore, *Internal Labor Markets*, 29–32, 165–167.

[10]Ibid., p. 28–29.

[11]See Becker, *Human Capital*, pp. 26–37; see pp. 11–12 of Paul Osterman, "The Nature and Importance of Internal Labor Markets," in Paul Osterman, ed., *Internal Labor Markets* (Cambridge, MA: MIT Press, 1984), pp. 1–22.

[12]Daniel Katz and Robert L. Kahn, *The Social Psychology of Organizations*, 2nd ed. (New York: John Wiley, 1978), pp. 43–44, 188–192.

[13]Ibid., p. 189.

[14]Nicholson and West, *Managerial Job Change*, p. 9.

[15]Ibid., pp. 8–15. Gabarro, in a study of managers who had moved to new positions, found predictable stages that the managers in new positions were required to go through before they could be said to have mastered a job. The stages were taking hold, immersion, reshaping, consolidation, and refinement. John J. Gabarro, "When a New Manager Takes Charge," *Harvard Business Review*, 63, no. 3 (May–June 1985), 110–123.

[16]Instrumental training is called "tuition" by social learning theorists.

[17]The term *instrumental* is used to indicate that in this type of training the learner, by choosing the behavior to be displayed, is instrumental (directly involved) in bringing about the reinforcement.

[18]See p. 136 of Jacob L. Gewirtz, "Mechanisms of Social Learning: Some Roles of Stimulation and Behavior in Early Human Development," in David A. Goslin, ed., *Handbook of Socialization Theory and Research* (Chicago: Rand McNally, 1969), pp. 57–212.

[19]Ibid., pp. 146–148. This type of learning is also called imitation learning and identificatory learning. See p. 219 of Albert Bandura, " Social-Learning Theory of Identificatory Processes," in Goslin, *Handbook of Sociali. ation Theory and Research*, pp. 213–262.

[20]Bandura, "Social-Learning Theory," p. 213.

[21]Neal E. Miller and John Dollard, *Social Learning and Imitation* (New Haven, CT: Yale University Press, 1941), pp. 10–11.

[22]Lawrence Kohlberg, "Stage and Sequence: The Cognitive-Developmental Approach to Socialization," in Goslin, *Handbook of Socialization Theory and Research*, pp. 347–380.

[23]Bandura, "Social-Learning Theory," p. 242.

[24]A. L. Miller-Tiedeman, *Individual Career Exploration, Picture Form: Manual of Directions* (Bensenville, IL: Scholastic Testing Service, 1977), p. 141, reprinted in David V. Tiedeman and Anna Miller-Tiedeman, "Career Decision Making: An Individualistic Perspective," in Duane Brown, Linda Brooks, and Associates, *Career Choice and Development* (San Francisco: Jossey-Bass, 1984), pp. 281–310. Miller-Tiedeman points out that not everyone follows the planned/analytical decision strategy posited by the model of Exhibit 9-2. Other strategies in frequent use are reluctant, compliant, postpone, fixed, and aimless.

[25]Readers familiar with models of managerial decision making will find the Miller-Teideman model similar but containing an experiential content almost nonexistent in those models.

[26]Hall calls career success a "facilitator of career decisions." See Douglas T. Hall, *Careers in Organizations* (Pacific Palisades, CA: Goodyear Publishing Co., 1976), p. 29.

[27]See especially pp. 311, 315–318 of Robert W. White, ""Motivation Reconsidered: The Concept of Competence," *Psychological Review*, 66 (1959), 297–323, cited in Hall, *Careers in Organizations*, p. 29.

[28]For the relationship between expansion in career identity and realism of aspiration levels, see Kurt Lewin, "The Psychology of Success and Failure," *Occupations*, 14 (1936), 926–930, cited in Hall, *Careers in Organizations*, p. 32. For the relationship between feelings of career success and realism of aspiration levels, see Abraham Korman, "Self Esteem as a Moderator of the Relationship Between Self-Perceived Abilities

and Vocational Choice," *Journal of Applied Psychology*, 51, no. 1 (February 1967), 65–67. Korman found that students with high-self esteem, unlike students with low self-esteem, tended to choose occupations in which they felt they had high abilities.

[29]Hall, *Careers in Organizations*, p. 31, explains the relationship between expansion in career identity and career involvement as follows: "As the career subidentity expands, proportionately more of the total identity is invested in the career role; i.e., the person becomes more ego-involved in his career. This *career involvement* is a measure of the strength of one's motivation to work in a chosen career role." [Emphasis his.] In a study by Cochran, persons with higher status professional aspirations also had stronger career orientations. Larry R. Cochran, "Level of Career Aspiration and Strength of Career Orientation," *Journal of Vocational Behavior*, 23, no. 1 (1983), 1–10.

[30]Hall, *Careers in Organizations*, p. 29, portrays the development of competent self-identity as causing improved self-esteem, which is logical, as improved self-esteem appears the more global of the two concepts. His diagram on p. 32, in which he shows improved self-esteem as causing the development of competent self-identity, appears to be a typographical error.

[31]Ibid., p. 31.

[32]Lewin, "Psychology of Success and Failure," p. 927.

[33]See Hall's "Proposition I," *Careers in Organizations*, p. 32.

[34]Ibid., pp. 32–33; Korman, "Self-Esteem as a Moderator," p. 65; and Lewin, "Psychology of Success and Failure," p. 927.

[35]Much of the research about effects of goal setting on motivation , in particular the work of Edwin A. Locke, Gary P. Latham, and Erez Miriam, may not be directly applicable to career-oriented employees because that work has been largely with blue-collar employees who are not likely to be career-oriented. However, these authors contend that goal commitment may decline when the goal becomes very difficult as employees see their chances of reaching the goal decline. See "The Determinants of Goal Commitment," *Academy of Management Review*, 3, no. 1 (January 1988), 23–39.

[36]According to Lewin, "Psychology of Success and Failure," feelings of success for a person achieving a goal were especially pronounced when the person set a challenging goal for himself or herself, set a goal important to his or her self-identity, and determined his or her own means of attaining the goal.

[37]See Rosenbaum, *Career Mobility*, pp. 14–15.

[38]These two foci of the matrix focus on different employee groups; the resulting matrices are termed a "supply push" matrix or a "demand pull" matrix , respectively.

[39]For more information about matrices, see Margaret A. Lial and Charles D. Miller, *Mathematics: With Applications in the Management, Natural and Social Sciences*, 4th ed. (Glenview, IL: Scott, Foresman, 1987).

[40]See Hall, *Careers in Organizations*, pp. 161–163, for a discussion of the negative consequences of the inability to move employees downward in organizations.

[41]The median value is arrived at by first listing all employees in a group by rank order of performance. The median value for the group is the level of performance of the employee in the middle of this ranked listing.

[42]For a person who left the organization, this was the last appraisal performed while the employee was a member of the organization.

[43]The data used for the complement ratio chart is not comparable to the data of the transitional matrix of Exhibit 9-6 and the flow tables of Exhibits 9-7 and 9-8. The complement ratio charts use data for all employees in jobs A, B, C, and D, and the transition-

al matrix and flow tables of Exhibits 9-6 through 9-8 use data for the 1985 cohort (all those who entered the organization in 1985) only.

[44]Stewman and Konda use the name "grade ratio charts." This name has the disadvantage of implying that complement ratio tables are useful only for analyzing opportunities for movement through grade levels in graded organizations, such as the military and the U.S. government. See Shelby Stewman and Suresh L. Konda, "Careers and Organizational Labor Markets: Demographic Models of Organizational Behavior," *American Journal of Sociology*, 88, no. 4 (1983), 637–685.

[45]This appears to be a typical pattern in organizations. See ibid., pp. 644–647, for a discussion of studies of complement ratios in a number of different organizations.

[46]A career cohort, in the sense used here, is that group of persons who entered an organization at approximately the same time.

[47]See Gewirtz, "Mechanisms of Social Learning," pp. 147–148; Bandura, "Social-Learning Theory," pp. 222–223.

Chapter 10

Planning for the Management of Human Resource Flows

The course of an organization is determined by the way its daily operations are managed. The human resource operations of an organization are guided by both strategic and maintenance considerations.

Maintenance considerations are those inherent in the technologies used by the organization, the markets or clients served, the environment occupied, and the size of the organization. Maintenance considerations give human resource activities and the way the activities are carried out commonalities such that the activities are similar in all organizations of similar size with similar technologies, markets or clients, and environments, regardless of the strategic objectives or the strategies of the organizations.[1]

Strategic considerations are those arising out of the strategic plans of the organization. Strategies serve to differentiate the operations of an organization and to give the organization its distinctive competence and competitive advantage. If the organization is to do well in its industry, it is important that these strategies are carried out in its everyday operations. A key to successful strategic management is to find a way to intervene in the day-to-day operations so that the overall direction or course of the organization is driven in the desired direction. Flows of human resources are key intervention points to allow the management of human resources to be directed toward human resource strategic objectives.

It is neither necessary nor desirable to manage all human resource activities strategically. Viewing human resource operations as flows of human resources allows the choice of activities that will drive the organization toward its human resource strategic objectives. There are flows that bring employees into the organization, flows that move employees within the organization, and flows that deplete the staff of the organization. Different strategies will require emphasis on different flows. The activities involved in each of these flows must be considered for their importance to human resource strategies and those chosen must be managed in ways that produce strategic effects.

This chapter discusses the ways that organizations may be driven strategically at the operational level while not interfering unnecessarily in the day-to-day affairs of the organization.

KEY INDIVIDUALS AND GROUPS

Human resource flows may be managed for strategic advantage by deliberately choosing persons, or groups of persons, who can bring about the effects required by organization strategies. These persons must be enlisted as agents to help ensure that the flows of human resources have their desired effects. Key individuals who can influence flows are persons moving between job states, mentors, and supervisors. For some strategies, other persons or groups of persons may be enlisted.

Persons Moving

People moving among job states who are chosen to influence flows must be empowered to act as agents. They must be told the larger, strategic purposes of the move—above and beyond its immediate and obvious purposes. They must be selected, trained, and supported in a way that will allow them to fulfill these larger purposes.

The aspects of empowerment may be illustrated by returning to the example of E. C. Corporation, a national chain of nursing homes, introduced in Chapter 7. An important strategic human resource objective of the corporation is "profits per employee" and one of its strategies is "promoting the development of employees."

John Brown is a graduate with an MBA from Syracuse University who has been working for the past 11 years in various managerial and staff positions at E. C. Corporation. He has been offered and has accepted the opportunity to move from his position as director of the human resource unit servicing corporate headquarters in Atlanta to the Boston regional office to fill an expected vacancy caused by the impending retirement of the regional director. John is informed that while the immediate purpose of the move, from the organization's viewpoint, is to fill a vacancy and to allow a raise in pay and rank for John, the larger purpose of the move, and of other moves such as this, is to build human capital in the organization. John has been told that, to achieve this purpose, organization support, both personal and financial, is available on request.

As the first step in his empowerment, John had been carefully selected for this position. The organization is satisfied that he has the required qualifications and can benefit from the training that will be necessary to prepare him for the position. John is enrolled in a training program that prepares him for tasks that will be new to him in the new position and instructs him on how to handle the most common problems of the transition from his present position into the upcoming position.

Evidence of the success of the attempt to empower John occurs when, as a result of the training, John requests additional training to enhance his interpersonal skills and reads additional material about the Boston facility. John asks to be transferred to the new job 3 months before the director's actual retirement in order to allow the director to help John adjust to the new job.

John and the director mutually agree, and corporate approval is given, that after the director's retirement, he will be available for several days a month, if needed, to help John during the transition period. The director will be paid from corporate funds set aside to support John's move to the new position, not from the budget for John's operations. It is anticipated that the director will come in to help with several tasks critical to effective operations that occur infrequently and with which John is not familiar.

At the end of a year, John has been fully assimilated into his new position and shows all signs that he will be one of the better regional directors. Moreover, John enjoys the work and appears to be a satisfied and loyal employee.

This example illustrates how moving employees may be empowered. The specific ways will vary, depending on the kinds of moves involved, the capabilities of the employee, the demands placed on the employee by the move, and whether other agents are used. Everyone in an organization moves at one time or another because everyone in the organization enters the organization; occupies at least one job, position, classification, and/or grade level; and leaves the organization. Organizations may decide to empower all employees for all moves between job states or a few employees for few moves between job states.

At E. C. Corporation, in carrying out the strategy "promoting employee development," special attention is devoted to moves by professional and managerial employees. If the strategy being supported were "creating employee commitment to the organization," all employees moving among job states might be empowered and the types of support given would necessarily differ.

Mentors

Mentors help to integrate persons into the mainstream of organization life.[2] They provide support for one or more proteges by performing some or all of the following functions:

Vocational support—sponsorship, exposure, visibility, protection, challenging work assignments, coaching

Personal support—acceptance and confirmation, counseling, role modeling, friendship[3]

The use of mentors may be an informal or formal arrangement. Informal arrangements may be initiated by the employee who recognizes a need for vocational or personal support and who identifies and enlists the aid of another within the organization who seems able to give this support. Or an experienced employee may recognize the need of another employee for support and will perform the mentoring function. Formal mentoring is initiated by the organization with designated persons to serve as mentors. Usually the employee is allowed the choice of mentor or mentors from this designated pool.

For formal mentoring, mentors should meet the following criteria:

- Occupy central positions in the organization in terms of respect and inclusion.[4]
- Have worked in a variety of jobs, positions, and locations in the organization. A minimum requirement would be two jobs in two positions in two locations of the organization.
- Can perform well most of the career support and personal support functions of the mentor.

Mentors usually receive no extra compensation but do command a measure of respect. Training should be made available to them to assist them in the performance of their functions. Much of this training should center on the transition cycle, described in Chapter 9. The mentor function should be continually evaluated and mentors should remain on the list only if their proteges report that they are helpful in both the vocational and personal support roles.

E. C. Corporation has designated a large number of persons as formal mentors. It also encourages the use of informal mentors. A critical feature of the mentor program at the corporation is to make formal mentoring unnecessary by fostering informal mentoring: Formal mentors are, in effect, told to "work themselves out of a job."

When John first came into the organization 11 years ago, he was told of the assistance a mentor could provide and of the importance of developing mentor relationships. After John had become somewhat familiar with the organization, he was given a list of officially designated mentors with background information on each and was asked to select from this list at least one person to be his official mentor. When John had been with E. C. Corporation for 8 months he selected Glenn Canaker, director of purchasing, to be his formal mentor, and Glenn promptly agreed.

John was also encouraged to develop a network of informal mentor relationships. A primary mentor can perform many mentor functions, but these persons are unlikely to be able to perform all the functions of a mentor.[5] Multiple mentor relationships are necessary.

The culture of E. C. Corporation facilitates the development of informal mentor relationships. Corporate managers have a "hands-on" style and are quite visible. And there are few social barriers separating people at work into occupational groupings. Social functions at the corporation are relaxed affairs to which everyone is invited. Such functions are held frequently at each location, and corporate officials frequently attend. Many informal mentor relationships arise out of these events.

John was given the following guidelines for choosing informal mentors:

- Persons should be chosen who can perform the functions of a mentor—position, rank, or age does not necessarily prevent a person from performing mentor functions.[6]
- Mentors should be accessible and strategically placed throughout the organization.
- Enduring relationships are reciprocal. John should be prepared to reciprocate support of various kinds to his mentors.[7]

After 11 years with E. C. Corporation, John still has Glenn Canaker as his formal mentor. This relationship has been a comfortable one for both of them. Although John has visited with Glenn in his office only once, and the two meet informally, usually by chance, John feels free to telephone Glenn at any time and has done so frequently. John also has eight other persons, most of whom he would describe as colleagues, who serve, in at least some aspect of their relationship, as mentors to him. He feels that much of his sense of being well informed about the organization and of being a part of it comes from his mentor relationships, both formal and informal.

This example illustrates what is probably an ideal mentor structure in an organization—a strong skeletal framework of formal mentoring surrounded by an elaborate network of informal mentoring. Because mentoring furthers the adjustment process by hastening development of job skills and integration of the individual into the organization,[8] a strong, organization-wide mentoring program is a powerful tool for ensuring that human resource flows have their desired effects.

Supervisors

Supervisors, because of their positions, often can further the effects of changes in job states by

- Mentoring moving employees
- Promoting the social learning of moving employees
- Functioning as a link between the organization communication system and the employee
- Helping the employee in a new job state to interpret and to reconcile the various role expectations communicated by the employee's role set
- Assigning specific tasks intended to shape the attitudes and values of the subordinate
- Managing any internal labor market within his or her unit

Mentoring is the most demanding of all people skills,[9] and it may not be feasible to require all supervisors to have proficiency in mentoring. With an effective mentoring system in place, it is not essential, although it is desirable, that a supervisor be able to mentor an employee who moves into his or her unit. Where a supervisor is able to mentor a subordinate, he or she should be able to fulfill most of the mentor functions. A supervisor can supplement well the role of a nonsupervisory formal mentor. What the mentor does with respect to the entire organization, the supervisor does with respect to the specific job state of an employee. And just as a mentor can hasten the integration of an employee into the organization, the supervisor, by performing the mentor functions, can hasten the integration of the individual into the supervisor's unit and into the new job state.

Supervisors can promote the social learning of subordinates in ways that others in the organization cannot. They have opportunities for positive reinforcement of desired behavior (instrumental training) because they distribute many of the rewards subordinates are eligible to receive. And because the subordinate often has considerable opportunity to observe the supervisor's behavior, supervisors often may be the most important role models that subordinates will experience.

Supervisors occupy key positions in organization communication networks and are better informed than nonsupervisory employees about aspects of the organization of direct importance to their units. If supervisors share information, subordinates are better informed and, in consequence, are better able to make choices about appropriate behaviors.[10]

Supervisors learn what others expect of their subordinates. These expectations can be overwhelming to an employee and can seem to be in conflict.[11] Supervisors can interpret roles and mediate conflicts.

Supervisors assign the tasks performed by employees. By selecting the tasks assigned, the supervisor can develop in the employee attitudes and values important to the organization.[12]

John Brown's earlier job experience in E. C. Corporation, prior to his promotion to regional director, may be used to illustrate the role of the supervisor in managing an internal labor market. When John was recruited out of graduate school, he had no clear sense of career direction other than that he thought he wanted to be a manager. Background information, interviews, and testing indicated that he might be suited eventually for a regional director position or even higher, depending on how he developed. John was assigned to Tim Schraeder's region. Tim, director of the Washington, D.C. region, both because of his innate characteristics and deliberate training on the part of the company, was exceptionally adept at developing managerial talent.

Tim Schraeder understood the importance to the organization of internal labor markets (ILMs), including the market culminating in his own position. This internal labor market was used exclusively for the staffing of nursing home superintendent positions and regional director positions. He had responsibility for the portion of this ILM in his area and considered it one of his most important functions.

The ILM used for staffing the nursing home superintendent and regional director positions extends throughout the organization. It begins at training positions in the nursing homes where each future supervisor is required to work for a time as part of a patient care team. It includes staff positions in cost accounting, human resources, and marketing, along with the positions of nursing home super-intendent and regional director.

E. C. Corporation wanted John to get to know some patients in person so that patients became real people with concerns and hopes and with families who cared about their well-being, not statistics on a percentage-occupancy report. John started work in a nursing home in Washington, D.C., and moved through a series of positions throughout the organization, culminating in the regional director position. In each of these positions, John was assigned to work for a supervisor and coworkers who recognized the uniqueness of this opportunity for John and who shared information with John and encouraged his questions about the work and how the work fit into the organization as a whole.[13] John stayed in each of these positions as long as he desired but at least until a job cycle had been completed and he could receive feedback on, and learn from, the results of his work.

Supervisors such as Tim Schraeder, who supervise large numbers of employees moving between job states, are skilled developers of people. They understand the jobs of their units, having performed many of these jobs themselves. They have received job instruction training—training in how to teach someone efficiently to carry out the tasks of a job—and have ensured, with the cooperation of the corporate training unit, that all their employees who frequently train new employees also have received such training. They are adept mentors, having received certification of successful completion of training provided by E. C. Corporation in performance of the primary functions of a mentor. They have received training that enables them to shape behavior through appropriate schedules of reinforcement. And these supervisors also model job behaviors that reflect core values and behaviors of the organization.

Tim Schraeder and supervisors like him are important agents for carrying out E. C. Corporation's human resource strategies. At a relatively low cost, they have developed an excellent nucleus of very capable employees in key positions in the organization.

Other Persons or Groups

In particular situations, a role set, a career cohort, or a work group might be active or passive agents influencing flows. For example, in an important port-of-entry position, it might be worthwhile to give all persons in the role set training in role theory so that they understand their impact on persons entering the organization and so that they learn ways to shape the behavior of persons entering. Or a work group containing an important port-of-entry position might be given team-building training to build the interpersonal skills of the group so they might more quickly assimilate and socialize new persons into the group. An entire career cohort—all new employees entering the organization in a given year—might be encouraged to maintain a loose association to exchange information and to provide mutual support for the adjustment process.

Special Case: Career Employees

Career employees need to be identified at time of hiring[14] Handled properly, they give a level of performance that frequently surpasses that of others in similar positions. They have capabilities and needs, however, that require special attention to allow them to be enlisted as agents for the desired effects of strategies adopted by the organization.

Career employees tend to be self-directed. They have plans that extend beyond the organization and will consider the organization as a place of work only if their experience in the organization fits into these plans. They have a great need for explicit information about what the organization needs and what it intends to do with them.

Career employees cannot reciprocate this candor about their own plans because it is difficult to project a career plan any distance into the future. Career decision making for most persons is an inherently experiential process. It is carried out in lock step with a "trying out" of the decision during which the employee changes and so, too, does his or her career plan. In fact, success experiences in the organization will be especially likely to produce growth and change in the employee. When organizations ask career employees how the organization fits into their career plans, they truly cannot say, for they do not know.

We return again to E. C. Corporation to illustrate the way human resource flows may be managed when career employees are involved. The same year that John Brown was hired, a classmate, Leah Boyle, was hired. Like John, she, too, had an MBA, and her background information, interviews, and testing indicated that she might be suited for a regional director position or even higher. However, these screening results also indicated that, unlike John, Leah was highly career-oriented.

After the preliminary screening information was assembled, Leah was informed that the results indicated that she was very career-oriented and that the organization felt it was important that it be candid about what it could offer her because she might have needs that it could not meet. The company told her the sequence of jobs she would move through and explained that, because of the narrow occupational structure of the organization, it was not possible to deviate greatly from this career path. It also told her the probabilities of promotion through the job sequence and the approximate times she should expect to spend in each position.[15]

When Leah decided to accept the position with the company, she was assigned a career counselor, Cindy House, who also served as one of her formal mentors. The assignment of a career counselor to serve as a mentor is the only major difference in the way career-oriented employees and other employees are handled at E. C. Corporation. This difference, however is significant. Cindy counseled Leah to solicit and to accept the help of others in the organization, including feedback on how she was doing, but, in addition to those objectives established by the organization, to establish her own objectives for learning, both overall, career-centered learning objectives and learning objectives related to specific jobs.

With Cindy's help, Leah worked out a set of overall learning objectives that included improving some career-related skills, such as communication skills; developing a deeper understanding of certain areas of management in which she felt deficient, such as strategic planning; and developing a better understanding of E. C. Corporation, such as understanding its evolution from a single nursing home to its current stature in the industry. Leah and Cindy also determined specific plateaus for each overall learning objective and specific measures of success in each area. For each position, they jointly developed specific, task-centered learning objectives. Cindy encouraged Leah, where given the choice, to avoid leaving each position until the job specific objectives had been fully satisfied.

The same year that John was promoted to regional director of the Boston area, Leah was promoted from her position as director of the Denver region to a newly established position of corporate director of strategic planning. At present, she cannot imagine wanting to work at any other organization. But she knows that where she will be in ten years is impossible to predict. After all, who would have predicted eleven years ago that she would be corporate director of strategic planning at age 38!

SUPPORT STRUCTURES FOR FLOWS

Formal organizations can be threatening for the newcomer. The newcomer is invading the turf of others who "belong" and who seem to have little place or need for the new arrival as they carry out myriad activities with an air of assurance. It can seem an impossible task to earn and to learn one's place in the organization. After a difficult period of adjustment, the newcomer becomes comfortable. It is tempting for the established employee to resist any further movement that will disturb this comfortable fit with the system.[16] But organizations need to move employees among job states. Movements of employees in an organization are necessary to

- Replenish human resource stocks.
- Rejuvenate employees who are no longer responding to their jobs. Research shows that employees who remain too long in the same job state, regardless of the nature of their jobs, become unresponsive to their jobs.[17]
- Allow adjustments to the changing needs of technologies, markets, and environments and to personal change and growth of employees.
- Allow correction of errors made in hiring and in job/person match.

If movements of employees among job states are to have their desired effects and to take place in sufficient numbers, a support system is necessary that will

- Cause the numbers of employees moving to increase by enabling and encouraging more employees to move and by lowering employee resistance to moving.[18] This will require help for employees to ease the discomfort of moves, and assistance for people in the organization to cope with the challenges posed by the moves.
- Raise the rate of learning and organization development caused by the movement[19] and lower the time required for new employees to reach proficiency.[20]

The support system for employee moves should be designed as a two-part system—a formal support system composed of formal policies, procedures, and programs, and an ambient support system that functions when the need arises.

Policies, procedures, and programs will be established for each of the major types of flows—organization entry, internal flows, and organization exit. Organization entry is the movement of persons from the outside labor force into the organization, either as full-time employees or as contingent employees.[21] Bringing about organization entry requires procedures and programs for employment planning,[22] choice of labor markets (where this is feasible), recruitment, selection, placement, orientation, and early job training.

Internal flows are movements of employees among job states within an organization. Some or all of the following procedures and programs may be directly involved in internal movements of employees: employment planning, transfer, job change, relocation, hiring-from-within, promotion/demotion, employee support, training, employee development, organization development, work design, research, and career management.

Organization exit is the movement of employees from employment status with the organization to other employment, to unemployed status, or out of the labor force. Procedures and programs involved in carrying out organization exit are employment planning, retirement, termination by discharge or resignation, outplacement, layoff, and alternative staff reduction procedures.

All of the procedures and programs named in this section are defined in Appendix 2 at the end of this chapter.

As employees move within the organization[23] and through work life and career stages,[24] their needs for support change. The full extent of needed support for flows cannot be anticipated. Different types of persons learn in different ways and need different kinds of support.[25] or have different life situations requiring different kinds of support.[26] And different agents of moves will need different mixes of support at different times and in different moves. The kinds of support needed for flows are so complex that formal, bureaucratized systems of support, even in highly developed systems, are often inadequate or inappropriate.[27]

An ambient support structure is one that is activated at time of need and with support appropriate to the moment. Three types of ambient support are necessary for employees in transition: financial and material support, information support, and social support.

The ability of an organization or its units to benefit fully from the arrival of a newcomer has been shown to depend on the existence of slack resources.[28] An organization or a unit that is overextended may not be able to give the needed support to a newcomer or benefit from the new ideas the newcomer may bring to the group. It is important, therefore, for organizations to set aside funds to enable a supportive response during employees' transitions among job states.[29]

By far the most expensive type of move for employees may be relocation, if relocation requires the movement of them and their families to a new residence. Such a move is likely to cost as much or more than the annual salary paid the employee.[30] Employees frequently refuse to relocate when they have suffered financially from an earlier move.[31] Helping with these moves is a necessary part of relocation. If the new job state requires that an employee move to a new residence, either to take a job for the first time with the organization or to relocate to another job in the organization, support usually will take the form of reimbursement for moving expenses; house-hunting trips for the family; absorption of mortgage payment penalties and maintenance and repair costs associated with the sale of a home; purchase costs (for example, "points" and attorney fees); temporary living expenses at the new location; mortgage interest differentials, if interest rates have risen; and other miscellaneous employee expenses associated with the move.

Other types of financial and material support also should be available on an as-needed basis. For example, it may be helpful in a particular move to have an employee who is retiring come in on occasion to help his or her replacement adjust to the new position.

Support in the form of detailed information—about the new job state, about why the employee is being asked to move, and about how the move is expected to affect the employee—should be complete, candid, and available on request. The efficiency of an information delivery system is lost if employees do not believe the information and must conduct independent checks of its validity. Credibility of information has a cost. Organizations must take the time to ensure that information given to employees is accurate, building credibility for the future.

If general information is presented first to employees, employees can decide for themselves when they need additional information. The information should be presented in a variety of forms, as employees will differ in their preference for a particular form of communication. Some possibilities are written materials and pamphlets, oral explanations, and videodiscs. Worksheets to guide employees in developing their personal plans for the move can indicate additional sources of information available. This information should be in a form that permits easy use by the employee.

Social support is very important to the adjustment process of employees in transition.[32] Social support requires that persons who are part of the social system of the new position, the "nonmoving employees," are willing and able to be supportive of the moving employee. If nonmoving employees are suspicious and afraid of newcomers and of new ideas, they will be unable to accept or to provide support for employees in transition among job states.

Employees who are relatively mobile have more active ties with the organization and gain information as a result of these ties. They can share this information with their less mobile colleagues. Nonmoving employees will have in-depth understanding of their smaller orbit that they can share with incoming employees. There is much to be gained from a social system made up of strong people who are generous with their support of each other. Organization cultures must value a variety of ideas and people.

STRATEGY-DRIVEN FLOWS OF HUMAN RESOURCES

Planning for management of the flows of human resources provides a vehicle for directing human resource management operations toward the achievement of strategic human resource objectives. To drive their operations strategically, organizations should *To drive strategic plans*

1. Choose the flows to be emphasized.
2. Find and enlist the support of key individuals or groups within the organization who can help to carry out the strategies in their daily activities.
3. Develop special operational policies, procedures, and programs for the flows that are to be emphasized.
4. Develop an ambient support system for these flows.

The following discussion describes how an organization would manage flows to carry out the strategy "facilitating technological change," one of those discussed in chapter 4.

An Example: Facilitating Technological Change

This strategy requires building a stable work force especially adept at applying new technologies. Two organizations will be described here: one, an established organization that realizes it must introduce technological change frequently to remain competitive; the other, a start-up organization that realizes that the nature of its business will require frequent technological change. The established organization has an existing culture, practices, work habits, attitudes, and beliefs to consider; the new organization will not be bound by existing traditions.

To implement this strategy, the established business will first identify the flows that should be emphasized. Internal movements of employees and organization exit are the two most likely to be emphasized in this case. The key individuals whose support will be necessary are likely to be

* Moving employees—employees who are moved to new jobs or new locations to accommodate technological change or employees who remain in the same unit but whose jobs are being changed
* Mentors who perform a personal support function[33]

- Supervisors of employees whose jobs are being changed or who are transferred or relocated to accommodate technological change
- Human resource function representative(s) to the technology management team

Moving employees will need to be empowered to effect both relatively minor changes and major changes in job states. Only their jobs, and thus their duties and roles, may be changed; or their jobs, duties, roles, role sets, organization units, and locations may be changed. The specifics and the extent of their empowerment needs will differ, depending on the extent of change involved. In any event, they need to be informed of changes in advance of their occurrence to enable the anticipatory stage of adjustment. This should include information about the kinds of technological change expected and the specifics of changes anticipated for their jobs. They need interpersonal skills training that allows them to adjust quickly to new work groups. They need job skills training that allows them to learn new tasks and that enables them to carry out the responsibilities of their new jobs. And they must be given the time needed to adjust to the new jobs.

If a mentoring program has not already been established, such a program will have to begin small and informally and then eventually be expanded and made formal. Established employees should be encouraged to extend help to employees in transition. The organization should provide opportunities for organization-wide contacts to allow these helping relationships to extend across functional areas, organization units, and hierarchical levels. As informal mentoring relationships develop, they can be recognized and encouraged.

When mentoring becomes a way of life in the organization, a formal mentoring program can be initiated for new employees. Mentors will need to perform the personal support functions that help proteges to take a broad institutional view, rather than a narrow parochial view, of the organization.[34] The formal program should be designed, as mentioned, to encourage further informal mentoring.

Supervisors in the established organization will need to redefine their supervisory roles. They will need to work in partnership with employees as agents promoting organization strategy. They must measure their accomplishments in part by how quickly and how well the employees of their unit are able to make use of new technologies. They will need interpersonal and group process skills that enable them to develop individual employees and to foster teamwork and cohesiveness in their work groups. Those supervisors who are able to do so should be encouraged to establish mentor relationships with employees.

The human resource function representative to the technology management team should be a member also of the futures committee. The representative serves as the link among the technological domain, human resource systems, and employees affected by the technology. The representative should participate in studies to define the future of the organization, so he or she is intimately aware of future technological changes expected and of the way these changes are expected to affect the organization. He or she should advise other human resource specialists on the design of all human resource systems to ensure that these systems foster, rather than inhibit, adjustments of employees to technological change. For example, the representative might advise that compensation systems not employ job-based systems, because jobs will change frequently, but should employ expertise-based systems to pay employees for the expertise brought to the job. And the representative should serve as liaison to employees, advising them or referring their concerns to others when employees have questions about changes in technology and its effects.

The key operational policy consideration for this strategy centers on the effect of technological change on job security. If employees believe that their jobs are at stake as new technologies are introduced they are unlikely to help with the introduction of new technologies. An organization pursuing this strategy must commit itself to a policy that does not allow the burden of technological change to be placed on employees.

Procedures and programs focused on internal moves of employees and organization exit will be emphasized.

Occasional transfers and relocations of employees are a necessary part of this strategy in order to

- Avoid stagnation of employees.
- Promote a broad view of the organization.
- Develop a multiskilled work force.
- Avoid layoff of employees whose jobs have been discontinued.

Extensive training may be necessary to supplement the basic skills of employees, such as reading and computation. Training also will be necessary to keep employees up to date with new technologies and to acquire the skills needed for new jobs.

Layoffs should not be used as a way to adjust to the changing work force requirements of technological change. Termination of persons who cannot adapt to technological change should be supported by comprehensive outplacement. Thorough employment planning, based on futures analysis and forecasts of technological change, will be necessary to plan for the employee complement needed for new technologies. Errors in futures analysis or forecasting may require work force reductions; these must be accomplished through alternatives to layoff, such as early retirement incentive programs, transfers and relocations, and attrition.

An ambient support system for this strategy should emphasize informational support and social support. Much of the information shared with employees will come from futures analysis and forecasting of technological change. Other information should be supplied by the management technology team. Particular attention will have to be paid to the credibility of information about the expected effects of technological change. This will require investments of time and effort to ensure that information is accurate and that promises are kept.

With extensive technological change, employees no longer have a stable, well-defined set of job duties. This can be unsettling for those who are accustomed to being defined by their jobs. Instead, their jobs revolve around the mastery of a class of technologies used by their employer. They must be able to do almost any job that evolves as the technology unfolds. A social support system must give these "new" employees social standing. This may require a new label for the job—"technologist." These employees must be recognized as occupying a central place in the organization and having skills basic to the identity of the organization.

The start-up organization will follow the same four steps to drive the organization strategically, but there will be differences in the way the steps are carried out. The primary difference is that the start-up organization can take advantage of the opportunity to build a work force from the ground up. It will emphasize the organization entry flows and related procedures and programs for selection, orientation, and early job training. The organization will

- Select employees who desire to learn and value variety in their work.
- Orient new employees to expect frequent change and variety in their jobs so that investments in basic skills training are not lost through early job turnover.
- Provide early job training to ensure that each employee has the basic skills needed to learn new technologies.

The start-up organization may make other modifications. For example, it can initiate a formal mentor approach immediately without an interim period of encouraging informal mentoring and developing acceptance of the mentoring function. In general, the organization can actively establish its culture, practices, work habits, attitudes, and beliefs.

This example has dealt with two types of organizations, both managing their flows of human resources to implement the same strategy. Each followed the same four steps to drive the organization operations strategically, but the choices for each step were made to satisfy the unique circumstance of each organization. This same approach may be used to guide other organizations in a creative search for a way to direct their operations toward their strategic objectives.

SUMMARY

The human resource operations of an organization are guided by both strategic and maintenance considerations. Maintenance considerations are those inherent in an organization's technologies, size, markets or clients, and the environment. Strategic considerations are those arising out of the strategic plans of the organization.

It is neither necessary nor desirable to manage all human resource activities strategically. Viewing human resource operations as flows of human resources allows the choice of activities that will drive the organization toward its human resource strategic objectives.

Flows of human resources are movements of employees into, through, and out of the organization. Key individuals who can help to ensure that movements of employees have their intended effects are persons moving between job states, mentors, and supervisors. These individuals must be empowered to act as agents. They must be told the strategic purposes of each move, and they must be selected, trained, and supported in a way that will allow them to fulfill these strategic purposes.

Support for moves of employees among job states can increase the numbers of persons moving and enhance the positive learning and organization development effects of the moves. A support system for moves must encourage moves of strategic importance to the organization, ease employee discomfort caused by moving, and assist people in the organization to cope with the challenges posed by the moves.

The support system for employee moves should be designed as a two-part system: a formal support system composed of formal policies, procedures, and programs, and an ambient support system that functions when the need arises. Policies, procedures, and programs will be established for each of the major types of flows, organization entry, internal flows and organization exit.

An ambient support structure is one that is activated at time of need and with support appropriate to the moment. Three types of ambient support are necessary for employees in transition—financial and material support, information support, and social support.

To drive their operations strategically, organizations should:

1. Choose the flows to be emphasized.
2. Find and enlist the support of key individuals within the organization who can help to carry out the strategies in their daily activities.
3. Develop special operational policies, procedures, and programs for the flows that are to be emphasized.
4. Develop an ambient support system for these flows.

LEARNING EXERCISES

Case Analyses

If you have the opportunity for small-group discussion, you may use the procedure suggested for Case 1 in Chapter 1.

Sun Microsystems, Inc.

"Sun Microsystems," Case 10, had an urgent need to manage more rationally the human resource function of the organization. Analyze the organization's needs by answering the questions or taking the actions listed here:

1. As background information for this analysis, first answer the study questions asked at the end of the case. You will need to review material from earlier chapters to answer the questions.
2. Recommend steps that Sun Microsystems should implement to identify and to analyze its human resource flows. (Material needed for this analysis is covered in Chapter 9.) What flows can you identify?
3. Use the strategy identified in question 2 of the background study. Make assumptions about human resource flows as needed and develop an operational plan for Sun Microsystems using the four steps described in Chapter 10 to drive operations strategically.

Chase Manhattan Bank   *strategic*

In Case 9, "Chase Manhattan Bank," does Mr. Lafley think primarily in strategic or maintenance terms concerning the management of human resources? What criteria did you use to decide this? Is the balance of his thinking appropriate for his position in the organization? Explain why or why not.

Activity

Arrange to interview someone who mentors other employees as part of his or her work. Determine

- Whether he or she enjoys the mentoring function
- Whether he or she feels rewarded by the employer for mentoring
- How many of the mentoring functions he or she can do well
- Which of the mentoring functions he or she feels is most important for the organization
- Which of the mentoring functions is most important to career success of employees mentored
- Whether he or she has one or more mentors

Did you have a mentor

Discussion Question

1. Should it be mandatory that every supervisor in an organization be able to perform all the mentoring functions? Why or why not? What considerations should enter into deciding this question?

APPENDIX 1: A GUIDE FOR AN ANALYSIS OF THE EFFECTS OF HUMAN RESOURCE FLOWS: KINDS, AGENTS, OBJECTS, TIMING, AND MEANS

Possible Effects of Flows

Changes In	Group performance
Behavior	Morale
Knowledge, skills, abilities	Human resource stocks
Understanding, attitudes, values	Quantities
Commitment	Qualities
Creativity	Varieties
Job satisfaction	Complementarities
Workload	Accumulations of HR stocks, rates
Relationships/compatibilities	Synergy/fit
Career success	Innovation, rates
Chances of career success	Organization learning/forgetting, rates
Effort to achieve career goals	Renewal/decay, rates
Quality of work life	Unit productivity/performance
Individual performance	Organization productivity/performance

Possible Agents of Effects

Key individuals	Employee support systems
Persons moving	Work rules
Mentors	Organization ambient structure
Supervisors	Material support availability
Key groups	Information support availability
Role sets	Social support availability
Work groups	Enabling conditions
Career cohorts	Change/rates of change
Job search networks	Move itself
Organization formal structure	Net imports/exports of energy
Culture	Combinations of above
Policies, programs, procedures	

People or Units Likely to Be Affected

Persons moving	Receiving career cohort(s)
Sending role set(s)	Sending work group
Receiving role set(s)	Receiving work group
Sending ILM(s)	Sending organization unit(s)
Receiving ILM(s)	Receiving organization unit(s)
Sending career cohort(s)	Organization as a whole

Possible Timing of Effects

Just before moves	Delayed after moves
During moves	Long delayed after moves
Immediately after moves	

Possible Means/Vehicles of Effects	
Social learning	Human capital gains/losses (ILM)
Instrumental training	Work experience
Observation learning	Discovery learning
Organization communication	Formal training/development programs
Role sending	Labor turnover
Career development	Systemic adjustments
Career decision making	Renewal effects
Career goal setting	Precipitating effects
Behavioral structuring	Combinations of above

APPENDIX 2
GLOSSARY OF PROCEDURES AND PROGRAMS USED IN THE MANAGEMENT OF HUMAN RESOURCES FLOWS GROUPED ACCORDING TO FLOWS

ORGANIZATION ENTRY

The movement of persons from the outside labor force into the organization, either as full-time employees or as contingent employees.

Employment Planning. The process of forecasting the numbers and kinds of persons needed for all positions in the organization and making specific plans for obtaining them. Employment planning must consider not only organization entry but also internal movements of employees and organization exit. Defining carefully the objectives of hiring and devising strategies for hiring are especially critical aspects of this planning.

Choice of Labor Market. Labor markets are places where employers and potential employees meet, figuratively speaking, and make decisions about whether to enter into an employment relationship. Labor markets should be well structured—have many efficient intermediaries who can bring employers and job candidates together—and have large supplies of labor suited to the needs of the organization. Start-up organizations and organizations making a decision about relocation of their operations or the location of new operations can choose to locate to allow access to favorable labor markets.

Hiring. That part of organization entry consisting of recruitment, selection, and placement.

Recruitment. Recruitment activities are intended to ensure that the organization "meets" in the labor market with better job candidates. Recruitment has two important aspects—choice of recruitment source and liaison with these sources. Sources are intermediaries that arrange meetings between job candidates and employers, such as another employee, a family member or friend of the potential employee, a help wanted advertisement placed by the employer or potential employee, or an employment agency.

Selection. The process of finding the best candidates from among those considering work in the organization and making carefully reasoned and timely job offers to those candidates.

Placement. The process of deciding which job, position, classification, and/or grade to offer a job candidate. Placement often is inseparable from selection in that the employer is selecting a candidate for a particular job or job state.

Orientation. A formal program for integrating the new employee smoothly into the organization.

Early Job Training. Training provided to develop in the new employee those attributes needed to perform the job in a satisfactory manner. Where it is economical to do so, employers usually prefer to hire job candidates already having those attributes.

INTERNAL MOVEMENT

The movement of employees among job states within an organization. These moves may involve a change in job, position, classification, or grade. A *job* is a unique set of tasks normally performed by one person. One or many persons in an organization may perform a given job. A *position* is used to distinguish the work done by different persons all doing the same job. Each employee in an organization normally is assigned to one position. Job *classification* is used to distinguish relatively minor differences in kinds of tasks performed within the same job. For example, two classifications of the job of secretary may be distinguished, with one classification performing somewhat more difficult tasks than the other. Alternatively, a classification may be used to distinguish among jobs on the basis of the kinds of tasks performed in the different jobs. For example, all jobs involving primarily customer contact tasks would be classified separately from all jobs involving primarily data analysis. A *grade* is used to distinguish among jobs on the basis of the level of the job on a scale measuring, most often, status attached to the job, worth of the job to the organization, and/or pay rate carried by the job.

Employment Planning. See "Organization Entry" section.

Transfer. Movement of an employee to a new position or job where the move is not across functional or organization unit boundaries. Transfer to a new job is likely to involve a change in classification and grade.

Job Change. Redesign of the job that an employee is performing.

Relocation. Movement of an employee to a new position or job and to a new function or organization unit. Relocation to a new job is likely to involve a change in classification and grade. An example of a relocation is a move from the position of secretary in a plant of a manufacturing company to the position of secretary in division headquarters.

Hiring-from-Within. The filling of a vacant position by selection of a suitable candidate from among present employees.

Promotion. The filling of a vacant position by moving an employee from a job carrying a lower classification and grade. Selection of the person for the promotion is based at least in part on performance in the previous job.

Demotion. The movement of an employee from a job, because of poor performance, to a job carrying a lower classification and grade.

Employee Support. The integrated system that provides tools and supplies, information, and personal amenities needed by an employee to do effective work. For the professional employee, a support system would include nonprofessional support personnel and communication system and computer access.

Training. A formal program to enhance the value of the employees of an organization by altering their values, attitudes, understandings, knowledge, and/or skills and thus their job behavior. Training is distinguished from development in that training is group-centered, development is individual-centered.

Development. An activity, project, or experience to enhance the value of an employee by altering the employee's values, attitudes, understandings, knowledge, and/or skills and thus job behavior.

Organization Development. The use of behavioral science knowledge and accompanying intervention skills to modify the social system of an organization to allow more efficient and/or more personally rewarding social interactions.

Work Design. The modification of a job or a family of jobs to improve job satisfaction, employee performance, and/or the integration of jobs. Work design may be done for any number of jobs ranging from a single job to all jobs within an organization.

Research. Careful systematic study to determine cause-and-effect relationships so that a problem can be solved or an activity can be performed better.

Career Management. An integrated set of related programs and procedures offered by an organization to support career planning and development of employees. These programs and procedures might include career screening, support for career planning (may be computer-assisted), career path design, mentoring, career development aids, informational services about career opportunities within the organization, career counseling, and feedback on career development.

ORGANIZATION EXIT

The movement of employees from employment status with the organization to other employment, to unemployed status in the outside labor force, or out of the labor force.

Employment Planning. See "Organization Entry" section.

Retirement. The voluntary or mandatory severance of employment because of the advanced age of an employee. Voluntary severance usually permits the employee to stop work while continuing to receive some compensation and benefits. Forced severance usually has the purpose of avoiding the retention of superannuated employees and may be based on individual performance or controlled by a policy of mandatory retirement at a predetermined age. Under federal law, mandatory retirement is prohibited in most occupational groups.

Termination. The severance of employment by discharge or resignation. Discharge is the forced severance of employment because the contribution of the employee does not warrant continued employment. Resignation is the voluntary severance of employment because the employee no longer wishes to continue the employment relationship. The term *quit* is sometimes used to distinguish the resignation in which the employee does not give notice.

Outplacement. A set of programs, such as counseling, training, and referral to vacant positions in outside organizations, to enable separated employees to secure suitable employment with another employer. These services may be provided by an outside firm, acting as a subcontractor, or by the human resource department of the employing organization. Outplacement services may be provided for individual employees or for all employees of an organization unit.

Layoff. Severance of employment because of a temporary reduction in the need for employees or because an operation is being permanently reduced in size or discontinued.

Alternative Staff Reduction Procedures. Various procedures, such as early retirement incentive programs and attrition, to avoid the layoff of employees. These procedures usually are sequenced and integrated to allow maximum reduction in payroll cost with minimum disruptions to operations and to the lives of employees.

Endnotes

[1]Baron finds weak support for hypotheses linking internal labor markets to organizational or sectoral "imperatives." At the job level, however, linkages between job ladders and technology and the institutional environment were found. James N. Baron, Alison Davis-Blake, and William T. Bielby, "The Structure of Opportunity: How Promotion Ladders Vary Within and Among Organizations," *Administrative Science Quarterly*, 31, no. 2 (June 1986), 248–273. See also Jeffrey A. Sonnenfeld and Maury A. Peiperl, "Staffing Policy as a Strategic Response: A Typology of Career Systems," *Academy of Management Review*, 13, no. 4 (October 1988), 588–600. For studies of job structures and human resource flows in specific industries, see David B. Bills, "Costs, Commitment and Rewards: Factors Influencing the Design and Implementation of Internal Labor Markets," *Administrative Science Quarterly*, 32, no. 2 (June 1987), 202–221; Thomas A. DiPrete and Whitman T. Sould, "The Organization of Career Lines: Equal Employment Opportunity and Status Advancement in Federal Bureaucracy," *American Sociological Review*, 51, no. 3 (June 1986), 295–309; Peter Allan, "Career Patterns of Top Executives in New York City Government," *Public Personnel Review*, 33, no. 2 (April 1972), 114–117; Yoav Vardi and Tove Helland Hammer, "Intraorganizational Mobility and Career Perceptions Among Rank and File Employees in Different Technologies," *Academy of Management Journal*, 20, no. 4 (December 1977), 622–634; James C. March.and James G. March, "Almost Random Careers: The Wisconsin School Superintendency, 1940–1972," *Administrative Science Quarterly*, 22, no. 3 (September 1977), 377–403.

[2]See Terry D. Piper and N. Jane Fullerton, "Preparing Entry-Level Professionals for Post-Entry-Level Positions," *Journal of College Student Personnel*, 26, no. 6 (November 1985), 566–567; Craig C. Pinder and Klaus G. Schroeder, " Time to Proficiency Following Job Transfers," *Academy of Management Journal*, 30, no. 2 (June 1987), 336–353.

[3]See Kathy E. Kram and Lynn A. Isabella, "Mentoring Alternatives," *Academy of Management Journal*, 28, no. 1 (March 1985), 110–132.

[4]For a discussion of the organizational dimension "inclusion," see Edgar H. Schein, *Career Dynamics: Matching Individual and Organizational Needs* (Reading, MA: Addison-Wesley, 1978), p. 38.

[5]James G. Clawson, "Is Mentoring Necessary?," *Training and Development Journal*, 39, no. 4 (April 1985), 36–39.

[6]Kram and Isabella, "Mentoring Alternatives."

[7]Ibid., p. 129.

[8]Piper and Fullerton, "Preparing Entry-Level Professionals."

[9]See "People Functions Scale," in Sidney A. Fine and Wretha W. Wiley, *An Introduction to Functional Job Analysis, Methods of Manpower Analysis No. 4* (Kalamazoo, MI: W. E. Upjohn Institute for Employment Research, 1971), pp. 34–39.

[10]Jepsen points out that a sense of personal control causes a heightened awareness of decision-making processes. See p. 93 of David A. Jepsen, "Comment on Symposium," *Character Potential: A Record of Research*, 9, no. 2 (December 1979), 93–94.

[11]See "Role Conflict," in Robert L. Kahn, Donald M. Wolfe, Robert P. Quinn, J. Diedrick

Snoek, and Robert A. Rosenthal, *Organizational Stress: Studies in Role Conflict and Ambiguity* (New York: John Wiley, 1964), pp. 55–71.

[12]This shaping of attitudes and values by requiring a set of behaviors may be termed behavioral structuring. For a discussion of the effect of work experience on values, see Jeylan T. Mortimer and Jon Lorence, "Work Experience and Occupational Value: A Longitudinal Study," *American Journal of Sociology*, 84, no. 6 (May 1979), 1361–1385.

[13]This on-the-job development process is especially effective where employees are enlisted as part of a development team and where opportunities for all employees to become part of a promotion chain are available.

[14]For suggestions about measuring career orientation, see Larry R. Cochran, "Level of Career Aspiration and Strength of Career Orientation," *Journal of Vocational Behavior*, 23, no. 1 (August 1983), 1–10; Raymond A. Noe, Ann Wiggins Noe, and Julie A. Bachhuber, "An Investigation of The Correlates of Career Motivation," *Journal of Vocational Behavior*, 37, no. 3 (December 1990), 340–356.

[15]For a discussion of points to consider in the negotiation of an (implicit) psychological contract with the career employee, see James F. Wolf and Robert N. Bacher, "Career Negotiation: Trading Off Employee and Organizational Needs," *Personnel*, 58, no. 2 (March–April 1981), 53–59.

[16]See Ralph Katz, "The Influence of Job Longevity on Employee Reactions to Task Characteristics," *Human Relations*, 31, no. 8 (August 1978), 703–725. Studies show that employees who have moved most are less likely to want to move in the future. See p. 42 of Betsy D. Gelb and Michael R. Hyman, "Reducing Reluctance to Transfer," *Business Horizons*, 30, no. 2 (March–April 1987), 39–43.

[17]Katz, "Influence of Job Longevity." Employees who move among job states, as compared to those left too long in the same job, perform better, are more innovative, are more satisfied, and understand their place in the organization better. See Robert T. Keller and Winford E. Holland, "Job Change: A Naturally Occurring Field Experiment," *Human Relations*, 34, no. 12 (December 1981), 1053–1067.

[18]Thomas A. DiPrete, "Horizontal and Vertical Mobility in Organizations," *Administrative Science Quarterly*, 32, no. 3 (September 1987), 422–444; Gelb and Hyman, "Reducing Reluctance to Transfer"; Sam Gould and Larry E. Penley, "A Study of the Correlates of the Willingness to Relocate," *Academy of Management Journal*, 28, no. 2 (June 1985), 472–478; Allan Proske and Charles David LaBelle, "At Manufacturers Hanover Trust, Human Resource Matrixing Builds Motivation Through Control," *Administrative Management*, 46, no. 1 (January 1976), 22–25; see pp. 183 and 185 of Robert N. Beck, "Adding Value: The Accountability of Human Resources for Impacting Business Results," *Human Resource Planning*, 8, no. 4 (December 1985), 173–191.

[19]John E. Ettlie, "The Impact of Interorganizational Manpower Flows on the Innovation Process," *Management Science*, 31, no. 9 (September 1985), 1055–1071; Keller and Holland, "Job Change"; Katz, "Influence of Job Longevity."

[20]Level of perceived support is one of most important factors affecting time to proficiency in a new job; see Craig C. Pinder and Klane D. Schroeder, "Time to Proficiency Following Job Transfer," *Academy of Management Journal*, 30, no. 2 (June 1987), 336–353. For a discussion of the importance of a support system, see Nancy K. Shlossberg and Zandy Leibowitz, "Organizational Support Systems as Buffers to Job Loss," *Journal of Vocational Behavior*, 17, no. 2 (October 1980), 204–217.

[21]Contingent employees are those with relatively low job security and variability of hours. For a discussion of contingent work, see Anne E. Polivka and Thomas Nardone, "On

the Definition of 'Contingent Work,'" *Monthly Labor Review*, 112, no. 12 (December 1989), 9–16.

[22]Employment planning supports all three flows: organization entry, internal moves and organization exit.

[23]See Edgar H. Schein, "The Individual, the Organization, and the Career: A Conceptual Scheme," *Journal of Applied Behavioral Science*, 7, no. 4 (July–August 1971), 401–426; Douglas T. Hall and Khalil E. Nougaim, "An Examination of Maslow's Need Hierarchy in an Organizational Setting," *Organizational Behavior and Human Performance*, 3 (1968), 12–35.

[24]Paul H. Thompson, Robin Zenger Baker, and Norman Smallwood, "Improving Professional Development by Applying the Four-Stage Career Model," *Organizational Dynamics*, 15, no. 2 (Fall 1986), 49–62; Erik H. Erikson, *Identity, Youth, and Crisis* (New York: W. W. Norton, 1968); Daniel J. Levinson, *The Seasons of a Man's Life* (New York: Knopf, 1978).

[25]Gib Akin, "Varieties of Managerial Learning," *Organizational Dynamics*, 16, no. 2 (Fall 1987), 36–48.

[26]For example, women have different needs for support during transfer among jobs. See "Failure to Transfer Women Hinders Their Advancement," *Employee Benefit News*, 1, no. 6 (November–December 1987), 26–27.

[27]DiPrete and Sould, "Organization of Career Lines."

[28]Ettlie, "Impact of Interorganizational Manpower Flows."

[29]Gelb and Hyman, "Reducing Reluctance to Transfer," p. 40, recommend a "cafeteria approach" to reimbursing employees for expenses associated with transfer.

[30]"Relocation Costs Average 104% of Salary," *Resource*, 2, no. 5 (May 1983), 9.

[31]Gelb and Hyman, "Reducing Reluctance to Transfer," p. 40.

[32]A study by Pinder and Schroeder, "Time to Proficiency," indicated that perceived support by supervisor and coworkers is one of the most important factors in the time to proficiency of employees moving among jobs.

[33]If the employees whose jobs are affected by technology have opportunities for promotion, mentors also should perform the vocational support functions.

[34]Piper and Fullerton, "Preparing Entry-Level Professionals for Post-Entry-Level Positions."

Closure

Business planning is an integrative learning/producing process. Strategic, tactical, and operational planning can take the organization from a vision of what the organization can be to the actual realization of that vision. When driven by the planning process through all stages of planning, organizations can become focused and vibrant.

Human resource planning is the dynamic core of business planning. It is people not fixed assets that will decide which organizations will lead in tomorrow's economies. Introducing human resource planning into the business planning process as a first priority consideration will be a challenge, but those who learn to do it will reap benefits for their diverse stakeholders.

Part 4

Cases

The cases in this section have their setting in a time period ranging from the late 1970s to the early 1990s. Cases from the earlier dates were chosen because they illustrate exceptionally well important principles of human resource planning. Several of the cases deserve to be called classics of case analysis. Examples are "Bolling Laboratories" and "Sun Microsystems."

Two cases are interviews with vice presidents of human resources in organizations that are known for their innovative human resource practices. At the time the interview was conducted, Robert Beck was just beginning his new position as head of human resources at Bank of America, and Alan F. Lafley was retiring from Chase Manhattan Bank. The two represent the modern professional human resource manager at the top of the human resource career ladder. Their views about planning-related topics are therefore important for students of human resources.

Cases have been paired with the chapter they best illustrate. Because these are all actual cases or are based on actual cases they often will illustrate material from several chapters. For example, "Bolling Laboratories" and "Shuckman Interiors" are suited to illustrate any of the chapters in Part I. "Chase Manhattan Bank" illustrates some of the material in almost all chapters of Parts II and III, and "Chase Manhattan" or "Apex Manufacturing" would have served equally well for Chapter 9. Seeing the same concerns and problems continue from one case to another strengthens the learning process by allowing the problem to be considered in more than one context.

As you analyze the cases, remember that your objective is to apply concepts. You may find this difficult at first. Continue to take specific ideas and try to apply them. You will begin to understand why events are occurring in the cases and you will learn how to intervene to change the course of events. In due time you will find you are comfortable with your ability to analyze and solve the case problems.

Case 1

Lehman Brothers[1]

NEW YORK—AFTER YEARS OF TRYING TO MESH ITS WARRING PARTS, SHEARSON LEHMAN HUTTON HOLDINGS, INC. IS ABOUT TO RESHAPE ITSELF, SPLITTING ITS INVESTMENT BANKING BUSINESS FROM ITS BIG BROKERAGE NETWORK.

Shearson, the nation's second-biggest securities firm, is expected as soon as next week to announce a series of organizational changes that could include a new corporate name and the uncoupling of Shearson's two main businesses: its brokerage business for individual investors and its investment-banking and institutional trading operations. The new investment-banking unit is likely to resurrect the magical Lehman Brothers name, employees briefed on the realignment said.

"We need a new identity," said one senior manager, one of many who have been briefed and debriefed in recent weeks by McKinsey & Co., a management consultant that has encouraged the splitting of Shearson into two main business halves.

People familiar with Shearson's plans say that the firm probably will change its name to Shearson Lehman Holdings, Inc. or S&L Holdings, Inc., with two separate divisions under it, and that each might eventually have its own internal profit-and-loss statements.

One division probably would be Shearson's retail brokerage business for individual investors; it would have nearly 10,000 stockbrokers and retain the Shearson name. The other division, which would include investment-banking and capital-markets operations, might operate under a resurrected name of Lehman Brothers.

Shearson, the struggling American Express Co. unit, acquired the venerable Lehman Brothers Kuhn Loeb, Inc. investment bank in 1984; that was after Lehman's traders and investment bankers split the firm in a civil war. Former Lehman partners never fully integrated into Shearson's corporate culture; some still announce themselves as "Lehman Brothers" bankers. And Shearson retains a separate Lehman brokerage operation for rich investors.

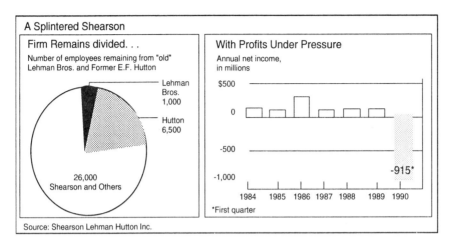

A Splintered Shearson

Firm Remains divided. . .

Number of employees remaining from "old" Lehman Bros. and Former E.F. Hutton

Lehman Bros. 1,000

Hutton 6,500

26,000 Shearson and Others

With Profits Under Pressure

Annual net income, in millions

$500

0

-500

-915*

-1,000

1984 1985 1986 1987 1988 1989 1990

*First quarter

Source: Shearson Lehman Hutton Inc.

Some Lehman veterans—there are about 1,000 still at Shearson, including brokers—aren't hiding their desire to resurrect their old firm, at least in name. "The Lehman name stands for something in investment banking and capital markets," said James Stern, a Shearson Lehman investment banker and Lehman veteran. "As for the Shearson name, I'm not sure it's the greatest name in the world. It's better than the ayatollah's." But some senior managers of Shearson are against the splitting of the brokerage business from investment banking, if only because it will fan speculation that Shearson's parent, American Express, is splitting up Shearson as a precursor to selling it.

Shearson executives briefed on the expected changes said such speculation is erroneous, although the timing of the split-up is nevertheless unfortunate. "I think the timing is wrong, but the philosophy is good," said one senior manager.

As part of the reorganization, Sherman R. Lewis Jr., Shearson's head of investment and merchant banking, and Richard S. Fuld Jr., head of capital markets, are expected to head the Lehman Brothers entity, people familiar with the plan said. (Mr. Lewis has Shearson roots, and Mr. Fuld is a Lehman veteran.)

The realignment would play down a separate identity for what remains of E. F. Hutton & Co., the well-known but deeply troubled brokerage firm that Shearson acquired in 1988, just after the stock-market crash. About 6,500 Hutton employees, mostly stockbrokers, remain at Shearson; many of them, too, have chafed at being part of Shearson. Most of the new Shearson names under consideration don't include "Hutton."

Howard L. Clark, Jr., a former American Express official installed as Shearson's chairman earlier this year, is known to favor a decentralization of authority at Shearson similar to the management philosophy at American Express. He declined to comment yesterday. A Shearson spokesman said: "We are considering a number of options on how we could regroup our businesses. We're still considering options."

In recent months, Shearson has been struggling to deal with financial and management problems, made worse by Wall Street's recession. American Express was forced to inject more than $1 billion into Shearson to prop up its capital levels. The parent has also had to increase its stake in Shearson, buying virtually all of it, rather than pulling away, as American Express has long wanted.

American Express plans to acquire the remaining publicly traded shares of Shearson, subject to a shareholders' vote expected in June.

Shearson took a huge restructuring charge in the first quarter to pay for thousands of layoffs, the closing of 67 U.S. branch offices and other cost-cutting efforts. That gave Shearson a $915 million first-quarter loss, a record for a U.S. securities firm. Shearson said that no new restructuring charge will be required for its latest changes.

Shearson officials said that under the expected realignment, Shearson's big Boston Co. money-management unit probably will report directly to the new Shearson holding company. A number of Shearson administrative staffers would report directly to the holding company as well.

How will the Shearson split-up play on Wall Street? The stock market has hammered Shearson's stock price to less than half of its 1987 issue price of $34. In New York Stock Exchange composite trading yesterday, Shearson stock closed at $13.875 a share, down 12.5 cents.

The initial reaction from a top securities-industry analyst was positive. "You know, one of their goals is to keep good people," said Lawrence Eckenfelder of Prudential-Bache Securities, Inc. "Well, if you create a separate investment bank, like the old Lehman, you could give guys incentives to stay. By giving them an identity, I just think you would help, longer term, as far as stemming some defections."

Some Lehman bankers are already hoping that Lehman is eventually taken public by American Express. "It gives [American Express] a hell of a lot more flexibility" as far as splitting off Lehman down the road, said Mr. Eckenfelder. American Express has vehemently denied it currently has any plans to sell Shearson or any of its parts.

American Express stock closed at $29.50 a share, up 25 cents in Big Board trading yesterday.

Case 2

Bolling Laboratories, Inc.[2]

Bolling Laboratories, Inc., is a medium-sized manufacturer of pharmaceutical products. It is known in the industry as a firm that takes very seriously its responsibilities both to its customers and its employees. It fulfills these responsibilities by maintaining good management, good products, and a favorable rate of growth.

Bolling has a broad product line covering most segments of a diversified national market. It sells both ethical drugs (those that may be purchased only with a doctor's prescription) and proprietary items (those sold over the counter). The company is also becoming known for its veterinary drugs in both ethical and proprietary forms. An organization chart for the company is shown in Exhibit 1.

At a meeting of the Pharmaceutical Manufacturers Association two years ago, R. M. Gerrard, president of Bolling, had a conversation with executives from other companies regarding the future of veterinary pharmaceuticals. One of the others brought up the subject. "At that time," Gerrard says, "I wasn't particularly interested. Bolling has a nice list of veterinary products. In fact, we were one of the first companies in this business."

During the months that followed this conversation, Gerrard

got to thinking about veterinary products. Our brands are well-known, but I know that we do not sell as effectively as we could. Our attention has always been rather negligible, because the total market for human pharmaceuticals was so much larger. You see, we have an overall goal of maintaining 15 percent of the total pharmaceutical market in the United States with gradual increase over ten years to 18 percent. With a fast growing market, this is not easy. The difficulty of achieving this market share is increasing, especially in the market for human pharmaceuticals. It is getting more and more difficult to clear drugs for sale through federal authorities. We can spend hundreds of thousands of dollars developing a drug and then not be able to put it on the market for three or four years, even if it is safe. Part of this, of course, is due to the fact that we do not experiment on human beings directly. In addition to this

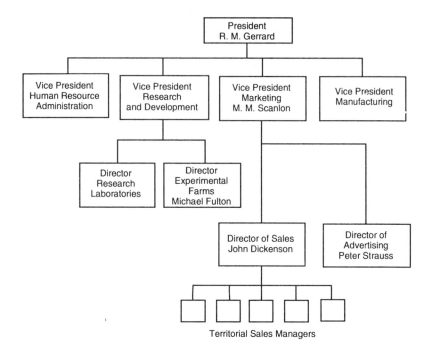

Exhibit 1.   Organization Chart, Bolling Laboratories, Inc.

factor, competition is becoming much stronger in the development of so-called wonder drugs for humans. With these reasons in mind, I instituted a project for the study of our veterinary products and operations. These products are subject to the same difficulties, but to a lesser degree.

Shortly after Gerrard announced this project, M. M. Scanlon, marketing vice president of Bolling, called a meeting

> to discuss the veterinary situation. I wanted to find out from our managers here in headquarters why we are not doing better in this area. Like Gerrard, I don't need a foundation grant to know that Bolling is not a leader. Present at the meeting were myself, Peter Strauss, director of advertising, John Dickenson, director of sales, and Mike Fulton, director of experimental farms.
>
> I started the meeting by saying that it is becoming more and more difficult to maintain Bolling's market share by promoting and selling human pharmaceuticals, that veterinary products represent one avenue for growth, and that we should take a hard look at either (1) what is wrong with our present operations or (2) what might be done to increase our effectiveness. I told them that Mr. Gerrard and I are thinking in terms of increasing our share of the ethical veterinary drug market from 15 to 18 percent.

John Dickenson was the first to speak:

> The most important key to most market-share problems is always the same. Selling. You cannot move products without sales representatives. The key people are the veterinarians. Ethical drugs are the place where the real sales potential exists. Proprietary drugs are strictly secondary. The overwhelming majority of ethicals sold are by veterinarians. Even when they don't carry inventory on their premises (most of them do), they, not the druggist, are the customer. I do not think we have enough sales representatives in the field. If we want to increase our market share from 15 to 18 percent, then it may mean hiring 20 percent more salespersons. We now have twenty-eight. That would mean an expansion of the sales force to thirty-four people.

Peter Strauss interrupted and gave his opinion on this issue:

> I wouldn't be sure of that. Advertising is important even in the ethical trade. The average veterinarian, like the average physician, reads professional journals constantly. We have a survey of the Advertising Association that shows that in the introduction of new drugs, veterinarians report that in 55 percent of the cases they first became acquainted with the product by seeing a professional advertisement, showing the various technical specifications and treatment results. I believe that we should increase the budget for advertising by an additional $150,000.

Dickenson answered.

> I suppose I agree with you, Peter, but I just don't see that advertising is nearly as important as selling. But I don't know how we'd ever prove that.

Scanlon said at this point that this was the kind of question that had to be settled, if possible. He questioned whether the company was selling to the big users, or wasting its time selling and advertising on small accounts.

Dickenson answered:

> An analysis of our sales shows that 20 percent goes to what we call the "wholesale doctor"—the very large clinics, such as those at Fort Collins, Colorado, and Ithaca, New York (to which animals are sent by veterinarians from all over the country), as well as large private animal hospitals in the suburbs of major cities. We have no trade association statistics on total consumption of ethical products by these institutions.

At this point, Mike Fulton, the director of experimental farms, spoke up. Fulton had been invited to the meeting, Scanlon said, "because he is a vast repository of information on veterinary products." It was fairly unusual for anyone from "the farms" to attend. These two farms were set up a number of years ago to house experimental rats and guinea pigs used in general research. Today the farms contain several thousand animals of various types and represent a large capital investment. Fulton is an extremely busy man as administrator of the farms. Of course, the actual research there is done by bacteriologists, pharmacologists, and other scientists from the research department. He was originally hired with a degree in veterinary medicine because the animals needed care. However, he has continually helped both the sales department people when they have an idea for using a drug, and the scientists when they have an idea for developing one.

Fulton said:

> I am worried about another thing. There is no one who can be called captain of the team when it comes to veterinary products. Over on the human side, the product managers of antibiotics, reproductive pharmaceuticals, intravenous solutions, and the like are always going to the research laboratories saying, "We must develop a product to compete with Talizene—the competition is killing us," or going to sales and saying, "The research people have just discovered a new and lower cost way to make our standard Thyroxin—get ready with an advertising campaign." I don't see that happening in veterinary products. Sure, we develop and sell them, but they seem to get lost, sometimes, in the development of all the wonder drugs for humans.

At that point, Scanlon spoke up. He said that in the area of research Bolling seemed to have a good record.

> We introduced fourteen products last year which were either completely new or major specification changes in existing products. That kind of record, at today's research costs, is good.

Events of the Next Four Months

At the end of the meeting, Scanlon suggested that this group become a formal task force for improvement of Bolling's veterinary operations, meeting each Monday for four months. At the same time, he obtained permission from the vice president for research to have Mike Fulton relieved as director of experimental farms for a period of three months, so that he could serve as staff investigator for the task force. "Dickenson and I," Scanlon said, "both noticed that he had a flair for selling. He always seemed to be suggesting alternatives that we had not thought of as means for overcoming problems. Often they are unworkable, but he hit on some that are of great benefit."

Over the four months, members of the task force seemed to report solid statistics, but none that could really pinpoint where Bolling had real opportunity for improvement. "It's like my statistics on new products or the question of whether we need more sales representatives or more advertising," Scanlon continued. "We all know that the company could probably improve with either, but the question is, which is more important?"

During this time, Fulton reported regularly on certain investigations he was making. Most of these involved getting Bolling sales representatives to request information from customers with whom they are personally acquainted. "There was a certain reluctance by representatives to take on this added paperwork," Fulton said, "but after clearing with Dickenson and their territorial managers I went straight to the representatives themselves, spent a lot of time showing them what we're trying to do, and then how it would pay off for them in increased commissions if they could get the information."

At the end of this period, Fulton requested a special meeting of the task force to explain some of his findings. "This wasn't easy, since they are busy men. But I went to each of their offices and gave them a small part of the total information. When they saw that there were going to be some new statistics, not just the same we've been over before, they seemed interested."

At the meeting, Fulton presented charts on each of the subjects shown in Exhibits 2 through 7. (See exhibits at end of case.) The meeting lasted for the full time available. There was not much time for discussion. Scanlon asked each man to study the data and to be prepared to recommend policy changes at the next meeting. As a final comment, he said that he also wanted the task force to look into several other matters at the next meeting:

(1) the nature of the training given to Bolling sale representatives, and
(2) the sales incentive/compensation system used by the company, particularly its effect on proprietary and ethical sales.

Bolling	32
Company A	30
Company B	25
Company C	28

Exhibit 2. Number of Sales Representatives Employed, Bolling and Three Similar Competitors[1]

Bolling	28
Company A	62
Company B	55
Company C	49

Exhibit 3. Number of New Products Introduced in the Past Two Years[2]

Bolling	26%
Company A	22%
Company B	28%
Company C	19%

Exhibit 4. Where 20 Wholesale Customers Purchase Their Supplies[3]

Question: Can you cite specific information from advertisements for any of these companies that appeared in the past month?

Bolling	41%
Company A	45%
Company B	32%
Company C	38%

Exhibit 5. Percent of Veterinary Doctors Who Could Cite Information from the Advertisement[4]

Question: Compared to these other firms, do Bolling's representatives spend more time, the same time, or less time when they call upon you? Please rank the companies from 1 (spends most time) to 4 (spends least time).

	Doctors	Druggists
Bolling	4	1
Company A	1	4
Company B	3	2
Company C	2	3

Exhibit 6. How Doctors and Druggists Rate the Sales Effort of Bolling and Three Competitors[5]

Question: In addition to quality and price, what factors influence you most in the choice of a supplier?

Factor	Responses Mentioning
Helpfulness of Salesman[6]	45%
Promptness of Delivery[7]	32%
Company Reputation[8]	31%
Appearance and Convenience of Packaging[9]	30%

Exhibit 7. Miscellaneous Factors Influencing Sales, Veterinary Pharmaceuticals[10]

Notes to Exhibits 2–7:

1. For Exhibits 2–6, Mike Fulton selected three competitive companies selling veterinary pharmaceuticals in approximately the same volume as Bolling.
2. Source of the data in Exhibit 3 is Federal Drug Administration Reports and professional veterinary journals.
3. For the data in Exhibit 4, salesmen interviewed 20 large clinics nationwide. These were both research clinics at schools of veterinary medicine and large suburban clinics in population centers. In each case, the customer was asked to estimate the percentage of his/her total use of pharmaceuticals purchased from each company.
4. The data in Exhibit 5 are based on responses of 100 doctors interviewed by salesmen. Twenty doctors were from the wholesale sample (Exhibit 4) and 80 were from the medium-sized sample (Exhibit 6).
5. The data of Exhibit 6 are based on responses of doctors and druggists in 80 medium-sized clinics nationwide. Values shown are average responses.
6. Item includes comments such as "actually helped me treat the animal" or "showed me how to prevent spoilage of solutions."
7. Item includes comments such as: "shipping department couldn't find my rush order' or "the salesman traced it right away."
8. For example: "My customers are impressed when I use well-known drugs."
9. For example, "Company always has the latest dispensers."
10. The question used for the data of Exhibit 7 was asked of the sample of 100 doctors of Exhibit 5. The question did not include a checklist. The exhibit summarizes answers and gives the percentage of doctors mentioning the item.

Case 3

Shuckman Interiors, Inc.[3]

Shuckman Interiors, Inc., is a small firm in Milwaukee, Wisconsin. Its business at present involves the installation of flooring, walls, and ceilings in commercial buildings. The company historically has been well run and profitable. When founded by the late John Shuckman, Sr., the company concentrated on installation and sales of floor tile. Shuckman, Sr., would approach potential buyers, acquire installation contracts, and then hire workers to install the tile. Noting the increased interest in acoustical tile, Mr. Shuckman diversified his business by adding it to his product-service mix. This decision was wise, for the new product soon exceeded the sales of floor tiles. Always on the alert for new products that would fit into the company's line, Shuckman added wall partition products to its list of installation services shortly thereafter.

A Family Firm

John Shuckman, Sr., had been a tile salesman for another firm, but he longed for the pleasures and pains of his own business. Psychologists have not often studied the motives of people to form their own firms. This decision often means that they will work longer hours for less money and with high risk that they will lose all their investments and have no job at all. The failure rate of small new businesses is high. But some people do have desire for independence and success that entrepreneurship can bring, and Shuckman seems to be one of them. He knew the construction business, and by watching cash contracts and careful bidding for jobs, he avoided the bankruptcy that most similar businesses experience.

In 1990, he became ill, and he died in June 1991, after a lengthy illness. He was succeeded in the presidency by his 26-year-old son, John. The younger Shuckman had received a bachelor of education degree from the University of Wisconsin, and spent three years in the Air Force before entering the business during his father's illness. His experience in the business was limited to part-time work while in high school and college.

The case writer interviewed young Shuckman and asked him what the out-look was for his business. He replied:

> I'm concerned about some aspects of our operations. It seems like a lot of inef-ficiencies and poor practices have crept into our work in recent years. Dad was in poor health much of that time, and I guess he just didn't realize what was happening.
>
> One main problem is that our jobs are poorly coordinated. We usually have three crews working on large projects: a floor crew, a wall crew, and a ceiling crew. Changes in work procedures and work schedules for one crew can com-pletely wreck the plans of the other crews. Yet, in most instances, none of the crews know what each of the other crews is doing. Sometimes it's like we're three different companies working on the same job.
>
> Another problem is a lack of good supervision. Often times I find workers just loafing around, waiting for some types of material or just waiting for fur-ther instructions. Invariably, the supervisor in charge is up to his elbows in another job—doing things that the project leader should be doing. This sort of thing may have been permitted in the past, but we're simply too big now. We need supervisors who will be supervisors.
>
> Yes, I'm anxious to get a few things straightened out—to really shake things up around here. The trouble is, any time I mention changes, I meet with resistance. For example, I met with the supervisors last week to try and iron out the problem I was just telling you about. They agreed to do a better job of supervision, but the last on-site visit I made revealed that the problem is worse, if anything.
>
> At first I thought that such resistance was due to the fact that I am fairly young and inexperienced. People seem to resent being told what to do by a newcomer. But now I'm beginning to think that some people around here are just plain stubborn. I can tell you one thing: a few heads are going to roll unless things improve pretty soon!

The case writer then asked Mr. Shuckman to describe briefly the business as he saw it in view of its history and possible future. He described it as follows:

> For the past, Shuckman served both residential and commercial customers. Presently, the company limits its business to commercial customers. You see, it is difficult to compete in the residential market, since the small contractors selling in that market are not unionized and are therefore able to do the job cheaper. And we didn't want to spread ourselves too thin. Typically we lay the floor, put up wall and ceiling work for medium-to-large stores and office buildings. We try to work out a "package" deal with our customers. That is, we prefer to do all the basic interior work—floors, walls and ceilings—ourselves. These three jobs require a certain amount of coordination, and it is usually bet-ter to have one outfit doing them rather than many. We do, on occasion, con-tract to do just a portion of the interior work. Profit-wise, these jobs have not been as satisfactory.

Mr. Shuckman continued:

We offer a total interior service, you see. The floor line consists of vinyl tile, carpeting, and other resilient coverings. The ceiling line includes acoustical board material, illumination panels, and suspension hardware. We do some plastering work, but most of the wall work involves installation of drywalls. The company has developed its own line of dry walls, which features metal studs and channels rather than the more common wood studs and bases. These light and nonpermanent wall partitions have been especially popular for us in remodeling.

How Shuckman Evolved

When the company began, Mr. Shuckman, Sr., performed a wide range of tasks himself. He did all the selling, ordered materials, scheduled and supervised operations, and handled all bookkeeping and accounting routines. He employed a secretary and four or five workers. More workers were added as the business grew. Then, as the company began taking on simultaneous projects, it became necessary to hire project leaders for each project, and supervisors to supervise the leaders. Salespeople were hired to help Mr. Shuckman find new business.

Presently, the organization consists of about 110 employees, 65 of whom are skilled or semiskilled laborers. At the management level there are two vice presidents, an accountant, and three production supervisors. Exhibit 1 shows what the organization presently looks like.

Mr. Thomas Oslin is vice president in charge of production and also serves as general manager. Forty-eight years old, Mr. Oslin began working for Shuckman Interiors about ten years ago. Before that, he worked for a firm which manufactures acoustical ceiling material. Besides having responsibility for all production activity, Mr. Oslin is in charge of the main office and accounting department. Mr. Howard, the office manager, reports directly to him.

Reporting to Mr. Oslin are three production supervisors. One is in charge of drywall construction, another supervises ceiling operations, and the third is responsible for floor installation. These persons schedule and control all production activity. Each supervisor assigns work crews to their jobs, ensures that needed supplies are on hand at the work sites, and coordinates work activities with the other two supervisors. The project leaders working on specific projects report to the supervisors. All three supervisors have worked for Shuckman for many years and have "risen through the ranks."

The vice president of sales is Glynn Rickers. Mr. Rickers worked in the construction business for 18 years before coming to Shuckman. He started as a sales estimator and was promoted to vice president four years ago. Mr. Rickers is knowledgeable in all aspects of the company's business and works closely with Mr. Oslin in planning and scheduling jobs.

Three sales estimators work directly under Mr. Rickers. These employees are responsible for locating new business and for preparing price estimates for bids.

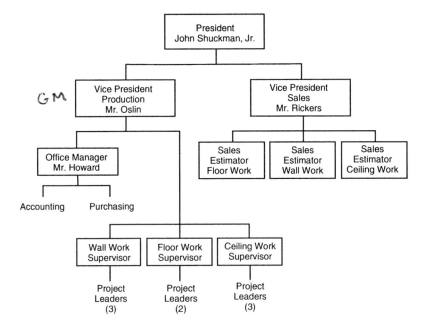

Exhibit 1.   Informal Organization Chart, Shuckman Interiors, Inc.

They also assist customers in selecting materials and color schemes. All three have had considerable experience in the interior finishing business. One previously owned an acoustical tile company.

The Shuckman Operation

Jobs at Shuckman Interiors are obtained either by bids or negotiated sales. Most Shuckman business is a result of bid jobs. Typically, a job is announced in a trade magazine, or in a construction service bulletin to which the company subscribes. When a potential job is announced, Mr. Rickers sends sales estimators to review the plans with the building owners and architects. Guided by the blueprint plans, the sales estimators compute the costs for materials and labor. Estimates of costs are made as close as possible to actual direct costs, with overhead, error allowance, and profit margin added on.

Mr. Rickers emphasized the importance of accurate cost estimation:

Most firms lose their shirts because they underestimate costs. A good estimator can determine almost exactly what the labor and materials needs will be from a good set of plans. A poor set of plans can throw estimates off seriously. We give ourselves a large error margin if plans are not specific. Overall, we've done a pretty good job of bidding most projects. Sometimes we're caught off guard by unforeseen hikes in wages or materials prices, but this is unusual.

Mr. Rickers said that they try to make a 13 percent operating margin on most projects. He added that it was not always possible to obtain such a margin, particularly if a number of other firms are anxious to obtain a given project.

A small proportion of jobs are obtained through direct negotiation with general contractors. In most such instances, contractors have worked with Shuckman in the past or desire a specific skill or material available only from Shuckman. Some interior materials businesses have salespeople who solicit sales by calling on architects and contractors. Mr. Rickers does not feel that this marketing approach is worthwhile, particularly since most of Shuckman's work involves rather large projects for which bids are necessary.

There are dozens of firms in the Milwaukee area that install floor, wall, or ceiling material. However, only four firms engage in all three types of activities on a large commercial scale. Mr. Shuckman said that his company has about 25 percent of the commercial market, and that this market percentage has remained fairly constant for the past five years. Shuckman presently limits its market to the immediate Milwaukee area.

The other three firms are Bischoff Construction Company, Arrighi Services, Inc., and Pulaski Interiors. Bischoff is the leading firm, having about 35 percent of the commercial market. But in addition, it has as much residential business as commercial. An old, well-established, and respected firm, it originated as a family concern but is no longer dominated by the family. Its bids are always competitive, yet it stresses quality workmanship as well. It does not do as much wall business as Shuckman.

The third firm, Pulaski Interiors, has about 20 percent of the commercial business. Its share of market has been declining. Mr. Pulaski seems to have lost interest in the business as he nears retirement. Pulaski's business in about the same size as Shuckman's.

The newest entry is Arrighi Services. At present it gets only 5 percent of the commercial business, but it has a fairly large residential business. It also offers wider services, including painting and decorating. The business is about two-thirds the size of Shuckman but is growing fast. Shuckman feels Arrighi cuts a few corners and has been getting more bids than he should have of late.

Like other firms tied to the construction business, these firms find that their business fluctuates considerably. Construction activity is both seasonal and cyclical. Seasonality does not affect firms doing interior work as much as it does firms doing outside work, since workers inside are afforded protection from the elements. Nevertheless, most companies such as Shuckman do a greater amount of work during the warm months. All construction activity is dependent on a number of political and economic variables, including interest rates, rate of business growth, and employment rates. Recessions in construction activity are often rather prolonged, and marginal companies are sometimes forced to go out of business during such periods. The level of employment in this labor-intensive industry fluctuates in proportion to the level of construction activity.

Once the job is obtained, a sales ticket and work ticket are completed. The sales ticket is sent to the accounting office, and the work ticket is sent to the production department. When production supervisors receive the work ticket, they begin planning operations. Materials for the job are ordered, and crew assignments are tentatively made. The production supervisor must keep in close contact with the general contractor to determine the exact date when the job will begin. When the job is ready for Shuckman to begin operations, the material is sent to the job site from the warehouse and labor is scheduled.

The accounting office records job expenses as they accrue. Actual material costs and labor costs are compared to bid cost estimates on a weekly basis. Wide variances between bid and actual costs are investigated immediately by Mr. Oslin, who takes corrective action, if necessary.

To explain more about his operations, Mr. Shuckman took the case writer on a visit of several work sites. He explained what he considers the production problems to be. He said:

> For one thing, our work crews can never seem to follow schedules. You see, work crews for the three basic operations (wall work, ceiling work, and floor work) are scheduled so that the needed workers are available for each successive phase of a project. But if one crew gets behind, this delays the starting time for the next crew. For example, if the wall crew is delayed in finishing a job, the ceiling crew cannot begin on time. Since there is often no more work for the ceiling crew to do, they are temporarily idle. This is not because of a lack of planning, but subsequent changes in work assignments throw projects off schedule. What happens is that the wall superintendent sees that he's getting a little behind on one project, so he shifts workers over from another. This delays work on the other project, and throws everything off schedule. Mr. Oslin and I have talked over the problems a great deal, but haven't come up with any workable solutions. He claims that you have to expect so much slack in the work schedule.

On a later day, the case writer visited with the production vice president, Mr. Oslin. Earlier a worker had told the case writer that he should talk to Mr. Oslin, since "he ran the whole place, anyway."

The case writer asked Mr. Oslin about the production problem mentioned by Mr. Shuckman. He replied rather sharply:

> No, I don't think we have poor supervision or poor work conditions. John seems to think that something is wrong when every single employee is not working every single minute of the day. But this just isn't always possible. Things happen which upset even the most carefully planned schedules. I try to keep in touch with the production supervisors about scheduling and work assignment changes. We work things out the best way we can.

But I'll tell you one thing, we do have a supervisor problem. Our three supervisors are spread too thinly. Right now, for instance, we have four major projects under way. It's impossible for each supervisor to be everywhere at once, although sometimes it's almost necessary for him to do so. We need more supervisors. That's the only solution.

The case writer asked several other questions and at one point commented that a worker had said he really ran the Shuckman company. Mr. Oslin replied:

Oh, sure, I guess you might say that I did run the place for quite a while. Mr. Shuckman, Sr., became so sick that he even stopped coming to work. He left everything in my hands. The business would have gone to pieces if someone hadn't taken over. But now that John, Jr., is here, things are different. There's only room for one leader at the top, and right now that's him. I'm careful not to infringe on his authority. Sometimes that's difficult, because many people still look to me for instructions and guidance. I discourage this. I'm trying to help John, Jr., all I can.

Asked to comment on Mr. Shuckman's abilities as president, he said:

Well, you can't learn everything there is to know about this business overnight, but John is working hard and learning fast. He's interested in the business. Sometimes, though, I think that there could be better communication between John and the rest of us. He makes a lot of decisions without talking them over with anyone. Some guys resent this. But I'm not going to say anything. As I said before, he's running this show, not me.

Financial Management

Mr. Howard, the company's accountant, told the case writer about the financial problems that are unique to the business.

For one thing, we must pay for materials and labor long before we receive payment from the customer. Furthermore, the customers retain a certain amount to assure the completion of a job. Usually, 10 to 15 percent of our accounts receivable consists of such funds. Because of these factors, we must manage our money more carefully. This involves sound financial planning. Also, it's imperative that we maintain a good relationship with the bank. Since there are relatively few fixed assets to serve as collateral in this business, most banks want prompt payment. Yes, many firms in this business fail because they lack financial management capabilities.

Mr. Howard stressed the importance of using accurate accounting and control procedures.

Mr. Howard's department also handles purchasing functions. Purchases are made for inventory and in response to specific job requests. All materials are stored in a new warehouse building having rail access. Mr. Howard explained that since there is ample storage space, he usually goes ahead and orders materials as soon as he finds out that they will be needed.

Some Final Comments

As the case writer was getting ready to leave, he was pondering the challenges and problems at Shuckman. Running through his mind were some of John Shuckman's earlier comments about his dream for the firm. He had said:

> I want to get things shaped up around here first—make the most of what we have now. But my real hopes are far beyond that period. I dream of a firm that is growing and expanding. We've entrenched ourselves—cut out our share of the pie. But we've been standing still—we still think of ourselves as a small outfit. It's about time our managerial thinking caught up to our size and do some long-range thinking instead of operating only on a day-to-day basis.

The case writer wondered if Shuckman Interiors was capable of fulfilling those dreams.

Case 4

Bank of America[4]

BOB BECK: AN INTERVIEW WITH THE NEW HEAD OF CORPORATE PERSONNEL

IBM is considered a leader in the personnel area. Can you tell us about your work there and about IBM's programs?

There are a lot of similarities between IBM and Bank of America. A. P. Giannini and Tom Watson, Sr., IBM's founder, were friends and had a lot of the same attitudes about corporations, about people, and about customers and service. When I was considering changing companies, I wanted a company whose culture and traditions were in keeping with the training and experiences I'd had at IBM.

Based on its personnel policies and practices, IBM is what I call an enlightened employer. There are many companies that offer good pay and good benefits, but the big difference to me is not the pay and benefits. What makes an employer distinctive in today's environment is something more. The big difference is the treatment of employees, how they're managed.

One thing that is a hallmark of excellence at IBM is their emphasis on good people management. They make a tremendous investment in their managers to make them people-oriented, good leaders of others. For instance, at IBM you can't be a manager of people anywhere in the U.S. without going to management school within 30 days of your appointment. These people go through a week's class, studying mostly people issues—not technical or business issues.

The three IBM basic beliefs are respect for the individual, the pursuit of excellence in everything you do, and the best customer service in the world. Mr. Watson started those back in the early 1900s, and IBM has built everything around them. Those beliefs are very compatible with what I've found here at Bank of America.

I was fortunate in my IBM career to have the opportunity to follow a career development path that led me through a variety of assignments and gave me a well-rounded experience. I went from headquarters to manufacturing to research laboratories, to field operations, back to headquarters, into an international job, and then back to headquarters again. I spent two-thirds of my time out of the U.S. for a couple of years. Because of that broad exposure, I feel I'm a better personnel generalist with a wide perspective, rather than a technical specialist.

What aspects of your experience at IBM do you feel are transferable to BofA?

Managing change and managing people are going to be the real tests of corporations in the decade of the '80s, and our people have to be prepared to deal with that change. That takes an investment in our managers through a strong management development program.

We're now putting together a worldwide management development strategy for the bank. This is something for which my experience at IBM—where we implemented a worldwide management development plan several years ago—has been very helpful.

Does IBM hire executives at your level?

No. Their basic philosophy is promotion from within. However, this requires a real investment in successions planning. We already have the beginnings of a succession planning system at the bank.

The goal is to develop an effective working tool so that senior executives won't have to be hired. We need to build our management team strongly enough so that all the key jobs will be filled from within. We'll soon be implementing a program that will oversee our management development plans on a worldwide basis— for international assignments, U.S. assignments, reentry assignments, and assignments across division lines. This will be part of the succession plan process.

What are your impressions so far of the personnel programs here at Bank of America? Can you share some of your ideas for possible change?

Well, overall it's clear that one of the reasons that Bank of America is the leader in its industry is because the bank has been developing the state of the art in personnel policies and practices. One of the concerns I have is that banks in general tend to look only among banks when comparing their programs. Companies like IBM or Xerox, however, look across all industries and try to glean the policies and practices that are best for them from a wider horizon. So when you compare Bank of America against all the leading banks, we look very good. While we have areas where we can make further enhancements, I think we are in a very positive position. We have programs such as our opinion surveys, Open Line, and other employee feedback channels that are very enlightening.

I plan to enhance the things we're doing, and at the same time further reduce bureaucracy. We still have a little bit too much bureaucracy, in my opinion, in terms of certain formal procedures and ways of getting things done.

One of the things I've seen here that has been so pleasing to me in the first few weeks on the job is the willingness to change, the open mind that Bank of America people have. I've been out talking to people at all levels—in senior management, in administration, and in the branches and regions—and there's really an open attitude. There's no one putting up a fight of "not invented here," or "you're an outsider coming in." In fact, from the beginning, I didn't feel at all like an outsider. I was concerned about that, coming in as I did at a high-level position....

With banking undergoing sweeping changes, training of our employees to meet the new demands of the marketplace and the work place is likely to become more critical. Will we be doing more training and career counseling to help our people meet these changes?

Another one of my top priorities is employee development. The financial services industry is going through at least a sweeping evolution, if not a revolution. We need to better understand how that is impacting people so we can anticipate future change and plan for it by redirecting people's careers. We'll be grouping all of our training, retraining, and development efforts under employee development. This means not just training, but development of people, so that when certain jobs aren't needed anymore, or product or technology changes dictate new positions, we will have people prepared for these new careers.

Development means having meaningful careers that people can move through. By that I'm not talking just about promotions, but about horizontal development as well. Keeping people growing—that's the kind of society we have. We have a much more educated work force today than we had 30 or 40 years ago. People today are demanding continual learning and growth.

I think most people come to the bank for a career. And that's why we want to develop better career path progressions. The supervisor has to sit down with each employee and ask, "Where do you want to go? What would you like to do? How much effort are you willing to invest?" Developing careers is not a one-way street—it's not just the company providing training and direction. Employees have to be willing to learn new jobs and take some risks if they want to advance or move into new career paths. There is always risk in change, but the payoff can be very rewarding.

In order to provide our employees with these development opportunities and career path progressions, we in Personnel need to have strategic plans that support the bank's strategic plans. This type of personnel planning is one of the key ingredients in making the whole process work. It is imperative that our planning process be closely aligned with the business planning process.

How about our benefits and salary policies? Is the bank considering so-called "cafeteria-style" or flexible benefits that enable employees to pick and choose benefits to meet their individual needs? Is our compensation package competitive with those of other organizations?

Let's take benefits first. We're in quite good shape with our benefits plans, especially our survivors' benefits and our pension and medical plans. In the benefit area, I'd like to see us become more flexible. Most benefit plans were designed in the 1930s and 1940s when the typical employee was male, had a non-working spouse, and three to five children. You don't find many of those anymore. You have a much wider range in the demographics of the work force. There are more single people and more working couples, there are employees with dependent parents. The traditional benefit package doesn't fit individual employees' needs as it once did.

But to go to a cafeteria-style, flexible benefits program overnight isn't easy. Some companies are trying it overnight, and it's turning out to be extremely difficult for them.

One of the most important things about any benefits program is to ensure that it's soundly funded and the company can afford it over the long haul. To have, for instance, a pension plan that's not properly funded is really unfair to the people who go on retirement. People want to be able to count on those benefits. So you should build your plans in a responsible manner, knowing you can afford them over the next 10, 20, and 30 years, not just today....

In medical, for example, we offer multiple HMOs. Why not consider offering three medical plans, some that are more preventive-oriented than major-illness oriented? That's what we're working on, trying to gradually build in more flexibility for individuals—in their time-off provisions, survivors' benefits, and medical programs. You can manage it plan-by-plan, but not all at once. To get there, we've got to walk before we can run.

On the pay side, it's a little early for me to comment on the competitiveness of our salary programs. I will say that I'd like to see a strengthening of our performance-based pay system. It's clear that over the past 15 to 20 years, pay schemes that are based on length of service are not successful. Even the U.S. government is moving off that system and going to a merit-based system. It's the key to productivity and the key to success in the future. We have to have a pay system that rewards performance and challenges people. As long as performance plans are fair and mutually set by the employee and the manager, and the employee knows where he or she stands and what is expected, then you can provide greater rewards to people who make more significant work contributions.

Our system at the bank is generally designed to do that, but we need to put more emphasis on the performance side. That's the feedback I've gotten from talking to people. And we need to make sure that people are challenged and that we expect more from them each year than the previous year because of their greater experience and training.

What are your thoughts on incentive programs to promote employee initiative and contributions to productivity and quality of service?

If you look at opinion survey data, you'll find that many people say that if the conditions were right, they could improve their performance. And often the things they're talking about are either better tools or equipment to do their jobs, or simply eliminating bureaucracy and unnecessary rules and regulations.

I'd like to see us develop more of a culture and climate that rewards people in a general sense for being part of—and contributing to—the success and well-being of the company. If their company is successful, profitable, and growing, employees are going to benefit from it. We'll be able to provide better training, better pay, better benefits, and more opportunities and promotions.

The environment has to encourage people to be creative. At many companies, when a manager gets a suggestion, it seems like his or her first thought is how do I knock this off? How can I get rid of this? Because, you know, I can't let other people be suggesting ideas, I'm supposed to think of them.

I'd like to get people's attitudes to something like, "Say, this is probably a good idea. I ought to try to find some way to implement it and reward the employee for being creative." And if the solution that they've suggested isn't exactly right, but it stimulates us to do something similar to it, we ought to try to find a way to reward the employee.

It's an attitude that recognizes our employees have good ideas, and we're all on the same team. The quality circle idea is what's bearing that out. Employees today are well educated. They have good ideas. They want to be heard. They want their company to be successful. It's to their benefit. It should be a team spirit that we foster in the bank.

This is such a competitive business, we need every good idea we can get. I welcome personnel policy ideas from all employees. Particularly those ideas that will help us run the business better and make us more human relations-oriented.

What is your philosophy of managing people? How would you describe your management style?

One thing is that I trust people. I give them as much lead and challenge as they can take on. If I find that they are having difficulties, then I step in and help them overcome the hurdles.

Another philosophy I have is to surround myself with the very, very best people. Some managers try to surround themselves with weaker employees, so they won't challenge the system. I feel, however, that if my people are successful, I'll be successful. Developing people is a basic responsibility of management. I spend a lot of time trying to challenge my people—to stretch them, to help them grow, and to help their ideas come to fruition.

I also feel very strongly about treating people fairly and with respect. I heard of a saying in a commercial that I'd like to paraphrase: "We don't treat our people like employees, we treat our employees like people."

Along the same lines, I believe in dealing on a first-name basis. We shouldn't get caught up in layers of bureaucracy so that, for example, I can't talk to someone three levels down from me simply because I'm supposed to go through two layers of management to get to them.

What do you see as the greatest challenge facing you at Bank of America?

I see a pent-up demand by the managers for many new personnel programs. Management development, strong succession planning, strong career-development programs—those kinds of things. The demand is here today—it's not as if they're saying, "Bob, you can take the next year to do these things at a gradual pace." It's more like, "Okay, you have some good solutions, let's do them tomorrow."

It's going to be difficult for the personnel community in the bank to move and do those things in the time frame that people want. It's going to be a major challenge for us. It's not a matter of finding out what to do, it's how to do it in an orderly fashion.

What would you like to accomplish in your first year?

First, I think I need to develop a good understanding of and appreciation for the tradition and the culture that made this bank great, so that I can help build on those strengths.

Second, I'd like to ensure that we have developed the strategic directions in our personnel policies and practices that will help the bank meet its business objectives. We need a game plan in the personnel side of the business just like the business side has for its programs and products.

And I'd like to feel comfortable that we have begun to build the personnel community as a professional part of the corporate whole—in California, in the U.S., and worldwide. That means we're going to put a lot of emphasis on development of the personnel team.

There is no university anywhere that could give me the kind of development and education in personnel management that I got at IBM. But that was a deliberate plan—a combination of seminars, developmental programs, rotational assignments, and career objectives that got me to where I am. That's my goal—to make sure we have that for all our personnel people worldwide. Then our personnel community will be ready to take on whatever challenges the bank faces.

What things attracted you to Bank of America?

One is the fact that the financial services industry is going through this rapid change. I see the financial business just getting ready to explode into whole new sectors. The customer set is different, the products and delivery systems are changing, and it's an exciting time for me to be in a new industry. And with a company that is committed to being number one.

Also, in my employment interview with Sam Armacost, I became convinced that he wants this bank to be the greatest place to work from a personnel standpoint, from a human relations standpoint. That was important to me.

I also was impressed with the attitude of flexibility and openness to change that I found here. You always read in personnel research studies about resistance to change—a kind of mind set that makes changing anything in an organization difficult—product changes, organizational changes, whatever. I don't see that here. The attitude of openness here is a unique gift that must have started back in the early 1900s when the bank was founded and continues to this day. That makes me excited about the future.

Case 5

Westview Company, Inc.[5]

The Westview Company manufactures parts for the automotive industry. Its one plant is located 20 miles outside of South Bend, Indiana.. The company is relatively small, employing 274 production workers, in addition to 118 office and sales employees and executives. Growth has been very rapid—from an initial 12 employees to the present number in 16 years. Between 1984 and 1991 its revenue has grown from $1.2 million to more than $30 million.

The founder and president, Barry Westview, also holds the title of sales manager in his company. Before organizing the company, he had been a salesman in a competitor that has since discontinued operations. Believing that his extensive contacts in the automobile industry and his proven sales ability would enable him to run his own company, he went into business for himself, after obtaining capital from three friends, each of whom owns a 15 percent interest in the firm.

Mr. Westview did not give much attention to internal operations. In fact, until 1990, he devoted most of his time to contacting important customers and the manufacturers' agents who represent the company in the southern and western states. In 1990, his plant manager retired and problems have escalated since then even though the replacement, the former assistant manager, seems to have continued practices much as they were under the previous manager. Mr. Westview found that internal matters needed more and more of his attention.

Seeking the help of an outside consultant, he was advised that he was the classic "entrepreneur" who enjoyed building but did not enjoy or have the patience to manage a business. On the advice of the consultant, he hired Mark Frankell to act as president and chief operating officer of the company. Mr. Westview will continue to wear the dual hats of Chief Executive Officer and Sales Manager. The consultant, Lenora Gambell, agreed to advise on organization design and to help select and staff the new structure.

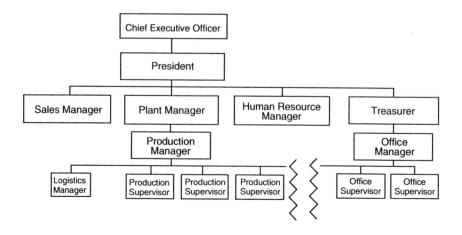

Exhibit 1.   Organization Chart of Westview Company, 1991

By the end of 1990, the new organization design was completed. A partial organization chart is shown in Exhibit 1. One addition to the chart was the creation of a human resource department. John Stoltz was hired to head the new department in January 1991. He was 36 years old in 1991. He had a bachelor of science degree in business with a major in personnel and labor relations. He had been employed as a college recruiter in the employment department of a large multiplant manufacturing concern until he lost his position as a result of a takeover of the company by another concern. He had worked as counselor for a large employment agency with branches throughout the United States until he accepted the position with Westview Company.

Lenora Gambell informed Mr. Stoltz that she had advised Barry Westview to initiate business planning as soon as possible. Ms. Gambell suggested that Mr. Stoltz begin gathering information to be used by the Business Planning Committee. She encouraged him to gather information about the organization himself since she believed he would have a fresh perspective of the organization. Mr. Stoltz filed his report with Barry Westview and Lenora Gambell. Mr. Stoltz later was informed that he was to be one of the eight persons serving on the Business Planning Committee.

Planning began at the enterprise level of the organization and then moved to the functional level. Mr. Stoltz was informed that he would take the lead in planning for human resources. Mr. Stoltz's background caused him to be familiar with external conditions in the human resource domain and it was felt that, with the information he had picked up about internal operations, he was the person most qualified to handle this task.

Mr. Stoltz assembled the information and strategic planning for human resources was finished in early 1992. When tactical planning began, Mr. Stoltz developed a briefing report which consisted of a list of items that he believed might have relevance for the committee in its deliberations. He intends to base his opening remarks to the committee on this report. A synopsis of the information contained in the report follows:

Briefing Report
Tactical Planning Committee
John Stoltz

& outcome

Human Resource Objectives: (agreed upon during strategic planning)

NO strate control to cost

- Maintain high product quality
- Control costs
- Maintain employee morale and satisfaction

how to obtain outcome

Human Resource Strategies: (agreed upon during strategic planning)

WORK DESIGN

- Keep employees satisfied
- Promote employee development

Major Problems or Issues: *HR*

- Conversations with several company officials and company employees seem to indicate that as the company grew in number of employees, morale appeared to degenerate. The "one-big-happy-family" spirit that was characteristic of the company in its early days has disappeared.
- It has been the practice of the company to allow each production and office supervisor to hire, discipline, transfer, promote, and otherwise make his or her own decisions about personnel matters within his or her own department.
- A number of employees expressed resentment about the discharge of an employee who had been with the company for many years. He was known to be an alcoholic but other employees believed that he should have been "carried" for a longer period of time in view of his long service and good record.
- Some employees have indicated "off the record" that they are afraid that a union will be brought in by disgruntled employees. Employees have resisted all union organizing attempts prior to this time.
- Personnel records are incomplete with little information about employees, other than that required for payroll and government reports. There is no provision for evaluating performance, determining individual strengths and weaknesses of employees, and for identifying departments with performance problems.
- Productivity appears to be declining in recent years and quality of the product is down while overtime costs and costs for temporary help (primarily in office positions) are up. At least one large order was lost recently because of poor quality. This matter is of particular concern since the company salespersons have been able to sell effectively largely because the firm has an excellent reputation for quality. While the

firm sells primarily to U.S. manufacturers, pressure on the U.S companies from the Japanese companies such as Honda and Mazda have forced the U.S. companies to pay more attention to the quality of the parts they use. This has proved advantageous to Westview and has contributed to their rapid growth to this point.

- There seems to be some increase in turnover, particularly among new hires. And absenteeism and lateness are high among these employees. The company has not previously experienced major problems of this kind.

- Rapid expansion has created staffing problems, resulting in some of the overtime and the hiring of temporary employees cited earlier. Supervisors appear to be spending much of their time hiring replacement employees.

- A number of supervisors in both the plant and the office are approaching retirement at the same time. This problem is compounded by the fact that turnover among this group of employees seems to be rising. If current trends continue during the next five years, approximately one-third of the managerial/supervisory staff will have left the company through retirement or otherwise.

- A number of the better managerial/supervisory employees are attending evening classes at a nearby university. In the past employees who have continued their education have left the company when they obtained their degrees. Westview Company has no programs to assist its employees to continue their education.

- There are no standard procedures for such things as vacations and employee leaves.

- Jobs have not been evaluated and pay of individual employees seems to be based largely upon an informal "negotiation" process between individual supervisors seeking increases for their employees and the payroll clerk in accounting. Compensation for all managerial/supervisory employees is established every two years by Mr. Westview.

Mr. Stoltz laid the report on his desk and tried to imagine the likely course of deliberations in the tactical planning committee. The first meeting was to be in two weeks. He knew that the committee would have to distinguish between those major policy areas of prime importance to strategies and those that could be decided during operational planning in each department of the plant and the office. He wondered how he should recommend that the committee proceed.

Case 6

Apex Manufacturing Company, Inc.[6]

Before his retirement, John Hadley had been President and General Manager of Apex Manufacturing Company, Inc., for fifteen years. Under his direction the company had grown from a small shop to a medium-sized corporation with 1,200 employees (see Exhibit 1).

Over the past eighteen months the profit picture of the company had a slow but continuous slide into the red. Morale and productivity had also followed this slow yet steady downward spiral. While it had been difficult to determine what the exact cause of the trend was, it appeared to have started at the first news of the offer by ARMCO Plastics to buy out 51 percent of the stock of the company. Although ARMCO had said that there would be no change in the status quo at APEX, there seemed to be a steady stream of ARMCO control being exercised over the company. The latest of these perceived changes was the early retirement of Hadley two months ago.

Hadley's successor was Bill Linden, a long-time employee of ARMCO and General Manager of their Cleveland plant. Upon coming aboard, he had taken little action, which had raised the anxiety level of everyone in the plant. While rumors of sweeping changes were rampant, no concrete actions had thus far been taken. The only actions that could be observed were the constant visits that the new GM was making to all areas of the plant.

On Monday of this week Linden had scheduled a Senior Manager's meeting to discuss the future of the company. This would be the first time that he would enumerate his expectations of the company and its managers. His speech was short and to the point.

> I am sure that you are well aware of the present situation in this company. I
> have taken the past two months to go around and confirm the problems I feel

	Present Organization Chart			
	General Manager			
Production Manager	Personnel/ Human Resource Manager	Sales/ Marketing Manager	Finance Manager	Customer Services Manager
1 Middle Manager	1 Middle Manager	1 Middle Manager	1 Middle Manager	1 Middle Manager
40 Supervisors	3 Supervisors	8 Supervisors	7 Staff	8 Supervisors
761 Staff	7 Staff	76 Staff		280 Staff
802 Total	11 Total	85 Total	8 Total	289 Total
	Projected Organization Chart			
	General Manager			
Production Manager	Personnel/ Human Resource Manager	Sales/ Marketing Manager	Finance Manager	Customer Services Manager
1 Middle Manager	1 Middle Manager	1 Middle Manager	1 Middle Manager	1 Middle Manager
5 First Level Managers	3 Supervisors	10 Supervisors	2 Supervisors	4 Supervisors
40 Supervisors				
997 Staff	7 Staff	100 Staff	2 Staff	140 Staff
1043 Total	11 Total	111 Total	5 Total	145 Total

Exhibit 1.   ARMCO/APEX Manufacturing Present and Projected (2 Years) Organization Chart and Personnel Assigned

are causing us to lose our competitive position in the market. The morale of the organization is low and continues to fall. Rumors of massive firings and sweeping changes abound. Our production rate is 80 percent of what it was two years ago and the number of time loss accidents has doubled in the last fourteen months.

I am not here to point fingers and direct blame. I am here to direct this company back to a competitive position in the market and into the profit column of our corporation's balance sheet. In light of that goal, I am recommending a six-point plan that I feel will start us back on the road of recovery.

My six-point plan is as follows:

1. The introduction of new manufacturing technology, which will begin in three months and be in place within the next eighteen months. The new techniques and machines will replace our old outdated processes and will affect approximately 75 percent of our work force.

2. In concert with my first point, we will be replacing two of our present product lines with updated versions that are presently being developed in the ARMCO R&D department. We are planning to replace our basic model with a version that will give our customers twice the capacity in half the time. The second line will be more expensive but it is virtually maintenance free. Our third line, which has been relatively unprofitable, will be dropped. As you can see, these changes will have a marked effect on our profitability as well as on the present work force. The changes tentatively projected are these:

- An overall increase in our current work force of 10 percent.
- A substantial change in the skill requirement of our present work force. This may entail a substantial number of personnel in certain areas being terminated.
- A reduction of 50 percent of our customer service personnel.
- An increase of 30 percent in the production areas.
- Training for all new production personnel as the machinery is state of the art.

The anticipated timing of this action is included in the paperwork on the table in front of you (Exhibit 2).

3. The advent of our improved product line will require an increase of staff in our sales/marketing department. I estimate this will be in the neighborhood of 30 percent. This will afford us the opportunity to recapture our market share and improve to the point where we have a total of 40 percent of the market in the next five years. As you know, our present market position is 25 percent.

4. We need to establish a promote-from-within policy whenever possible. I want this program implemented within four months. This program will ensure not only that we keep our best people but that we think ahead of time about what type of skills our people will need for their next career move.

5. As all of you are well aware, there is a massive problem with low morale in this organization. While we all could make guesses as to the cause, I feel that all it would be is guessing. I therefore want to find out what exactly is causing the problem of low morale and develop recommendations for combating it.

6. We will establish a different performance appraisal system based upon Management By Objectives (MBO). Our present system is all but nonexistent. It is backward looking and in most cases serves as a tool for punishment rather than as a support technique for improved performance. This MBO system should also be tied to the merit pay system that we implemented last year. If this system works well, it should also give us insight into the third point. This system should be implemented and working well within the next twelve months.

I would like your comments on these recommendations within the next twenty working days. I am also interested in seeing tentative implementation schedules at the same time. If you have any problems or concerns about this program as it is proposed please make an appointment with me before the deadline and let's talk about it. I feel that at this time it would be inappropriate to take questions before each of you has had an opportunity to digest this plan. Please keep foremost in your mind that this is only a plan and if you see changes that need to be made we can discuss them. Please feel free to make an appointment with me at any time and let me emphasize that if you do have problems with this approach, I want to know why as well as what alternatives you are proposing. If there is nothing else, this meeting is concluded.

Jayne Mico, the Director of Human Resources Management, called a meeting of the key people in her department to discuss the matter. Attending the meeting were Robert Armstrong, the Assistant Personnel Manager for OD; Joy Storm, the head of Administration; and Jeff Gilby, the Assistant Personnel Manager and Director of Human Resource Development.

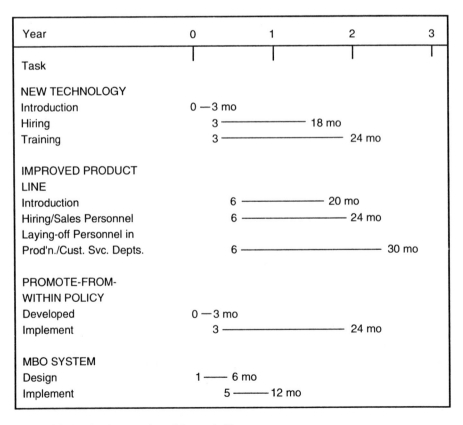

Exhibit 2.   Implementation of Strategic Plan

Jayne explained the situation as best she could and asked the meeting atten-
dees to have their inputs ready within the next ten working days. She closed as follows:

> You now have all the information that I have. I need not tell you that this pro-
> ject is massive in scope and has many potential pitfalls. My major concern at
> this point is that it appears that Mr. Linden has not thoroughly thought the pro-
> gram through. Of course it may also be that he is just testing us to see what
> changes we will recommend to his plan. At any rate, we must give him the best
> information possible to support any changes we would recommend to the plan.
>
> This is Monday. Give me your recommendations by COB Friday. If there
> are any areas where you need more information, please let me know.

Jeff Gilby walked back to his office. There were definite problems with the
plan, given what he knew about the organization.

Jeff sat back and thought:

> I have been with the company for ten years and for the past seven I have been
> Assistant Personnel Manager and Director for Human Resource Development.
> This plan may be the most difficult undertaking I have had thus far in my
> career. The issues as I see them are these:
>
> 1. The morale seems to be the key factor to trying to increase productivity
> but some of the changes that are going to take place are going to affect morale
> even more adversely than doing nothing. The staff and managers feel that it is
> only a matter of time before they are replaced by ARMCO personnel and that
> these technology innovations are just one of a series of changes that will afford
> them (ARMCO) the opportunity to accomplish that goal. ("These ARMCO
> people don't care about us like Mr. Hadley did," was a comment he had heard
> no few number of times.)
>
> 2. It is true that over the past few years innovations in our product line have
> only been cosmetic in nature and the market share that we once held has dwin-
> dled to half of what it was. The new technology and updating of our product
> line are good ideas. Even with their reservations about the new owners most
> employees will be in agreement with those needed changes. The other associat-
> ed issue is demographics; where will we get the people to fill all these new
> positions?
>
> 3. The promote-from-within policy would tend to indicate that APEX was
> serious about not firing large numbers of people. At the least, it was trying to
> keep those personnel who were the most productive. However, the changes in
> technology and major cuts in our customer service department will be psycho-
> logically devastating to the plant as a whole. There are a lot of good people
> who will be let go if this portion of the plan comes to fruition.
>
> 4. I have thought for a long time that the implementation of an MBO type
> of performance appraisal system would be helpful in increasing productivity
> and improving morale. However, given the general morale problems and some
> of the other tasks in the plan, now might not be the appropriate timing to
> implement such a system. The staff might perceive that this appraisal system is

just a mechanism for "setting enough unachievable goals to fire us." Even though our other performance appraisal system is basically not working, people at least use it. I wonder if the implementation of this program is the right thing now? But if we have to go forward with it, what would be the best way to implement it given the rest of the plan? Is the timing right? That is a crucial point.

5. Are the aspects of the plan that impact me thoroughly tested? We really have not done a thorough needs assessment to see if the proposed plan is truly what is needed—at least from a Human Resource Development standpoint.

After two days of anguish over this, Jeff decided to seek more information from the Director of the Human Resources Management group. It appeared that everyone was as perplexed as he was. The decision was made to meet the next day and look for the solution jointly.

Case 7

Northeast Data Resources, Inc.[7]

George Wellington closed the door behind him and slumped into his desk chair with an air of resignation. He had just returned from a meeting of the Executive Committee of Northeast Data Resources where personnel layoffs had been decided upon. As director of personnel at NDR, he realized that he would be responsible for both developing the process by which the layoffs would take place and assisting the managers responsible for the actual implementation. It wasn't a pleasant task, particularly in light of the human resources program that he had begun to implement over the past four years.

Wellington pulled out a pad of paper from the top desk drawer and began to scribble notes. He had found that in times of pressure it was best to get some perspective on the situation before taking action. The drastic character of this situation required a review of the growth of Northeast Data Resources from its inception in 1969 to the present. It was the first crisis the young company had been forced to face.

Background of the Company

In 1969, four young engineers formed a partnership to form the basis of NDR. Three of them had worked for a large, national data-processing company. They had recognized the high potential in the computer industry particularly for a product which filled a vital need in this growing field. Another engineer working in a research program with a large university was asked to join them because of his expertise in the computer field.

Jack Logan was the prime mover of the new company. He had been working for nearly five years on a project within the large company to develop ways to protect its computer systems from being copied by competitors. The primary objective in this project was to ensure that a customer would have to purchase the entire system rather than being able to make use of a number of different systems. Jack saw the opportunity to sell a service to customers that would do just the opposite—provide a mechanism that would link various competing systems into an integrated unit.

He and a colleague, Charlie Bonner, developed a "black box" which had the capacity to connect at least two types of computer systems already on the market. They had worked in Jack's basement over a two-year period to perfect this instrument. Another six months of testing found that it was very effective. The two other engineers had begun to work with them in order to expand the box to tie together three other systems with which they had experience.

The four men decided to strike out on their own and found that their innovation and daring paid off. The first two years were both exhilarating and demanding. NDR subcontracted the production of the black box to a small manufacturing company while the partners divided responsibilities between marketing and continuing research. Jack and Charlie carried the marketing and organizational functions while George Miller and Al Grant worked to streamline the instrument itself.

Early success in securing contracts with some key customers and fears about loss of the exclusive information about the unpatented invention led to a decision to go into full production. An old plant was leased and renovated and workers were hired to begin the process of building the black box for distribution. Within two years the company had grown from four partners to nearly 100 people. By 1976 NDR had expanded to about 700 people and had become the focus of attention for a number of investors. The invention, now dubbed Omega I, had become a product competitors emulated but with little success.

Logan assumed the responsibilities of chairman and president with Bonner as executive vice-president in charge of operations. Miller and Grant stayed in the lab with more interest in research and development, being willing to act more in advisory capacity on managerial decisions.

Logan saw the need to consolidate and expand the overall operations of the company. Production and distribution now overflowed into three buildings separated by nearly ten miles. He negotiated a contract with the economic development committee of Newbury, a New England town about forty miles away, to help construct a new building to house headquarters and plant. The town agreed to help NDR through reduced taxes, water, and sewage hookups at a minimal charge, arrangements with local banks to secure a loan for construction of the plant, and development of a federal grant to train new workers at the plant. In exchange NDR agreed to move its entire operation to Newbury within the next two years. It helped Newbury in its search for new industry while assuring NDR of a secure base of operations for the future.

The Newbury headquarters was only forty miles from the old facilities so NDR lost few of its present staff because of the change. But the growth in business demanded an increase in personnel. Engineers with sophisticated skills in computer science were hired to expand the system capability. Often, international engineers were the only ones available and the importation of English and Australians with a spattering of Europeans gave an international flair to the small company. New factory workers from Newbury and surrounding towns were hired so that the production shifts could be expanded from one to two. The training grants secured by the town helped to equip new workers and the integration with more experienced workers moved smoothly. Empty managerial slots required hiring from the outside mostly. A new vice-president of manufacturing came from a large industrial company in the Midwest. The new vice-president of finance had a solid resume which included most recently financial experience with a large conglomerate but before that two stints with growing companies much like NDR. The staffing of the growing company proceeded professionally.

Future of the Company

The phenomenal growth of NDR in old industrial New England rivaled the computer companies developing in California's Silicon Valley. The work force had evolved from 4 in 1969 to 100 in 1971, 700 in 1976, and 1,350 by 1982. Sales increased from two small initial contracts in 1969 of $75,000 to nearly $59 million by 1982. In 1975, NDR went public and was listed on the New York Stock Exchange in 1980. The opening price of 7 moved to between 8 and 9 and hovered there in 1981. But a feature article in a national stock advisory report about NDR led to an upward move in the summer of 1982 to 15. Even without paying a dividend in its thirteen years of existence, it had become an attractive investment.

Logan had taken time during the summer of 1982 to begin the process of strategic planning. Convinced that he and his executive committee could and should do this alone, he decided not to engage outside consultants to develop a costly set of plans. His projection was that the computer industry would grow nearly ten times in size over the next decade. Conservatively the company could expect to hold its share of the market which meant a doubling of sales in five years to $120 million and up to $210 million by 1992. Expansion was the key to maintaining market share and holding its own against the handful of competitors which had begun to appear by 1982.

In shaping the strategy, Logan began to map out a new marketing plan which would guarantee NDR's position in the national market instead of the eastern market alone. He saw new customer possibilities in the fields of insurance, financial institutions, and state and local governments. He negotiated an option to buy the factory of a watch company moving South. Its building was about thirty-five miles away in the heart of another old industrial New England town with a pool of skilled workers available to be retrained. He began to develop some ideas about how many new staff would be needed and the kind of capital necessary to finance this expansion.

George Wellington's Career at NDR

George stopped his writing and reviewed the rapid growth of NDR up to this point. He remembered vividly his first few months at the company in 1977. He had moved to a nearby town to retire in the serenity of New England. His career had begun immediately after completing his MBA from a leading eastern university where he had concentrated on management and personnel. He had begun work in the personnel area with a major corporation located in New York. Six years in the field had led him next into marketing and then strategic planning with another company. The last seven years had been with a prestigious consulting firm in New York where he had focused on a variety of problems for a host of clients. His decision to retire had been prompted by a dislike for traveling and a desire to settle down in the area where his children had located.

While retirement continued to bring part-time consulting work, George still found the travel excessive. But his ideas of relaxation in retirement quickly exposed his own need to be fully active in business to be happy. His search for a part-time job was successful as Jack Logan met him at a Chamber of Commerce luncheon in Newbury and hired him as a consultant to help with the transition from the old to the new facilities. He remembered the challenges associated with coordinating not only the efforts of NDR personnel but outside contractors and town officials as well.

The flawless nature of the transition into the new plant made the president recognize that he needed George full-time. Wellington agreed to stay only another six months as a special assistant to Logan. He carried out a variety of projects for Logan and quickly became an integral part of the management team at NDR.

The president called in George one day and showed him an organization chart which he was reworking. "George, I know that your six months are nearly up but I need you around here on a permanent basis. I just don't know where to put you on this chart. How about becoming director of personnel for NDR? That is the only important position which we haven't filled here in the past few months and it would allow me to have you close at hand for help on those big decisions."

George asked for some time to think through his decision and within a week agreed to a full-time position. While Logan still saw personnel as a somewhat unnecessary staff function, there would be a chance for George to help him understand the importance of human resources to this company.

Wellington began immediately to develop a plan for human resources at NDR. Logan encouraged him but wasn't excited about the use of the term "human resources." "I don't understand why you have to complicate this whole business of personnel with a new name. Why not still use the old 'personnel' for the department?" Logan asked. George saw a futile battle in this naming process so he clearly defined his function as that of director of personnel.

His plan for that function at NDR had three major elements:

1. The Program

Gathering Employee Information. He had his staff develop a file on each employee with a record of hiring date, previous experience and employers, salary, job title, etc. This was stored in a computer so that he could have rapid recall for evaluation.

Performance Appraisal System. He developed a new appraisal system which incorporated a three-page form to be completed twice a year by immediate supervisors. The annual review was tied to salary and bonus decisions. He experimented with it in two engineering sections over a two-year period and then was able to get Logan to mandate it for all of NDR beginning in 1981. The results from the 1981–82 year were compiled and filed for future use.

Personnel Policy Manual. In 1981, a new personnel policy manual was developed that detailed the policies and procedures as well as benefits for all personnel at NDR. There was some initial negative reaction by those who had enjoyed a variety of benefits from the early days of the company. But the imprint of Logan on the manual quelled the complaints and ensured uniformity in the policies.

EEO and Affirmative Action (AA) Program. The highly technical character of the NDR business and its presence in a small New England town made both EEO and AA difficult to pursue. A visit to Wellington by an EEO field investigator regarding the case of a former worker led him to move quickly to formulate this program. The data was gathered on minority hiring and promotion and then a plan designed for increasing the percentage of minorities in all categories and the number of women in management in particular. Logan resisted the immediate implementation of the program with the argument that the Reagan administration would soft-pedal civil rights in employment so that business people did not need to worry. George accepted this decision with reluctance but got an agreement to update the plan periodically as well as pursue informally a goal of more integration of the work force.

Management Development Program. The rapid growth of NDR created many new managerial positions. Hiring from the outside became one method by which to increase the number of managers, but George believed that the key to the company's future lay in developing them from within. He negotiated a contract with a professor of management at a local university to design and teach a course in management for selected employees. George and the professor team-taught a six-week course for twenty middle level managers in 1980. Its success led to an offering three times a year to both managers and potential managers.

2. The Staff

George became director of personnel in the spring of 1979. He selected four professionals and two secretaries to work with him. Two professionals came from outside of NDR and two from within. All four had human resources management experience but needed more training. One was encouraged to enter an MBA program on a part-time basis with a concentration on human resource management. The other three were sent to local and national seminars to upgrade skills and understanding in the various areas of HRM. But at the heart of their training was George Wellington, drawing on his vast experience and encouraging his younger colleagues to learn through experimentation and discussion.

3. The Office Location

The final design of the NDR headquarters had not been decided when George became a consultant to the project so he had taken primary responsibility for the design of the corporate office area. Later, as director of personnel, he negotiated some changes in the office assignments so that personnel was located at one of the major entrances and exits of the building. It was a primary thoroughfare for engineers and managerial personnel arriving in the morning and leaving at night. It was also a stop along the way to the new cafeteria that had just opened.

George had chosen this location for a reason. He felt that human resources departments must have high visibility and availability. Being in the middle of a key thoroughfare allowed people to recognize the central function of personnel in the operation of NDR. It encouraged questions about policies and procedures. It also gave the HRM staff the chance to get to know all of the managers and professionals within a short period of time. This provided instant recognition and a capacity to deal with problems on a much more personal basis. George himself was always at his desk working before most of the staff arrived and usually left after 6:00 p.m. This gave him considerable visibility with managerial personnel who often worked late.

The images of the first few years were succeeded by thoughts about the past two months with his staff. He had begun to engage them in the planning process by asking them to think about NDR for the next five years. He had sketched out the growth projections of Logan and then provided some parameters within which to think about staffing. Each of his professional staff was to develop a short presentation on four consequences for HRM:

1. Impact on the size of our work force
2. Impact on the mix of skills needed in the work force
3. Impact on the recruitment efforts from outside NDR and development efforts from within
4. Impact on the working conditions within the company itself, both physically and organizationally

The first meeting four weeks ago had produced some very good reports. With one exception, the four had done a lot of homework and some imaginative thinking about the future with regard to how HRM plans would fit into the NDR overall strategic plan. George had collated and refined the projections and redistributed them to the professional staff asking for further thought and more specific targets for the next five years. He asked for input for his own report to the president, which he had hoped would be ready by December 1982.

The Present Dilemma

That work had now come to an abrupt halt although he had not alerted the staff to the discussion taking place within the executive committee until the day before. Logan's projections about the future had been overly optimistic.

Two weeks ago, Logan had asked George to meet him at 8:00 p.m. He laid out a report on the results from the first quarter of this fiscal year and then a chart which traced the sales of the last nine quarters. The last two quarters showed a significant decline. Logan indicated to George that "the decline is now a trend and not simply a blip on the screen as I had thought." The loss of five key contracts totaling nearly $5 million dollars over the past six months plus the entry of a new competitor in the southeastern market had been responsible for the dramatic sales drop. At the same time, profits had suffered as well because of the increased expenses from a decision to increase the size of the engineering and financial service departments. The president admitted that his projections had been too optimistic and that something had to be done immediately. The cash flow problem had emerged as the most important pressure in this situation. The budget had to be pared while efforts to increase revenue were intensified.

George studied the figures carefully and agreed reluctantly to both the conclusions and recommendations reached by Logan. The two men took some time to sort through the various options available but it always came back to drastic cuts in personnel. He urged Logan to call a meeting of the executive committee in the morning and provide the data to them with encouragement to diagnose the problem and solutions to it. He argued that any solution must be a product of consensus of the committee.

The meeting caught everybody by surprise as they had accepted the president's projections of growth despite a temporary decline in sales. Two weeks of intensive debate among the executives led to the meeting this morning which defined the exact personnel cuts to be made. It was agreed that twenty-five engineers, fifty production personnel (workers and supervisors), and twenty-five others from various departments would be laid off within the next two weeks. In addition, fifteen new marketing and sales personnel would be added as soon as possible to carry out a new marketing thrust aimed at a different market segment.

There had been heated discussion about the exact number to be laid off and hired, with considerable friction between the vice-presidents of production, engineering, and marketing. The blame for the crisis was shouldered by Logan who asked that the executives recognize that they had to work together to resolve this problem if the future of NDR was to be assured. Wellington as the director of personnel was given the task of coordinating the identification of the people to be laid off although the actual decision would rest in the hands of the three vice-presidents. There were no criteria for the decisions although all agreed that loyal and trusted employees who had been with NDR for a number of years should be released only as a last resort.

The Director's Responsibility

The acrimonious debate of the morning still echoed in George's ears that afternoon. He tore the pages on which he had been writing off the pad and began a new one as he started to determine how the layoffs should be handled. It was a far cry from the exuberance with which he had begun the process of developing a five-year human resource plan just two months ago. Cutbacks in personnel demanded the same precision and careful thought in planning and action as hiring and promotion. There was less excitement about retrenching than growing because it affected the livelihood of so many people.

George jotted down the important questions in three different areas as he mapped out his thinking on this problem.

1. The Layoffs
   - Criteria to be used?
   - Data available on employees?
   - Impact of EEO and AA on decisions?
   - Severance pay and benefits?
   - Procedure for layoffs?

2. The New Hires
   - Skills needed in marketing and sales?
   - Available resources for positions?
   - Salary and benefit package?
   - Procedure for hiring?

3. The HRM Plan
   - Immediate impact on HRM five-year plan?
   - What if only temporary reversal of growth trend? (Commitments to rehire or not?)
   - Impact on employee morale now and in future?

George recognized that he had a lot of work to do. He struggled to regain his sense of professionalism as he began to detail the options available to each of the questions. His days as a consultant and manager had given him little experience in the arena of layoffs. But Logan had given him the responsibility and he knew that the future of NDR would depend heavily on how it handled this crisis.

Case 8

Deft Research
and Development, Inc.[8]

Karl Rhodes sat back in his chair. On his desk was a short memo from DR&D's new President, Glenn Richards, announcing the upcoming Management Committee meeting of all the DR&D's Vice-Presidents and the President to discuss the future plans for the Personnel function.

Rhodes beamed as he looked at the green countryside outside his corner office. As he stood, he knew that the President's office would come into view, a mere 400 yards down the quiet country road that crossed the rural setting which DEFT had chosen ten years ago as the ideal site for its R & D facility.

A look of great anticipation washed over his face as he thought about Personnel's role in helping the company plan and carry out its ambitious strategic plans for the 1980s. He reached for the phone and began dialing. In a few seconds he would have the President of DR&D on the line.

The time is now.

Background

DR&D is a high technology subsidiary of a large multinational corporation (DEFT Co.). As the research and development arm of the total corporation, it employs some 3,000 scientists and engineers.

Personnel, the department of DR&D in charge of employee matters, is headed by a manager who oversees some fifty professionals with functional managers of Recruitment, Labor Relations, Compensation and Benefits, Manpower Planning, Affirmative Action, and Training and Development. Exhibit 1 diagrams the formal structure of Personnel and its reporting line in DR&D.

The founding of the Personnel Department is attributed to Robert McKinnon, a very creative and controversial scientist employed by the former Consolidated

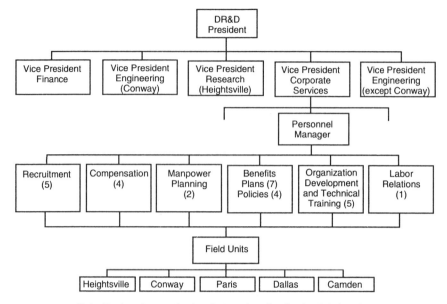

Note: Numbers in parenthesis reflect number of professionals in function.

Exhibit 1.   Formal Structure, Personnel Department of DR&D

Development Company. While holding a high-level position within the organization, McKinnon began building the personnel function in the mid-to-late 1930s. This signified forward thinking for its time, reflecting McKinnon's paternalistic orientation toward the function. At the same time that this HR function was developing, DR&D was becoming the first major industrial research company.

During the 1940s and 1950s innovative employee relations policies and programs were developed, which at the time were considered to be at the cutting edge of personnel management.

With the creation of scientific personnel salary scales and a maturity curve system, technical employees could now climb the rungs of a dual career/recognition ladder. New and rewarding opportunities became available to them; talented scientists were able to get recognition without becoming managers themselves. This allowed DR&D to attract and retain top individuals within their fields. Textbooks were written about the DEFT system by former personnel employees.

Throughout most of the innovative period and/or through the '60s, Lyle Johnson served as the manager of HR. He ran a dynamic, "hard hitting" department, continually producing innovative employee policies and programs. Organization Development (OD) was the key practice of the Johnson era. "All of the big names in the field either worked or consulted there." In fact, only TRW was doing as much in OD as DR&D at the time.

Although Johnson and his staff were energetic and dedicated, they were also unpredictable and unconventional. Johnson's image was far from professional: he was said to call staff meetings by the blow of a whistle as he paced the corridors, occasionally wearing his volunteer fireman's uniform or his hunting outfit from a weekend camping trip. There were a number of internal political controversies towards the end of his tenure which ultimately contributed to his decision to leave in 1965. Apparently Personnel, as a function, both prospered and suffered under Johnson's leadership.

The late '60s served as a transition phase for the Personnel Department. Alan Boyden followed Johnson as acting Personnel Manager for the next one and a half years. Boyden lost a number of good professionals from Johnson's staff and the personnel function was forced to adjust to a new and very different image and style.

Two critical events followed Johnson's departure. First, all four members of the Personnel Department's OD function left DR&D to form a consulting company (commonly referred to as the "Brown-Frasca split out"). The OD function was not rebuilt. As a result, division heads at DR&D expected to carry on with OD efforts on their own or with the help of outside consultants. Everyone felt that the dissolution of OD was a disaster for Personnel. Most thought that OD in the hands of line managers would spell "chaos."

The other critical event that followed Johnson's departure was the decentralization of the Personnel Department. Field units were created in the late '60s to provide employee services on site instead of relying on a single corporate staff. Corporate staff had mixed feelings about the decentralization, complaining mostly of a loss of control and dysfunctional relationships with field units. However, Personnel staff in the field units, as well as technical employees, felt that Personnel could respond better to employee and line management needs by the creation of the field units.

Matt Dembinsky was named Manager of Personnel in 1967 and stayed until his retirement in 1977. Characterized as "competent and nice," Dembinsky led the department through a series of budget cutbacks, reduced resources, and other recessive measures.

After a rare layoff of DR&D in 1972, manpower needs increased sharply in 1973. This demand together with the advent of additional federal legislation (EEO, Affirmative Action, ERISA) increased hiring in Personnel.

At the same time, Personnel corporate staff moved from Conway to Heightsville, closer to the main research site of DR&D.

Personnel Today

Karl Rhodes became Manager of Personnel in January of 1978, eight months after the arrival of DR&D's new President, Glenn Richards. The transition from Dembinsky to Rhodes was characterized as "smooth and well-managed," partially due to four months of overlap by the managers. The impact of the change was, however, enormous. With Rhodes came a new definition of the role of Personnel— from a reactive, maintenance role to a proactive, growing, and fast-paced one.

During Rhodes's first few months as Personnel Manager, several significant events occurred. Many of these events have been interpreted as being indicative of Personnel's future role in the company.

Operational

- Reopening of the Organization Development unit; Ray Wiggins returns to head the function, Wiggins having been on the OD staff in DR&D at the time of the Brown-Frasca split-out.
- Bob Kopcke transferred into Personnel to renew activity in EEO and to start a Manpower Planning Area.
- Establishment of new Personnel field units on site in Paris, Dallas, and Camden.
- Expansion of the Personnel staff.
- Budgets increased, producing a marked contrast when comparing ability to operate today to the cost control of the previous ten years which precluded anything but maintenance of established programs.
- New compensation and performance appraisal systems introduced (DEFT Company policy changes).

Consultants Called In

Aware of difficulties he would face in turning the function around, Karl Rhodes sought guidance from a team of consultants with expertise in human resource management. At their request, Rhodes called an exploratory meeting between the consultants and the eleven administrators of Personnel (see Exhibit 1).

As the meeting progressed, it became clear to the consultants that the administrators had different visions of Personnel's role in DR&D, and the direction it should go in. To explore the differences , they used a round-robin nominal group technique to generate a list of goals for the department. When the tally was done, the only clearly agreed-upon goal for the department was stated by Rhodes as:

> Have the Personnel Department become (and be perceived as) an influential force in the management of human resources at DR&D.

The Administrator's Viewpoint

The consultants talked with a few of the administrators. Although Karl Rhodes seemed widely respected, a few other comments were made:

> Rhodes, hell, he's still on his way up in DEFT. He'll relate well to the Management Committee since he's tied in so well, but I'm worried that he will be looking for a promotion before he is completed here and leave us cold.
>
> How much he has our interest at hand, I don't know. He wants change and more influence for the department which may end up just making our life a little more difficult. He's quite political, but also a very knowledgeable and expert personnel manager.

Some were distressed at the changes taking place. One administrator captured a common feeling when he said:

> I can't assimilate the changes fast enough. Never mind new ideas—
> let's try to catch up with last week's plans. There is an incredible
> workload—good for the most part, but also a lot of pressure.

The consultants explored further the different Personnel goals and strategies that had been put forth at the exploratory meeting.

Fred Perella, in charge of Training, saw Personnel as a service department.

> Our job is to implement programs which come through the system and to
> provide advice to line management on the spectrum of Personnel topics.

Maurice Flint, Administrator of Labor Relations, saw Personnel's role as primarily a question of negotiating a good contract. "As long as I keep the big unions out of DR&D, then I'm doing a good job."

Field Unit Personnel Staff

Two field units had existed when Rhodes arrived: at Conway, on site with the refinery, and the major field unit at Heightsville (down the road) where most of DR&D's research was done.

Soon after his arrival, Rhodes started three new field unit operations in Paris, Dallas, and Camden, with one or two professionals in each.

The Heightsville field unit had a staff of twelve professionals and ten support personnel. Ricky Maier was the Personnel Administrator of Heightsville, reporting to Rhodes.

In conversations with corporate administrators, the consultants discerned some problems in the relationship with field units, especially Heightsville.

> Field units act like we don't exist. They want complete control. Rhodes
> tells me I'm in charge of compensation for all of DR&D, but the next
> thing I hear is Maier making unilateral promises to his line managers in
> engineering that are 10 percent or 20 percent above DEFT guidelines.
>
> Maier runs a one-man show down there. But Karl's not going to put
> up with it. The problem is he wanted Rhodes's job and was pretty disappointed when he didn't get it. Turns out Maier had worked for
> Rhodes ten years back in Dallas. Back then he was Rhodes's fair-
> haired boy. Now he wants to show off to daddy, so to speak.

Jerry Hall, head of Recruitment, thought Personnel's most vital function was to make sure the company got the best people it could. "DR&D's only resource is its people. So we'd better make damned sure it's got the best."

The consultants spoke with Karl Rhodes in his office. As they began discussing the role of Personnel, Rhodes reached into a drawer and pulled out a sheet of paper. "It's all here." Exhibit 2 presents the formal mission statement Rhodes had developed and was about to distribute through the department.

> Personnel Department's overall role is stated as follows:
>
> The Personnel Department advises and assists line management in the effective recruitment, development, utilization, and motivation of human resources needed to achieve Company objectives.
>
> Discharge of this responsibility requires an understanding of the immediate and long-range goals of the organization and the effects of the internal and external environment on the attainment of these goals. Within this framework, the Personnel Department will develop policies, programs, and plans to create an environment which will optimize employee motivation.
>
> In order to advise and assist line management on the best means of utilizing human resources, the Personnel Department must be knowledgeable of the line organization's business plans and objectives, and develop human strategies in support of them.

Exhibit 2. Personnel's Mission Statement

Corporate Personnel Jobs

In talking with the different administrators and other employees, it was clear that the jobs in Personnel were varied. Administrators coordinated the jobs of professionals under them, and had support staff to assist with clerical work.

Most of the administrators did not shy away from actually doing the grunt work in the department. At peak periods, they pitched in. Some professionals even thought they did too much.

One young professional, who had recently joined the Organizational Development group, blamed the older professionals for not wanting to change.

> A number of people here are POPO's (Pissed On and Passed Over). They have nowhere to go. It would be great if we could just get rid of them, but of course it's not the DEFT way. So we have to carry the driftwood right along with us.

Each function had its own schedules, with peak periods that varied throughout the year. Recruitment, for instance faced its heaviest activity from June to September. August and September were especially hectic in running training sessions for all the recruiters drawn from DR&D (about 100 volunteers for one week each year). Throughout October they were out on the road, interviewing potential DR&D recruits across North American campuses.

Support staff seemed somewhat alienated from the professionals. When asked to comment on some of the recent events in Personnel, one secretary responded:

> I haven't the faintest idea what they're up to. They just put me in recruiting and told me to type my letters.

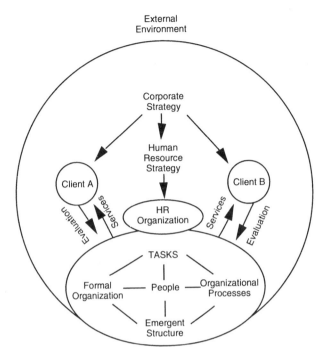

Description of Components.

Corporate Strategy: This includes the organization's reason for being, its basic approach to carrying out its mission, its strategy, and its criteria for effectiveness.

Tasks: This refers to the technology by which the organization's work is accomplished.

People: This includes the characteristics of the manners of the organization, background, motivational patterns, managerial style, etc.

Emergent Structure: These are the structures and processes which inevitably emerge in the organization and link together individuals and groups.

Formal Organization: This refers to the explicitly designed social structure of the organization. It includes the organization of subunits, communication, and authority networks as well as structural mechanism for integrating the organization.

Organizational Processes: These are the mechanisms (communication, decision-making, conflict management, control, and reward) which enable the organization to carry out the dynamics of work.

Exhibit 3.   The Human Resource Audit

Human Resource Audit

In order to more systematically assess the internal dynamics and the effectiveness of the Personnel Department *vis–à–vis* its clients and users, the consultants undertook a comprehensive HRMA.[9] The HRMA is designed on the premise that all organizations have a range of service needs in the human resource area. The audit, therefore, takes an overall organizational perspective, focusing on the human resource function as a service unit in the organization, delivering these services to an internal market place of client users. Exhibit 3 depicts the outlook that guides the HRMA.

At the core of the model is the human resource strategy of the organization which guides the kind of human resource function that is created. The human resource strategy stems from and intersects with other elements of the corporate strategy of the organization.

The human resource or personnel function is depicted as an organization in its own right. Tasks have to be done (selection, training, compensation), people are hired to do them, placed in a structure, make decisions, get into conflict, build their own networks. The result is a distinct package of services that are provided to the clients. These clients in turn evaluate them and provide a mechanism for assessing their performance. Presumably, the more "compatible" (or the higher the "fit" between them) the people, task, structures, and processes are, the more effective the human resource organization is likely to be in servicing its clients.

The HRMA uses this framework to try to answer such questions as:

1. Is the personnel organization's mission and strategy designed in keeping with its environment—both its external environment and its internal markets?
2. Does the design of the human resource organization enhance its ability to accomplish the strategy?
3. Are the kinds of people in the human resource function good choices for the ongoing tasks, structures, and processes?

Data Collection. The data collection involved three distinct steps. The first was an assessment of the human resource organization. Data were collected using interviews, questionnaires, documents, and observation.

The second step consisted of surveying the clients of the human resource function. Questionnaires were used to access areas of agreement and disagreement over work priorities, activities, and the role of the human resource function in the larger organization. Finally, the third step consisted of interviewing upper line management around issues related to the personnel strategy of the whole organization, and perceptions of the personnel organization's role.

Vice-Presidents' Viewpoints

As part of the HRMA, the vice-presidents of DR&D were interviewed by the consultants. Questions were asked that dealt with five areas: Personnel's mission in DR&D, appropriate activities for it to pursue, how Personnel's performance should be evaluated, its strengths and weaknesses as an organization, and the vice-presidents' overall impression of Personnel.

The consultants were surprised at the diversity of the responses from the five vice-presidents. Exhibit 4 summarizes the results of the interviews.

The vice-presidents were asked what criteria should be used to evaluate Personnel's performance. The responses covered a wide range. One vice-president felt

Personnel's Mission

DR&D vice-presidents were asked to read Personnel's role statement (see Exhibit 2) and comment on its appropriateness. Two of the five vice-presidents interviewed said that the role statement reflected their beliefs about what Personnel should be doing and stated that a Personnel unit operating with that role statement could effectively meet their needs. One vice-president felt it did not reflect his beliefs and would not meet his needs. Two vice-presidents did not respond to the scaled question because they felt there was some ambiguity in the role statement. They commented, "The basic problem is that they think they have major charter but they are fighting a 'no-win' battle unless Glenn supports it." "Are they servants or are they going to lead? Glenn will resolve it. "

Personnel Activities

The vice-presidents were asked to evaluate the appropriateness of twelve activities Personnel is pursuing over the next year. Four of the five vice-presidents responded to the scaled questions. Of the twelve activities, only four were considered appropriate by all respondents. These were:

• Bring about an ongoing salary communications program tied to orientation of new employees and training of new managers/section heads.
• Conduct studies assessing impact of the Ossipee move on DR&D work force.
• Help DR&D management make effective use of human resources, and have employees believe this is true.
• Establish and actively maintain an effective relationship between management and the bargaining agencies representing company employees.

One was viewed as inappropriate by all four vice presidents.

• Redesign starting level and early career assignments in a manner to make them attractive and challenging for DR&D employees.

The seven remaining activities reflected a lack of consensus on the part of the vice-presidents.

Exhibit 4. Summary of Vice-Presidents' Perceptions of Personnel

the same criteria used to evaluate DR&D's performance should be used to evaluate Personnel—productivity, creativity, and cost effectiveness. Another implicitly ruled out creativity when he stated the criterion should be "How well do they perform delegated tasks." Two vice-presidents suggested that the information or advice Personnel provides to management is the critical factor—"should give us advice on salary levels of scientists." "...how promptly they give us advice and how quickly they can do a study to support it." One stated that his criterion for evaluating Personnel's performance was "Do they make my life easier."

The vice-presidents were asked about the strengths and weaknesses of Personnel. Some of the items viewed as strengths by some were thought by others to be weaknesses, reinforcing the pattern of "mixed messages" from the vice-presidents.

The underlying differences in the pattern of responses is reflected in the comments made by the vice-presidents when they were asked their overall impression of Personnel. For some the impression is basically negative as borne out by the following responses: "They don't stand out—arrive at 8:30 and leave at 4:30." "They haven't won our confidence—(they) don't always do their homework." This contrasts with one vice-president who stated, "Overall, I would give them a 4 on a 5-point scale." Another said, " I think they are quite good but they are hampered by the fact that they frequently do not get the support they need—especially from the Managerial Board."

Summary of Audit Results

The consultants summarized their findings from the HRMA in Exhibit 5.

Component	Summary Diagnosis
Environment	Quite complex and changing, multiple markets with need for multiple services.
Mission/Strategy	Formally written mission quite organic, not fully understood or agreed to by many staff and not seen as accurate by many clients and users.
	Strategy same as mission.
Tasks	OK at the operational level (mechanistic and appropriate). At the managerial and strategic levels not well developed.
Prescribed Organization	Generally mechanistic, reliance on simple integrating mechanisms.
	Some medium-range integrating mechanisms but no complex ones.
People	Technically competent at the operational level (with a few exceptions); motivational needs not well matched with organizational rewards, especially career mobility.
	Lack strategic orientation.
Emergent Networks	Non task-related; very separated by professional vs. support; few participants.
Processes	Conflict OK, communication around goals needs to be improved, rewards need to be changed, control needs to be upgraded.

Exhibit 5.   Summary of Audit for Components of Model.

The consultants had shared these reports with Karl Rhodes and his administrators and were now ready to propose an action strategy for Karl and his Personnel Department.

A Surprise Telephone Call

Eager to discuss the results of the audit with Rhodes, the consultants headed straight for his office. As they entered they found him pacing back and forth, an angry frown on his face.

> How the hell are we going to have an effective strategic role with the Management Committee if we can't even get this shop running right. You know what just happened? That idiot Maier just quit on us, now that we need him in Heightsville! I should have listened to everyone and fired him a long time ago.

> The consultants sat down. It was going to be a long meeting.

Case 9

Chase Manhattan Bank[10]

A CONVERSATION WITH ALAN F. LAFLEY

Borucki: As a starting point, what impact can the human resources executive have on an organization?

Lafley: The human resources executive can have a major impact on an organization's performance and success. The degree of impact depends on a number of factors. It depends mostly on the CEO and the president's view of what a human resources function can contribute to the development and achievement of business plans and results, and on the credibility and performance of the person in the human resources executive position. The ability of the human resources executive to add value in determining the strategic direction of the corporation with particular focus on the human resources issues is very important. It is my opinion that most corporate executive officers recognize the important contribution to be made by the human resources function, and are seeking this level of contribution from their human resources executives. Unfortunately, many CEOs are experiencing a problem finding the human resources managers and professionals capable of meeting their standards for this critical business function.

Borucki: Alan, can you briefly highlight what is required of today's human resources executive?

Lafley: The requirements begin with the fact that human resources capacity will be a critical factor for most corporations in the attainment of business objectives in the years ahead. That capacity is being stretched today and the demands on it can be expected to continue to grow. There is an increasing need for human resources executives to bring into question both the adequacy and relevance of recruiting, selection, appraisal, development, and reward systems as the breadth and depth of managerial and professional skills required to complete effectively in our markets continue to grow and change. In this context, it is crucial for them to highlight priorities and guide human resources planning and development efforts as they go forward. As we assess our strategic positioning in relation to the anticipated environment of the 1980s, human resources capacity, more than financial capacity, lies on the critical path to meeting our business objectives in the years ahead.

Borucki: As background, would you comment on Chase's philosophy of human resource management?

Lafley: I believe that managers must be delegated more responsibility and authority, with corresponding accountability for human resource management. At the same time it must be made clear to managers that they are expected to perform to high standards on all significant elements of human resource management. In order for them to carry out these responsibilities, managers must possess the knowledge and skills required to be effective. They must understand the corporation's human resources philosophy, be prepared to carry it out, and be measured on their performance.

The core Chase philosophy for managing its people is to ensure its employees that they will be respected and treated as individuals and enjoy individual dignity at all times. This declaration of what employees can expect of Chase is paralleled by an equally clear declaration of what it has a right to expect of the employees in return. This kind of mutual understanding is fundamental to effective human resource management.

Successful managers clearly take the leadership in managing their human resources based on this fundamental philosophy. They do not hand over the responsibility and accountability to the human resources function. At the same time, the successful managers demand human resources functional support that provides the professional expertise and added value to ensure that human resource management will be competitive business strength for the organization.

It's the responsibility of the human resources executive to ensure that the human resource function is highly competent from a professional standpoint, has the relationships with top management to influence the human resource management of the company—including a reward system for managers that is heavily influenced by human resource management performance, and provides the quality of support needed and expected by managers.

Borucki: When you entered into the EVP position at Chase, it appeared that you were advocating breaking away from the Chase tradition of developing and promoting people from within. Now it's my understanding that you are returning to the practice of growing people within the organization. Would you comment on this apparent contradiction?

Lafley: When I joined Chase, it soon became apparent to me that we had to go outside the corporation to search for and attract particular managerial and professional talent of the highest quality to correct identified deficiencies. This was necessary because we had not recruited at the entry level the quantity, quality, or type to satisfy certain needs, had failed to develop the competencies required, made some poor placements as a result of our selection process, and had not achieved the performance results required because of our performance evaluation process and our reward system.

The CEO and president were convinced that the success of Chase, both short and long term, depended on the identification and placement of the very best people available in the particular positions at that point in time. And if that necessitated going to the outside to achieve the best placements, then we should do so.

There are significant problems, however, in assimilating outside hires into an organization at other than the entry level. Individuals within the organization are disappointed when there is no opportunity for promotion from within. Higher salaries that often need to be paid to attract outstanding talent from a competitor can cause inequities. Furthermore, it takes time and considerable managerial attention to assimilate an individual into a new organization. And, the failure rate of outside hires is high no matter how well the selection and assimilation of the individuals is done. We realized these risks inherent in external recruiting and fortunately managed the situations with considerable success.

Today, our external recruiting is focused primarily on the entry level, with much improved human resources planning and development efforts. And our policy is clearly to promote from within whenever possible. There has not been a change in our belief about the positive influence on employee morale of promotion from within, but it still must not be accomplished by sacrificing quality and suitability when filling the position. Because of the critical importance of strength and depth relative to key general manager and key professional positions, we will continually stay in the external market on a very selective basis to identify and attract top talent with the experience and competencies suited to our corporate-wide needs.

Borucki: At a recent symposium, you were quoted as saying, "In order to get the best, you've got to pay for the best." Would you please elaborate on this comment? Do you feel that this compensation philosophy should apply to internal promotions as well as external hires?

economics

Lafley: Chase at one time made the mistake of cutting salary budgets, as a part of expense reductions to a level where they were not competitive with the market, and they could not attract or retain the most competent and highly qualified individuals. In many cases they got what they paid for—adequate people for adequate salaries, but not the best managers or professionals. Compensation plans and salary structures must be competitive with your major competitors in each business. In Chase we are in that position today, and we will make certain that we remain there. At the same time, the compensation paid, both salaries and incentive payments, is managed so as to significantly differentiate the amounts paid to the better and to the lesser performers.

Let me add a comment that not only must pay be competitive, but the total reward system must be equal to or better than the competitor's. The opportunities for personal development and promotion, challenging work, a satisfying work environment, a good manager, a successful and well-respected company, are all important factors in attracting and retaining the highest-quality employees.

Borucki: One problem that many organizations are constantly dealing with, and often unsuccessfully, is removing politics from the selection process, especially at senior level and executive positions. The political element is often troublesome not only in terms of patronage and internal promotions, but also in relation to external recruiting. How does Chase deal with politics in selecting individuals for senior level positions?

Lafley: We have taken the staffing of senior level positions out of any political process without question, and, I believe, have a very effective approach to making decisions for staffing key managerial positions throughout the corporation worldwide. Staffing decisions for general manager and other key managerial positions are the responsibility of the president or chief executive officer. They are made after consideration of the sector executive's recommendations and a discussion of candidates identified and evaluated relative to the open position's agreed-upon specifications. The candidates are discussed relative to the position requirements in a very open and forthright manner in the meetings of the sector or equivalent executive with the human resources executive and the president and/or chief executive depending on the level of the position. The individuals recommended have been identified and evaluated previously as candidates for the position during the quarterly management resource review sessions with the president and his direct reports, and at the annual management resource review sessions with the chief executive, president, vice-chairman, and executives at the sector level. The human resources executive is the coordinator and an active participant in all management resource review sessions.

Borucki: How do you feel about the Boston Consulting Group's matrix as an instrument for identifying and fitting a manager to an operation's growth phase? They use the star, cash cow, question mark, and dog categories to identify growth phases and have complementary growers, caretakers, harvesters, and undertakers as manager "types." Is this matrix or a similar method used at Chase?

Lafley: I think that such an approach is an oversimplification of the general manager staffing process. Successful staffing of a position is highly dependent on arriving at a clear understanding and agreement on what the job is; that is, what needs to be accomplished in the particular general manager position over the next two to five years. And then it is necessary to interpret those needs into staffing specifications in terms of competencies, experience, and individual characteristics required. More staffing failures, in my opinion, come about because of lack of careful thought and agreement on the position requirements than are caused by poor assessments of an internal candidate's strengths and weaknesses.

The strategy for a business and knowledge of where we want to take it are important in determining the staffing requirements for the manager, but it's much more than assigning a generic strategic category. There may be a need to rethink the strategic direction of the business, and the position therefore requires a general manager who has outstanding ability to think strategically. You may need both an excellent strategic thinker and one who can bring costs in line. Does the business require strong marketing experience, or is the focus on technical strengths regardless of the growth phase? Do we need product development leadership or production strength? A business may have need for an unusual inspirational leader because of the circumstances in the organization, regardless of the strategic direction.

So my point is that although strategic direction is an important consideration in making the staffing decision, many other factors about the business are important in determining the position specifications and individual requirements.

Borucki: Alan, to follow this train of thought a bit further, is there some mystique about the "perfect" manager?

Lafley: In my opinion there is no perfect manager or singular model of a successful manager. I think that it is now very clear, since it has been proven over the years in numerous situations, that professional managers for all seasons do not exist. Companies have found that the concept of professional managers who can successfully manage any business is unsound, and it has resulted in numerous failures. There is a need to know the particular business and have sufficient experience in it to become a successful general manager. It is true for a functional manager as well. Unless you have knowledge of the function, you cannot successfully manage it. The concept of the professional manager was overstated and overtaught at one time. Fortunately, some of the companies who preached and taught the role of the professional manager have had their book burnings and the concept has passed.

Borucki: What do you consider to be the important components of strategic staffing?

Lafley: To answer your question on strategic staffing and to bring some of our previous comments on staffing into focus, let's discuss the linkage of staffing with development as key elements of human resource management to provide the strength and depth of talent required to meet the needs of the corporation in a timely fashion.

Based on some fundamental assumptions about Chase's development needs, a framework has been developed around a concept of "core" and "specialized" development streams. A development stream depicts a progression pattern for a particular "population" or family of jobs. "Core development streams" represent the job families which have the broadest application across the corporation and typically lead to general management roles; "specialized development streams" relate to more specialized job families and most often lead to functional management roles or the management of a more specialized business.

Each development stream is made up of the following elements; a recruiting profile which represents the "starting point" in development; development stages relating to one's position in the career cycle and general organizational level; development activities (including both on-the-job experiences and formal training) for each development stage; and a series of development targets, or outcomes, representing attainment of the "core competencies" required of the fully qualified professional or manager at various stages in the development stream.

Once defined, development streams must be supported by a number of staffing and development practices. These include manpower needs forecasts linked with longer-range business plans; a selection process targeted to ensure the appropriate qualitative inputs; assessment processes and manpower reviews to identify the most promising and their development needs; the placement process to match the development needs of the most promising with the best development opportunities; and reward systems to reinforce development objectives.

We see the development task requiring agreement on the critical competencies needed in our key professional and managerial population today and in the years ahead. With agreement on these profiles, we can use them to drive our staffing, recruiting, selection and placement, and our development strategies and practices. This approach emphasizes the interdependence of the staffing and development elements of human resource management.

Borucki: Let's turn to the topic of culture. Several articles and a few books have emerged recently in the literature espousing the significance of culture in relation to organizational performance and effectiveness. How should culture, in your opinion, be considered in the staffing strategy and the selection process?

Lafley: Before specifically answering your question, I would like to express a word of caution about all of the focus on culture of an organization. I have a concern that too much time can be spent on assessing the corporate culture and becoming overly sensitive to the organization's faults that the corporate management becomes immobile. It's somewhat analogous to a person worrying about all their little pains and aches to a point where they can no longer physically or mentally handle life's problems.

Certainly, the culture of the corporation impacts all elements of human resource management. It affects the approaches to selection, appraisal, development, reward, and the total work environment. It is an important consideration in determining staffing strategy and the selection process, and in deciding on needed changes in approach.

Borucki: Alan, what selection criteria do you use at Chase for recruiting and selection at the entry level?

Lafley: The selection process is crucial. It involves careful planning and effective implementation to ensure that we not only recruit the quality of individuals we want in Chase, but that we recruit enough of the core professional competencies we require, and a sufficient number of individuals who appear to have the qualities needed to grow into key managerial positions. The human resources development job is manageable if a sufficient number of entry-level hires have the basic qualities to be effective in broad managerial roles.

Chase's entry-level selection criteria includes certain *core criteria*. These are the qualities which, if found in sufficient measure, will provide the raw material for general management, and are, in most cases, relevant for our functional and professional populations. The core criteria include interpersonal skills—the ability to communicate ideas persuasively, understand the viewpoint of others, and relate effectively to a broad range of people; mental abilities—the intellectual breadth and versatility, in addition to the depth of mental capacity; achievement motivation—the high individual achievement needs involving the "desire to do better" that are the foundation for strong on-the-job performance; adaptability—to change and cross components. The rapid rate of change in our markets and in technology makes this quality extremely important; cross-cultural adaptability is becoming increasingly important as more of our businesses become "global" in scope; and leadership ability/potential—a significant proportion of our entry-level hires should rate high against this criterion, since in many cases our assessment will prove to be incorrect and in others it will prove irrelevant due to the individual's career interests and the problems of fit to position needs as careers develop.

The other entry-level selection criterion is *population and component-specific criteria.* These are the additional criteria which, if consciously recruited for, will make the development job more manageable and enable us to focus our early-career development on the special professional skills and abilities which will give Chase a competitive edge. These are functional skills/knowledge—the in-depth academic training and/or experience in a functional discipline which is fundamental to the work of a professional population. This can mitigate our development investment in a raw recruit substantially; and market knowledge/experience—knowledge or experience related to a particular customer segment or geographic market—can substantially reduce orientation time and permit us to bring someone "on-line" more rapidly. Special qualifications, such as fluency in a particular language or competence in a specific product or technical area, also enhance development.

Borucki: How are individuals targeted as candidates for higher-level positions within Chase? How does one "move" upward in the organization?

Lafley: Chase's strategy for selection and development is to focus on the most promising for both managerial and professional roles. Initial judgments are made about the long-term promise of the individual as early as possible in their Chase careers. While these initial judgments are necessarily tentative, and need to be reviewed continuously throughout an individual's career, it is critical that the most (and least) promising be identified early to permit focused assessments and individual attention. Among those identified as "most promising," assessments have different development implications. In the case of the promising future general managers, we begin broadening within and across core development streams early in their careers. The promising professionals are given more intensive development within specialized development streams.

Discussions with the individual are particularly important to ensure compatibility of individual goals with the company's manpower development plans. In addition, it is important for the corporation to identify and focus on the "key development jobs" which are seen to be most effective in developing and testing those competencies required in greatest measure in our general managers. Senior management concurrence with corporate human resources involvement is required in staffing them to maximize their development value. And, as with the development of key professionals, the selection of strong "mentoring" managers is important right along with job content.

Chase's disciplined approach to management resource reviews and candidate slates for key positions helps to ensure worldwide consideration of the most promising and best qualified individuals for open positions. The recruiting, selection, and placement process has deep involvement by senior managers. The selection process is targeted to ensure the appropriate qualitative inputs. Assessment processes and manpower reviews are focused on identifying the best performers, the most promising in each development stream, and giving individual development attention to those with the greatest potential. The placement process is geared to matching the development needs of the most promising with the best job development opportunities. And the reward systems reinforce managers' responsibility for development of quality talent to meet the corporation's needs.

Borucki: Alan, there has been much discussion on the utility of career ladders for individual development within organizations. Do you feel that this concept is important as a developmental tool and is it used within Chase?

Lafley: I am concerned about many of the approaches to career planning and some of the references to career ladders or career paths. An individual moving along a defined or planned career path, or up a ladder which connotes vertical, upward progress as ideal development and the way to promotion and increased responsibility, disturbs me.

Sound individual development planning and successful moves to positions of increased responsibility must optimize the fit between individual career goals, solid assessments of strengths and weaknesses based on performance, and the organization's needs.

Too many individuals get all hung up over unrealistic career plans developed by them. Seldom does a career progress as one plans, particularly in the job sequence and on the time schedule expected. Some of the best individual development moves are to a lateral or even lower-position levels. Too many failures are a result of climbing straight upward on a career ladder without sufficient experience, development, and testing at each rung. This has resulted in large numbers of executives falling off when they reach the top.

One of the situations that we had to turn around at Chase was the problem of too many people on career paths where they would spend two to three years on each job in a sequence of positions, each at a higher level until they reached an executive position and a senior officer title, only to then find their performance unsatisfactory because the job moves neither provided the development experiences or the assessments required for sound growth and promotion.

Borucki: How far into the future are your staffing plans made?

Lafley: Staffing strategy and plans must be an integral part of the Chase business strategies and plans. A corporate staffing strategy and plan cannot stand alone. Staffing and other human resource issues must be part of the particular business plans, but modified accordingly and summarized in a corporate staffing plan to ensure that the long-term staffing requirements of the corporation are met in terms of numbers, skills, and management competencies.

Chase staffing plans are reviewed on a six-month rolling basis with a focus on requirements twelve to eighteen months in the future. I believe that staffing and planning is much more dynamic than we tend to recognize, because both the internal and external environments are much more difficult to forecast than we admit in our business planning, particularly in banking and financial services.

Borucki: Alan, how does human resource management link with strategic business planning? Is the staffing element the only significant human resources consideration in determining strategic business objectives?

Lafley: Staffing is certainly not the only element of human resource management that needs to be addressed in strategic business planning. It is an area, however, where there needs to be a major focus in the initial strategic considerations. The planning involves consideration of compensation and reward systems to satisfy the business strategy being considered. The work environment considerations relative to location, facilities, and employee relations is another major human resources focus in the strategic business planning process.

Borucki: Handling staffing issues in troubled times can be problematic. Experts on Wall Street and in the banking industry have commented favorably on your handling personnel associated with Drysdale and Penn Square in a firm, decisive manner. Can you elaborate on the actions you have taken to resolve these issues? Is this the normal approach you take when such circumstances occur?

Lafley: I do not believe that we would have made different decisions, or handled the personnel actions differently were we to replay the same scenario tomorrow. We calmly investigated the situations before we took any personnel actions. We deliberately and thoughtfully gathered the facts. We carefully reviewed them, and then moved quickly. We made our decision on each personnel case on one day, communicated the decisions and took action the next day. We did not dribble out our findings and leave our people wondering whether or not another shoe was going to drop. Our approach was consistent with the way we normally handle difficult personnel situations.

Borucki: What is the role or responsibility of human resource management when poor performance of this nature surfaces and becomes problematic?

Lafley: When business performance is not up to expectations, we must focus on the core elements of human resource management: (1) staffing—the recruiting, selection, and placement process, (2) training and development, (3) performance appraisal and measurement, (4) reward systems and practices, and (5) the work environment. If the problem is poor staffing, and particularly in key manager positions, the poor placements have to be corrected in an uncompromising manner as soon as the evidence is clear. Related organization structure and staffing actions must be taken without delay, accompanied by appropriate discussions and communications. We must not contribute to increasing the anxieties of individuals by dragging out the process unnecessarily. This is where the culture of the organization is a factor in successful implementation. Staffing actions that impact individuals negatively must be handled with sensitivity and fairness to the people affected. Transfer, outplacement, and termination policies and practices must provide alternatives for the positive support that individuals need under these circumstances. It has been my experience that necessary staffing changes due to performance or future business needs can be made with firmness in a decisive and timely manner so that most individuals feel that they have been treated fairly by the company, and have located a new position much better suited to their interests and strengths. I sincerely believe that the greatest injustice that we can do to an individual, as well as the company, is to let a person remain in a position for which he is unqualified and where he becomes increasingly unhappy.

Borucki: What do you consider to be the lessons that Human Resources at Chase has learned from these events?

Lafley: These events have caused us to reflect on selection, placement, compensation, and training issues, and on management culture. Should we have made staffing changes sooner? Should we allow an incentive plan to be put into place if it can be mismanaged? We have been reminded that there are some things we need to do better in manager training. We are putting all of our present managers and those appointed in the future through a newly designed Manager Awareness Program. Its purpose is to provide the knowledge that a manager must possess before he is placed in a position of significant managerial responsibility. And there are management culture issues to reflect on. Can we improve management communications upward and horizontally, and the way in which managers "manage" their subordinates? These are some of the areas where human resources lessons may be learned.

Borucki: What has been the impact of the Drysdale and Penn Square incidents on the culture of Chase?

Lafley: The impact on the bank's people has been different than that experienced as a result of the problems in the mid-1970s. There was more anger and disappointment because individuals bankwide were performing well; the bank was meeting or exceeding its performance goals in nearly all its businesses in a very difficult external environment. Morale was high, employees were proud of their performance; they were with a winner. Unlike the mid 1970s, these were isolated incidents involving a handful of people out of more than thirty thousand. Their actions, however, had significant negative impact on Chase, not only on its profitability but its reputation. It was a very different kind of situation.

It's fortunate that Chase people today still view themselves as part of a winning team. They have gone back to work with even greater resolve. They have a positive attitude and are working hard to demonstrate that we at Chase will come back stronger than ever. I believe that Chase people have been able to handle adversity considerably better than others who have faced similar problems.

Borucki: A recent article mentioned that Citicorp was changing its organizational structure once again, abandoning the matrix concept for a market or geographically oriented structure, I believe. Chase is maintaining the matrix structure, which appears to work quite well. Can you elaborate on Chase's adherence to this structure and its implications for human resource management?

Lafley: First, let me make it clear that Chase's organization structure is not matrix form. And, we are not a proponent of the matrix as the best form of organization structure. It is a complex organization form and should be avoided whenever possible.

We have organized and staffed Chase to best fit our business strategies. We will continue to modify our structure and staffing to best fit our evolving business strategies and plans, and our executive manpower planning and development needs.

It is our opinion that the nature of Chase's business requires a high degree of integration, however, and considerable collaboration, teamwork, and communication between all businesses and functions. Our corporate culture therefore must encourage that type of work environment.

As part of our selection criteria which we addressed previously, in our performance appraisal process and in our training and development activities, we strongly encourage and reward teamwork and collaboration. This cultural element is so important to the success of any organization structure suited to managing closely integrated businesses such as Chase.

Borucki: It seems that Chase managers have acquired a good deal of human resource management skills. Have the requirements for good human resource management filtered down to all levels of line management?

Lafley: That's a very good question. The foundation of our whole approach to human resource management is that the primary responsibility for all the elements of excellent human resource management must be with the line manager. This is reinforced by the human resources function that must have the professional expertise to provide managers with the counsel and support, along with the training and development that they demand in order to fulfill their human resource management responsibilities.

An effective human resources function is one that works hard behind the scenes to help managers do their job. The person who is very good in human resources is constantly able to add value that the line managers want very much and need. The human resources professional helps managers to develop the skills necessary to perform their human resources responsibilities at a high standard of excellence. This is how human resource management gets filtered down to all levels of line management and ultimately impacts an entire organization. I might add that line manager responsibility and accountability for staffing, as for every element of human resource management, is absolutely essential for successful results.

Borucki: Looking toward the future, Alan, what changes in direction do you see Chase taking in terms of strategic staffing?

Lafley: Before we focus too quickly on the need for change in strategic staffing to meet future needs, let me emphasize that the most important need in Chase and most companies is to do what we've been talking about much better. There is greater need to improve our implementation of current staffing strategies and plans than to change our course.

I am not suggesting, however, that we should not be continually assessing the future staffing requirements of our businesses and modifying our recruiting, selection, training and development strategies, plans, and methods to meet changing needs.

Increased emphasis on selection, training, and development of the most capable and best performing specialists or professionals is one change I see taking place in Chase and other companies. There is greater realization that this population is increasingly important to the success of the business. It has also become more evident that the best source for potentially successful general managers is from within the group of high-performing professionals and specialists who have demonstrated excellent results over a significant period of time. We should not be identifying and selecting the candidates for general manager development who have not demonstrated outstanding performance as individuals in challenging assignments.

Borucki: As our final question, is Chase's human resource management philosophy and approach, including its strategic orientation, firmly in place, or will the function and its contributions change significantly at the time of Alan Lafley's retirement in 1984?

Lafley: Much of what Chase has accomplished in human resource management has been the result of deep involvement of the CEO and President, initially David Rockefeller and Bill Butcher and now Tom Labreque, with the Human Resources Executive. They have strongly encouraged and have taken a leadership role in putting in place a professionally competent function to support the line managers in carrying out their human resources responsibilities.

The senior management of Chase has focused on the improvement of every element of human resource management: staffing, development, appraisal, reward, and the total work environment. They have reinforced the need to delegate the responsibility and authority, with accompanying accountability, to Chase managers.

This was confirmed and reinforced this past May when Chase was fortunate in having Steve Drotter join the human resources function as Deputy Corporate Human Resources Executive reporting to me and preparing to take over on my retirement in 1984. Our approach to Steve's entry provides for the continuity to ensure that Chase progress in human resource management continues and makes even greater strides in reaching its future goals.

Sun Microsystems, Inc.[11]

INTRODUCTION

Scott McNealy, president and chairman of Sun Microsystems, ordered two more beers at the Dutch Goose Bar in Menlo Park, CA. It was June 3, 1986, four years and a few months since he and three other 27-year-olds had founded Sun, which was regarded as one of Silicon Valley's hottest startups. At 31, Scott was reflecting on his company's meteoric growth with an old college friend, John Bartlett.

Bartlett—Last time we got together, you were heading up operations at Onyx Systems. How'd you get involved with Sun?

McNealy—One of the other founders, Vinod Khosla, was a classmate of mine at Stanford Business School. He got the four of us together. The other two were Andy Bechtolsheim and Bill Joy, the engineers of the group. While working on his doctorate at Stanford, Bechtolsheim built what came to be Sun's primary product: a high powered technical workstation for engineers and other sophisticated users. Because of its unique design and low cost, a lot of companies were interested in it. Bechtolsheim turned them all down because he wanted to build a new company around his product. He teamed up with Khosla, and they recruited Joy and me. Joy, who was at Berkeley at the time, was our software guru. We raised $4.6 million in venture capital and started Sun, an acronym for Stanford University Network.

Bartlett—What's the status of the four of you today at Sun?

McNealy—Bechtolsheim's title is vice president of technology and Joy's is vice president of research and development. They're both in rather unique positions here, off on their own doing research. No one reports to them and they report to no one. Khosal left in 1985 to retire at the age of 30. He gets his kicks from starting companies. Once that was accomplished at Sun, he was ready to go. He's still a major stockholder, a director of the company, and a dabbler in venture capital.

Bartlett—I can imagine that in the first couple of years the excitement of working for a startup kept everyone going. But you're no longer the new kid on the block. Is it more difficult now to attract and retain the same kind of people that made Sun what it is?

McNealy—What Sun is—that's what I'd like to know. We know we're a different company today from what we were a year ago. We just need to figure out how. Last year, we recruited a vice president for human resources who's developed a system to define our "corporate culture."[12] Once I figure out who we are, I'll let you know how we intend to react to all the changes. There's no doubt in my mind that the human resource function is much more important at Sun today than it was a few years ago. We used to be able to recruit outstanding people for salaries much lower than what they were getting somewhere else. Our benefits package wasn't up to par. We didn't have time for things like formal training programs or performance appraisals. The excitement of the startup definitely kept the momentum going for the first few years. But things have changed a lot in the last few years. We've got over 2,000 employees and are hiring 150 new people a month. We're a public company. We are shipping at a rate greater than $300 million per year. We started in half of one building and now occupy more than eight buildings in Mountain View alone. In the past year, we've made our salary and benefits package competitive with the market. But we've got to spend a lot more time and money putting all the systems into place that will enable us to continue to attract and hold on to the best people.

The conversation went on, but this part of it stayed on McNealy's mind long after he dropped Bartlett off at his hotel. He knew that Sun could not maintain the entrepreneurial spirit that permeates a young startup. But he was convinced that something could be done so that the increase in bureaucracy did not change Sun as it had other high-tech startups. Employees at Sun overwhelmingly described Sun as a *fun* place to work. Despite his goal of reaching a billion dollars in sales, McNealy was intent on keeping Sun that way.

THE TECHNICAL WORKSTATION MARKET

In 1986, Sun's product line was primarily limited to workstations used by engineers, scientists, and other technical professionals. Sun's workstations were high-powered microcomputers that offered, on average, four times the processing speed and ten times the memory of a PC, as well as more sophisticated graphic capabilities. They were usually linked through a network that allowed, for instance, a team of engineers working on a new automobile to coordinate their designs. Because of the workstation's ability to increase productivity enormously, and a declining price, demand for Sun's systems was high.

The pioneer of the technical workstation market was not Sun but Apollo Computer, a company started in 1980 in Chelmsford, Massachusetts. By 1986, there were over two dozen producers, with Apollo and Sun controlling over 60% of the world market. According to Dataquest, a California market research firm, Apollo's market share fell from 50% to 39% in 1985. That same year, Sun's market share rose from 16% to 20%. Sun's installed base in June 1986 was approximately 17,000 machines, compared to Apollo's 20,000. The total number of systems in use was expected to increase from 40,000 in 1986 to nearly 2 million in 1990. Revenues over the same period were expected to grow from $1.1 billion to over $3 billion. A *Business Week* article of March 1986 described Sun's growth as "meteoric," listing Sun as one of the new "post-industrial" corporations because it relies on other companies for manufacturing and many crucial business functions. Considering that there are 5 million engineers in the world as well as other applications for the product, Sun and other producers of workstations had only reached a small portion of the potential market.

In May 1985, Digital Equipment Corporation entered the market with a stripped-down, low-cost machine that competed with Sun's low-end system. An even greater threat to Sun and Apollo was IBM, which introduced the RT PC in January 1986. The machine used a simplified design approach, known as Reduced Instruction Set Computer (RISC) architecture. Although the RT PC did not compete in performance with the Sun or Apollo products, IBM was expected to introduce a more sophisticated machine in late 1986 or early 1987. Because the typical workstation user was a knowledgeable scientist or engineer rather than an analyst or manager, several industry observers believed that IBM would not enjoy its traditional advantage of sales in the technical workstation market based primarily on the IBM name.

SUN'S PRODUCT STRATEGY: "OPEN SYSTEMS FOR OPEN MINDS"

Sun's product strategy was focused in two closely linked areas: industry standard technologies and open systems architecture. Under these conditions, Sun was an assembler of existing high performance systems rather than a manufacturer of components. Bechtolsheim's objective when designing the workstation was to combine low cost with high performance. To reduce production costs, he used standard components produced by other Silicon Valley manufacturers when possible. This strategy of purchasing "off-the-shelf" components from local suppliers differed greatly from that of Apollo and others that used components manufactured solely for their machines. This "art of making a Ferari out of spare parts," as

McNealy described it, enabled Sun to price its products approximately 20% to 40% lower than Apollo.

Tied to a strategy of low-cost production was Sun's commitment to an open systems architecture. Sun's founders agreed that because of the diversity in computing, no vender could supply equipment to serve every need of every user. As a result, Sun promoted standards that made it possible for the equipment of many vendors to work together. Because of Joy's and Bechtolsheim's involvement at Berkeley with the development of the Berkeley version of the UNIX operating system and early design of 32-bit microprocessor systems, Sun's initial product development team was able to achieve a high level of hardware and software integration. In addition to supporting the UNIX standard, Sun's systems were designed to support a number of other significant industry standards. In 1985, Sun began working with AT&T to develop jointly a next generation operating system that would combine Sun's version of UNIX with AT&T's latest operating system, System V.

Since its conception, Sun has introduced three generations of the Sun workstation—the Sun-1, the Sun-2, and the Sun-3 product families. Sun-2 was introduced in November 1983. Two years later, in November 1985, Sun began shipment of the Sun-3 product line. At this time, the Sun-1 product line was no longer available. Most Sun-1 systems were upgraded to Sun-2. According to a company executive: "Probably the most significant problem for us in product design is the speed at which we improve and replace our own technology. Since we plan to bring out a new product in approximately an 18-month time frame, it becomes crucial to meet that deadline so that the product doesn't become obsolete before it has a chance to go to the marketplace properly."

In 1986, approximately 40% of the systems were sold to OEMs (original equipment manufacturers); the rest were sold to end users. Sun's largest OEMs included Computervision and Eastman Kodak; a list of its large end-user customers included such companies as EDS, General Electric, Hughes Aircraft and AT&T Bell Labs. Although most of its systems were used by engineers, there was a growing market in the financial services industry for high-powered workstations that allowed simultaneous display of information on a single screen.

OWNERSHIP AND FINANCING THE GROWTH

Ownership of Sun changed as the company sought additional financing for expansion. When Sun was started, the four founders had similar levels of ownership. By June 1986, none of the founders owned more than 8% of the company. Explained McNealy: "Here I am, a founder, with less than 5% of the company after only four years in business." Shortly after it began, Sun raised $4.6 million in venture capital from four firms in return for almost half the company.

Each of the founders strongly believed in ownership by employees. As a result, when hired every employee was given stock options, regardless of his or her position. For employees hired before the public offering, the price of the stock option was the company's book value. In early 1985 the book value of Sun's stock was approximately $2 per share.

A second round of private financing took place in the summer of 1984. The largest investor was Eastman Kodak, a customer of Sun, which purchased 7% of Sun for $20 million.

Faced with increased competition, Sun management agreed that the company needed to go public to acquire the funds necessary to finance new product development. The board had originally planned the initial public offering (IPO) for the summer of 1985, but held off because of slumps in both the computer and stock markets. The IPO was finally announced in March 1986, when Sun offered 4 million shares of stock at $116 per share.

After the IPO, venture capital firms owned approximately 27% of the stock. Eastman Kodak owned 5.7% of Sun's stock. The four founders became multimillionaires, with holdings valued between $15 and $26 million each. Over 50 other employees also became millionaires after the public offering.

SALES AND PROFITABILITY

In the period of slow growth in high-tech that began in mid-1984, Sun remained one of the leaders in terms of sales growth and profitability. Sun turned its first profit just three months (August 1982) after it started shipping systems. In June 1983, the company ended its first full fiscal year of business with net income of $654,000 on revenues of $8.7 million. In 1984, revenues grew fourfold to $39 million and earnings climbed to $2.7 million. In 1985, revenues tripled to $115 million. They topped the $200 million mark in 1986, and the estimates for 1987 ranged from $350 to $450 million.

Several industry observers were wary of Sun's rapid growth. They were surprised that Sun's sales and profits continued to grow through 1984 and beyond as other high-tech companies faced difficult financial times. In Silicon Valley, the failure rate of startup companies in the first 12 to 15 months of operation was almost 80%. Bob Smith, chief financial officer at Sun, attributed the company's financial performance to the skill of the young management. According to Smith:

> Since joining Sun, I've been amazed at the perceptiveness of the management team in catching problems early on. The recession in the computer business is a perfect example. Instead of waiting until massive employee layoffs were necessary, we took smaller steps earlier. Hiring was done at a slower pace, production schedules were cut back, facility expansion was lessened, and fewer business trips were scheduled. Sun was one of a handful of computer companies that remained profitable throughout the computer slump. By eliminating perks like parties and picnics, which had gotten way out of hand in terms of cost in the Valley area, we were able to retain pay raises and other items with high value to the employee. We never had to lay off any employees.

DEVELOPMENT OF THE MANAGEMENT TEAM

Because of the company's continuous rapid growth, the organization at Sun was never the same for long. In the early days, the company was very informal: the founders were the only real managers within the company. For the first year, the majority of employees hired were engineers. During that time, the company's primary concern was getting the product out the door, so little time was spent worrying about adding layers of management. During the second and third years, when orders were coming in faster than the company could respond, concern about the organization of management in the company heightened. An early hire in operations commented:

> Things were happening so quickly around here that no one had time to devote to the kind of training we needed for middle management positions. As a result, a lot of young inexperienced people were promoted before they were ready to handle the additional responsibility. This also led to a weak middle management and heavy top management later on.

As Sun grew, top management underwent a number of changes. Initially, Vinod Khosla served as president and chief operating officer. McNealy was vice president of operations, Bechtolsheim headed up the hardware group, and Joy managed the software development. In 1983, Khosla became chairman and an outsider from Digital Equipment Corporation was brought in as president. He stayed only 10 months after facing difficulty blending in with the existing management team. McNealy then became president and chief operating officer. In McNealy's words:

> The decision that I would serve as president came almost by default. We decided on me because Joy and Bechtolsheim had no interest in running the show. They enjoy devoting their time to research—managing no one and being managed by no one. With Khosla leaving, I was given the job temporarily until we could find a "real" president. It never happened, and I was formally elected CEO six months later.

In 1984, McNealy realized that Sun needed not only the best engineers, but also the best management, and began to devote much more of his time to recruiting seasoned management from other high-tech companies. Bob Lux, recruited from Apollo in early 1986 as vice president of customer support, described McNealy's winning recruitment philosophy: "McNealy operates under the theory that if you always hire people better than yourself, you'll be successful."

McNealy spent a great deal of time pinpointing the one individual he wanted for each management position, and did not give up until he had recruited that person. Many of those eventually hired said that they hardly considered the opportunity at first. While they were impressed by Sun's rapid growth and quality products, they were wary of the young founders and the company's viability for the long term. Moreover, most of the high-level recruits were offered base salaries up to 50% lower than than what they were currently making. Bob Smith, former chief operating officer and vice president of finance at Xerox Office Products Division, described his decision to take the chief financial officer position at Sun:

> I was involved in the startup of the Xerox Office Products Division. I always knew that I'd someday be ready to join another startup, and had a friend who was a venture capitalist who told me that when I was ready, he'd find me the right place. I received a Christmas card from him in 1984 saying, "I think the time is right—I've got the company for you." He was talking about Sun, and at that point, I wasn't interested. It was such a small company, run by such young guys that I doubted it needed what I could bring to a company. This friend of mine convinced me to consider it more seriously, so I did. I was extremely impressed by the foresight of the founders, and very attracted to the fast-paced environment. After talking to the senior staff, learning the product strategy, and reviewing the numbers, I was convinced that Sun would be a major part of an important industry. I gave up half my salary and all of my retirement fund, and have never worked so hard in my life.

An even more unlikely recruit was Crawford Beveridge, vice president of human resources, who came to Sun from Analog Devices in early 1985. Beveridge had worked at Analog for three and a half years, (before Analog he had been with both Hewlett-Packard and DEC in Europe) and was very happy in his position when he received a phone call from McNealy in November 1984. Beveridge described his decision to go to Sun:

> I picked up the phone and heard, "Hello, this is Scott McNealy, president of Sun Microsystems. I hear you can walk on water." He then went on to tell me a little about Sun, and that he wanted me as the vice president of human resources. I was impressed with Sun's growth, and flattered by his interest, but I told him I wasn't ready to leave Analog. I did tell him that I could suggest some good candidates in the Valley. Since I was going out west for the Christmas holidays, I agreed to meet with him to discuss possible candidates. I met with him and some other members of the management team, and gave them some names to pursue. A month later, I got another call from McNealy. This time his words were, "Well, are you coming?" I was amused by his persistence, but thought I'd make it clear that I wasn't interested. Then he replied that Bernie LaCroute, executive vice president, was on his way to Boston to make me an offer, and it would be rude if I didn't at least meet him for breakfast. The offer was what I had expected—considerably less money than I was making, but a great deal of stock. Although I thought my position was still firm, I began to think about the opportunities at Sun. At Analog, the founder had done an excellent job of articulating the company's values, and it was my responsibility to translate the philosophy into behavioral changes. At Sun, I could take a step backward, and work on defining the company's culture. I was intrigued by this, but it was actually a television program that made my decision to work at Sun final. It was a PBS special on *In Search of Excellence*, which included a short segment on Apple Computer. I was enthralled by the

fast pace and excitement level at Apple. All of a sudden it occurred to me this was just what I had seen at Sun. Although I did underestimate the effort it takes to install sanity in a company growing so fast, I've never once regretted my decision.

Bob Lux, vice president of customer support and former vice president at Apollo, said that when he was first approached by Sun, he had three major concerns: McNealy's youth, the "instant millionaire syndrome," and Sun's ability to sustain its growth. While he admitted that he was attracted by the stock options, he emphasized the importance of McNealy's reputation within the company. According to Lux:

> Scott is by far the most influential person inside Sun. The employees love his personable nature—that he gives you the high five rather than shaking your hand. For me, it's actually refreshing working for someone so young. He doesn't bring any baggage along since he's not tied to another corporate philosophy. He's got a lot of good ideas, but most important, he knows his limitations. He's told us more than once that he'd move over in a minute if his staff thought he wasn't the right person for the job. It's that kind of attitude that drew me to Sun.

By February 1986, there were thirteen vice presidents on McNealy's staff, aside from Joy and Bechtolsheim. With what he described as a strong management team intact, McNealy was able to spend more time with long-range planning, something he felt he never had time for before. In McNealy's words:

> For the first couple of years, Sun was moving so quickly and was so short-staffed that no one had time to think about the future. It's actually quite amazing that we've gotten where we have today with so little planning. With the influx of some heavy new competitors, and technology changing so rapidly, sound strategic planning is critical. Although I rely on my staff to manage day-to-day activities, I also depend on them heavily for planning for the future. They're all experts in their fields, with a lot more experience than I have.

THE ENGINEERING DOMAIN

Despite the strong management team, it was widely reported that the engineers remained the dominant force within Sun. An administrative assistant who had been with Sun since the beginning stated, "The engineers run this place today, just as they did four years ago. It will always be that way. We're a technology-driven company and they're the ones who drive the technology."

The dominance of the engineers was reflected in the lifestyles they led at the company. While Fridays were designated as "jeans day" throughout the company, tee shirts, jeans and sneakers were the everyday garb for the engineers; a sport jacket might be worn when meeting with a client. Most of the engineers kept unusual hours, coming in at 10:00 a.m. and working well into the night. Many of the engineers had terminals at home to work from as well. Like people in other departments, most engineers worked at least part of the weekend, especially in the early years.

The engineering department had something of an "off-the-wall" reputation within the company. When asked to describe the department, one employee in the marketing department alluded to the engineers' enthusiasm on April 1:

> The engineering department is becoming notorious for its April Fools' Day stunts. It started last year when a bunch of them came in the night before and moved the entire office of Eric Schmidt, vice president and general manager of the Software Products Division, into the middle of the brook in the courtyard outside. They just didn't move the stuff out there, however. You have to remember we're talking about engineers. They wired the whole thing up so his phone and computer worked. He actually spent the day out there! This year, they put a real "software bug" in his office—a completely assembled Volkswagen Beetle.

SALES ORGANIZATION

Sun marketed and distributed its products to end users and OEMs through a direct sales force and independent distributors. At the end of 1985, Sun had 33 sales offices in the United States and nine abroad. The sales staff was composed of approximately 350 people. In addition to the direct sales organization, Sun used approximately 15 independent distributors to cover over 25 foreign countries. Sales to foreign customers accounted for about 18% of total sales in 1985.

Much of the attention of the sales organization was focused on Sun's 10 national accounts. Each of these accounts purchased at least $2.5 million, and combined made up 20–25% of Sun's revenue. A team of five senior sales people managed two national accounts each. Building a direct sales channel was difficult in this business, and required a very aggressive sales force. In June 1986, Sun's top salesperson, who had no previous sales experience, had brought in $6 million in sales, and the average sales per sales person was two and a half times the industry average. "We have an outstanding sales force," stated an officer of the company.

McNealy was strongly committed to the notion of "close to the customer." He and Joe Roebuck, the vice president for sales, were out in the field at least weekly to instill a reputation for service and support and determine the user's future needs. Although most employees welcomed the involvement of senior management in sales and customer support, some believed that there was a lack of effective middle management in the field.

MANUFACTURING

Because Sun bought all its parts from outside suppliers, the focus in manufacturing was on the assembly of parts. Five divisions reported into the vice president of operations. These included the operations group, new product growth, quality assurance, materials management, and production cost management. As Sun grew, management within the operations department found themselves extremely overworked. One manager commented: "The outlook in this department has to be very short term—like the next day. We don't have time for strategic planning. I know, for instance, that if I'm out sick some very important items won't get done. I guess that's what keeps us going over here. There's a great deal of personal pride and responsibility, knowing how important our work is to the success or failure of the business." Many of the complaints by the operations managers focused on the poor documentation and design from engineering. The operations department usually took the blame when a product was late in going out, even if the problem was traceable to engineering.

This frustration was also felt at the production level. In this group, there were three groups of workers: technicians, testers, and assemblers. In the summer of 1986, 30% of the production crew were temporary employees. Management had decided to increase the number of temporary hires to achieve greater flexibility in scheduling and reduced costs. The length of stay of a temporary employee averaged between three to six months. The public offering and subsequent rise in temporaries contributed to the decreasing morale of the department. One operations manager commented:

> Before the public offering, most of the production employees were permanent and received stock. Now with employees coming and going all the time, the morale seems to be a lot lower.

Compounding the morale problem was the overcrowding of facilities that resulted from growth in staff and materials. During the summer of 1986, half of the manufacturing department was moved to the East Bay, about 10 miles from the main location. Curt Wozniak, director of operations, explained the significance of the move:

> The planned expansion of facilities has had a major impact on the department. This place has been far too overcrowded, with no place for anyone to get their work done. In addition to alleviating this problem, the expansion is important because it gives the department its own place. Manufacturing has always taken a back seat to engineering; this investment is giving more credibility to our department.

EMPLOYEE RETENTION

The watershed for Sun came as the officers prepared for the company's first public sale of stock. McNealy and his team knew that once the company was public, recruitment of seasoned management and top engineers would be more difficult than before. In addition, Sun no longer had the same hold on some very valuable employees who would be millionaires after the IPO. McNealy and other officers were extremely concerned about the effect of the IPO on recruiting and maintaining valuable employees. In 1986, Sun's turnover rate averaged only 3 to 5%.

After the IPO, McNealy felt even stronger about retaining the spirit that made Sun a fun place to work. He believed the environment at Sun had played an important part in attracting some of the company's most valuable employees. A senior manager at Sun described the values of Sun's engineers:

> Engineers at Sun like the notion of a startup and the control they are given over their work. They like to see that their efforts have such a tremendous and immediate impact on the market. They don't like work environments such as IBM's where a new product idea takes months before a decision to go with it is made. Probably what really motivates many of them is the opportunity to work with some of the world's top engineers.

What, then, would keep these people from joining a new startup, or starting a company themselves? One member of the human resource staff commented:

> I think management is and should be concerned about losing some key software and hardware engineers. Those people are highly sought after, and once we're public, the risk of losing them is greater. I don't think this is the primary reason anyone would leave, however, I think the real threat is the growth of Sun. You don't find the same enthusiasm for reaching a billion in revenues with the engineers that you do with the officers. Obviously, the technical people want to see the company grow, since it means their efforts have been successful. On the other hand, they place a high value on autonomy and freedom in their work environment. The fact that Sun is growing at the rate of 150 employees per month is a real turnoff to some of the engineers, who came to Sun for the small-company, non-bureaucratic environment. Control has always been in the hands of the engineers here, and if that changes too much, I think we'll lose a lot of key people.

One attempt by McNealy to retain the "small company" atmosphere was the reorganization of Sun's operations into five divisions in early 1986. Another goal of the divisionalization was to create a wider career ladder for employees striving for management positions within the company.

The new divisions, each its own profit center, were Workstation, East Coast, Federal Systems, Customer Services, and Software Products. The company's sales, administrative, customer services, and European operations continued to report to McNealy. Sun brought in Barry Folsom from Digital Equipment Corporation and Bob Lux from Apollo Computer to run two of the divisions, bringing the number of vice presidents to 15.

THE HUMAN RESOURCE FUNCTION

The focus of the human resource (HR) function has changed continuously as Sun has grown. In the early days, the officers did the hiring. There was no time for training, benefits design, and many other traditional HR functions. Recognizing the importance of this function, however, McNealy brought in Beveridge to organize and manage the HR department. While much of Beveridge's early efforts also focused on hiring, the department expanded to develop such functions as compensation and benefits, communications, and training and development. As of June 1986, the department consisted of 40 members.

Compensation and Benefits

McNealy knew that by the time Sun went public, salaries and benefits would have to be competitive. In the early years, the company had been able to offset its low salaries with stock incentives, and frequently new hires would accept a 30 to 50% salary cut in exchange for stock. But as Sun made the transition to a public company, with enormous needs for new people, it became critical to implement a more attractive compensation package, since the company could no longer offer stock below the market price.

The terms of the option were as follows: Nonexempt employees and grade 4 (the lowest grade) exempt employees received options to purchase between 100 and 200 shares; the exact number was based on the importance of the hire at a certain point in time, rather than the position or individual alone. Above grade 4, the number of options offered corresponded to the grade level. In addition to this plan, employees with the company for two years could purchase half the amounts appropriate for their grade level based on their performance. Approximately 85% to 90% of the employees eligible for this plan were offered stock.

Both plans were to be in place until January 1, 1987. After the IPO, however, instead of receiving options to purchase stock for $2 to $3 per share, options would be granted at the market price of the stock, which opened at $16. In January 1987 Sun management planned to put a new stock plan into place. Only new hires and employees of grade 7 or higher were eligible to receive stock options. Management expected this plan to be further constricted later in the spring of 1987 as the amount of stock reserved for this plan was depleted. These changes would include a reduction in the number of shares offered at each grade level, and a higher grade cutoff point.

In 1985, Sun implemented a bonus plan for its high-level executives. The plan was based on the performance of the organization rather than on an individual or department, and was offered at the director level or higher.[13] Bonuses were determined annually as a percentage of salary, ranging from 15% to 40% based on the individual's position within the company. The percentage varied depending on the yearly corporate results and varied from 80% to 140%. For example, if the company received 100% of its target profit, the president of the company would receive 40% of his salary as a bonus, while a director would receive 15%.

In 1986, Sun also made significant improvements in its benefits plan. The most notable improvements were in the area of medical coverage. Before the changes, Sun had offered employees a choice of three Health Maintenance Organizations (HMOs) or a self-insured plan. Employees paid no premium for the self-insured plan, but from $4 to $50 per month for the HMOs depending on the plan and the number of family members. The deductible for the self-insured plan, was

$100, and employees paid 20% of all medical expenses. Under the redesigned plan, called the Sun Plan, the company paid 100% (instead of 80%) for many common services. These services generally included types of preventive care, or alternative methods of health care delivery that offered cost savings while retaining the level of quality. Examples of these included outpatient preadmission testing, outpatient surgery, and birthing centers.

Another significant improvement in the Sun Plan was a reduction in the yearly maximum cost after the deductible from $5,000 to $2,000. This resulted in a maximum out-of-pocket cost to the employee dropping from $1,100 [$100 deductible + (20% x $5,000)] to $500 [$100+ (20% x 2,000)].

Other changes to the benefits plan were implemented in the following areas: vision, dental, accidental death or dismemberment, business travel accident, employee disability, and stock purchase. As a result of the improvements in the Sun Valley Plan, the percentage of employees enrolled in the plan rose from 73% to 83%.

Communications

With the tremendous growth came the inevitable expansion of Sun's facilities and a growing communications problem. When the company was started, the founders wondered if the building they had leased (45,000 square feet) was too large for them. In four years (1982-1986), Sun expanded into eight buildings at the Mountain View facility (each within walking distance of the others), and moved part of the manufacturing to a larger building about 10 miles from the main location. Many of the old timers attributed the changes in the environment at Sun to the physical separation of employees. According to one engineer:

> Things have really changed a lot around here with all this moving. I've moved three times, and this probably isn't even permanent. When there were just a hundred or so employees under one roof, everyone knew each other and there was a real sense of camaraderie. You realize how few people you know now when we have social gatherings like the Friday beer busts. We used to all hang out together no matter what department we worked for. Now there are a bunch of small cliques that only mix with each other.

Sun's primary tool in keeping the lines of communication open was the electronic mail system (known as e-mail), used daily by virtually every Sun employee: 85% of the employees had electronic mail terminals at their desks, and the remainder had access to one. The system enabled employees to send messages electronically to other employees, whether they were at the next desk or in a foreign office:

> The e-mail system is a tremendous time saver. I used to spend hours playing telephone tag, or tracking people down around the office. With e-mail, I can send one message to the whole company in seconds if I want. It's also a great replacement for memos and letters, since you don't have to be as formal. It's amazing how much time can be saved when you're not concerned with how something is worded.

Although the e-mail system was a great productivity booster, its easy accessibility also created some problems. Because there were no controls on the messages sent, any employee could send an "all-home" message (a message to all other terminals in the network), at a cost of between $500 and $600. Reflecting on the use and misuse of e-mail, one senior manager said:

> E-mail is convenient. It saves time, phone calls and meetings. But e-mail is not a perfect vehicle. It sacrifices a whole realm of communication devices that assist in the transition of ideas. Facial expressions, body language, and intonation are lost when e-mail is used. If the message is very important, controversial, confidential, or one that can easily be misunderstood, I think we should think twice about sending it via e-mail. I have come to the view that e-mail is a good way to communicate but that it is not necessarily the best way to communicate every message.

The detachment and semi-anonymity of e-mail occasionally created an environment where bad manners seemed acceptable. Privacy, for instance, might be violated because it was so easy to access someone's mail or mail record. "Carbon copying" of messages too might be overdone or done for the wrong reasons. Finally, there had been occasional "flaming" messages from angry employees.

HIRING A COMMUNICATIONS EXPERT

Senior management at Sun was convinced that to avoid becoming "just another large company," communications within Sun, including e-mail, should be given considerably more attention. From his experience at Analog, Beveridge was convinced that at this stage of growth, a communications person was most effective within the human resources department, rather than the traditional marketing communications or public relations department. Beveridge recruited Jan Fry from Analog to develop a communications area within the human resources department.

Fry's mission upon joining Sun was twofold: to ensure that company information was readily available to employees and that the proper channels were in place so that employees could give feedback to the company. Fry's first priority was to develop a process to communicate to employees the details and implications of the new benefit package that was to be be introduced in August 1986. In doing this, Fry organized focus groups to test the effectiveness of the communication process. She developed brochures, videotapes, and employee meetings to provide information on the new benefits package. The groups were asked to comment on the clarity of the brochures and other mediums of communication. In addition to improving the communication process, Fry was sure that the focus groups improved employee relations:

> The focus groups turned out to be a real success and will undoubtedly be used for communications more in the future. Employees really enjoyed being a part of the decision-making process and were impressed that management had taken the time to organize a program that invited so much feedback from employees.

A second priority for Fry was developing guidelines for use of the e-mail system. In their effort to limit bureaucratization, many of the senior managers wanted to avoid placing physical constraints on the system. However, because of the high cost of sending messages to all desks and the potential misuse of this capacity, guidelines on e-mail etiquette were needed. An e-mail protocol was distributed to employees in the spring of 1986.

Soon after Sun went public, management discovered another communications problem that became one of Fry's priorities. After the company went public, SEC rules restricted Sun from releasing any financial data to employees before the information was made available to the investment community. Before the public offering, financial information had been readily available to all employees. Beginning in August 1986, Sun decided to hold quarterly meetings for the purpose of sharing financial information, future plans, and company goals with employees. Each VP was responsible for running his or her own meeting, but Fry would be involved in preparing the leaders for these meetings.

Another of Fry's responsibilities was to improve communications with potential Sun employees. As it became increasingly difficult to attract outstanding candidates, this role was given even greater attention. Specifically, Fry made sure that each piece of Sun literature and correspondence sent to a potential employee reflected Sun in a positive and accurate manner.

Fry was also heavily involved in the culture project that Beveridge designed to articulate the company's goals and values.

HIRING

In Sun's infancy, the investment in the human resources function was not significant. Human resources was far below the level of growth of the corporation as a whole, especially in terms of its personnel needs. The HR function had also remained centralized when the company changed to a divisionalized structure. With an overwhelming number of open job requisitions (a fairly constant 200 openings for approximately four recruiters), it was natural that the ability of the HR organization to meet these needs or to be available to its clients was very low.

As a result of the shortage of recruiters, human resources was not involved in most hiring decisions. Overwhelmed managers often could not find enough time to conduct interviews and screen carefully, especially for "cultural fit." In many cases, managers turned to outside employment agencies, which had driven hiring costs up to $2 million a year.

In order to bring the hiring problem under control, several programs were instituted. The HR organization was decentralized and HR resources were dedicated to specific functional or divisional groups. Some of the money formerly spent on outside recruiters was used to hire in-house contracting employment people. These were individuals brought in to Sun from hiring agencies on a contract basis to offer full-time assistance in the hiring of new personnel. More rigid policies were introduced requiring higher levels of authority to use external agencies and limiting the fees the company was prepared to pay when agencies were used. An applicant tracking system was introduced to make managers better aware of the status of candidates in the hiring process. Over a twelve-month period, these changes resulted in Sun's ability to handle a constant backlog of nearly 400 requisitions. It also gave the company more control over the hiring process, slashing costs by two-thirds.

TRAINING AND DEVELOPMENT

A natural outcome of the company's growth was that many people were brought into supervisory and management positions above others who had been with the company for a longer period of time. Beveridge described the implications of this:

> Because individuals frequently associate their own growth with the growth of the company, they tend to believe that their careers are not being appropriately managed if they are not rapidly promoted at a place like Sun. In addition, growth means bringing in many experienced people from a variety of cultures. Without understanding "how things get done around here," they tend to bring their prior ideas with them, thus causing much confusion for employees who see vastly different approaches to the same issues by different managers. Finally, our rate of growth means that the time people need to spend on their own jobs leaves very little time for them to think about the development for their next jobs.

When the company reached about 1,000 people, a dedicated training and development organization was instituted. The basic charter was to understand the critical transitions that people need to go through when changing from individual contributor to supervisor, from supervisor to manager and so on. The purpose was to ensure that employees were equipped with appropriate skills and the appropriate cultural understanding to be able to function effectively within the company. In addition, a series of peripheral programs dealt with such things as career management, negotiating skills, and effective presentations. According to Jan Becker, training and development manager:

> Due to rapid growth of the company, the initial focus of training and development was the orientation program—a program dedicated to helping the large number of new employees quickly adjust and become effective in the Sun environment. This was particularly important as an opportunity to help operationalize the values articulated in the value study.

THE VALUE STUDY

In light of all the changes—the IPO, reorganization, building expansion, new competition—the culture at Sun had become much more difficult to define. Crawford Beveridge believed that in order to maintain the spirit that drove Sun in the early days, a formal assessment of the company's present culture was needed. In early 1986, using a model developed by Professor Stanley Davis of Boston University, Beveridge organized what came to be known as The Value Study. According to Beveridge, the purpose of the project was to define whether it was in line with the company's long-term goals.

Beveridge believed that much of Sun's success had resulted from the culture that had emerged in its early years. He had been told that the mood at Sun in its first year in business was one of high energy, free spirit, and risk taking. There had been a tremendous feeling of worth throughout the company, since even the smallest task completed increased the chances of survival. An administrative assistant described the environment at Sun during its first year:

> We were all pretty big fish in quite a small pond back then. I can't say that there weren't some murky spots, but for the most part, the high-flying atmosphere really permeated the place. I don't think any of us have ever worked so hard, so many long hours, but no one cared. The "I really do make a difference" feeling was a thrill that kept us all going. I don't know if I could be involved in another startup, but I wouldn't give up those early days at Sun for the world.

A technical support person had a similar view of Sun in the early days:

> Things around here are quite different from the early days. Back then there was no time for bureaucracy, no time for planning, not even time for lunch! We were overworked and underpaid, but there were few complaints. We had a common goal—survival—and that's what really kept us all moving so quickly. It's sort of ironic that once survival was no longer an issue, the problems began to develop.

When asked to describe the culture at Sun, many employees focused on the approachability of senior management. A customer service representative compared the management at Sun with former employers:

> The senior management here is very visible and approachable. I've worked for other high-tech companies where you rarely saw the top officers, let alone the president. Scott makes a real effort to get around and keep in touch with all departments here. When Sun had just a couple of hundred employees, he knew almost everyone's name. Now that we've expanded into so many different buildings, it's more segregated, since most of the officers are in the same building. Scott and some others are always at the Friday beer busts, so the effort is still there.

One of the company's telephone operators recalled an effort by the president to stay close to the employees. "On Halloween last year a bunch of employees came to work in costume. The word got around that I had a pretty good costume, and Scott came over, dressed up himself, to check my costume out. It's little things like that that keep me here when I could be making more money somewhere else."

At an offsite meeting in May 1986, the executive staff (e-staff) came up with a group of general ideas that described the culture at Sun. With these ideas, Beveridge designed a questionnaire that included a number of statements about Sun's culture. The e-staff was asked to rate the importance of each statement to the business strategy of Sun and put in order of importance those statements that they believed to be important to the strategy. They were also asked to consider how compatible each statement was with Sun's present culture.

In addition to distributing the questionnaire to the e-staff, the human resources department organized representative groups of employees (Fry's focus groups) who were also asked to complete the questionnaire. According to Beveridge: "The results from the focus groups were remarkably similar to those from the offsite meeting."

At a second offsite meeting, the culture statement was again discussed, using an outside consultant as a facilitator for the meeting. Few problems were encountered as the group integrated the different responses and designed a third version of the value statement. Managers at Sun decided that the term value was more appropriate than "culture" since the statement described goals that the company strived for rather than what it was like to work at Sun. The new statement was sent out by electronic mail to all employees with an invitation for comments. A large number of employees responded, and a final value statement was produced. Commenting on this development, one officer said: "Considering that it took companies such as HP and DEC many years to put their values in writing, our development of the value statement was very rapid. Some here, in fact, think it was too quick."

Conclusion

As McNealy headed home, he gave some more thought to Bartlett's questions. He felt that the value statement did a good job of describing Sun's objectives, but wondered if and how much the company's values would change as it continued to grow. In the area of compensation and benefits, Sun was certainly competitive and perhaps even above par for the market. But McNealy was concerned that even the most attractive salary and benefits package would not lure the same type of employee the company had drawn in its early days. McNealy wondered what other action might be taken to ensure that the company continued to hire the "entrepreneurial type" that had been so important to Sun's initial success.

SUN MICROSYSTEMS, INC., STUDY QUESTIONS

1. Identify and evaluate Sun's business strategy.
2. Identify and evaluate Sun's human resources strategy.
3. What future human resources issues would you suggest Crawford Beveridge should be discussing with Scott McNealy? Why?

Endnotes

[1] This case appeared as an article in the *Wall Street Journal*: William Power and George Anders, "Shearson to Reorganize, Splitting Banking, Brokerage Operations," *Wall Street Journal*, Friday, May 18, 1990, pp C1, C5. Reprinted by permission of *The Wall Street Journal*, © 1990, Dow Jones and Company, Inc. All Rights Reserved Worldwide.

[2] This case is an adaptation of a case published in William H. Newman, Charles E. Summer, and E. Kirby Warren, *The Process of Management: Concepts, Behavior, and Practice* (Englewood Cliffs, NJ: Prentice Hall, 1972), pp. 345–353. Reprinted and adapted by permission.

[3] This case was written by William F. Glueck. It has been adapted and reprinted by permission of the publisher from William F. Glueck, *Business Policy: Strategy Formation and Management Action*, 2nd ed. (New York: McGraw-Hill Book Co. 1976), pp. 602–609. The case is based on a real company situation, but the identity of the company has been disguised.

[4] Doug Bartholomew, "Bob Beck: An Interview with the New Head of Corporate Personnel," *BankAmerican*, November 1982. Reprinted with permission.

[5] This case was written by Donald W. Jarrell for class use in 1991. It is based on an actual company situation, but the identity of the company has been disguised.

[6] This case was written by Neal M. Nadler, George Washington University, and was published in Randall S. Schuler and Stuart A. Youngblood, *Case Problems in Personnel and Human Resource Management* (St. Paul, MN: West Publishing Co., 1986), pp. 179–183, under the title "Case Study in Human Resource Development." Reprinted by permission of the author.

[7] This case was written by D. Jeffrey Lenn, School of Government and Business Administration, George Washington University, and was published in Randall S. Schuler and Stuart A. Youngblood, *Case Problems in Personnel and Human Resource Management* (St. Paul, MN: West Publishing Co., 1986), pp. 3–10. The case is not meant to be an example of effective or ineffective personnel and human resource management but an example for teaching and discussion purposes. Reprinted by permission of the author.

[8] This case is a human resource management teaching case prepared by Charles Fombrun, Noel Tichy, and Mary Anne Devanna for use in class discussion rather than to illustrate either effective or ineffective handling of a particular situation. Names were changed to protect confidentiality. The case was published in Randall S. Schuler and Stuart A. Youngblood, *Case Problems in Personnel and Human Resource Management* (St. Paul, MN: West Publishing Co., 1986), pp. 10–19. Reprinted by permission of the publisher.

[9] Human Resource Management Audit. See M. A. Devanna, C. Fombrun, N. Tichy, "Human Resource Management: A Strategic Approach," *Organizational Dynamics*, vol. 9, no. 1. (1981).

[10] Chester C. Borucki, "The Importance of Strategic Staffing as a Component of Human Resource Management: Conversation with Alan F. Lafley," *Human Resource Management*, vol 22, no. 3, Fall 1983, 298-312. Reprinted by permission of John Wiley and Sons, Inc.

[11] This case was prepared by Ellen M. Cain, under the direction of Professor Fred K. Foulkes, as the basis for class discussion rather than to illustrate either an effective or ineffective handling of an administrative situation. © Human Resource Policy Institute, School of Management, Boston University, 1988.

[12]The project, first dubbed the "culture project," was later transformed into the "value study," discussed in detail in a later section.

[13]Positions that were eligible for bonuses included directors, vice presidents, vice president/officers, executive vice presidents, and president. In June 1986, this group totaled approximately 100 individuals.

Index

Activity areas (*see also* Tactical
  human resource activity
  areas)
  defined, 174
  list of, 175
Activity-specific approach to evaluation, 225-26, 245
Activity stance, 30
  proactive/reactive, defined, 30
Allopoietic systems, 15
American Express, 52
American Management Association
  survey, 122
Analysis of filed data, 237-38
  methods of analysis, 238
  value of data, 237
Anthropomorphous, organizations
  seen as, 32
Artificial intelligence, defined, 192
ASA cycle (*see* Attraction-selection-
  attrition cycle)
Assessment center, 232-34
  defined, 232
  learning effect, 233
  on assessed employees, 233
  on manager assessors, 233
  modified for planning, 233-34
  and operational planning, 232-33
AT&T, 114
Attitude and opinion surveys, 238-39
  modified for planning, 238
  to promote learning, 238-39
  whom to survey, 238
Attraction-selection-attrition (ASA)
  cycle, 83-84
Attributes (*see* Employee attributes)
Audit (*see* Human resource audit)
Autopoiesis:
  example of, 14-15
  in self-producing systems theory,
    14
  Autopoietic systems, 15

Bank of America, 223-24

Barry (R. G.) Corporation, 197
Behavioral change:
  kinds of change (*Exhibits*), 56, 57
  participants affected, 54-56
  in strategic planning, 54-58
  techniques, 56-58
  glossary (*Appendix*), 63-65
Behaviorally anchored rating scales
    (BARS), 144, 230-31
  illustrated (*Exhibit*), 231
  process for developing, 230
Benchmark:
  defined, 81, 229
  for evaluation of structure, 81
  for human resource evaluation,
    229
  procedure, 81
Boston Consulting Group, 27
Boundary agent:
  defined, 210
  managing surprises, 210
Brooks, Linda, 263
Brown, Duane, 263
Budgets (*see* Financial budgets)
Buffering, 210-11
  defined, 210
  examples, 210-11
Business planning:
  defined, 3
  in free-enterprise economies, 3
  functions involved, 4
  levels of, 8-10
    and complexity of organization
      structure, 9
    described, 8
    illustrated (*Exhibit*), 9
    and the managerial hierarchy,
      8-10
  by organization units, 10
  stages, 5-7
    compared to military (*Exhibit*),
      12
    described, 5-6
    and the managerial hierarchy, 6

    and time periods, 6-7
      illustrated (*Exhibit*), 7
    terms, defined, 11-12
    theoretical foundations, 15
  in the United States, 4-5
    development of, 4
    functional areas involved, 4
    in well-managed firms, 4-5
    universality, 16
Business planning concepts, 10-15
  evolution of, 10
  terms, 11-12
  theories, 12-15
    compared, 15
    open systems, 12-14
    self-producing systems, 14-15
Business planning practice, 3-10

Career, defined, 140, 262
Career cohort:
  as agent of strategic effects, 287
  defined, 287
Career decision theory, 262-64
  and the Miller-Tiedeman model,
    262-64
  illustrated (*Exhibit*), 263
Career employees:
  as agents of strategic effects, 288-
    89
  defined, 140, 262
Career management, defined, 140
Career path, 264-66
  and career plateaus, 145
  defined, 141
  design of, 141-45
  illustrated (*Exhibit*), 265
  and job duties, 142-43
  learning principles, 141-45
  organization support, 145-46
  ownership, 142
Career success:
  dynamics of, 264
  process, 264
    illustrated (*Exhibit*), 264

Causal analysis, 225, 238
Chandler, Alfred, 75-76
Change:
    management of, 60-61
    in operations, 96
    and organization identity, 44
Change agent, 60-61
Chemical Bank, 123
Chief executive officer:
    role in strategic human resource
        planning, 111, 148
    role in strategic planning, 54-56
Chief human resource officer:
    role in strategic human resource
        planning, 111-13, 148
    role in strategic planning, 52-53
Chrysler Corporation, 114
Classical approach to evaluation, 226
Commitment (see Organization com-
    mitment)
Complement ratio, 271, 272
    illustration of use (Exhibits), 271,
        272
    table, 270-72
    and vacancy chains, 270
Computer:
    for human resource management,
        187, 190, 192-94
    role in human resource planning,
        190, 192-94
Computer-aided management, kinds,
    192
"Conscripted clerk" behavior, 125,
    126
Continuing development, 123
Continuous model, for study of envi-
    ronment, 33
Control of variables, 208-9
Cost-benefit analysis, 239, 240
    competencies of evaluators, 245
    defined, 239
    extended by utility analysis, 239
    use to planners, 239, 240
Cotton, John L.., 134
Crescive approach, 45-47
Culture (see Organization culture)
Customer service, role of employee,
    124-27

Dachler, Peter, 134
Dahl, Henry L., Jr., 198
Davis, Stanley, 83
Dead-end positions:
    classification, 120-21
    defined, 120
Decision support systems (DSS), 192-
    94
    components, 193
    defined, 192
Defining the future:
    control of variables, 208-9
    forecasting, 211-16
    futures analysis, 204-8
    neutralization of variables, 209-11
Delta Air Lines, 114, 131
Departmentation, bases of, 78
Development (see Employee develop-
    ment)
Distinctive competence, 23-25

and customer service, 124-25
    defined, 23-24
    respecting human resources, 150
    and strategic orientation, 24-25
    use in strategic planning, 22, 24-
        25
Distributive structure (see also Tacti-
    cal structures)
    defined, 74
    as a tactical planning concept, 74
Duty:
    basis for job description, 142-43
    as basis for performance
        appraisal, 230-31
    and career appraisal, 143-44, 146
    and career planning, 142-43
    and information about work, 196-
        97

E. C. Corporation:
    career employees, 288-89
    description of, 206
    empowerment of moving employ-
        ees, 282-83
    environmental study report
        (Exhibit), 37
    futures analysis, 206-8
    managing an ILM, 286-87
    mentoring, 284-85
    planning variables (Exhibit), 205
    role of supervisors, 286-87
Empirical selection:
    of activity areas, 177-79
    examples of measures used, 177-
        79
    and policy development, 180
    process, 177-79
Employee attributes:
    glossary (Appendix), 249-50
    group, 227, 250
    individual, 227, 249-50
    use in evaluation, 227-28
Employee development (see also
    Training)
    assessment center experience,
        233
    continuing, 123, 124
    defined, 122, 300
    effect of work experience, 141
    over life span, 260
    remedial, 123-24
Employee mobility, factors affecting,
    271-72
Employee movement:
    reasons for, 289
    support for, 290-91
Employee participation, 132-37, (see
    also Participatory deci-
    sion making)
    forms of, 134-36
        combinations (Exhibit), 134
    and the manager, 137
Employee productivity:
    defined, 127
    and employee participation, 135
    improvement of, 127-30
        examples, 128-30
        successful program focus, 128
Employee satisfaction, 137-40

benefits for organization, 140
    and candidate selection of organi-
        zation, 139
    career employees, 140
    defined, 137
    and employee participation, 135-
        36
    and employee selection, 138
    and employee treatment, 139-40
Employee selection (see also Selec-
    tion)
    and desired culture, 85
    to promote service to customers,
        125-27
    promoting employees' satisfac-
        tion, 138
Employee service orientation (see
    Service orientation)
Employees:
    as agents of strategic effects, 282-
        83
    as information repositories, 188,
        189, 194-95
Empowerment, 282-83, 286, 293, 296
Entry positions:
    classification, 120-21
    defined, 120
Environment:
    defined, 11
    as a "mirror," 14, 38-39
Environmental analysis (see also
    Environmental study)
    defined, 13
Environmental study, 32-36
    conducting, 32-36
    interpretation of results, 35-36, 37
    objectives of study, 33
    of relationships, 34
    scope, 33
    of sectors, 34-35
    study models, 33
    summarizing results, 36
        example (Exhibit), 37
Evaluation (see also Evaluation of
    human resources)
    of an HRIS, 195-96
    of human resource function, 222-
        23
    in operational planning, 95-96
    and stages of planning, 221
    of strategic human resource plan-
        ning, 152, 153
        direct outcome, 152
        indirect outcome, 152
    of strategic planning, 47-49
        evaluation forms (Exhibits),
            48, 49
        of planning outcomes, 47
        of planning process, 47
Evaluation of human resources:
    activities to evaluate, 222
    approaches, 225-27
        combinations of (Exhibit), 227
    and employee attributes, 227-28
    evaluators, 244-45
        choice of, 244-45
        desirable characteristics, 245
        and learning, 244
        third party, 244

Evaluation of human resources (con't.):
  guidelines for forecast method,
    215-16
  measures used, 227-28
    final, 228
    intermediate, 228
  methods (see Evaluation methods
    for human resources)
  need for, 221
  nonroutine, 245
  philosophy, 224-25
  points to consider, 221
  role in planning, 221-23
  routine, 245
  standards for, 228-29 (see Stan-
    dard)
  supportive setting for, 223-24
  in support of planning, 222
  use of, 245-46
  what to measure, 227-28
Evaluation methods for human
    resources, 229-43
  formal, 230-43
    analysis of file data, 237-38
    assessment centers, 232-34
    attitude and opinion surveys,
      238-39
    cost-benefit analysis, 237-40
    experiment, 240-43
    external peer review, 236, 237
    human resource audit, 234-36
    performance appraisal, 230-32
    reputation assessment, 236-37
    utility analysis, 237-40
  informal, 229
Evaluator (see Evaluation of human
    resources, evaluators)
Experience curve, 25, 27
  defined, 27
  use in strategic planning, 22, 27
Experiment, 240-43
  competencies required, 245
  control of unintended influences,
    241-43
    control groups, 242
    repeated measurements, 242
    standardized activities, 242-43
    statistical/judgmental tech-
      niques, 243
  defined, 240-41
  example of, 241-42
    illustrated (Exhibit), 241
  interpretable/generalizable results,
    241-42
  role of experimenter, 241
Expert systems, defined, 192
External labor markets:
  comparison with internal, 257-58
  defined, 257
External peer review, 236, 237
  areas involved, 237
  defined, 237
Extrapolation:
  defined, 213
  methods, 213-14
  use in forecasting, 213-14

Fahey, Liam, 33
Falsey, Thomas A., 187

"Feeling rules:"
  and customer service, 125
  defined, 125
Ferry, Diane L., 80, 81
Field experiment (see also Experi-
    ment)
  defined, 240-41
Financial budget, 86-89
  defined, 86
  kinds:
    appropriation, 86
    capital, 86
  as a tactical process, 86-87
    employee participation in, 87-
      89
  as a tactical structure, 74, 86-89
First National Bank of Chicago, 83,
  92
Five-year-average hiring, 210-11
Flows of human resources (see
    Human resource flows)
Flow table, 268-70
  defined, 268
  illustrated (Exhibits), 269, 270
  and quality indexes, 268-70
Forecasting, 211-16
  defined, 211
  methods, 212-16
    extrapolation, 213-14
    forecast models, 214-15
    guidelines for use, 215-16
    how determined, 212
    measuring intentions and opin-
      ions, 212-13
  when needed, 211-12
Forecast models, 214-15
  defined, 214
  qualitative, 214, 215
    example (Exhibit), 215
  quantitative, 214-15
Further definition of variables, 208-16
  control, 208-9
  forecasting, 211-16
  neutralizing, 209-11
Futures analysis, 204-8
  nominal group meeting, 205-8
  scenario analysis, 207-8
Futures committee, 204-5

General Motors Corporation, xi, 128-
  30
Giant Food, 125
Goal-constrained approach to evalua-
    tion, 226
Goal-free approach to evaluation, 226
Goals:
  and career path learning, 141
  and career success process, 264
  distinguished from objectives, 11-
    12
  and time-period planning, 7
Godet, Michael, 218
Gomez-Mejia, Louis, 235
Good citizen characteristics, 126
Gordon, George, 53

Hain, Tony, 151
Hall, Douglas T., 264
Hawthorne effect, 242

Hax, Arnoldo, 152
Henderson, Bruce D., 27
Hiring, defined, 299
Holland, John, 126
Hrebiniak, Lawrence, 24
HRIS (see Human resource informa-
    tion system)
Human capital:
  and internal labor markets, 258-59
  investments in, 258-59
  theory, 258
  in U. S. economy, 122
Human factors engineering, 118
Human resource accounting, 197
Human resource audit, 234-36
  described, 234
  extended analysis, 235
    Gomez-Mejia method, 235
  selection of measures, 234
  sources of data, 234
  traditional use, 234-35
Human resource department:
  role in operational planning, 97
  role in strategic human resource
    planning, 111-13, 150
  role in strategic planning, 51-61
  role in tactical planning, 91-93
Human resource domain:
  defined, 148
  sector variables, 149-50
Human resource executive (see Chief
    human resource officer)
Human resource flows:
  analysis, 272-74
    guide for, (Appendix), 298
  along career paths, 262-66
  description of, 256
  through economic systems, 257-59
  effects of, 273-74
    kinds, 273
    time of occurrence, 274
    on whom, 273
  extent, 274
  identification of, 266-72
    data assembly/presentation,
      267-72
    data collection, 267
    key individuals and groups, 282-
      89
      mentors, 283-85
      others, 287
      persons moving, 282-83
      supervisors, 285-87
    kinds, 272-73
  organization need for, 289
  planning for:
    career employees, 288-89
    examples, 292-95
    maintenance considerations,
      281
    policies, 290, 294 (see also
      Tactical policy set)
    procedures and programs, 290,
      294
      glossary, (Appendix), 299-
        301
  selection of key individuals and
    groups, 282-89
  strategic considerations, 281

support structure (*see* Support structure for human resource flows)
through social systems, 259-62
strategically-driven, 281
    intervention points, 281
    steps to achieve, 292
    views of, 257-66
        compared, 266
Human resource function:
    objectives of, 116
    strategies of, 116-46
Human resource information system (HRIS), 187-89
    defined, 187
    management, 194-96
        choice of repositories, 194-95
        information needed, 194
        promoting effectiveness, 195-96
    for planning, 190, 192-94
    role of computer, 190, 192-94
    in selection of tactical planners, 93
    suggested improvements, 196-99
        human resource valuation, 197-99
        work analysis, 196-97
Human resource objectives (*see* Strategic objectives, human resource)
Human resource professionals:
    relationships with line managers, 113, 151
    specialist support:
        for operational planning, 97
        for strategic planning, 53-61
        for tactical planning, 92-93
    and technological change, 293-94
Human resource specialists (*see* Human resource professionals)
Human resource stocks:
    and buffering, 210-11
    defined, 256
    and human resource flows, 256, 289
Human resource strategic objectives:
    examples, 116
    purpose of, 116
    selection, 150
Human resource strategies:
    examples of, 117-46
        employee commitment, 130-32
        employee development, 122-24
        employee participation, 132-37
        employee productivity, 127-30
        employee satisfaction, 137-40
        focus on career employees, 140-46
        service to customers, 124-27
        supply of human resources, 120-22
        technological change, 117-20
    formulation, 116, 150-51
    implementation, 151

Human resource valuation, 197-98
    investments, 198-99
    measures (*Exhibit*), 198

IBM Corporation, 32, 52, 114, 131
Identification learning, 261-62
Imitation learning, defined, 261
Incremental learning, 95
Information:
    for human resource planning, 190, 194
        kinds (*Exhibit*), 191
    importance for planning, 187
    official/unofficial, 189
        examples (*Exhibit*), 189
    public/private, 189
    repositories, 188-89
        kinds, 188-89
        linkages, 190, 192
        for human resource planning, 194-95
Information system (*see also* Human resource information system (HRIS); Information)
    defined, 187
    functions, 188
    role of computer, 187, 190, 192-94
Instrumental training, 261
    defined, 261
Insulating the organization, 210-11
    defined, 210
    example, 211
Insuring against risk, 211
Intention:
    accuracy of measure, 213
    defined, 212
    how gathered, 212
    use in forecasting, 212-13
Internal labor market (ILM):
    as buffer and insulator, 211
    comparison with external, 257-58
    defined, 257
    and E. C. Corporation, 286-87
    and human capital, 258-59
    and turnover, 259
Irregular model, for study of environment, 33
Issues:
    causes of, 50
    defined, 50
    for evaluation of planning, 50, 153
    indicating need for forecast, 211
Issues management, 50-51
    defined, 50
    purposes, 50
    steps, 50
    in strategic human resource planning, 147, 153
Issues management team:
    role in accommodation, 51
    role in managing surprises, 210
    submission of budget proposals, 86

Job analysis, 230 (*see also* Work analysis)

Job duty (*see* Duty)
Job positions (*see* Positions)
"Joe," as self-producing system, 14-15
Judgmental selection:
    of activity areas, 175-77
    and policy development, 179-80
    process, 176
    role of outside facilitator, 176

Kast, Fremont E., 13
King, William, 33

Labor markets (*see* External labor markets; Internal labor markets)
Levels of planning (*see* Business planning, levels)
Lewin, Kurt, 44
Likert, Rensis, 197
Line managers, role in strategic human resource planning, 11, 113, 148
Locke, Edwin, 134
Long-term employment policy, and employee development, 123

Maintenance considerations, in human resource operations, 281
"Make-or-buy" decisions, 123-24
Management by objectives (MBO), 144, 230
Management information systems, 192
Managing surprises, 210
McKinsey and Company, 58
Mentors, 283-85, 292, 293
    as agents of strategic effects, 283-85
    for career employees, 145, 288-89
    formal, 283, 284, 285
        criteria for, 284
        functions, 284
    informal, 283-84, 285
    and the supervisor, 285-86
    training of, 284
Meyer, Marshall W., 62
Miles, Raymond, 24
Military planning stages, compared to business (*Exhibit*), 12
Miller-Tiedeman, Anna L., 263
Miller-Tiedeman model, 262-64
Mobility (*see* Employee mobility)
Model, defined, 214
Modeling, a forecast method, 314-16

Neutralizing variables, 209-11
    buffering and insulating, 210-11
    insurance against risk, 211
    managing surprises, 210
    promoting organization agility, 209-10
New York Telephone Company, 124
Nicholson, Nigel, 260
Nominal group meeting:
    defined, 205
    example, 206-8

Nominal group meeting (con't.):
  and futures analysis, 205-8
  steps, 206-8
Nonentry positions:
  classification of positions as, 120-21
  defined, 120
Nonroutine evaluations, 245-46

Objectives (see also Planning objectives; Strategic objectives)
  defined, 11
  distinguished from goals, 11-12
  for environmental study, 33
Observational learning, 261-62
  defined, 261
  identification, 261-62
  imitation, 261
  and simple observation, 262
Ohmae, Kenichi, 58, 59, 60
On-the-job training, as an investment, 258-59
Open systems theory, 12-14, 38
  compared to self-producing systems theory, 15
  as guide to organization identity, 38-39
Operational planning, 93-97
  concepts, 94-96
  described, 5, 93-94
  for different operations, 96
  distinctive features, 95
  and evolutionary/revolutionary change, 96
  guidelines for, 97
  human resource department role, 97
  illustrated (Exhibit), 95
  process, 96-97
  and repetitive cycles, 94, 95, 185, 221
Operational planning committee, 96
  function, 97
  skills needed, 96
Operations:
  defined, 11
  illustrated (Exhibit), 94
Opinion (see also Attitude and opinion surveys)
  accuracy of measure, 213
  defined, 212
  how gathered, 212
  use in forecasting, 212-13
Organ, Dennis, 140
Organization, defined, 11, 82
Organization agility, 209-10
  defined, 209
  and organization alertness, 209-10
  and organization flexibility, 209
Organization commitment, 130-32
  defined, 130
  fostered by, 131-32
  as organization asset, 130-31
  and turnover, 131-32
Organization culture, 82-86
  and attraction-selection-attrition (ASA) cycle, 83-84
  defined, 82, 250

evolution of, 83-84
expression of, 82
formation process, 83
and informal mentoring, 284
and organization identity, 83, 93
origins of, 83
for study of organization identity, 40-42
tactical management of, 85-86
as a tactical structure, 74, 82-86
ways to study, 40
Organization identity, 36, 38-44
  defined, 11, 36, 38
  and organization subsystems, 13, 38
  illustrated (Exhibits), 13, 39
  respecting human resources, 150
  study of, 36, 38-44
    through culture, 40-42
    through environmental mirror, 38-39
    by introduction of change, 44
    through participant observation, 43-44
    through semantics, 42-43
  and technological change, 118, 119-20
Organization objectives (see Strategic objectives)
Organization philosophy:
  choice of, 31-32
  basic points, 32
  defined, 11, 31
  need for, 31
  respecting human resources, 114-16
    drafting of, 148
    and employee needs, 115
    need for, 114-15
    and organization needs, 115
    substance of, 115-16
  substance of, 31
  tenure of, 32
Organization strategies, 44-47 (see also Human resource strategies)
  choice of, 44-45
  defined, 11
  implementation of, 45-47
    according to planning level, 44-45
Organization structure, 74-82
  defined, 74-75
  relationship to strategy, 75-77
  and strategic business units, 22-25
  and strategic orientation (Exhibit), 79
  tactical design of, 74-82
    comparison of approaches, 81-82
    design steps, 77
    prospective approach, 80-81
    retrospective approach, 77-80
Osgood, Charles, 42, 43

Participant observation, 43-44
Participatory decision making:
  advantages, 133
  defined, 133
  forms, 133-36

requirements for success, 136-37
Performance appraisal, 230-32
  of career employees, 144, 46
  for control, 230
  defined, 230
  methods:
    behaviorally anchored ratings, 230-31
    combined for planning, 232
    objective-determined ratings, 230, 231
  for planning, 230, 231, 232
Philosophy, of evaluation, 224-25
  (see also Organization philosophy)
Pierce, Jon, 84
Planned-change approach to evaluation, 226, 245
Planners:
  selecting (see Selection, of planners)
  training (see Training, of planners)
Planning (see also Business planning)
  in centrally-directed economies, 3
  in free enterprise economies, 3
Planning objectives:
  choice of, 28-29
  criteria, 29
  process, 28, 29
  product, 28-29
Policy, for tactical areas, 174, 179-80
Policy-capturing models, defined, 192
Policy set (see also Tactical human resource policy set)
  defined, 174
Policy statement:
  as official store of information, 189
  as a tactical structure, 74
Porter, Michael, 58, 59-60
Port-of-entry position, 211, 287
Positions:
  classification, 120-22
  dead end, 120
  entry, 120
  nonentry, 120
  port-of-entry, 287
Process objectives, 28-29
Productivity (see Employee productivity)
Product objectives, 28-29
Products, Inc:
  aligning structure with strategy, 75
    illustrated (Exhibit), 76
  creation of strategic business units, 22, 23
    illustrated (Exhibit), 23
  description, 22
  prospective approach, 80-81
  retrospective approach, 77-80
    new structure illustrated (Exhibit), 79
Promotion chain, as a buffer, 211
Prospective approach, to organization design, 80-81
Pulakos, Elaine, 138
Pygmalion effect, 242

Quality circles, 135

Quality index, 268-70
  defined, 268
  in flow tables, 268-70
    illustrated (*Exhibit*), 270
  kinds, 269-70

Regular model, for study of environment, 33
Remedial development, 123-24
  and "make-or-buy" decisions, 123-24
Repositories of information (*see* Information, repositories)
Reputation assessment, 236-37
  description, 236
  outsiders involved, 236
Retrospective approach, to organization design, 77-80
Role(s), social:
  defined, 259
  and instrumental training, 261
  interlocking, 259-60
  and transition cycle, 259-60
    illustrated (*Exhibit*), 260
Role set:
  as agent of strategic effects, 287
  defined, 259
Rosenzweig, James E., 13

Satisfaction (*see* Employee satisfaction)
Scanlon plans, 135
Scenario analysis, in futures analysis, 207-08
Schein, Edgar, 41
Schmitt, Neal, 138
Schneider, Benjamin, 83, 84
Schweiger, David, 134
Selection (*see also* Employee selection)
  defined, 299
  of planners, 30-31, 58-59, 92-93, 97
Self-producing systems theory, 14-15
  compared to open systems theory, 15
  as guide to organization identity, 39-44
  and implementation of objectives and strategies, 45-47
Selznick, Philip, 41
Semantic differential (*see also* Semantic differentiation)
  example, 42
Semantic differentiation, 42-43
Semantics, for study of organization identity, 42-43
Service orientation, 126-27
  defined, 126
  prediction of, 126
Service Orientation Index, 126
Sherwin-Williams, 129-30
Simple observation learning, 262
Skinner, Wickham, 110, 120
Smith, Alan, xi
SmithKline Beecham Corporation, 52
Snow, Charles, 24
Social learning, 260-62

defined, 260
  instrumental training, 261
  observational learning, 261-62
  role of supervisors, 286
  and transition cycle, 260-61
Social learning theory, 260-62
Social role (*see* Role(s))
Social system, defined, 259
Staffing, defined, 120
Stages of planning (*see* Business planning, stages)
Staines, Graham, 132
Stakeholders, of organization, 31, 32, 114, 148
Standard:
  benchmark, 229
  comparative/absolute, 228-29
  defined, 228
  need for, 228
  setting of, 229
Stocks, human resource (*see* Human resource stocks)
Strategic business units, 22-23
  defined, 22
  an example of (*Exhibit*), 23
  use in strategic planning, 22-23
Strategic considerations, in human resource operations, 281
Strategic group mapping, 22-25
  example (*Exhibit*), 26
  role in strategic planning, 22, 25-27
  steps, 25
Strategic human resource planning:
  and directional stability of organization, 110-11
  elements of, 113
  key people, 111-13
  long term nature, 110
  necessary conditions, 110-11
  role of chief executive officer, 111, 148
  role of chief human resource officer, 111-13, 148
  role of line managers, 111, 113, 148
Strategic human resource planning process, 146-53
  establishment of planning objectives, 147-48
  evaluation of planning, 152
  formulation of strategies, 150-51
  implementation of strategies, 151
  initiation, 147
  management of issues, 153
  organization identity respecting human resources, 150
  participant identification, 148
  philosophy respecting human resources, 148
  selection of strategic objectives, 150
  steps, 146-47
  study of setting, 148-50
Strategic objectives, 44-47 (*see also* Human resource strategic objectives)
  choice of, 44
  human resource, 116, 150

implementation, 45-47
  crescive approach, 45-47
  according to planning level, 44
Strategic orientation:
  classification, 24-25
  and distinctive competence, 24-25
Strategic planning (*see* Strategic human resource planning)
  described, 5
  human resource department role, 51-61
    the human resource executive, 52-53
    the human resource specialist, 53-61
  participation in:
    a cause of behavioral change, 54
    extent of, 29-30, 54-56
    kinds, 29-30
Strategic planning committee:
  composition and control (*Exhibit*), 55
  role of human resource executive, 52-53
  selection, 30-31
Strategic planning concepts, 21-27
  distinctive competence, 23-25
  experience curve, 27
  strategic business unit, 22-23
  strategic group mapping, 25-27
Strategic planning process, 27-51
  choice of organization philosophy, 31-32
  design for behavioral change, 54-58
  environmental study, 32-36
  establishment of organization identity, 36, 38-44
  establishment of planning objectives, 28-29
  evaluation of planning effort, 47-49
  formulation of organization objectives and strategies, 44-47
  implementation of objectives and strategies, 45-47
  management of issues, 50-51
  participant identification, 29-31
  steps, 28
Strategies, 44-47 (*see also* Human resource strategies)
  choice of, 44-45
  defined, 11
  human resource, 116-46, 150-51
  implementation, 45-47
    crescive approach, 45-47
    according to planning level, 44-45
Strickland, A. J. III, 26
Subsidiary storage devices, as information repositories, 189, 195
Suci, George, 42, 43
Supervisors:
  as agents of strategic effects, 285-87
  of career employees, 145-46

Supervisors (*con't.*):
  as mentors, 285-86
  managing internal labor markets,
    285, 286-87
  role for moving employees, 285
Support structure for human resource
    flows, 289-92
  ambient, 290-91, 294-95
  formal, 290, 294
  reason for, 290
Systems approach to evaluation, 225,
    226

Tactical human resource activity
    areas, 175-79
  development of policies for, 179-
    80
  for selected strategies (*Exhibit*),
    178
  selection, 175-79
    empirical, 177-79
    judgmental, 175-77
    methods compared, 179
Tactical human resource planning:
  committee, 180-81
  concepts, 174-80
  defined, 174
  process, 180-81
Tactical human resource policies,
    relation to objectives,
    174
Tactical human resource policy set,
    179-80
  development of, 179-80
  guidelines for design of, 181
  relation to objectives, 174
  as a tactical structure, 74
Tactical planning:
  committee, 89
    composition, 89, 90
    role of human resource execu-
      tive, 91
  described, 5
  human resource department role,
    91-93
    the human resource executive,
      91
    human resource specialists, 92-
      93
  and other planning stages, 73, 74
Tactical policy set (*see* Tactical

human resource policy
    set)
Tactical structures:
  guidelines for design of, 89-91
  kinds:
    financial budget, 74, 86-89
      (*see also* Financial bud-
      get)
    organization culture, 74, 82-86
      (*see also* Organization
      culture)
    organization structure, 74-82
      (*see also* Organization
      structure)
  managed change of, 93
Tactics, defined, 11
Tannenbaum, Percy, 42, 43
Task inventory method:
  described, 196
  for planning, 196-97
Technological change (*see also* Tech-
    nology management
    team)
  effects, 117-18
  management, 118-20
Technologies, as information reposi-
    tories, 188-89, 195
Technology:
  defined, 52, 117, 188
  human content, 117
  technical content, 117
Technology management team, 118
  role of human resource representa-
    tive, 118-20
Theory of human capital (*see* Human
    capital, theory)
Thompson, Arthur A., Jr., 26
Tiedeman, David V., 263
Training:
  audit measures for, 234
  defined, 124, 300
  experimental evaluation of, 242-
    43
  to facilitate technological change,
    119
  instrumental (*see* Instrumental
    training)
  on-the-job, 258-59
  organization-specific, 259
  of planners, 6, 10, 30-31, 59-60,
    113

human resource policy
    set)
Transaction processing systems,
    defined, 192
Transitional matrix, 267-68
  illustration of basic (*Exhibit*), 268
Transition cycle:
  of employee adjustment, 259-60
  illustrated (*Exhibit*), 260
Triandis, Harry, 43
Tuition (*see* Instrumental training)
Turnover:
  and employee development, 123,
    124
  and investments in human capital,
    259
  and organization commitment,
    131-32

Union Oil, 109
United Automobile Workers (UAW),
    129
Upjohn Company, 197-98
U.S. Air Force Human Resources
    Research Laboratory,
    196
Utility analysis, 239-40
  and cost-benefit analysis, 239, 240
  defined, 239
  formula, 240
  use to planners, 240

Vacancy chain:
  defined, 270
  and opportunity for advancement,
    271-72
Valuation (*see* Human resource valua-
    tion)
Van de Ven, Andrew H., 80, 81
Van de Ven/Ferry organization design
    modules, 80-81
  illustrated (*Exhibit*), 80

Watson, Thomas J., Sr, 32
West, Michael, 260
Wilpert, Bernhard, 134
Work analysis, 196-97
  defined, 196
  task inventory method, 196-97
Work group, as agent of strategic
    effects, 287

Zucker, Lynne G., 62